Arabian Sands

ARABIAN SANDS

Wilfred Thesiger

HarperCollins*Publishers*

HarperCollins*Publishers*
77–85 Fulham Palace Road,
Hammersmith, London w6 8jb

www.**fire**and**water**.com

Published by HarperCollins*Publishers* 2000
1 3 5 7 9 8 6 4 2

First published in Great Britain by
Longmans, Green and Co Ltd 1959

Previously published by
William Collins Sons and Co Ltd 1983

A catalogue record for this book
is available from the British Library

ISBN 0 00 217005 1

Maps redrawn for this edition
by Leslie Robinson

Set in Postscript Linotype Janson by
Rowland Phototypesetting Ltd,
Bury St Edmunds, Suffolk

Printed and bound in Great Britain by
Clays Ltd, St Ives plc

*To bin Kabina and
bin Ghabaisha*

Contents

Preface   xiii
Introduction   xvii
Prologue   xxi

1 Abyssinia and the Sudan   1
2 Prelude in Dhaufar   24
3 The Sands of Ghanim   39
4 Secret Preparations at Salala   61
5 The Approach to the Empty Quarter   87
6 On the Edge of the Empty Quarter   103
7 The First Crossing of the Empty Quarter   121
8 Return to Salala   143
9 From Salala to Mukalla   169
10 Preparations for a Second Crossing   192
11 The Second Crossing of the Empty Quarter   211
12 From Sulaiyil to Abu Dhabi   231
13 The Trucial Coast   252
14 A Holiday in Buraimi   269
15 The Quicksands of Umm al Samim   286
16 The Wahiba Sands   296
17 The Closing Door   310

Arabic and Botanical Names of Plants Mentioned
   in the Book   323
A List of the Chief Characters on the Various
   Journeys   324
Index   327

Illustrations

Bin Kabina in the Sands
Qarra tribesmen of Dhaufar
A cave-dwelling in the Qarra Mountains
The northern slopes of the Qarra Mountains
Trilithons on the northern slopes
The southern slopes
Salim bin Kabina
Two boys of the Bait Kathir
Sultan, a shiekh of the Bait Kathir
Ghaf trees near Mughshin
A herdsboy of the Manahil
Manahil raiders
The Empty Quarter: the steep side of a 600-foot dune
The Wadi Umm al Hait
Al Auf, the Rashid guide
The Empty Quarter
A camp in the Sands
Vegetation in the Sands after rain
Bin Anauf of the Bait Kathir
Bin Kabina by the crest of a great dune
Cleaning out a well
Preparing a meal

Salim bin Ghabaisha
A woman of the Harasis
The girl from the Saar at Manwakh well
One of the bin Maaruf Saar
A Saar family on the move
In the Hadramaut: Shibam, from the wells
Shibam: a mosque and houses

A Saar encampment
The author's party loading up in the Sands
The Empty Quarter: descending a great dune
Sulaim, the *rabia* from the Mahra
Rashid: Amair, bin al Mamam, Salim bin Mautlauq and Muhammad bin
    Kalut
Dhiby well
The author during the second crossing of the Empty Quarter
Bin Ghabaisha pouring coffee
A Rashid boy milking a camel

Travelling eastwards from Jabrin
In the Wadi Jaub
Crescent dunes near the Sabkhat Mutti
Sand massifs near the Liwa oasis
A settlement in the Liwa oasis
The sea journey to Bahrain
Wind-towers on a house at Dibai
Falconers of Zayid bin Sultan
A Kuwaiti boom returning from Zanzibar
A mounted falconer
Peregrines on their blocks
The Imam's representative
One of the Junuba
Some of the sheikh's retainers at Abu Dhabi
The Omani-type of camel-saddle
A boy of the Wahiba
Al Jabari of the Awamir
One of the Wahiba
Huaishil, a sheikh of the Duru
A settlement in Liwa oasis
A camel of the Wahiba
A camel of the Batima
Bin Kabina riding a thoroughbred Wahiba camel
Travelling northwards to Muwaiqih
The Oman Mountains: Jabal Kaur and Jabal al Akhadar
Bin Kabina and bin Ghabaisha in Oman

Maps

	page
The Empty Quarter	xxii–xxiii
Danakil Country	8
The Sudan	18
Arabia	26
Tribal Map of Southern Arabia	55
The Empty Quarter: First Crossing	104
The Mahra Country	171
The Empty Quarter: Second Crossing	212
Oman: The Interior	287

Preface

Arabian Sands describes the journeys I made in and around the Empty Quarter from 1945 to 1950, at which time much of that region had not yet been seen by a European. I returned to Arabia in 1977 at the invitation of the Oman Government and Emir Zayid of Abu Dhabi.

Even before I left Arabia in 1950, the Iraq Petroleum Company had started to search for oil in the territories of Abu Dhabi and Dubai. They soon discovered it in enormous quantities, and as a result the life I have described in this book disappeared for ever. Here, as elsewhere in Arabia, the changes which occurred in the space of a decade or two were as great as those which occurred in Britain between the early Middle Ages and the present day.

I was aware before I returned to Oman that considerable changes, both economic and political, had taken place there. In 1954 Muhammad al Khalili, the xenophobic Imam of Oman, had died. He was succeeded by his son, Ghalib, but the following year the Omani Sultan, Sayid Said bin Timur, took the opportunity to invade and occupy his domains and to abolish the Imamate. This caused great resentment and Talib, Ghalib's brother, backed by Sulaiman bin Hamyar of the Bani Riyan and a considerable following, rebelled. After their forces had been defeated in 1957 they withdrew into the almost impregnable Jabal al Akhdar; however, the British SAS Regiment, acting on behalf of the Sultan, scaled the mountain and overcame their resistance.

In 1965 a rebellion in Dhaufar, instigated and actively supported by the communist regime of the People's Democratic Republic in South Yemen, led to years of fierce fighting in the Jabal Qarra, which was finally suppressed in 1976 with the help of British and Persian troops. Meanwhile, in 1970 Qaboos had deposed his reactionary father, Sayid Said bin Timur and, as the new Sultan of Oman, he immediately set about developing and modernizing the country.

I was anxious to see the ancient Arab seaport of Muscat which I had not yet visited, to climb the Jabal al Akhdar, the unattainable goal of my last journey in Arabia and, above all, to meet once more the Rashid and Bait Kathir who had accompanied me on my journeys; but I was filled with misgivings at going back.

In this book I have described a journey in disguise through Inner Oman in 1947 and I wrote: 'Yet even as I waited for my identity to be discovered I realized that for me the fascination of this journey lay not in seeing this country but in seeing it under these conditions.' The everyday hardships and danger, the ever-present hunger and thirst, the weariness of long marches: these provided the challenges of Bedu life against which I sought to match myself, and were the basis of the comradeship which united us.

For the three weeks I was in Oman, aeroplanes, helicopters, cars and even a launch were put at my disposal; during this time I covered distances in an hour that previously had taken weeks. Soon after my arrival in Muscat I was flown to Salala, from where I had started my journeys into the Empty Quarter. Salala had been a small Arab village adjoining the Sultan's palace; now it was a town with traffic lights. Bin Kabina and bin Ghabaisha met me when I landed. They had been my inseparable companions during the five most memorable years of my life. When I had parted from them in Dubai in 1950 they had been young men; now they were the grey-bearded fathers of grown-up sons. I was deeply moved to meet them again. I had thought of them so often. They went off next day to prepare a feast for me at their tents in the desert. Meanwhile, old friends from the Bait Kathir, led by Musallim bin Tafl, escorted me in a procession of cars, with blaring horns, up the highway to the new town on the top of Jabal Qarra, where they entertained me in the concrete houses in which they now lived, near the military airfield.

The following day I was flown in a helicopter, accompanied by a television crew, to bin Kabina's black tents near Shisur. Here the

Rashid were assembled, their Landrovers and other vehicles parked behind the tents. None of them now rode camels, though some still lived in tents and owned camels. Many of them had travelled with me on my journeys to the Hadhramaut, but several of my old companions had died or been killed. Bin Kabina had slaughtered a camel and provided a lavish meal; while we ate the television cameras whirred. I flew back to Salala in the evening, accompanied by bin Kabina and bin Ghabaisha, who remained with me while I was in Oman. Together we climbed the Jabal al Akhdar; here, too, was an airfield with jet planes and helicopters landing and taking off. I realized that after all these years and under these changed conditions the relationship between us could never again be as in the past. They had adjusted themselves to this new Arabian world, something I was unable to do. We parted before I went to Abu Dhabi, which I found an Arabian Nightmare, the final disillusionment.

I am happy that HarperCollins are publishing this new edition of *Arabian Sands*; for me this book remains a memorial to a vanished past, a tribute to a once magnificent people.

WILFRED THESIGER

Introduction

During the years that I was in Arabia I never thought that I would write a book about my travels. Had I done so, I should have kept fuller notes which now would have both helped and hindered me. Seven years after leaving Arabia I showed some photographs I had taken to Graham Watson and he strongly urged me to write a book about the desert. This I refused to do. I realized that it would involve me in much hard work, and I did not wish to settle down in Europe for a couple of years when I could be travelling in countries that interested me. The following day Graham Watson came to see me again, and this time he brought Mark Longman with him. After much argument the two of them persuaded me to try to write this book. Now that I have finished it I am grateful to them, for the effort to remember every detail has brought back vividly into my mind the Bedu amongst whom I travelled, and the vast empty land across which I rode on camels for ten thousand miles.

I went to Southern Arabia only just in time. Others will go there to study geology and archaeology, the birds and plants and animals, even to study the Arabs themselves, but they will move about in cars and will keep in touch with the outside world by wireless. They will bring back results far more interesting than mine, but they will never know the spirit of the land nor the greatness of the Arabs. If anyone goes there now looking for the life I led they will not find it, for technicians have been there since, prospecting for oil. Today the desert where I travelled is scarred with the tracks of lorries and littered with discarded junk imported from Europe and America. But this material desecration is unimportant compared with the demoralization which has resulted among the Bedu themselves. While I was with them they had no thought of a world other than their own. They were not ignorant savages; on the contrary, they were the lineal heirs of a very ancient civilization, who found within the framework of their society the personal freedom and self-discipline for which they craved. Now they are being driven out of the desert into towns where the qualities which once gave them mastery are no longer sufficient. Forces as uncontrollable as the droughts which so often killed them in the past have destroyed the economy of their lives. Now it is not death but degradation which faces them.

Since leaving Arabia I have travelled among the Karakoram and the Hindu Kush, the mountains of Kurdistan and the marshlands of Iraq, drawn always to remote places where cars cannot penetrate and where something of the old ways survive. I have seen some of the most magnificent scenery in the world and I have lived among tribes who are interesting and little known. None of these places has moved me as did the deserts of Arabia.

Fifty years ago the word Arab, generally speaking, meant an inhabitant of Arabia, and was often regarded as synonymous with the Bedu. Tribesmen who had migrated from Arabia to Egypt and elsewhere, and still lived as nomads, were spoken of as Arabs, whereas others who had become cultivators or townsmen were not. It is in this older sense that I use the word Arab, and not in the sense that the word has acquired recently with the growth of Arab Nationalism, when anyone who speaks Arabic as his mother-tongue is referred to, regardless of his origin, as an Arab.

The Bedu are the nomadic camel-breeding tribes of the Arabian desert. In English they are usually called Beduin, a double plural which they themselves seldom use. I prefer Bedu and have used this word throughout the book. They generally speak of themselves as 'al Arab', and when referring to them I have used Bedu and Arab indiscriminately.

In Arabic, Bedu is plural and Bedui singular, but, for the sake of simplicity, I have used Bedu for both singular and plural. So as not to confuse the reader, I have done the same with the names of the tribes: Rashid, singular Rashdi; and Awamir, singular Amari.

I have used as few Arabic words as possible. Most of the plants mentioned in the book have no English name and I have called them by their local names in preference to the Latin equivalents; for most people, *ghaf* is easier to remember than *Prosopis spicigera*, and as intelligible. At the end of the book is a list of the Arabic and scientific names of all the plants mentioned.

Inevitably, this book contains many names which will sound strange to anyone unfamiliar with Arabia. I have included in the text several sketch-maps showing the places mentioned in the accounts of each journey, and I have also included at the end a list of the chief characters.

The maps were specially drawn by K. C. Jordan, and I am grateful to him for all the care and trouble he has taken. He compiled the large one from those drawn by the Royal Geographical Society from my traverses in Arabia, and used some information derived from Thomas and Philby. I decided not to correct or amplify this map from work done since I left Arabia.

Any transliteration of Arabic words leads to dispute. I have tried to simplify as much as possible and have consequently left out the letter ' *Ain*, usually represented by '. In any case, few Englishmen can pronounce this letter correctly; to the majority of readers the frequent recurrence of this unintelligible ' would be both confusing and irritating. For the other difficult letter, *Ghain*, I have used the conventional 'gh'. Experts say that this soft guttural sound is pronounced like the Parisian 'r'. This letter occurs in the name of one of the chief characters in the book, bin Ghabaisha.

Only I know what my mother's interest and encouragement have meant to me. I was nine months old when she took me from Addis Ababa to the coast, the first of many long childhood journeys with camels or mules. Having herself known the fascination of African travel before it was made easy, she has always understood and sympathized with my love of exploration.

In writing this book I owe a great debt of gratitude to Val ffrench Blake. He read the first chapter as soon as it was written, and since then has read the whole typescript, not once, but many times. His understanding and encouragement, as well as his excellent advice and criticism, have been invaluable to me. My brother Roderic has also read the text with the greatest care and patience and offered many valuable suggestions. To John Verney and Graham Watson I also owe much: John Verney for invaluable advice, and Graham Watson for his faith in the outcome of the task on which he launched me. W. P. G. Thomson of the Permanent Committee on Geographical Names was kind enough to check and approve the spelling of the Arabic names. I am most thankful to him for doing so. I am also extremely grateful to James Sinclair & Company, of Whitehall, for the great trouble they have taken over my photographs for many years. I also wish to thank the Royal Geographical Society for the help and encouragement which they gave me before I started on these journeys.

Although it would be pointless to thank them in a book which none of them will ever read, it will be obvious that I owe everything to the Bedu who went with me. Without their help, I could never have travelled in the Empty Quarter. Their comradeship gave me the five happiest years of my life.

Prologue

A cloud gathers, the rain falls, men live; the cloud disperses without rain, and men and animals die. In the deserts of southern Arabia there is no rhythm of the seasons, no rise and fall of sap, but empty wastes where only the changing temperature marks the passage of the year. It is a bitter, desiccated land which knows nothing of gentleness or ease. Yet men have lived there since earliest times. Passing generations have left fire-blackened stones at camping sites, a few faint tracks polished on the gravel plains. Elsewhere the winds wipe out their footprints. Men live there because it is the world into which they were born; the life they lead is the life their forefathers led before them; they accept hardships and privations; they know no other way. Lawrence wrote in *Seven Pillars of Wisdom*, 'Bedouin ways were hard, even for those brought up in them and for strangers terrible: a death in life.' No man can live this life and emerge unchanged. He will carry, however faint, the imprint of the desert, the brand which marks the nomad; and he will have within him the yearning to return, weak or insistent according to his nature. For this cruel land can cast a spell which no temperate clime can match.

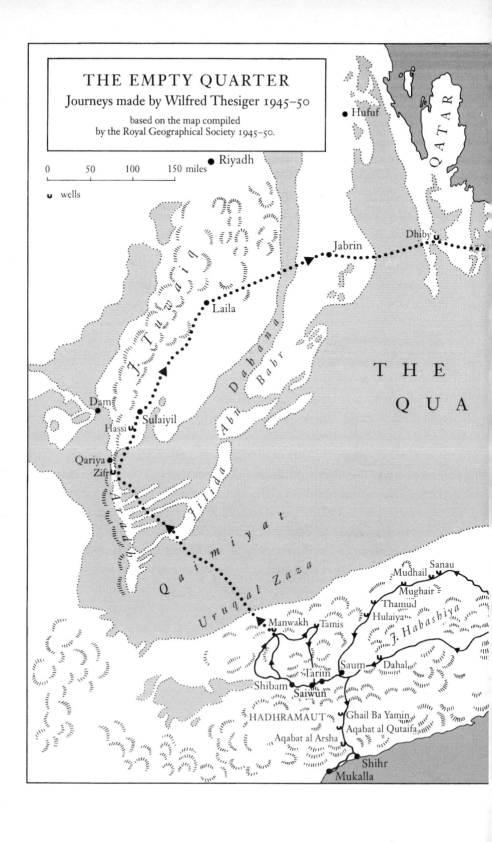

THE EMPTY QUARTER
Journeys made by Wilfred Thesiger 1945-50
based on the map compiled
by the Royal Geographical Society 1945-50.

0   50   100   150 miles

ᴗ wells

● Riyadh

● Hufuf

QATAR

Dhiby ᴗ

Jabrin

Laila

Dam

Hassi   Sulaiyil

Qariya
Zifr

J. Tuwaiq

Dahana   Bahr

Abu

Jilida

Qaimiyat

Uruq al Zaza

THE

QUA

Sanau
Mudhail
Mughair
Thamud
Hulaiya   J. Habashiya

Manwakh   Tamis

Tarim   Saum   Dahal

Shibam   Saiwun

HADHRAMAUT   Ghail Ba Yamin
Aqabat al Qutaifa

Aqabat al Arsha

Shihr
Mukalla

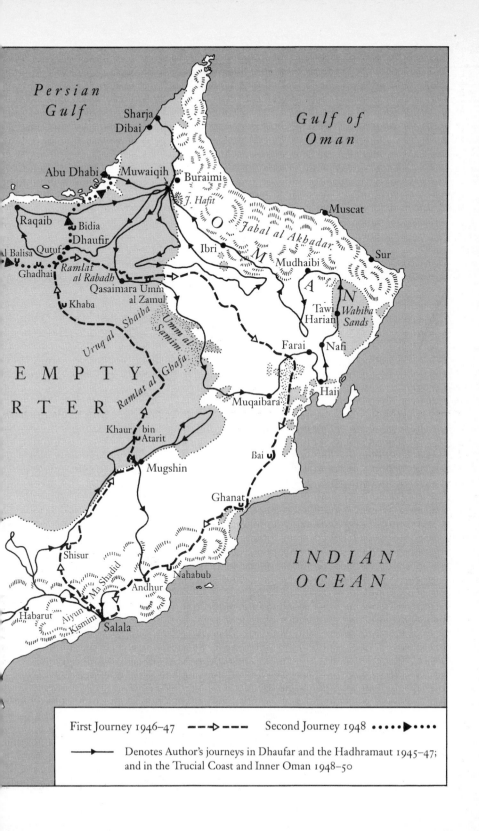

First Journey 1946–47 — ▷ — — —   Second Journey 1948 •••••▶••••

———▶ Denotes Author's journeys in Dhaufar and the Hadhramaut 1945–47;
and in the Trucial Coast and Inner Oman 1948–50

ONE

Abyssinia and the Sudan

A childhood in Abyssinia is followed by a journey in
the Danakil country and service in the Sudan. The
opportunity to travel into the Empty Quarter of
Arabia comes from a wartime meeting with the
head of the Middle East Locust Control.

I first realized the hold the desert had upon me when travelling
in the Hajaz mountains in the summer of 1946. A few months
earlier I had been down on the edge of the Empty Quarter.
For a while I had lived with the Bedu a hard and merciless life,
during which I was always hungry and usually thirsty. My companions had been accustomed to this life since birth, but I had been
racked by the weariness of long marches through wind-whipped
dunes, or across plains where monotony was emphasized by the
mirages shimmering through the heat. There was always the fear
of raiding parties to keep us alert and tense, even when we were
dazed by lack of sleep. Always our rifles were in our hands and our
eyes searching the horizon. Hunger, thirst, heat, and cold: I had
tasted them in full during those six months, and had endured the
strain of living among an alien people who made no allowance for
weakness. Often, in weariness of body and spirit, I had longed to
get away.

Now, in the Assir, I was standing on a mountain-side forested
with wild olives and junipers. A stream tumbled down the slope;
its water, ice-cold at 9,000 feet, was in welcome contrast with the

scanty, bitter water of the sands. There were wild flowers: jasmine and honeysuckle, wild roses, pinks and primulas. There were terraced fields of wheat and barley, vines, and plots of vegetables. Far below me a yellow haze hid the desert to the east. Yet it was there that my fancies ranged, planning new journeys while I wondered at this strange compulsion which drove me back to a life that was barely possible. It would, I felt, have been understandable if I had been working in some London office, dreaming of freedom and adventure; but here, surely, I had all that I could possibly desire on much easier terms. But I knew instinctively that it was the very hardness of life in the desert which drew me back there – it was the same pull which takes men back to the polar ice, to high mountains, and to the sea.

To return to the Empty Quarter would be to answer a challenge, and to remain there for long would be to test myself to the limit. Much of it was unexplored. It was one of the very few places left where I could satisfy an urge to go where others had not been. The circumstances of my life had so trained me that I was qualified to travel there. The Empty Quarter offered me the chance to win distinction as a traveller; but I believed that it could give me more than this, that in those empty wastes I could find the peace that comes with solitude, and, among the Bedu, comradeship in a hostile world. Many who venture into dangerous places have found this comradeship among members of their own race; a few find it more easily among people from other lands, the very differences which separate them binding them ever more closely. I found it among the Bedu. Without it these journeys would have been a meaningless penance.

I have often looked back into my childhood for a clue to this perverse necessity which drives me from my own land to the deserts of the East. Perhaps it lies somewhere in the background of my memory: in journeys through the deserts of Abyssinia; in the thrill of seeing my father shoot an oryx when I was only three; in vague recollections of camel herds at water-holes; in the smell of dust and of acacias under a hot sun; in the chorus of hyenas and jackals in the darkness round the camp fire. But these dim memories are almost gone, submerged by later memories of the Abyssinian highlands, for it was there that I spent my childhood until I was nearly nine.

It was an unusual childhood. My father was British Minister in Addis Ababa, and I was born there in 1910 in one of the mud buildings which in those days housed the Legation. When I returned to England I had already witnessed sights such as few people had ever seen. I had watched the priests dancing at Timkat before the Ark of the Covenant to the muffled throbbing of their silver drums; I had watched the hierarchy of the Ethiopian Church, magnificent in their many-coloured vestments, blessing the waters. I had seen the armies going forth to fight in the great Rebellion of 1916. For days they passed across the plain in front of the Legation. I had heard the wailing when Ras Lul Seged's army was wiped out trying to check Negus Michail's advance, and had witnessed the wild rejoicing which proclaimed the final victory. I had seen the triumphant return after the battle of Sagale, where the armies of the North and the South had been locked throughout an entire day in desperate hand-to-hand fighting, only fifty miles to the north of Addis Ababa.

Each feudal lord was surrounded by levies from the province which he ruled. The simple fighting men were dressed in white, but the chiefs wore their full panoply of war, lion's-mane head-dresses, brilliant velvet cloaks stiff with silver and golden ornaments, long silk robes of many colours, and great curved swords. All carried shields, some embossed with silver or gilt, and many carried rifles. The Zulu impis parading before Chaka, or the dervishes drawn up to give battle in front of Omdurman, can have appeared no more barbaric than this frenzied tide of men which surged past the royal pavilion throughout the day, to the thunder of the war-drums and the blare of war-horns. This was no ceremonial review. These men had just returned after fighting desperately for their lives, and they were still wild with the excitement of those frantic hours. The blood on the clothes which they had stripped from the dead and draped round their horses was barely dry. They came past in waves,

3

horsemen half concealed in dust and a great press of footmen. Screaming out their deeds of valour and brandishing their weapons, they came right up to the steps of the throne, whence the Court chamberlains beat them back with long wands. Above them, among glinting spear points, countless banners dipped and danced. I can remember one small boy who seemed little older than myself being carried past in triumph. He had killed two men. I can remember Negus Michail, the King of the North, being led past in chains with a stone upon his shoulder in token of submission, an old man in a plain black burnous, with his head wrapped in a white rag. The most moving moment of that wildly exciting day was when the drums suddenly stopped and in utter silence a few hundred men in torn, white, everyday clothes came slowly down the long avenue of waiting troops, led by a young boy. It was Ras Lul Seged's son bringing in the remnants of his father's army, which had gone into battle five thousand strong.

It is not surprising that I dreamt of Africa during the years I was at school. I read every book that I could find on African travel and adventure, by Gordon-Cumming, Baldwin, Bruce, Selous, and many others. I pored over Rowland Ward's *Records of Big Game* and I could easily have passed an examination on African animals, while I was failing repeatedly in Latin. During sermons in chapel I could picture again the scenes of my childhood, conjure up the mountains that had ringed my horizon, Zuquala, Fantali, Wuch-acha, Furi, and Managasha. These are names which have always held a nostalgic fascination for me. Until I went to school I had hardly seen a European child other than my brothers. I found myself in a hostile and incomprehensible world. I was ignorant of the rigid conventions to which schoolboys conform and I suffered in consequence. I spoke of things which I had seen and done and was promptly called a liar. I felt little confidence in my ability to compete with my contemporaries and was often lonely. Fortunately I went on to Eton, for which I acquired a deep and lasting affection.

I returned to Abyssinia when I was twenty. Haile Selassie had never forgotten that during the critical days of the great Rebellion my father had sheltered his infant son, the present Crown Prince, in the Legation. He sent me, as my father's eldest son, a personal invitation to attend his coronation, and I went out to Ethiopia attached to the Duke of Gloucester's mission. We landed at Jibuti. I do not think I have ever felt so intoxicatedly happy as I did that night in the train on my way to Addis Ababa. When I arrived back at the Legation more than half my life simply vanished from my mind. It needed an effort to remember even the immediate past. It was impossible to believe that eleven years had passed since I had last climbed the hill behind the Legation, watched the blue smoke rising into the cold clear air above the servants' quarters, or listened to the kites shrilling above the eucalyptus trees. I recognized every bird and plant, even the shape of the rocks themselves.

During ten hectic days I took part in processions, ceremonies, and state banquets, and finally I watched while the Patriarch crowned Haile Selassie, King of Kings of Ethiopia. Crowned, robed, and anointed, he showed himself to his people, another king in the long line that claimed descent from Solomon and Sheba. I looked on streets thronged with tribesmen from every province of his empire. I saw again the shields and brilliant robes which I remembered from my childhood. But the outside world had intruded and the writing was on the wall. I realized that traditions, customs, and rites, long cherished and revered, were soon to be discarded; that the colour and variety which distinguished this scene were to disappear from the land for ever. Already there were a few cars in the streets, harbingers of change. There were journalists, who forced themselves forward to photograph the Emperor on his throne and the priests as they danced. I was thrust aside by one of them who shouted 'Make room for the Eyes and Ears of the World.'

I had grown up dreaming of big-game shooting and exploration, and was determined, now that I was back in Africa, to get away into the wilds. I had brought a rifle out with me. One day, standing on the Legation steps during a lull in the coronation festivities, I asked Colonel Cheesman, the well-known explorer, if there was anywhere left in Abyssinia to explore. He told me that the one problem left unsolved was what happened to the Awash river, which, rising in the mountains west of Addis Ababa, flowed down into the

Danakil desert and never reached the sea. This conversation turned my thoughts to the Danakil country, where the people were head-hunters who collected testicles instead of heads. I was expected back at Oxford in six weeks' time, but could at least get down to the edge of this country and have a look at it. Helped by Colonel Sandford, an old family friend, I collected my caravan. Just as I was ready to start, Sir Sidney Barton, the British Minister, said that he was unhappy about my travelling by myself in this completely unadministered and dangerous area, and suggested that, instead, I should join a shooting trip which he was arranging. I was grateful to him for this offer, but I knew that acceptance meant turning my back for ever on the realization of my boyhood dreams, and that then I should have failed even before I had started. I tried fumblingly to explain what was at stake; how I must go down there alone and get the experience which I required. He understood at once and wished me well, and added as I left the room, 'Take care of yourself. It would be awkward if you got yourself cut up by the Danakil immediately after the coronation. It would rather spoil the effect of it all.'

My first night in camp, as I sat eating sardines out of a tin and watching my Somalis driving the camels up from the river to couch them by the tent, I knew that I would not have been anywhere else for all the money in the world. For a month I travelled in an arid hostile land. I was alone; there was no one whom I could consult; if I met with trouble from the tribes I could get no help; if I were sick there was no one to doctor me. Men trusted me and obeyed my orders; I was responsible for their safety. I was often tired and thirsty, sometimes frightened and lonely, but I tasted freedom and a way of life from which there could be no recall.

This was the most decisive month in my life. When I returned to Oxford the pictures crowded back into my mind. I saw once more a group of Danakil leaning on their spears, slender graceful figures, clad only in short loin-cloths, their tousled hair daubed with butter; an encampment of small dome-shaped huts and the sun's rays slanting through the clouds of dust as the herds were brought in at sunset; the slow-flowing muddy river and a crocodile basking on a sandbank; a waterbuck stepping out of the tamarisk jungle on its way down to drink; a kudu bull with magnificent spiral horns silhouetted on a skyline against fast failing light; the scrambling rush of an oryx shot through the heart; vultures planing down on rigid wings to join others hopping clumsily about the kill; a frieze of baboons sitting on a cliff against the sky. I could feel once more the sun scorching through my shirt; the chill of the early dawn. I could taste camels' urine in water. I could hear my Somalis singing round the camp-fire; the roaring of the camels as they were loaded. I was determined to go back and to discover what happened to the Awash river; but it was the attraction of the unknown rather than any love of deserts which was luring me back. I still thought that my heart was in the Abyssinian highlands; and, certainly, if there had remained any unknown country there I should have chosen them in preference to the desert.

Three years later, accompanied by David Haig-Thomas, I returned to Abyssinia to explore the Danakil country. We travelled first with mules for two months in the Arussi mountains, for we wished to test under easy conditions the men who were going with us before we took them down into the Danakil desert. We camped high on mountain-tops, where the slopes around us were covered with giant heath, or higher still among giant lobelias where clouds formed and re-formed, allowing only glimpses of the Rift Valley seven thousand feet below. We travelled for days through forests, where black and white colobus monkeys played in the lichen-covered trees, and rode across the rolling plains near the head-waters of the Webbi Shibeli. We passed through some of the finest mountain scenery in Abyssinia. Then we dropped off the Chercher mountains to the desert's edge. Breaths of warm air played round us and rustled the dry leaves on the acacia bushes, and that night my Somali servants brought me a bowl of camel's milk from a nomad encampment near by. I was filled with a great contentment. The desert had already claimed me, though I did not know it yet.

The Danakil desert lies between the Ethiopian plateau and the Red Sea, north of the railway line connecting Addis Ababa with Jibuti on the coast. It was a grim land with a grim reputation.

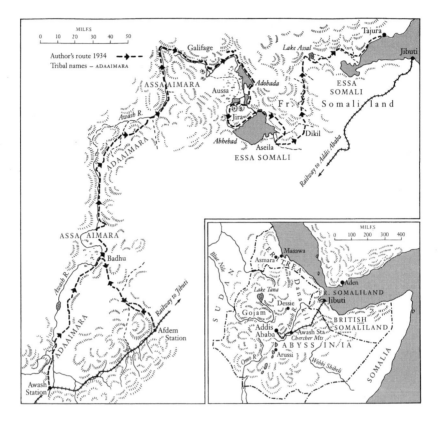

Danakil Country

Somewhere in this country towards the end of the last century the three expeditions of Munzinger, Giulietti, and Bianchi had been exterminated. Nesbitt and two companions had crossed it from south to north in 1928. They were the first Europeans to return alive from the interior of the Danakil country, but three of their servants were murdered. Nesbitt later described this remarkable journey in his book *Desert and Forest*. He had been prevented from following the Awash river for a large part of its course by the hostility of the tribes, and he had not explored the Aussa Sultanate nor solved the problem of the river's disappearance.

The Danakil are a nomadic people akin to the Somalis. They own camels, sheep, goats, and cattle, and the richer tribes have

8

some horses which they keep for raiding. They are nominally Muslims. Among them a man's standing depended to a very large extent on his reputation as a warrior, which was judged by the number of men he had killed and mutilated. There was no need to kill another man in fair fight; all that was required to establish a reputation was to collect the necessary number of severed genitals. Each kill entitled the warrior to wear some distinctive ornament, an ostrich feather or comb in his hair, an ear-ring, bracelet, or coloured loin-cloth. It was possible to tell at a glance how many men anyone had killed. These people buried their dead in tumuli, and erected memorials, resembling small stone pens, to the most famous, placing a line of upright stones in front of each memorial, one stone to commemorate each victim. The country was full of these sinister memorials, some of them with as many as twenty stones. I found it disconcerting to be stared at by a Danakil, feeling that he was probably assessing my value as a trophy, rather as I should study a herd of oryx in order to pick out the animal with the longest horns.

Unfortunately, David Haig-Thomas developed acute laryngitis during our journey in the mountains. As he was too ill to accompany me into the Danakil country, I left the Awash station without him on 1 December with forty Abyssinians and Somalis, all armed with rifles. We obviously could not force our way through the country ahead of us, but I hoped that we should appear too strong a force to be a tempting prey. We had eighteen camels to carry our provisions. As I planned to follow the river, I did not expect to be short of water. We started as quickly as possible since I heard that the Ethiopian Government intended to forbid my departure.

A fortnight later we were on the edge of Bahdu district, where the country was very disturbed; the village in which we stopped had been raided two days before and several people killed. The Danakil are divided into two groups, the Assaaimara and the Adaaimara. The Assaaimara, who are by far the more powerful, inhabit Bahdu and Aussa, and all the tribes through whom we had passed were terrified of the Bahdu warriors. The Adaaimara warned us that we should have no hope of escaping massacre if we entered

Bahdu, which was guarded from the south by a pass between a low escarpment and some marshes. This we picketed at dawn and were through it before the Assaaimara were aware of our movements. We then halted and, using the loads and camel-saddles, quickly built a small perimeter round our camp, which was protected on one side by the river. We were soon surrounded by crowds of excited Danakils, all armed – most of them with rifles. Two Greeks and their servants had been massacred here three years before. Expecting an attack we stood-to at dawn. Next day, after endless argument, we persuaded an emaciated and nearly blind old man, who possessed great influence in Bahdu, to provide us with guides and hostages. Everything seemed to be satisfactorily arranged, when just before sunset a letter arrived from the government. It had been passed on from one chief to another until it reached us. Its arrival roused great excitement among the Danakil, who collected in large numbers round their old chief. The letter was written in Amharic, and I had to have it translated, so there was no possibility of concealing its contents. It ordered me to return at once, since fighting had broken out among the tribes, and emphasized that in no circumstances must I try to enter Bahdu – the very place where I now was. Half my men insisted that they were going back, the others agreed to leave the decision to me. I knew that if I ignored this order and continued my journey with a reduced party we should be attacked and wiped out. I realized that I must return, but it was bitter to have my plans wrecked, especially when we had successfully entered Bahdu, and by so doing had overcome the first great difficulty in our way.

On the way back we passed the ruins of a large Adaaimara village. The Assaaimara had sent a deputation of seven old men to this village to discuss a dispute about pasturage. The villagers had feasted them and then set upon them during the night. Only one man, whose wounds I doctored in Bahdu, had escaped. The Assaaimara then attacked the village and killed sixty-one men. It was the incident that had started the recent fighting among the tribes.

* * *

I went up to Addis Ababa and wasted six weeks before I could induce the government to let me return, and then only after I had given them a letter absolving them from all responsibility for my safety. I returned to find my men suffering from fever, which is prevalent along the banks of the Awash. They were demoralized, and a few of them insisted on being paid off. In return for the letter which I had given them, the government had agreed to release from prison an old man, Miram Muhammad, and to allow him to accompany me. He was the head chief of the Bahdu tribes. Some months before, he had visited the government and had been detained as a hostage for the good behaviour of his tribes. It was his refusal to guarantee my safety while in Bahdu which had led to my recall. His presence with me ensured us a favourable reception there and at least an introduction to the Sultan of Aussa.

While we were in Bahdu I stayed for several days in the village of a young chief called Hamdu Uga. He had a charming smile and a gentle manner and I enjoyed his company. Though little more than a boy, he had lately murdered three men on the borders of French Somaliland and was celebrating his achievement with a feast when I arrived at this village. He wore, with amusing affection, the ostrich feather to which he was now entitled. Two days after we left, his village was surprised by another tribe, and when I asked about Hamdu Uga I heard that he had been killed.

Six weeks later I was at Galifage on the borders of Aussa, camped on the edge of dense forest. The tall trees were smothered in creepers; the grass was green and rank; little sunlight penetrated to my tent. It was a different world from the tawny plains, the thirsty thorn-scrub, the cracked and blackened rocks of the land through which we had passed. It was here that Nesbitt had met Muhammad Yayu, the Sultan. Nesbitt had received permission to continue his journey but his object was to travel across the lava desert to the north, not to penetrate into the fertile plains of Aussa. Muhammad Yayu, like his father before him, feared and mistrusted all Europeans. This was natural enough. He had seen the French and the Italians occupy the entire coastline, which consists of nothing but lava-fields and salt-pans, and he naturally believed that any

European power would desire to seize the rich plains of Aussa if it learnt of their existence. No European before Nesbitt had been given the Sultan's safe conduct and all had been massacred in consequence. Until I arrived in Aussa I had been faced with conditions of tribal anarchy, but now I was confronted by an autocrat whose word was law. If we died here it would be at the Sultan's order, not through some chance meeting with tribesmen in the bush.

I was ordered to remain at Galifage. The camp was full of rumours. On the evening of the third day we heard the sound of distant trumpets. The forest was sombre in the dusk, between the setting of the sun and the rising of the full moon. Later a messenger arrived and informed me that the Sultan was waiting to receive me. We followed him deeper into the forest, along twisting paths, until we came to a large clearing. About four hundred men were massed on the far side of it. They all carried rifles, their belts were filled with cartridges. They all wore daggers, and their loin-cloths were clean – vivid white in the moonlight. Not one of them spoke. Sitting a little in front of them on a stool was a small dark man, with a bearded oval face. He was dressed completely in white, in a long shirt with a shawl thrown round his shoulders. He had a silver-hilted dagger at his waist. As I greeted him in Arabic he rose, and then signed to me to be seated on another stool. He waved his men away. They drew back to the forest's edge and squatted there in silence.

I knew that everything, even our lives, depended on the result of this meeting. It was different from anything I had anticipated. The Sultan spoke very quietly; my Somali headman interpreted. We exchanged the customary compliments and he asked me about my journey. He spoke little and never smiled. There were long intervals of silence. His expression was sensitive, proud, and imperious, but not cruel. He mentioned that a European who worked for the government had recently been killed by tribesmen near the railway line. I learnt later that this was a German who was working with the Ethiopian boundary commission. After about an hour he said he would meet me again in the morning. He had asked no questions about my plans. I returned to camp without an idea of what the future held for us. We met again next morning in the same place. By daylight it was simply a clearing in the forest with none of the menace of the previous night.

The Sultan asked me where I wished to go and I told him that I wanted to follow the river to its end. He asked me what I sought, whether I worked for the government, and many other questions. It would have been difficult to explain my love of exploration to this suspicious tyrant, even without the added difficulties of interpretation. My headman was questioned, and also the Danakil who had accompanied me from Bahdu. Eventually the Sultan gave me permission to follow the river through Aussa to its end. Why he gave me this permission, which had never before been granted to a European, I do not know.

Two days later I climbed a hill and looked out over Aussa. It was strange to think that even fifty years earlier a great part of Africa had been unexplored. But since then travellers, missionaries, traders, and administrators had penetrated nearly everywhere. This was one of the last corners that remained unknown. Below me was a square plain about thirty miles across. It was shut in on all sides by dark barren mountains. To the east an unbroken precipice fell into the water of Lake Adobada, which was fifteen miles long. The northern half of the plain was covered with dense forest, but there were wide clearings where I could see sheep, goats, and cattle. Farther south was a great swamp and open sheets of water, and beyond this a line of volcanoes.

We followed the river, through the forest, past the lakes and swamps, down to the far side of Aussa. It was fascinating country, and I would gladly have remained here for weeks, but our escort hurried us on. I had permission from the Sultan to pass through this land, but not to linger. The Awash skirted the volcanoes of Jira and re-entered the desert, and there it ended in the salt lake of Abhebad. The river had come a long way from the Akaki plains to end here in this dead world, and it was this that I myself had come so far to see – three hundred square miles of bitter water, on which red algae floated like stale blood. Sluggish waves slapped over the glutinous black mud which bordered the lake, and hot water seeped down into it from among the basaltic rocks. It was a place of shadows but not of shade, where the sun beat down, and the heat struck back again from the calcined rocks. Small flocks of wading birds only emphasized the desolation as they passed crying along the shore, for they were migrants free to leave at will. A few pigmy crocodiles, stunted no doubt by the salt water in which they lived, watched us with unblinking yellow eyes – symbolizing, I thought, the spirit of the place. Some Danakil who were with me told me it was here that their fathers had destroyed an army of 'Turks', and thrown their guns into the lake. No doubt this was where Munzinger's expedition had been wiped out in 1875.

I crossed the border into French Somaliland and stayed with Capitaine Bernard in the fort which he commanded at Dikil. He and most of his men were to die a few months later when they were ambushed by a raiding force from Aussa. From Dikil I travelled across the lava desert to Tajura on the coast. So far it had been the tribes that had threatened us, now it was the land itself. It was without life or vegetation, a chaos of twisted riven rock, the debris of successive cataclysms, spewed forth molten to scald the surface of the earth. This dead landscape seemed to presage the final desolation of a dead world. For twelve days we struggled over the sharp rocks, across mountains, through gorges, past craters. We skirted the Assal basin four hundred feet below sea-level. The blue-black waters of the lake were surrounded by a great plain of salt, white and level as an icefield, from which the mountains rose in crowded tiers, the lava on their slopes black and rusty red. We were lucky. Some rain had fallen recently and filled the water-holes, but fourteen of my eighteen camels died of starvation before we reached Tajura.

I was restless. For three years I had been planning this journey, and now it was over and the future seemed empty. I dreaded a return to civilization, where life promised to be very dreary after the excitements of the last eight months. At Jibuti I played with the idea of buying de Monfried's dhow. I had read his *Aventures de*

Mer and *Secrets de la Mer Rouge* and had talked to the Danakil who had sailed with him. I was fascinated by his accounts of a free and lawless life.

I returned, however, to England, joined the Sudan Political Service, and went to Khartoum at the beginning of 1935. I was twenty-four. I had spent nearly half my life in Africa, but it was an Africa very different from this. Khartoum seemed like the suburbs of North Oxford dumped down in the middle of the Sudan. I hated the calling and the cards, I resented the trim villas, the tarmac roads, the meticulously aligned streets in Omdurman, the signposts, and the public conveniences. I longed for the chaos, the smells, the untidiness, and the haphazard life of the market-place in Addis Ababa; I wanted colour and savagery, hardship and adventure. Had I been posted to one of the towns I have no doubt that, disgruntled, I should have left the Sudan within a few months, but Charles Dupuis, Governor of Darfur, had anticipated my reaction and had asked that I should be sent to his Province. I was posted to Kutum in northern Darfur, where I served under Guy Moore, a man of great humanity and understanding. He had come to the Sudan from the deserts of Iraq, where he had been a Political Officer at the end of the First World War. He loved talking of those days among the Arabs, and his reminiscences made a great impression on me. We were the only Englishmen in the District, which was the largest in the Sudan and covered more than 50,000 square miles. It was desert country with a small but very varied population of about 180,000. There were nomadic Arab tribes, others of Berber origin, Negro cultivators in the hills, and in the south some of the Baggara, the cattle-owning Arabs, who had won fame as the bravest fighting men in the Dervish army.

I spent most of my time on trek travelling with camels. In the Danakil country I had used camels for carrying loads; here for the first time I rode them. District Commissioners usually travelled with a baggage train of four or five camels loaded with tents, camp furniture, and tinned foods. Guy Moore taught me to travel light and eat the local food. I usually travelled accompanied by three or four of the local tribesmen; I kept no servants who were not from the district. Where there were villages, the villagers fed us, other-wise we cooked a simple meal of porridge and ate together from a common dish. I slept in the open on the ground beside them and learnt to treat them as companions and not as servants. Before I left Kutum I had some of the finest riding camels in the Sudan, for I bought the best that I could find; they interested me far more than the two horses I had in my stable. On one of the camels I rode 115 miles in twenty-three hours, and a few months later I rode from Jabal Maidob to Omdurman, a distance of 450 miles, in nine days.

During my first winter in the Sudan I travelled for a month in the Libyan desert. I planned to visit the wells of Bir Natrun, one of the few places in this desert where there was water. It was not in Kutum district, not even in the same province, but as no officials ever went there, and as I had been told I should be refused if I did ask permission from Khartoum, I decided to visit it and say nothing. I started from Jabal Maidob with five companions. As we topped a rise on our first day and saw the stark emptiness before us I caught my breath. There were eight waterless days ahead of us to Bir Natrun and twelve more by the way we planned to return. For the first two days we saw occasional white oryx and a few ostriches; after that there was nothing. Hour after hour, day after day, we moved forward and nothing changed; the desert met the empty sky always the same distance ahead of us. Time and space were one. Round us was a silence in which only the winds played, and a cleanness which was infinitely remote from the world of men.

On my return I went into Fasher – the Provincial Headquarters – for Christmas. At dinner there was talk of the Italians having occupied Bir Natrun. Recently they had seized the small oasis of Uainat on the Sudan–Libyan frontier which had been assumed to belong to the Sudan. This incident had led to protests and the exchange of notes. Now I heard that Dongala had reported to Khartoum that some Arabs had recently seen white men at Bir Natrun, and that this was assumed to be further aggression by the Italians. 'Emergency measures' had been taken and aircraft had been moved to Wadi Halfa. I interrupted to say that I could not believe this since I had just returned from Bir Natrun, where I had only seen a few Arabs. A stunned silence followed, and then the CO of the Western Arab Corps said grimly, 'I suppose *you* are the Italians.' A little later, when I went through Khartoum on leave, it was pointed out to me firmly but sympathetically by the Civil Secretary that it was not customary to travel in someone else's district without the DC's consent, and certainly not to tour in another province without the Governor's permission.

At the end of 1937 I heard that I was to be transferred to Wad Medani, the headquarters of the Blue Nile Province and the centre of the Gezira Cotton Scheme. I was appalled at the idea of spending two years or more in this African suburbia. On my way through Khartoum on leave I persuaded the Civil Secretary to let me resign from the permanent Political Service and rejoin as a contract DC on the understanding that I should not be asked to serve except in the wilds. This meant that I should no longer be eligible for a pension, but I doubted that I really wished to spend the rest of my active life in the Sudan. I had been happy in Darfur. I had found satisfaction in the stimulating harshness of this empty land, pleasure in the nomadic life which I had led. I had loved the hunting. It had been exciting to stalk Barbary sheep among the craters of Maidob, or kudu in the Tagabo hills, or addax or oryx on the edge of the Libyan desert. It had been wildly exciting to charge with a mob of mounted tribesmen through thick bush after a galloping lion, to ride close behind it when it tired, while the Arabs waved their spears and shouted defiance, to circle round the patch of jungle in which it had come to bay, trying to make out its shape among the shadows, while the air quivered with its growls. I had grown fond of the people among whom I lived. I valued the qualities which they possessed and was jealous for the preservation of their way of life. But I knew that I was not really suited to be a DC as I had no faith in the changes which we were bringing about. I craved for the past, resented the present, and dreaded the future.

I was posted to the Western Nuer District of the Upper Nile

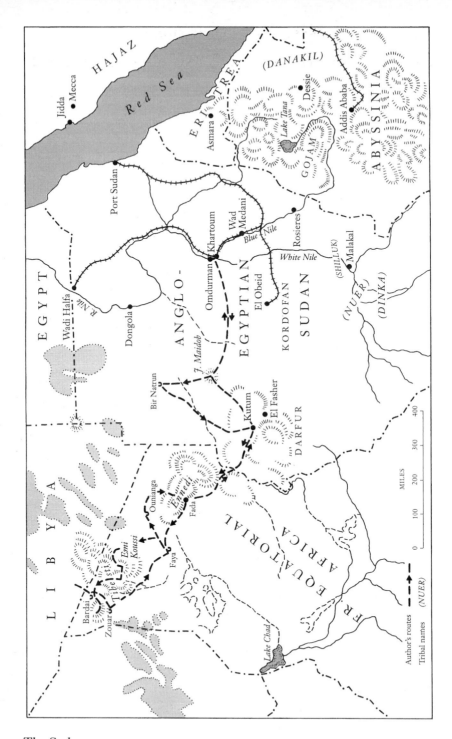

The Sudan

Province. I went there on my return from leave, part of which I had spent in Morocco.

The Nuer are Nilotics, kin to the Dinka and Shilluk, and they live in the swamps or Sudd which borders the White Nile to the south of Malakal. A pastoral people who own great herds of cattle, they are a virile race of tall, stark-naked savages with handsome arrogant faces and long hair dyed golden with cow's urine. The District had only been administered since 1925, and there had been some fierce fighting before they had submitted, but they were a people who had exerted a fascination over nearly all Englishmen who had encountered them.

I lived on a paddle-steamer with Wedderburn Maxwell, my District Commissioner. We were left to ourselves; all that the Governor asked was that he should get an occasional letter to say that we were all right. We kept a few files for our own convenience, but were not bothered with the mass of paper which accumulated on office desks in more conventional districts. We were happily out of touch with the rest of the Sudan, for there were no roads anywhere in the district; it was only possible to get there by steamer and to travel in the district with porters. The country was full of game. I once saw a thousand elephants in one vast herd along the river's banks. There were buffalo and white rhinoceros, hippopotamus, giraffe, and many kinds of antelope, and there were leopards, and a great number of lions. I shot seventy lions during the five years I was in the Sudan.

This was the Africa which I had read about as a boy and which I had despaired of finding in the Sudan when I first saw Khartoum: the long line of naked porters winding across a plain dotted with grazing antelope; my trackers slipping through the dappled bush as we followed a herd of buffalo; the tense excitement as we closed in upon a lion at bay; the grunting cough as it charged; the reeking red shambles as we cut up a fallen elephant, a blood-caked youth grinning out from between the gaping ribs; white cattle egrets flying above the Nile against a background of papyrus, such as is depicted in the Pharaohs' tombs; Lake No and the setting sun reflected redly in water that shone like polished steel; hippopotamus grunting close by in a darkness that was alive with other sounds; smoke rising over Nuer cattle camps; the leaping, twisting forms caught up in the excitement of a war dance; the rigid figures of young men undergoing the agony of initiation. Earlier in my life this would have been all that I could have asked, but now I was troubled with memories of the desert.

In 1938 I spent my leave in the Sahara and visited the Tibesti mountains, which were unknown except to French officers who had travelled there on duty. I left Kutum early in August accompanied by a Zaghawa lad, who had been my servant since I came to the Sudan, and an elderly Badayat who knew the language of the Tibbu, having lived in Tibesti. I hired camels in Darfur to take us as far as Faya; after that we should need camels used to the mountains. We travelled light, the distances being great and the time short.

Among the Nuer I had lived in a tent apart from my men, waited on by servants; I had been an Englishman travelling in Africa, but now I could revert happily to the desert ways which I had learned at Kutum. For this was the real desert where differences of race and colour, of wealth and social standing, are almost meaningless; where coverings of pretence are stripped away and basic truths emerge. It was a place where men live close together. Here, to be alone was to feel at once the weight of fear, for the nakedness of this land was more terrifying than the darkest forest at dead of night. In the pitiless light of day we were as insignificant as the beetles I watched labouring across the sand. Only in the kindly darkness could we borrow a few square feet of desert and find homeliness within the radius of the firelight, while overhead the familiar pattern of the stars screened the fearful mystery of space.

We did long marches, sometimes riding for eighteen or twenty hours. At last we saw, faint like a cloud upon the desert's edge, the dim outline of Emi Koussi, the crater summit of Tibesti. As we drew near it dominated our world, sharp blue at dawn, and dark against the setting sun. We climbed it with difficulty, and stood at last upon the crater's rim, 11,125 feet above sea-level. Beneath us in the crater's floor was the vent, a great hole a thousand feet deep.

To the north were range upon range of jagged peaks, rising from shadowed gorges, an awe-inspiring scene of utter desolation. Everywhere the rocks were slowly crumbling away, eroded by sun and wind and storm. It was a sombre land, black and red and brown and grey. We travelled across wind-swept uplands, over passes and through narrow gorges, under precipices, past towering peaks. From Bardai we visited the great crater of Doon, 2,500 feet in depth. We camped in the Modra valley beneath Tieroko, the most magnificent of all the Tibesti mountains. When we returned to Darfur we had ridden over two thousand miles in three months.

In the desert I had found a freedom unattainable in civilization; a life unhampered by possessions, since everything that was not a necessity was an encumbrance. I had found, too, a comradeship inherent in the circumstances, and the belief that tranquillity was to be found there. I had learnt the satisfaction which comes from hardship and the pleasure which derives from abstinence: the contentment of a full belly; the richness of meat; the taste of clean water; the ecstasy of surrender when the craving for sleep becomes a torment; the warmth of a fire in the chill of dawn.

I went back to the Nuer, but I was lonely, sitting apart on a chair, among a crowd of naked savages. I wanted more than they could give me, even while I enjoyed being with them. The Danakil journey had unsuited me for life in our civilization; it had confirmed and strengthened a craving for the wilds. The Nuer country would have met this need, but three years in Darfur and my recent journey to Tibesti had taught me to ask for more than this, for something which I was to find later in the deserts of Arabia.

I had been posted back to Kutum, but was still on leave when the war started, and being without a district I was allowed to join the Sudan Defence Force in April 1940. For me the Abyssinian campaign had the quality of a crusade. Ten years earlier I had watched the Emperor Haile Selassie being crowned in Addis Ababa; six years after this I had seen him descend from the train at Victoria into exile. I am proud to have served in Abyssinia with Sandford's mission which prepared the way for Haile Selassie's restoration, and to have fought in Wingate's Gideon Force which took him back

from the Sudan through Gojam to Addis Ababa. From Abyssinia I
was sent to Syria, where I served in Jabal al Druze and later worked
for a year among the tribes.

The deserts in which I had travelled had been blanks in time
as well as space. They had no intelligible history, the nomads who
inhabited them had no known past. Some bushmen paintings, a few
disputed references in Herodotus and Ptolemy, and tribal legends of
the recent past were all that had come down to us. But in Syria
the patina of human history was thick along the edges of the desert.
Damascus and Aleppo had been old before Rome was founded.
Among the towns and villages, invasion after invasion had heaped
ruin upon ruin, and each new conquest had imposed new conquerors upon the last. But the desert had always been inviolate.
There I lived among tribes who claimed descent from Ishmael, and
listened to old men who spoke of events which had occurred a
thousand years ago as if they had happened in their own youth. I
went there with a belief in my own racial superiority, but in their
tents I felt like an uncouth, inarticulate barbarian, an intruder from
a shoddy and materialistic world. Yet from them I learnt how welcoming are the Arabs and how generous is their hospitality.

From Syria I went to Egypt and then to the Western Desert,
where I was with the Special Air Service Regiment. We travelled
in jeeps and were divided into small parties which hid in the desert
and attacked the enemy's lines of communication. We carried food,
water, and fuel with us; we required nothing from our surroundings.
I was in the desert, but insulated from it by the jeep in which I
travelled. It was simply a surface, marked as 'good' or 'bad going'
on the map. Even if we had stumbled on Zarzura, whose discovery
had been the ambition of every Libyan explorer I should have felt
no interest.

In the last year of the war I was again in Abyssinia, where I
was Political Adviser at Dessie in the north. The country required
technicians but had little use for political advisers. Frustrated and
unhappy I resigned. One evening in Addis Ababa I met O. B.
Lean, the Desert Locust Specialist of the Food and Agriculture
Organization. He said he was looking for someone to travel in the

Empty Quarter of Arabia to collect information on locust movements. I said at once that I should love to do this but that I was not an entomologist. Lean assured me that this was not nearly as important as knowledge of desert travel. I was offered the job and accepted it before we had finished dinner.

All my past had been but a prelude to the five years that lay ahead of me.

TWO

Prelude in Dhaufar

The Wali of Dhaufar collects a party of Bait Kathir
at Salala to escort me to the sands of Ghanim.
While waiting for their arrival I travel in the Qarra
mountains.

The deserts of Arabia cover more than a million square miles,
and the southern desert occupies nearly half of the total
area. The southern desert stretches for nine hundred miles
from the frontier of the Yemen to the foothills of Oman, and for
five hundred miles from the southern coast of Arabia to the Persian
Gulf and the borders of the Najd. The greater part of it is a wilderness of sand; it is a desert within a desert, so enormous and so
desolate that even Arabs call it the Rub al Khali or the Empty
Quarter.

In 1929 T. E. Lawrence wrote to Lord Trenchard, Marshal of
the Royal Air Force, suggesting that either the R100 or R101 should
be deviated on its trial flight to India to pass over the Empty
Quarter. He wrote 'to go over the empty quarter will be an enormous advertisement for them. It will mark an era of exploration.
Nothing but an airship can do it, and I want it to be one of ours
which gets the plum.' Nevertheless in 1930 Bertram Thomas
crossed this desert from south to north, and a few months later
another Englishman, St John Philby, crossed it again, this time
from the north. Thomas and Philby had proved that the Empty
Quarter could be crossed with camels, but when I went there fifteen

years later they were the only Europeans who had travelled in it, and vast areas between the Yemen and Oman were still unexplored.

When I was at Oxford I had read *Arabia Felix* in which Bertram Thomas described his journey. The month which I had already spent in the Danakil country had given me some appreciation and understanding of desert life, and Lawrence's *Revolt in the Desert* had awakened my interest in the Arabs; but while at Oxford I longed only to return to Abyssinia. It was not until later that my thoughts turned more and more insistently to the Empty Quarter. Although I had travelled in the deserts of the Sudan and the Sahara, others had been before me and the mystery was gone: the routes and wells, the dunes and mountains were marked on maps; the tribes were administered. The thrill that I had known when travelling in the Danakil country was missing. The Empty Quarter became for me the Promised Land, but the approaches to it were barred until this chance meeting with Lean gave me my great opportunity. I was not really interested in locusts. I certainly would not have volunteered to go to Kenya or the Kalahari to look for them, but they provided me with the golden key to Arabia.

Nowadays one of the chief obstacles to travel in the few unexplored places of the world that remain is getting permission from the governments which claim them. It would have been difficult, perhaps even impossible, for me to have approached the Empty Quarter without the initial backing which I received from the Middle East Anti-Locust Unit, but once I had been there and had made friends with the Bedu I could travel where I wished, I had no need to worry about international boundaries that did not even exist on maps.

I had already seen plenty of locusts in the Sudan, and during the year I was at Dessie I had watched swarms rolling across the horizon like clouds of smoke as they arrived on the Abyssinian uplands from their breeding places in Arabia. I had watched them going past, long-legged in wavering flight, as thick in the air as snowflakes in a storm. I had seen branches broken from trees by the weight of the settled swarms, and green fields stripped bare in a few hours; but although I knew how destructive they could be, I

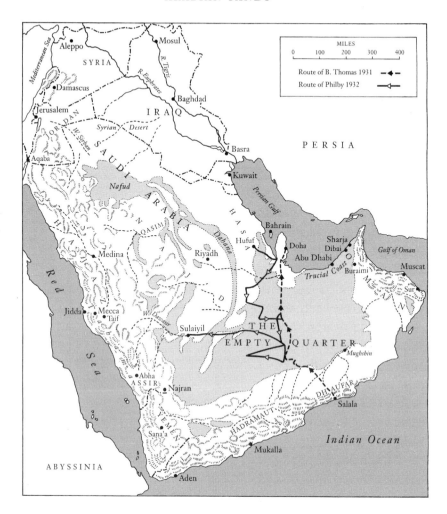

Arabia

knew practically nothing about their habits. Therefore, before going to the Empty Quarter, I was sent to Saudi Arabia for two months to learn about locusts from Vesey FitzGerald, who was running a campaign there. Few Europeans had previously been allowed to enter Saudi Arabia, and almost all of them had been confined to Jidda, the port on the Red Sea, where the diplomats and the commercial community lived. Locust officers, however, were allowed to travel freely in nearly all parts of the country.

During the war a species of locust called the 'desert locust' had threatened the Middle East with famine. It was known that one of the main breeding grounds was the Arabian peninsula, and in 1943–4 the Middle East Anti-Locust Unit was given permission by King Abd al Aziz ibn Saud to carry out a campaign against them in Saudi Arabia.

Vesey FitzGerald told me of the discoveries which had been made in recent years and which were the reason for my journey into the Empty Quarter. Dr Uvarov, who was head of the Anti-Locust Research Centre in London, had discovered that both the desert locust and a large solitary grasshopper belonged to the same species, although they differed in their habits, their colours, and even in the structure of their bodies to such an extent that naturalists had named and described them as separate species. These solitary grasshoppers occasionally developed gregarious habits that were probably due to overcrowding. Their numbers would increase after a season of plentiful vegetation, and then in the next dry season when they were confined to a smaller area they would swarm and migrate, ceasing to be solitary grasshoppers and becoming desert locusts. The small initial swarms increased very rapidly, for locusts breed several times a year, and each locust lays as many as a hundred eggs at a time. The eggs hatch in about three weeks and the young locusts or hoppers reach maturity in about six weeks.

In Saudi Arabia with Vesey FitzGerald I saw densely packed bands of hoppers extending over a front of several miles and with a depth of a hundred yards or more, and yet he told me that these were only small bands. I knew that with favourable wind locusts can cover enormous distances, but I was amazed when he told me that swarms can breed in India during the monsoon, move in the autumn to southern Persia or Arabia, breed there again, and then pass on to the Sudan or East Africa. Some of these swarms cover two hundred square miles or more. Eventually disease attacks them and they vanish as quickly as they had appeared. Then for a time there are no more desert locusts in the world, only solitary grasshoppers.

Doctor Uvarov believed that the 'outbreak centres' were restricted to certain definite areas and that if these could be located and controlled it would be possible to prevent the solitary grasshoppers from ever swarming. The first thing to do was to locate all these outbreak centres. He thought that some of them might be in southern Arabia, especially at Mughshin,* where Thomas had discovered that the great watercourses which ran inland from the coastal mountains of Dhaufar ended against the sands of the Empty Quarter. Dhaufar was known to get the monsoon, and it seemed probable that enough water flowed inland each year to produce permanent vegetation along the edge of the sands. If this were so, the area would almost certainly be an outbreak centre. I was to go there and find out, but so little was known about this part of southern Arabia that wherever I went I could collect no useful information.

I arrived in Aden at the end of September 1945, visited the mountains along the Yemen frontier, and on 15 October flew to Salala, the capital of Dhaufar, which lies about two-thirds of the way along the southern coast of Arabia. It was from there that I was to start my journey. While at Salala I stayed with the RAF in their camp outside the town. It was on a bare stony plain which was shut in by the Qarra mountains a few miles away, and had been set up during the war when an air route from Aden to India was opened. This route was no longer used, but once a week an aeroplane came to Salala from Aden.

Dhaufar belonged to the Sultan of Muscat, and he had insisted, when he allowed the RAF to establish themselves there, that not one of them should visit the town or travel anywhere outside the perimeter of the camp unless accompanied by one of his guards, and that none of them should speak to any of the local inhabitants. These restrictions also applied to me while I was staying in the camp. In the case of the RAF they seemed to me to be reasonable, designed to prevent incidents between airmen who knew nothing

* See map on page 26.

of Arabs, and tribesmen who were armed, quick-tempered, and suspicious of all strangers; but applied to me, who had come to travel with the people, they were extremely irksome. They meant that I had to make all my arrangements through the Wali, or Governor.

About 1877 Dhaufar had been occupied, after centuries of tribal anarchy, by a force belonging to the Sultan of Muscat, but in 1896 the tribes rebelled, surprised the fort that had been built at Salala, and murdered the garrison. It was several months before the Sultan was able to reassert his authority, which, however, has since remained largely nominal except on the plain surrounding the town.

The morning after my arrival I went into Salala to call on the Wali. Salala was a small town, little more than a village. It lies on the edge of the sea and has no harbour, the rollers from the Indian Ocean sweeping on to the white sands beneath the coconut palms that fringe the shore. When I arrived fishermen were netting sardines, and piles of these fish were drying in the sun. The whole town reeked of their decay. The Sultan's palace, white and dazzling in the strong sunlight, was the most conspicuous building, and clustered around it was the small *suq* or market, a number of flat-roofed mud-houses, and a labyrinth of mat shelters, fences, and narrow lanes. The market consisted of only a dozen shops, but it was the best shopping centre between Sur and the Hadhramaut, a distance of eight hundred miles. On my way to the palace I passed the mosque, near which were some old stone buildings and also an extensive graveyard. Scattered on the plain around the town were various ruins, all that remained of the legendary past, for some have claimed that Dhaufar was the Ophir of the Bible.

The successive civilizations whose prosperity caused the Romans to name all this part of Arabia 'Arabia Felix' had been farther to the west. The Minaeans had developed a civilization as early as 1000 BC in the north-eastern part of the Yemen. They were traders, with colonies as far north as Maan near the gulf of Aqaba, and they depended for their prosperity on frankincense from Dhaufar which they marketed in Egypt and Syria. They were succeeded by the Sabaeans, who in turn were succeeded by the

Himyarites. This southern Arabian civilization, which lasted for 1,500 years, came to an end in the middle of the sixth century AD, but while it lasted this remote land acquired a reputation for fabulous wealth. For centuries Egypt, Assyria, and the Seleucids schemed and fought to control the desert route along which the frankincense was carried northwards, and in 24 BC the Emperor Augustus sent an army under Aelius Gallus, prefect of Egypt, to conquer the lands where this priceless gum originated. The army marched southwards for nine hundred miles, but lack of water eventually forced it to retire. This was the only time any European power had ever tried to invade Arabia.

As I entered the town of Salala I passed a small caravan, two men with four camels tied head to tail, and when I questioned the guard who was with me he said that these camels were carrying *mughur*, or frankincense. Today, however, the trade is small and of little value, hardly more important in the market at Salala than the buying and selling of goats and firewood.

My attention was caught by the men who led the camels. They were small and wiry, about five feet four inches in height, and were dressed in a length of dark-blue cloth wound round their waists, with an end thrown over one shoulder; the indigo had run out from the cloth and smeared their chests and arms. They were bare-headed, and their hair was long and untidy. Both of them wore daggers and carried rifles. My guard said that they were Bedu from beyond the mountains and that they belonged to the Bait Kathir. In the market-place were more of them, while others waited outside the palace gates. They reminded me of the tribesmen whom I had seen recently at Dhala on the Yemen border, and seemed very different to the Arabs from the great Bedu tribes I had met in Syria and the Najd.

The palace gates were guarded by armed men dressed in long Arab shirts and head-cloths. Some of them were from Oman and the rest were slaves; none were local tribesmen. One of them took me into the reception hall, where I met the Wali. He was a townsman from Oman, large and portly. He was dressed in a white shirt reaching to the ground, a brown cloak, embroidered with gold, and a Kashmiri shawl which was loosely wrapped round his head. He wore a large curved dagger at the middle of his stomach. I greeted him in Arabic, and before we started our discussion I ate a few dates and drank three cups of bitter black coffee handed to me by one of his retainers.

The Wali told me that he had been instructed by the Sultan to collect a party of Bedu with camels to take me to Mughshin. He said that he had arranged for forty-five Bedu to go with me and that now he would send messengers into the desert to fetch them. I thanked him, but suggested that forty-five were far more than I needed, and that a dozen would be quite enough. I knew that the British Consul in Muscat, when he got permission for me to do this journey, had agreed with the Sultan that the size of the party should be fixed by the Wali, and that I was to pay the equivalent of ten shillings a day to each man who went with me. I realized that everyone here regarded my journey as a heaven-sent opportunity to enrich himself, and that they would all try to make my party as large as possible. The Wali now insisted that, as there was a serious risk of my meeting raiders, he could not take the responsibility of allowing me to go to Mughshin with fewer than forty-five men, and that the Bedu themselves would not agree to go with a smaller party. I knew there had been raiding near Mughshin when Bertram Thomas went there in 1929, but as he was the only European who had ever crossed the Qarra mountains, which I had seen that morning six or eight miles beyond the camp, I was completely ignorant of what conditions were now like in the desert beyond. Eventually, after several meetings with the Wali I agreed to take thirty Arabs. The Wali told me they would be from the Bait Kathir tribe, and added that they would be ready to start in a fortnight.

I arranged to spend this time travelling in the Qarra mountains, which had been explored by Theodore and Mabel Bent in 1895 and by Bertram Thomas in 1929. The Wali said that he would send four of his retainers with me, two Omanis and two slaves, and that we should have to hire camels from the Qarra, who live in the mountains, changing them every time we crossed from one valley into the next, since each valley was owned by a different section of the tribe, and all of them were jealous of each other and much divided by feuds. He warned me: 'Don't trust them. These mountain folk are not like the Bedu from the desert. They are treacherous and thievish; altogether without honour.'

It was obvious that, although the Qarra lived only a few miles from Salala, the Sultan of Muscat had little control over them. Arabs rule but do not administer. Their government is intensely individualistic, and is successful or unsuccessful according to the degree of fear and respect which the ruler commands, and his skill in dealing with individual men. Founded on an individual life, their government is impermanent and liable to end in chaos at any moment. To Arab tribesmen this system is comprehensible and acceptable, and its success or failure should not be measured in terms of efficiency and justice as judged by Western standards. To these tribesmen security can be bought too dearly by loss of individual freedom.

Two days later we rode our camels across the stony plain of Jarbib; we passed some cultivation and went on towards Jabal Qarra, which is about two thousand feet high, and is flanked on either side by much higher mountains which close in on the sea. Some peculiarity in the shape of these mountains draws the monsoon clouds, so that the rain concentrates upon the southern slopes of Jabal Qarra, which are in consequence covered with mist and rain throughout the summer and were now dark with jungles in full leaf after the monsoon. All the way along the south Arabian coast for 1,400 miles from Perim to Sur, only these twenty miles get a regular rainfall. The mountains on either side are often beautiful, especially at dawn and sunset when borrowed colours soften the austerity of rock and sand, but they are seldom touched with green. Usually the few camel-thorns, which throw a thin mesh of shadow over the darkly patinated rock, rustle dryly in the breeze. But on Jabal Qarra the jungle trees are wreathed with jasmine and giant convolvulus and roped together with lianas. Massive tamarinds grow in the valleys, and on the downs great fig-trees rise above the wind-rippled grass like oaks in an English park.

We camped in the mouth of a valley near a Qarra village. To

my unpractised eye these tribesmen were similar in appearance to the Bait Kathir whom I had seen in Salala, but they spoke their own language, whereas the Bait Kathir spoke Arabic. Three tribes, the Qarra, Mahra, and Harasis, as well as the remnants of others like the Shahara, speak different dialects of a common origin and are known to the Arab-speaking tribes as the Ahl al Hadara. Bertram Thomas had made some study of these dialects, sufficient to establish that they were closely related to the ancient Semitic languages of the Minaeans, Sabaeans, and Himyarites. He suggested that Hadara may perhaps be identified with Hadoram, who is given in Genesis as one of the sons of Joktan, a descendant of Shem, and that Hadhramaut, the present-day name of the country immediately to the west of the Mahra country, could be connected with Hazaramaveth, the brother of Hadoram.

As we climbed the mountain-side I noticed paradise flycatchers, rufous and black, with long white streamers in their tails, and brilliant butterflies. They were in keeping with the jungles which surrounded us, and as unexpected in Arabia. Then we came out on to the downs and camped near the top of the mountain. I walked to the watershed, anxious to see what lay beyond, and found myself standing between two worlds. To the south were green meadows where cattle grazed, thickets, and spreading trees, whereas a stone's throw to the north was empty desert – sand, rocks, and a few wisps of withered grass. The transition was as abrupt as it is between the irrigated fields and the desert in the Nile valley. Here the dividing line followed the crest of the mountains.

The Qarra were camped in family groups on the downs. They owned small humpless cattle, a few camels, and flocks of goats, but no sheep, horses, or dogs. Most of the families owned twenty to thirty cows. Thomas mentioned in his book that when a man died his family sacrificed half his cows. He thought that this custom was peculiar to them, but apparently the Wahiba, a Bedu tribe in Oman, do the same. They also had another strange practice which hitherto I had seen only among the Nuer in the southern Sudan. Before a man milked a cow – women were forbidden even to touch the udders – he would sometimes put his lips to the cow's vagina and blow into it to induce the cow to lower her milk. These Qarra told me that they would remain here till January and then move down to the foot of the mountain and collect in large cattle camps – one of which we had passed on the way – small grass shelters crowded together in the mouth of the valley. When the monsoon started they would move back into the valleys and shelter their animals in caves in the limestone cliffs, or in low dark byres made of stones and roofed with matted grass.

I stayed there for ten days. Then I heard rumours that the Bait Kathir, who were to go with me, were in Salala, and I decided to go back. Some Qarra came with us. They carried butter, firewood, and a pot of wild honey which they would sell in the market. They said they would buy dried sardines, which they feed to their animals later in the season when the grazing gets scarce.

On my return the Wali invited me to meet some of the Bait Kathir who were to go with me. There were eight of them sitting with him when I arrived. Six wore head-cloths and Arab shirts reaching half-way down their calves; two were bareheaded and dressed only in loin-cloths. All wore daggers and cartridge belts; they had left their rifles outside the audience hall. While we drank coffee and ate dates I wondered how I should get on with these people. An old man with a fringe of white beard and twinkling eyes, Salim Tamtaim, was their head sheikh. The Wali said he was eighty, but still vigorous, having just married another wife; and the old man exclaimed 'Eh, by God, I can still ride and shoot.' I noticed especially a man called Sultan who looked more like a Red Indian than an Arab. The others deferred to him rather than to Tamtaim, and I remembered that the Qarra had said: 'Sultan has arrived in Salala with the Bait Kathir.' It was obvious that he was their leader. He had a striking face, austere, lined, and hairless, except for a few hairs growing in a curl on his chin. The Wali pointed to another of them and said: 'Musallim will shoot meat for you. He is famous as a hunter.' The man of whom he spoke was dressed in a clean white shirt, and an embroidered head-cloth. He was a small man, like all the others, but he was more solidly built and slightly bow-legged. He looked more of a townsman than a Bedu. I arranged with them that they should fetch me next morning from the RAF camp.

They arrived after breakfast accompanied by a large crowd from Salala. They were a wild-looking lot, most of them wearing only loin-cloths, and all of them armed with rifles and daggers. I showed old Tamtaim and Sultan the food I had provided for the journey – rice, flour, dates, sugar, tea, coffee, and liquid butter. With the help of the RAF storeman I had done it up in sacks in what seemed to me suitable-sized loads, but Sultan said at once that they were too heavy. They undid them and started to repack, pouring the rice, flour, and sugar into dirty-looking goatskin bags. They argued endlessly among themselves, shouting in harsh voices. The camels were led up and couched, but they struggled roaring to their feet, and were couched again. An unkempt savage with inflamed eyes and a tangled mop of hair refused to allow a camel to be loaded, and started to lead it away. Someone else seized the camel's halter, and I thought they were going to fight. Everyone else gathered round and shouted. I could understand little of what they said. Eventually the camel was led back and loaded.

When they were nearly ready I went into the hut where I had been staying and put on my Arab clothes. To have worn European clothes would have alienated these Bait Kathir at once, for although a few of them had travelled with Bertram Thomas, most of them had not even spoken to an Englishman before. I wore a loin-cloth, a long shirt, and a head-cloth with the ends twisted round my head in their fashion. None of these Bait Kathir wore the black woollen head-rope which is a conspicuous feature of Arab dress in the north.

As this was the first time I had worn Arab dress I felt extremely self-conscious. My shirt was new, white, and rather stiff, very noticeable among the Bedu's dingy clothes. They were all small men, and as I am six foot two I felt as conspicuous as a lighthouse, and as different from them as one of the RAF.

On previous journeys I had commanded respect as an Englishman, and in the Sudan I had the prestige of being a government official. When I had travelled in the desert there I had tried to break through the barrier that lay between me and my companions, but I had always felt rather condescending. Now for the first time

I was travelling without a servant. Quite alone among a crowd of Arabs whom I had never seen before, I should be with them for three or four months, even for six if I undertook the second journey to the Hadhramaut which I was already planning. At first glance they seemed to be little better than savages, as primitive as the Danakil, but I was soon disconcerted to discover that, while they were prepared to tolerate me as a source of very welcome revenue, they never doubted my inferiority. They were Muslims and Bedu and I was neither. They had never heard of the English, for all Europeans were known to them simply as Christians, or more probably infidels, and nationality had no meaning for them. They had heard vaguely of the war as a war between the Christians, and of the Aden government as a Christian government. Their world was the desert and they had little if any interest in events that happened outside it. They identified me with the Christians from Aden, but had no idea of any power greater than that of Ibn Saud. One day they spoke of a sheikh in the Hadhramaut who had recently defied the government and against whom the Aden levies had carried out some rather inconclusive operations. I realized that they thought that this force was all that my tribe could muster. They judged power by the number and effectiveness of fighting men, not by machines which they could not understand.

I shall always remember the first camp at the foot of the Qarra mountains. We had stopped in a shallow watercourse which ran out into the plain, and we had dumped our kit wherever there was room for it among thorn bushes and boulders. The others were soon busy, greasing water-skins, twisting rope, mending saddles, and looking to their camels. I sat near them, very conscious of their scrutiny. I longed to go over and join them in their tasks, but I was kept awkwardly apart by my reserve. For the first and last time I felt lonely in Arabia. Eventually old Tamtaim hobbled over and invited me to drink coffee with them, and Sultan fetched my blankets and saddlebags and put them down beside the fire. Later Musallim cooked rice and six of us fed together.

I asked them about the Rub al Khali, or the Empty Quarter, the goal of my ambitions. No one had heard of it. 'What is he talking about? What does he want?' 'God alone knows. I cannot understand his talk.' At last Sultan exclaimed 'Oh! he means the Sands', and I realized that this was their name for the great desert of southern Arabia. I have heard townsmen and villagers in the Najd and the Hajaz refer to it as the Rub al Khali, but never Bedu who lived upon its borders.

I found it difficult to understand their talk. In the Sudan I had learnt Arabic among tribes who spoke it as their second language. I had really only begun to speak it when I was in Syria during the war. But there was a great difference between Syrian Arabic and the dialect of the Bait Kathir, whose pronunciation and intonation were entirely different from anything I had heard before, and many of whose words were archaic. The Bait Kathir were equally puzzled by my speech, but this did not stop them from asking questions about 'The Christians'. 'Did they know God? Did they fast and pray? Were they circumcised? Did they marry like Muslims or just take a woman when they wanted one? How much bride-price did they pay? Did they own camels? Were they tribesmen? How did they bury their dead?' It was always questions such as these that they asked me. None of them had any interest in the cars and aeroplanes which they had seen in the RAF camp. The rifles with which they fought were all that they had accepted from the outside world, the only modern invention which interested them.

They spoke of Bertram Thomas who had travelled with them. Bedu notice everything and forget nothing. Garrulous by nature, they reminisce endlessly, whiling away with their chatter the long marching hours, and talking late into the night round their camp fires. Their life is at all times desperately hard, and they are merciless critics of those who fall short in patience, good humour, generosity, loyalty, or courage. They make no allowance for the stranger. Whoever lives with the Bedu must accept Bedu conventions, and conform to Bedu standards. Only those who have journeyed with them can appreciate the strain of such a life. These tribesmen are accustomed since birth to the physical hardships of the desert, to drink the scanty bitter water of the Sands, to eat gritty unleavened bread, to endure the maddening irritation of driven sand, intense

37

cold, heat, and blinding glare in a land without shade or cloud. But more wearing still is the nervous tension. I was to learn how hard it is to live crowded together with people of another faith, speech, and culture in the solitude of the desert, how easy to be provoked to senseless wrath by the importunities and improvidence.

Bertram Thomas had reason to be impatient. He lost precious months of the cold weather waiting in Dhaufar for his guide, bin Kalut, and the other Rashid to arrive. The previous year he had reached Mughshin, and there, upon the threshold of the Sands, had been thwarted by his Bait Kathir companions. He was far from being a Bedu by nature, and yet I never heard these Bedu speak a disparaging word about him. I have known them criticize him for tiring their camels with the heavy foreign saddle on which he rode, or comment on his preference for sleeping apart from his companions; but these were idiosyncrasies which they accepted even if they never understood them, things which they now recalled with a smile.

He was the first European to come among them and he won their respect by his good nature, generosity, and determination. They remembered him as a good travelling companion. When I went among these exclusive tribesmen sixteen years after he had left them, I was welcomed because I belonged to the same tribe as Thomas. I had only met him twice, in Cairo during the war, and then only for a few minutes. I should have liked to meet him again before he died, to tell him how much I owed to him.

THREE

The Sands of Ghanim

⁓

After travelling to the sands of Ghanim and
Mughshin we return to Salala. There I meet
the Rashid for the first time and travel with them
to the Hadhramaut.

This first journey on the fringes of the Empty Quarter was
only important to me as my probation for the far longer
and more difficult journeys that were to follow. During the
next five months I learnt to adapt myself to Bedu ways and to the
rhythm of their life.

My companions were always awake and moving about as soon
as it was light. I think the cold prevented them from sleeping,
except in snatches, for they had little to cover them other than the
clothes they wore, and during these winter nights there was often
a ground frost. Still half asleep, I would hear them rousing the
camels from their couching places. The camels roared and gurgled
as they were moved, and the Arabs shouted to each other in their
harsh, far-carrying voices. The camels would shuffle past, their
forelegs hobbled to prevent them straying, their breath white on
the cold air. A boy would drive them towards the nearest bushes.
Then someone would give the call to prayer:

> God is most great.
> I testify that there is no god but God.
> I testify that Muhammad is the Prophet of God.

Come to prayer!
Come to salvation!
Prayer is better than sleep.
God is most great.
There is no god but God.

Each line except the last was repeated twice. The lingering music
of the words, strangely compelling even to me who did not share
their faith, hung over the silent camp. I would watch old Tamtaim,
who slept near me, washing before he prayed. Every act had to be
performed exactly and in order. He washed his face, hands, and
feet, sucked water into his nostrils, put wet fingers into his ears,
and passed wet hands over the top of his head. The Bait Kathir
prayed singly, each man in his own place and in his own time,
whereas the Rashid, with whom I later travelled, prayed together
and in line. Tamtaim swept the ground before him, placed his rifle
in front of him, and then prayed facing towards Mecca. He stood
upright, bent forward his hands on his knees, knelt and then bowed
down till his forehead touched the ground. Several times he performed these ritual movements, slowly and impressively, while he
recited the formal prayer. Sometimes, after he had finished his
prayers, he intoned long passages from the Koran, and the very
sound of the words had the quality of great poetry. Many of these
Bedu knew only the opening verse of the Koran:

In the name of God, the Compassionate, the Merciful.
Praise be to God, Lord of the worlds!
The Compassionate, the Merciful!
King on the day of reckoning!
Thee *only* do we worship and to Thee do we cry for help.
Guide us on the straight path,
The path of those to whom Thou hast been gracious;
With whom Thou are not angry, and who go not astray.

This verse they repeated several times as they prayed. Muslims
should pray at dawn, at noon, in the afternoon, at sunset, and after

dark. The Bait Kathir prayed at dawn and sunset, but most of them neglected the other prayers.

A little later I would hear bell-like notes as someone pounded coffee in a brass mortar, varying his stroke to produce the semblance of a tune. I would get up. In the desert we slept in our clothes so that all I had to do was to adjust my head-cloth, pour a little water over my hands, splash it over my face, and then go over to the fire and greet the Arabs who were sitting round it: 'Salam alaikum' (Peace be on you), and they would stand up and answer 'Alaikum as salam' (On you be peace). Bedu always rise to return a salutation. If we were not in a hurry we would bake bread for breakfast, otherwise we would eat scraps set aside from our meal the night before. We would drink tea, sweet and black, and then coffee, which was bitter, black, and very strong. The coffee-drinking was a formal business, not to be hurried. The server stood as he poured a few drops into a small china cup, little bigger than an egg cup, which he handed to each of us in turn, bowing as he did so. Each person was served until he shook the cup slightly as he handed it back, signifying that he had had enough. It was not customary to take more than three cups.

The camels were now rounded up and brought in to be saddled and loaded. Sultan went over to fetch Umbrausha, the camel I was riding. She was a magnificent animal, a famous thoroughbred from Oman. The other camels seemed to me to be very small, judged by Sudanese standards, and all of them were in poor condition. Sultan had told me that there had been no proper rain in the desert for the last three years, and that their animals were weak from hunger.

The camels which these Bedu rode were females. In the Sudan I had always ridden on bulls, since both there and in those parts of the Sahara where I had travelled the females are kept for milk and never ridden. Throughout Arabia, however, females are ridden from choice. The tribes which carry goods for hire use the bulls as pack animals, but the Bait Kathir slaughter nearly all the male calves at birth. They live largely on camels' milk, and have no desire

41

to squander food on animals which can make no return, since there is no carrying trade in this desert. Bull camels to act as sires are consequently very rare. Later, when I travelled to the Hadhramaut, I was accompanied by a man who rode one. We were continuously pursued by tribesmen with females to be served. We had a long journey in front of us and this constant exercise was visibly exhausting my companion's mount, but he could not protest. Custom demanded that this camel should be allowed to serve as many females as were produced. No one even asked the owner's permission. They just brought up a camel, had it served, and took it away.

Loading the camels was a noisy business, for most of them roared and snarled whenever they were approached, and especially when the loads were placed on their backs. I asked Sultan how they managed on raids when silence was important, and he told me that they then tied the camels' mouths. The noise which our camels were making would have been heard two miles away or even farther in the desert stillness. Sultan had brought Umbrausha over to the place where I had slept, leading her by her head-rope. He now jerked downwards on it, saying 'Khrr, khrr', and she dropped to her knees; she then swayed backwards, and after settling her hind legs under her, sank down on to her hocks; she then shuffled her knees forward until she was comfortably settled on the ground, her chest resting on the horny pad between her forelegs. Sultan tied one of her forelegs with the end of the head-rope to prevent her rising while he was loading her. Umbrausha was properly trained and this was not necessary, but an Arab near us was having a lot of trouble with a young animal. She struggled back to her feet after he had couched her, and even after he had tied her knees she half rose and then pivoted round among the loads which he had been trying to put on her back. She snarled and gurgled, spewing half-chewed green cud over his shirt. 'May raiders get you,' he shouted at her in exasperation. She looked as if she would bite his head off at any moment, but female camels are really very gentle and do not bite. Male camels will bite, especially when they are rutting, and they inflict appalling injuries. I had treated a man in the Sudan

42

who had been bitten in the arm and the bone was splintered to fragments.

The southern Bedu ride on the small Omani saddle instead of on the double-poled saddle of northern Arabia to which I was accustomed. Sultan picked up my saddle, which was shaped like a small double wooden vice, fitted over palm-fibre pads, and girthed it tightly over Umbrausha's withers just in front of the hump. This wooden vice was really the tree on which he now built the saddle. He next took a crescent-shaped fibre pad which rose in a peak at the back and, after fitting it round the back and sides of the camel's hump, attached it with a loop of string to this tree. He then put a blanket over the pad, and folded my rug over this, placed my saddle-bags over the rug, and finally put a black sheepskin on top of the saddle-bags. He had already looped a woollen cord under the camel's stomach so that it passed over the rear pad, and he now took one end of this cord past the tree and back along the other side of the saddle to the original loop. When he drew the cord tight it held everything firmly in place. He had now built a platform over the camel's hump and the fibre pad which was behind it. Sitting on this, the rider was much farther back on the camel than he would have been if riding on the northern saddle, which is set over the camel's withers.

My saddle-bags were heavy with money and spare ammunition, and the small medicine-chest which I took with me. Most of the other riding camels carried forty or fifty pounds of rice or flour; all of them would be heavily laden when we were travelling long distances between wells and all our goatskins would be filled with water. I had hired four baggage camels, and these carried between a hundred and fifty and two hundred pounds.

When all was ready we set off on foot. We always walked for the first two or three hours. While we were still in the mountains each of us led his camel, or tied her by her head-rope to the tail of the one in front. Later, when we were on the gravel plains or in the sands, we turned them loose to find whatever food they could as they drifted along. We would walk behind them with our rifles on our shoulders, held by the muzzle. This is the way Bedu always carry their rifles. At first I found it disconcerting, for I knew that all the rifles were loaded. Then I got used to it and did the same myself. When at length the sun grew hot we rode. The Bedu never bothered to stop their mounts and make them kneel before they got up, but pulled down their heads, put a foot on their necks, and were lifted up to within easy reach of the saddle. At first they insisted on couching my camel when I wished to mount. This was meant as a kindness. So it was when they begged me to ride instead of walking as we started in the morning, and when they frequently offered me a drink, but I found this constant attention irksome, because I was only anxious for them to treat me as one of themselves.

A Bedu who is going to mount a couched camel stands behind her tail. He then leans forward and catches the wooden tree with his left hand as he places his left knee in the saddle. Immediately the camel feels his weight she starts to rise, lifting her hindquarters off the ground, and he swings his right leg over the saddle. The camel then rises to her knees and with another jerk is on her feet. The Bedu either sit with a leg on either side of the hump, or kneel in the saddle, sitting on the upturned soles of their feet, in which case they are riding entirely by balance. They prefer to ride kneeling, especially if they mean to gallop. It is an extraordinary feat of balance, for riding a galloping camel, especially over rough ground, is like sitting on a bucking horse. A Bedu usually carries his rifle slung under his arm and parallel with the ground, which must add greatly to the difficulty of balancing. I could not ride kneeling; it was too uncomfortable and too precarious even at a walk. I had therefore to sit continuously in one position, which became very tiring on a long march. The first time I rode a camel in the Sudan I was so stiff next day I could scarcely move. This had not happened to me again, but I was afraid that it might when I started on this journey, for it was seven years since I had last ridden any distance. It would have been humiliating, for I had claimed that I was already an experienced rider.

In Darfur I had fed my camels on grain and had trotted them. A good camel travelling at about five or six miles an hour is very comfortable, but when walking even the best throw a continuous and severe strain on the rider's back. In southern Arabia the Bedu never trot when they are on a journey, for their camels eat only what they can find, which is generally very little, and have to travel long distances between wells. I had already learnt on the journeys to Bir Natrun and to Tibesti not to press a camel beyond its normal walking pace when travelling in the desert. I was soon to discover how considerate the Bedu were of their camels, always ready to suffer hardship themselves in order to spare their animals. Several times while travelling with them and approaching a well, I have expected them to push on and fill the water-skins, as our water was finished, but they have insisted on halting for the night short of the well, saying that farther on there was no grazing.

Whenever we passed any bushes we let our camels dawdle to strip mouthfuls of leaves and thorns, and whenever we came to richer grazing we halted to let them graze at will. I was making a time-and-compass traverse of our route and these constant halts were frustrating, making it difficult to estimate the distance which we had covered. On good going, where there was no feeding to delay us, we averaged three miles an hour, but in the Sands, where the dunes were steep and difficult, we might only do one mile an hour.

It often seemed incredible to me, especially when I was on foot and conscious of the steps I was taking, that we could cover such enormous distances going at this pace. Sometimes I counted my footsteps to a bush or to some other mark, and this number seemed but a trifle deducted from the sum that lay ahead of us. Yet I had no desire to travel faster. In this way there was time to notice things – a grasshopper under a bush, a dead swallow on the ground, the tracks of a hare, a bird's nest, the shape and colour of ripples on the sand, the bloom of tiny seedlings pushing through the soil. There was time to collect a plant or to look at a rock. The very slowness of our march diminished its monotony. I thought how terribly boring it would be to rush about this country in a car.

We drifted along, our movements governed by an indefinable common consent. There was seldom much discussion; we either halted or we went on. Sometimes we would start in the morning, expecting to do a long march, come unexpectedly on grazing soon after we had started, and halt for the day. At other times we planned to stop somewhere, but finding when we got to our destination that there was no grazing, we would push on without a halt till dark or even later. If we stopped in the middle of the day we would hurriedly unload the camels, hobble them, and turn them loose to graze. Then we might cook bread or porridge, but more often we ate dates. Always we drank coffee, which my companions craved for as a drug. Some of them smoked, and this was their only other indulgence. No one ever smoked without sharing his pipe with the others; they would squat round while one sifted a few grains of tobacco from the dust in the bottom of a small leather bag which he carried inside his shirt next to his skin. He would stuff this tobacco into a small stemless pipe cut out of soft stone, or into an old cartridge case open at both ends, light it with a flint and steel, take two or three deep puffs and hand it to the next person. If we were travelling when they wished to smoke, they stopped, got off, squatted down, smoked, and then climbed back into their saddles.

We always camped crowded together. All around us was endless space, and yet in our camps there was scarcely room to move, especially when the camels had been brought in for the night and couched around the fires. When we started on this journey we had divided ourselves into messes of five or six people, who each carried their own food. I fed with old Tamtaim, Sultan, and three others. One was Mabkhaut, a slightly built man of middle age; he was good-humoured and considerate, but he seldom spoke, which was unusual among these garrulous Bedu. Another was Musallim bin Tafl, who had been pointed out to me by the Wali as a skilful hunter. He was avaricious even by Bedu standards, quick-witted and hard-working. He was often in Salala, hanging about the palace, and had had in consequence the unusual experience of some contact with the outside world. He volunteered to do the cooking for our party.

When we had enough water he would cook rice, but generally he made bread for our evening meal. He would scoop out three or four pounds of flour from one of the goatskin bags in which we carried our supplies, and would then damp this, add a little salt and mix it into a thick paste. He would divide the dough into six equal-sized lumps, pat each lump between his hands until it had become a disc about half an inch thick, and would then put it down on a rug while he shaped the others. Someone else would have lighted the fire, sometimes with matches but generally with flint and steel. There was plenty of flint in the desert and the blade of a dagger to use as steel. They would tear small strips off their shirts or head-cloths for tinder, with the result that each day their clothes became more tattered in appearance. Musallim would rake some embers out of the fire to make a glowing bed, and then drop the cakes of dough on to it. The heat having sealed the outside of the cakes, he would turn them over almost immediately, and then, scooping a hollow in the sand under the embers, would bury them and spread the hot sand and embers over them. I would watch bubbles breaking through this layer of sand and ashes as the bread cooked. Later he would uncover the cakes, brush off the sand and ashes and put them aside to cool. When we wished to feed he would give one to each of us, and we would sit in a circle and, in turn, dip pieces of this bread into a small bowl containing melted butter, or soup if we happened to have anything from which to make it. The bread was brick hard or soggy, according to how long it had been cooked, and always tasted as if it had been made from sawdust. Sometimes Musallim shot a gazelle or an oryx, and only then did we feed well. After we had eaten we would sit round the fire and talk. Bedu always shout at each other, even if they are only a few feet apart. Everyone could therefore hear what was being said by everyone else in the camp, and anyone who was interested in a conversation round another fire could join in from where he was sitting.

Soon after dinner I would spread out my rug and sheepskin and, putting my dagger and cartridge belt under the saddle-bags which I used as a pillow, lie down beneath three blankets with my rifle beside me. While I was among the Arabs I was anxious to behave as they did, so that they would accept me to some extent as one of themselves. I had therefore to sit as they did, and I found this very trying, for my muscles were not accustomed to this position. I was glad when it was night and I could lie down and be at ease. I had sat on the ground before, but then I had been travelling with men whom I knew well, and with them I could relax and lie about. Now I would get off my camel after a long march and have to sit formally as Arabs sit. It took me a long time to get used to this. For the same reason I went barefooted as they did, and at first this was torture. Eventually the soles of my feet became hardened, but even after five years they were soft compared with theirs.

It hardly occurred to the Bedu that there could be other ways of doing things than those to which they were accustomed. When they fetched me from the RAF camp at Salala they had seen an airman urinating. Next day they asked me what physical deformity he suffered from which prevented him from squatting as they did. In the mountains it was easy to go behind a rock to relieve myself. Later, on the open plains, I walked off to a distance and squatted as they did, with my cloak over my head to form a tent. Except when we were at a well, we used sand to scrub our hands after we had fed, and to clean ourselves after we had defecated. Bedu are always careful not to relieve themselves near a path. In the trackless sands Arabs who stopped behind to urinate turned instinctively aside from the tracks which we ourselves had made before they squatted.

Muslims are usually very prudish and careful to avoid exposing themselves. My companions always kept their loin-cloths on even when they washed at the wells. At first I found it difficult to wear a loin-cloth with decency when sitting on the ground. Bedu say to anyone whose parts are showing, 'Your nose!' I had this said to me once or twice before I learnt to be more careful. The first time I wiped my nose thinking that there was a drip on the end of it, for the weather was very cold.

At first I found living with the Bedu very trying, and during the years that I was with them I always found the mental strain greater than the physical. It was as difficult for me to adapt myself to their way of life, and especially to their outlook, as it was for them to accept what they regarded as my eccentricities. I had been used to privacy, and here I had none. If I wanted to talk privately to someone it was difficult. Even if we went a little apart, others would be intrigued and immediately come to find out what we were talking about and join in the conversation. Every word I said was overheard, and every move I made was watched. At first I felt very isolated among them. I knew they thought that I had unlimited money, and I suspected that they were trying to exploit me. I was exasperated by their avarice, and wearied by their importunities. Whenever during these early days one of them approached me, I thought, 'Now what is *he* going to ask for?' and I would be irritated by the childish flattery with which they invariably prefaced their requests. I had yet to learn that no Bedu thinks it shameful to beg, and that often he will look at the gift which he has received and say, 'Is this all that you are going to give me?' I was seeing the worst side of their character, and was disillusioned and resentful, and irritated by their assumption of superiority. In consequence I was assertive and unreasonable.

Some rain had fallen three months earlier on the northern slopes of the Qarra mountains, and there was a little green grazing in some of the valley-bottoms where freshets had run down. The Bedu were loath to leave this grazing and push on into the empty wastes which they knew lay ahead. They dawdled along doing one hour's marching one day, and perhaps two the next, while my exasperation mounted. Whenever we came to a patch of grazing they vowed that it was the last and insisted on stopping; and then next day we would find more grazing and stop again. Anyway, most of this grazing did not seem to me to be worth stopping for. Usually it was only a few green shrubs. I did not yet realize how rare any fresh vegetation was in this desert. I still thought in terms of so many marching hours a day, which had been easy to do in the Sudan where we hand-fed our camels. I fretted at the constant delays, counting the wasted days instead of revelling in this leisurely travel. Unfairly, I suspected that the Arabs were trying to lengthen our journey in order to collect more money from me. When in the evenings I would protest and insist that we must do proper marches,

Sultan and the others would add to my exasperation by saying that I knew nothing about camels, which was true. I would, however, explain indignantly what a lot of experience I had had with them in the Sudan. I found it difficult to understand what they were saying and this added to my frustration.

Bedu, attracted from afar by the fresh grazing, were herding camels and goats in the valleys through which we passed. They were hungry, as Bedu always are, and they collected each evening in our camp to feed at our expense. Everyone had heard that the Christian had great quantities of food with him. These unwanted guests never waited for an invitation before sitting down with us to feed. They just joined us and shared whatever we had for as long as they were with us. Many of them followed us, turning up evening after evening. My companions accepted their presence with equanimity, since they would have done the same; and, anyway, no Bedu will turn a guest away unfed. But I was irritated by their assumption that we should feed them, and disturbed by their numbers. I realized that we had not brought enough food with us and that we were going to be short before we returned to Salala. In my more bitter moments I thought that Bedu life was one long round of cadging and being cadged from.

It was three months before I returned to Salala. They were hard months of constant travel during which I learnt to admire my companions and to appreciate their skill. I soon found these tribesmen far easier to consort with than more progressive town Arabs who, after discarding their own customs and traditions, have adopted something of our ways. I myself infinitely preferred the Bedu's arrogant self-assurance to the Effendi's easily wounded susceptibilities. I was beginning to see the desert as the Bedu saw it, and to judge men as they judged them. I had come here looking for more than locusts, and was finding the life for which I sought.

Two memories in particular remain with me of this journey. I had turned aside into the sands of Ghanim with a dozen Arabs, while the others went on to Mughshin. It was eight days since we had left the well at Shisur and our water had been finished for twenty-four hours. We were near Bir Halu, or 'the sweet well', when we came on clumps of yellow-flowering tribulus, growing where a shower had fallen a few months before. We grazed our camels for a while, and I then suggested going on to the well, for I was thirsty. Eventually Tamtaim, Sultan, and Musallim came on with me; the others said they would join us later after feeding their camels. We arrived at the well, unsaddled our camels, watered them, and then sat down near the well. No one had yet drunk. I was anxious not to appear impatient, but eventually I suggested we should do so. Sultan handed me a bowl of water. I offered it to old Tamtaim, but he told me to drink, saying that he would wait till the others came, adding that as they were his travelling companions it would be unseemly for him to drink till they arrived. I had already learnt that Bedu will never take advantage over a companion by feeding while he is absent, but this restraint seemed to me exaggerated. The others did not arrive until five hours later, by which time I was thoroughly exasperated and very thirsty. Though the water looked deliciously cold and clear, it tasted like a strong dose of Epsom salts; I took a long draught and involuntarily spat it out. It was my first experience of water in the Sands.

A few days later we passed some tracks. I was not even certain that they were made by camels, for they were much blurred by the wind. Sultan turned to a grey-bearded man who was noted as a tracker and asked him whose tracks these were, and the man turned aside and followed them for a short distance. He then jumped off his camel, looked at the tracks where they crossed some hard ground, broke some camel-droppings between his fingers and rode back to join us. Sultan asked, 'Who were they?' and the man answered, 'They were Awamir. There are six of them. They have raided the Junuba on the southern coast and taken three of their camels. They have come here from Sahma and watered at Mughshin. They passed here ten days ago.' We had seen no Arabs for seventeen days and we saw none for a further twenty-seven. On our return we met some Bait Kathir near Jabal Qarra and, when we exchanged our news, they told us that six Awamir had raided the Junuba, killed three of them, and taken three of their camels. The only thing we did not already know was that they had killed anyone.

Here every man knew the individual tracks of his own camels, and some of them could remember the tracks of nearly every camel they had seen. They could tell at a glance from the depth of the footprints whether a camel was ridden or free, and whether it was in calf. By studying strange tracks they could tell the area from which the camel came. Camels from the Sands, for instance, have soft soles to their feet, marked with tattered strips of loose skin, whereas if they come from the gravel plains their feet are polished smooth. Bedu could tell the tribe to which a camel belonged, for the different tribes have different breeds of camel, all of which can be distinguished by their tracks. From looking at their droppings they could often deduce where a camel had been grazing, and they could certainly tell when it had last been watered, and from their knowledge of the country they could probably tell where. Bedu are always well informed about the politics of the desert. They know the alliances and enmities of the tribes and can guess which tribes would raid each other. No Bedu will ever miss a chance of exchanging news with anyone he meets, and he will ride far out of his way to get fresh news.

As a result of this journey I found that the country round Mughshin was suffering from many years of drought. If there had been grazing we would have found Arabs with their herds, but we had just travelled for forty-four days without seeing anyone. I asked my companions about floods and they told me that no water had reached Mughshin from the Qarra mountains since the great floods twenty-five years before. It was obviously not an 'outbreak centre' for desert locusts. I now decided to travel westwards to the Hadhramaut along the southern edge of the Sands,* where I would be able to find out if floods ever reached these sands from the high Mahra mountains along the coast. No European had yet travelled in the country between Dhaufar and the Hadhramaut.

I had met with one of the Rashid sheikhs, called Musallim bin al Kamam, on my way to Mughshin, and had taken an immediate

---

* See map on page 26.

liking to him. I had asked him to meet me with some of his tribe in Salala in January, and to go with me to the Hadhramaut. I found bin al Kamam and some thirty Rashid waiting for me when I arrived in Salala on 7 January. I decided to keep Sultan and Musallim bin Tafl with me from the Bait Kathir and agreed to pay for fifteen Rashid, but bin al Kamam said that thirty men would come with us and share this pay. He explained that the country through which we should pass was frequently raided by the Yemen tribes. He had news that more than two hundred Dahm were even then raiding the Manahil on the steppes to the east of the Hadhramaut.

The Rashid were kinsmen and allies of the Bait Kathir, both tribes belonging to the Al Kathir. They were dressed in long Arab shirts and head-cloths which had been dyed a soft russet-brown with the juice of a desert shrub. They wore their clothes with distinction, even when they were in rags. They were small deft men, alert and watchful. Their bodies were lean and hard, trained to incredible endurance. Looking at them, I realized that they were very much alive, tense with nervous energy, vigorously controlled. They had been bred from the purest race in the world, and lived under conditions where only the hardiest and best could possibly survive. They were as fine-drawn and highly-strung as thorough-breds. Beside them the Bait Kathir seemed uncouth and assertive, lacking the final polish of the inner desert.

The Rashid and the Awamir were the tribes in southern Arabia who had adapted themselves to life in the Sands. Some of their sections lived in the central sands, the only place in the Empty Quarter with wells; others had moved right across the Sands to the Trucial Coast. The homelands of both the Rashid and the Awamir were on the steppes to the north-east and to the north of the Hadhramaut. The Bait Imani section of the Rashid still lived there, and we should pass through their territory on our way to the Hadhramaut. The Manahil lived farther to the west, between there and the Awamir. Beyond the Awamir were the Saar, bitter enemies of the Rashid. The Mahra, divided into many sections, lived in the mountains and on the plateau along the coast; beyond them were the Humum to the north of Mukalla.

The Bedu tribes of southern Arabia were insignificant in numbers compared with those of central and northern Arabia, where the tents of a single tribe might number thousands. In Syria I had seen the Shammar migrating, a whole people on the move, covering the desert with their herds, and had visited the summer camp of the Rualla, a city of black tents. In northern Arabia the desert merges into the sown and there is a gradual transition from Bedu to shepherds and cultivators. Damascus, Aleppo, Mosul, and Baghdad exert their influence on the desert. They are visited by Bedu, who see in their bazaars men of different races, cultures, and faiths. Even in the Najd the Bedu have occasional contact with towns and town life. But here scattered families moved over great distances seeking pasturage for a dozen camels. These Rashid, who roamed from the borders of the Hadhramaut to the Persian Gulf, numbered only three hundred men, while the Bait Kathir were about six hundred. But these Arabs were among the most authentic of the Bedu, the least affected by the outside world. In the south the desert runs down into the sea, continues into the kindlier deserts of the north, or ends against the black barren foothills of the Yemen or Oman. There were few towns within reach of the southern Bedu, and these they rarely visited.

My ambition was to cross the Empty Quarter. I had hoped that I might be able to do so with these Rashid after we had reached the Hadhramaut, but I realized when I talked with them that by then it would be too hot. I was resolved to return, and was content to regard this first year as training for later journeys. I knew that among the Rashid I had found the Arabs for whom I was looking.

It was on this journey that I met Salim bin Kabina. He was generally known as bin Kabina, 'the son of Kabina', who was his mother. In other parts of Arabia it is common practice to call a man the son of his father; here it is more usual to use his mother's name. Bin Kabina was to be my inseparable companion during the five years I travelled in southern Arabia. He turned up while we were watering thirsty camels at a well that yielded only a few gallons an hour. For two days we worked day and night in relays. Conspicuous in a vivid red loin-cloth, and with his long hair falling round

Tribal Map of Southern Arabia

his naked shoulders, he helped us with our task. On the second day he announced that he was coming with me. The Rashid sheikhs advised me to take the boy and let him look after my things. I told him he must find himself a camel and a rifle. He grinned and said that he would find both, and did. He was about sixteen years old, about five foot five in height and loosely built. He moved with a long, raking stride, like a camel, unusual among Bedu, who generally walk very upright with short steps. He was very poor, and the hardships of his life had marked him, so that his frame was gaunt and his face hollow. His hair was very long and always falling into his eyes, especially when he was cooking or otherwise busy. He would sweep it back impatiently with a thin hand. He had a rather

55

low forehead, large eyes, a straight nose, prominent cheek-bones, and a big mouth with a long upper lip. His chin, delicately formed and rather pointed, was marked by a long scar, where he had been branded as a child to cure some illness. He had very white teeth which were always showing, for he was constantly talking and laughing. His father had died two years before and it had fallen on young bin Kabina to provide for his mother, young brother, and infant sister. I had met him at a critical moment in his life, although I only learnt this a week later.

We were walking behind the camels in the cool stillness of the early morning. Bin Kabina and I were a little apart from the others. He strode along, his body turned a little sideways as he talked, his red loin-cloth tight about his narrow hips. His rifle, held on his shoulder by its muzzle, was rusty and very ancient, and I suspected that the firing-pin was broken. He was always taking it to pieces. He told me that a month earlier he had gone down to the coast to fetch a load of sardines, and on the way back his old camel had collapsed and died. He confessed: 'I wept as I sat there in the dark beside the body of my old grey camel. She was old, long past bearing, and she was very thin for there had been no rain in the desert for a long time; but she was my camel. The only one we had. That night, Umbarak, death seemed very close to me and my family. You see, in the summer the Arabs collect round the wells; all the grazing gets eaten up for the distance of a day's journey and more; if we camped where there was grazing for the goats, how, without a camel, could we fetch water? How could we travel from one well to another?' Then he grinned at me and said, 'God brought you. Now I shall have everything.' Already I was fond of him. Attentive and cheerful, he eased the inevitable strain under which I lived, anticipating my wants. His comradeship provided a personal note in the still rather impersonal atmosphere of my desert life.

Two days later an old man came into our camp. He was limping, and even by Bedu standards he looked poor. He wore a torn loin-cloth, thin and grey with age, and carried an ancient rifle, similar to bin Kabina's. In his belt were two full and six empty cartridge-cases, and a dagger in a broken sheath. The Rashid pressed forward to greet him: 'Welcome, Bakhit. Long life to you, uncle. Welcome – welcome a hundred times.' I wondered at the warmth of their greetings. The old man lowered himself upon the rug they had spread for him, and ate the dates they set before him, while they hurried to blow up the fire and to make coffee. He had rheumy eyes, a long nose, and a thatch of grey hair. The skin sagged in folds over the cavity of his stomach. I thought, 'He looks a proper old beggar. I bet he asks for something.' Later in the evening he did and I gave him five *riyals*, but by then I had changed my opinion. Bin Kabina said to me: 'He is of the Bait Imani and famous.' I asked, 'What for?' and he answered, 'His generosity.' I said, 'I should not have thought he owned anything to be generous with', and bin Kabina said, 'He hasn't now. He hasn't got a single camel. He hasn't even got a wife. His son, a fine boy, was killed two years ago by the Dahm. Once he was one of the richest men in the tribe, now he has nothing except a few goats.' I asked: 'What happened to his camels? Did raiders take them, or did they die of disease?' and bin Kabina answered, 'No. His generosity ruined him. No one ever came to his tents but he killed a camel to feed them. By God, he is generous!' I could hear the envy in his voice.

We rode slowly westwards and watered at the deep wells of Sanau, Mughair, and Thamud. There should have been Arabs here, for rain had fallen, and there was good grazing in the broad shallow watercourses which run down towards the Sands across the gravel plains. But the desert was empty and full of fear. Occasionally we saw herdsmen in the distance, hurriedly driving their animals away across the plain. Some of the Rashid would get off their camels and throw up sand into the air, an easily visible signal and the accepted sign of peaceful intentions. They would then ride over to ask the news. Always it was of the Dahm raiders who had passed westwards a few days before. They were in several parties, returning to their homelands in the Yemen with the stock they had captured. Sometimes we were told that they were three-hundred strong, and sometimes that they were a hundred; all we knew was that they were many and well-armed. Some Manahil women with a herd of goats told us that forty of them had slaughtered eight of their goats for food three days before. They described how the raiders had lain on the sands and milked the goats into their mouths. These women knew some of the Rashid who were with me and urged us to be careful, but we boasted that we were Rashid, and '*Ba Rashud!*' (the Rashid war-cry) we were not afraid of the Dahm, who were dogs and sons of dogs. The women answered, 'God give you victory.'

It was late one evening. We had watered that day at Hulaiya, and now we were camped on a plain near some acacia bushes, among which our scattered camels were grazing guarded by three men. Half a mile away to the west were limestone ridges, dark against the setting sun. The Rashid were lined up praying, their shadows long upon the desert floor. I was watching them and thinking how this ritual must have remained unchanged in every detail since it was first prescribed by Muhammad, when suddenly one of them said, 'There are men behind that ridge.' They abandoned their prayers. 'The camels! The camels! Get the camels!' Four or five men ran off to help the herdsmen, who had already taken alarm and were hurriedly collecting the grazing camels. Bin Kabina started towards them, but I called to him to remain with me. We had seized our rifles and were lying behind the scattered loads. A score of mounted men swung out from behind the ridge and raced towards our animals. We opened fire. Bin al Kamam, who lay near me, said, 'Shoot in front of them. I don't know who they are.' I got off five rapid shots, firing twenty yards in front of the racing camels, which were crossing in front of us. The dust flew up where the bullets struck the hard sand. Everyone was firing. Bin Kabina's three rounds were all duds. I could see the exasperation on his face. He lay a little in front of me to the right. The raiders sought cover behind a low hill. Our camels were brought in and couched. 'Who were they?' There was general uncertainty. It was agreed that they were not Dahm or Saar. Their saddles were different. Some said they were Awamir, perhaps Manahil. No, they were not Mahra; their clothes were wrong. A Manahil who was with us said he would go forward and find out. He got up and walked slowly towards the low hill, silhouetted against the glowing sky. We saw a man stand up and come towards him. They shouted to each other and then went forward and embraced. They were Manahil and a little later they came over and joined us. They told us that they were a pursuit party following the Dahm, had seen our camels and had mistaken us for yet another party of Dahm raiders. They had realized their mistake when they heard us shouting to the camel guards, for our voices were not the voices of the Dahm. We had bought a goat that morning, which we had meant to eat for dinner; instead we feasted the Manahil, who were now our guests.

The Rashid had collected round the fire, anxious to hear the latest news of this raid. Eventually I went to lie down, but it was difficult to sleep, for these excited Arabs were shouting at each other within a few yards of where I lay. They were planning a raid on the Dahm to recover their lost stock. The Rashid and Manahil were allies, and both tribes had suffered much in the last few years from Dahm raiders. Bin al Kamam had explained to me the difficulty of opposing them. In this desert, lack of grazing forced the Bedu to live and move about in widely scattered family groups. Two or three men herding a dozen camels were powerless to resist raiders. All they could do was to escape on the fastest of their animals. They could abandon their women and children, for they knew that the raiders would not harm them. The raiders would pick up a dozen camels here and half a dozen there. They had no chance of making a large haul in one day. They knew that as soon as they had been seen the alarm would spread throughout the desert, and that their enemies, after driving their herds southwards into the more broken country which lay towards the coast, would collect in pursuit. The longer the raiders delayed and the farther they went eastward looking for unsuspecting families, the more certain it was that they would have to fight before they could get home. But bin al Kamam said that it was difficult for the Rashid and Manahil to muster sufficient men to oppose raiders who were two hundred strong. Some of these raids covered a thousand miles and lasted for two months.

A week later we were in the valley of the Hadhramaut and rode slowly up it to Tarim. I was interested to see this famous valley and these unspoilt Arab cities with their curious architecture. We were lavishly entertained, sitting in cushioned ease in spacious guest-rooms; we ate well-cooked food and drank water which did not taste of goatskins. My companions, however, were anxious to be gone – they fretted about their camels, which would not eat the lucerne that they were offered. I persuaded them to remain for a few days more, for I was desolate at the thought of parting with them. The privacy for which I had craved while I was with them was there behind a door, but now it was aching loneliness.

FOUR

Secret Preparations at Salala

~~~

The next year I return to Salala and make plans to
cross the Empty Quarter with the help of the
Rashid. I assemble a party of Bait Kathir to take me
as far as Mughshin.

I had no inclination to return to England. I decided instead to
go to Jidda, to visit the anti-locust unit, whose headquarters
were outside the town, and then to travel in the Hajaz mountains; I had longed for years to visit this little-known corner of
Arabia.

For three months I travelled there, riding a thousand miles,
partly on a camel and partly on a donkey, accompanied by a Sharifi
boy from the Wadi al Ahsaba. Together we wandered through the
Tihama, the hot coastal plain that lies between the Red Sea and
the mountains, passing through villages of daub-and-wattle huts
reminiscent of Africa. The people here were of uncommon beauty,
and pleasantly easy and informal in their manners. We watched
them, dressed in loin-cloths and with circlets of scented herbs upon
their flowing hair, dancing in the moonlight to the quickening
rhythm of the drums at the annual festivals when the young men
were circumcised. We stayed with the Bani Hilal, destitute descend-
ants of the most famous of all Arab tribes, in their mat shelters in
the lava fields near Birk, and with the nearly naked Qahtan, who
bear the name of that ancestor who sired the Arab race, and who
live today in the gorges of the Wadi Baish. We visited weekly

61

markets which sprang up at dawn in remote valleys in the mountains, or just for a day packed the streets of some small town. We saw towns of many sorts, Taif, Abha, Sabyia, and Jizan; we climbed steep passes, where baboons barked at us from the cliffs, and lammergeyer sailed out over the misty depths below, and we rested beside cold streams in forests of juniper and wild olive. Sometimes we spent the night in a castle with an Amir, sometimes in a mud cabin with a slave, and everywhere we were well received. We fed well and slept in comfort, but I thought ceaselessly of the desert which I had left, remembering bin al Kamam, bin Kabina, Sultan, and Musallim.

At last I returned to London, wondering anxiously whether I should be able to persuade the Locust Research Centre to send me back to the Empty Quarter. I knew that my last journey had cost a great deal of money. Would Dr Uvarov think another journey worth while? If not, how should I get back?

As soon as I arrived in London I went to see him at the Natural History Museum, and, on one of the maps which covered the walls of his office, showed him where I had been. In answer to his questioning I assured him that floods from the coastal mountains very seldom reached the edge of the southern sands. He pointed to the Oman mountains and asked, 'Do you think that floods from there reach the sands?' Here was my chance, and I answered, 'I have no idea but I will go and find out.' Dr Uvarov said regretfully, 'I wish you could, but the trouble is we have already asked the Sultan for permission, and he would not hear of it. He was very definite in his refusal. I am sure it will be useless to ask again.' I said, 'Ask the Consul in Muscat to get me permission to go to Mughshin, and leave the rest to me, but for God's sake don't mention Oman, or indeed anywhere but Mughshin.' At last Dr Uvarov agreed, and I came out of his office thinking triumphantly, 'Now I shall be able to cross the Empty Quarter.' But I was determined to say nothing about my plans. I did not want a journalist to get hold of the story and write an article that might turn up in Muscat and prevent my journey.

I knew that the Sultan claimed that Mughshin and the Ghanim

sands immediately to the north of it belonged to him; but north of Ghanim was the Empty Quarter, to which he laid no claim. Nominally he was Sultan of Muscat and Oman, but in fact the interior of Oman was not under his control. It was ruled by a religious leader known as the Imam, who was hostile to him and fanatically opposed to all Europeans. I realized, because of this, that it would be in Oman that he would be most reluctant to let me travel.

I arrived back in Salala on 16 October 1946. I planned to cross the Empty Quarter from Mughshin to the Trucial Coast, and to return to Salala across the gravel steppes at the back of Oman, but I realized that if a hint of my plans reached the Wali he would forbid the Bedu to take me farther than Mughshin. All that I could do was to make arrangements as though that were as far as I intended to go, and hope that when I got there I should be able to persuade some of the Bedu to cross the Sands with me. I therefore agreed with the Wali that the same number of Bait Kathir should accompany me as the year before.

The Bait Kathir live in the mountains and on the gravel plains to the south of the Empty Quarter. Only one section of the tribe, the Bait Musan, ever enter the Sands, and even they only know the area round Ghanim. Bertram Thomas had made his first attempt to cross the Empty Quarter with Bait Kathir and had been forced to turn back after going a short way. He had succeeded in his second attempt with the Rashid. I knew that if I were to cross the Sands I must get hold of the Rashid.

One day while buying clothes in the market I met a young Rashid, called Amair, who had been with me the year before. Until I met him I had seen no Rashid in the town and was wondering how to get in touch with them. I knew that Bait Kathir from jealousy would not be willing to help me. After I had greeted Amair I took him aside and asked him to fetch bin al Kamam, bin Kabina, and two other Rashid whom I named. I promised that I would take him with me if he found me the people I wanted. He said that bin Kabina was at Habarut, four days' journey away. He believed that bin al Kamam had gone to the Yemen to seek a truce for the Rashid with the Dahm. We arranged that he should fetch bin Kabina and meet me at Shisur in ten days' time. I was now certain that more Rashid than I required would meet me there, as indeed they did.

While I was talking to Amair, one of the Wali's slaves came up and told me rudely that I was forbidden to speak to strangers. I answered that Amair was not a stranger and instructed him to mind his own business. He went off muttering. Slaves belonging to men of importance are often overbearing and ill-mannered, trading on their master's position. Arabs have little if any sense of colour-bar; socially they treat a slave, however black, as one of themselves. In the Hajaz I was sitting in the audience chamber of an Amir who was a relation of Ibn Saud's, when an expensively dressed old Negro belonging to the king came into the room. After rising to greet him, the Amir seated this slave beside him, and during dinner served him with his own hands. Arab rulers raise slaves to positions of great power, often trusting them more than they do their own relations.

I left Salala on the afternoon of 25 October, with the twenty-four Bait Kathir who were to accompany me. Nearly all of them had been with me the year before. Old Tamtaim was there, and he told me with pride that his wife had just produced a son. I remembered how after a long march he had shuffled round in a war-dance when he got off his camel, to prove that he at any rate was still as fresh as ever. I also remembered that he had once gone to sleep on his camel and fallen off, and how relieved I had been when he had got to his feet shamefaced but unhurt. I was glad that he was with me now; he would give good advice, and would keep the main party together while I was away, for I intended to cross the Sands with only a few Arabs. Sultan was also there. I knew that ultimately the decision about crossing the Sands would rest with him, and I felt confident that he would support me. He had been invaluable to me the year before. Already I was sure that he guessed my purpose, for when I commented on the poor condition of the camels he said, 'They will get us to Mughshin and we can change some of them there before we go farther.' Musallim Tafl was with them; while he was with us I knew that we should feed on fresh meat if there was any to be had. Mabkhaut bin Arbain was also there, and Salim bin Turkia, his kinsman, with his fifteen-year-old son, whom he wished to take with him, a handsome youth with brooding eyes and a curious cock's-comb of hair, a sign that he was still uncircumcised.

We camped at Al Ain, a spring at the foot of the Qarra mountains and spent the next day there sorting and arranging loads. I had provided two thousand pounds of flour, five hundred pounds of rice, and also clarified butter, coffee, tea, sugar, and some packages of poor-quality dates. There were very few dates to be had in the market at this time of year, for the dhows did not arrive with new supplies from Basra until December. I planned to be away for three months, and I intended to enlist six Rashid so that our party would number thirty-one, but it was possible that there would be more. We had enough flour for each of us to have a daily ration of three-quarters of a pound. I knew, however, that the Bedu would leave half this supply to feed their families while we were away; and I also knew from bitter experience that while we were in inhabited country every Bedu for miles around would come to feed at our expense. It would be impossible to refuse them food: in the desert one may never turn a guest away, however unwanted he may be. Even here many people had turned up, mostly from Salala, all hoping to get a meal. I refused, however, to agree to this, saying that we were going into the desert and that their own homes were only a few miles away across the plain. We got rid of most of them before evening.

We camped under some cliffs on a small level space among tumbled boulders and divided ourselves into parties of six or seven for feeding. It was difficult to move about, for the camels were couched wherever there was room for them. Many of them were being hand-fed with sardines, and the penetrating stench of the half-dried fish hung round our camp for days, until the last sardine had been eaten. The smell of decay attracted clouds of flies, which we later carried with us into the desert, clustered on our backs as we rode along. I had bought a goat for dinner, and we fed well, with boiled rice and rich savoury soup. Then Musallim brewed coffee, and Sultan produced a bowl of frothing camel's milk, warm from the udder; like all camel's milk, it tasted slightly salty. The light of the fires played over the men's bearded faces, and silhouetted the heads and necks of camels staring out into the darkness. Their eyes shone greenly. I thought of the first time I had camped here. Then I had been a stranger and lonely; now I felt that I was half accepted. I remembered the aching nostalgia for this comfortless yet satisfying life which had come over me a few months before on the slopes of the Hajaz mountains.

Where had I been? What had I done since I had left them? The Hajaz? Where was that? Were they Bedu there? The questions poured in, and I in turn asked others. Where was bin Lawi? Where was Bakhit bin Karaith? Had the Dahm raided the Rashid? Had any rain fallen at Mughshin? Where was Umbrausha? Sultan answered that she was dead, having fallen among some rocks two months before and broken her shouldder. And so the hours passed, and then one by one we rose and sought a place to sleep. I had left my possessions behind a pile of rocks, near a small level spot which I had chosen, but I now found a camel couched there. I decided that there was just room for the two of us, and spread my rug and sheepskin beside her. I had brought blankets with me the year before, but, for very shame, I had given them one by one to my companions, till I was left shivering with only one. It can be very cold in the desert during the winter nights. This year I had brought a sleeping-bag. I had a few things with me but they were all that I needed. I had the clothes which I wore – a coloured loin-cloth and a long shirt that was still white but which I intended to dye russet-coloured as soon as I got into the desert and could find an *abal* bush from which to make the dye. Round my loins under my clothes I had fastened a leather cincture of many strands, such as every Bedu wears to support his back. My shirt was girded in at the waist with the belt of my heavy silver-hilted Omani dagger, so that I had a natural pocket between my shirt and skin where I could carry my compass, a small notebook, and anything else I required. I had a head-cloth from Oman, like a Kashmiri shawl, and a brown Arab cloak from the Hajaz. I had my rifle and cartridge belt. Inside my saddle-bags were spare ammunition, my camera, films, an aneroid and thermometer, a large notebook, a volume of Gibbon and *War and Peace*, a press for plants, a small medicine chest, a set of clothes for bin Kabina, since I knew that he would be in rags, the dagger which I had worn last year and which I had replaced with the one I was now wearing, and several bags of Maria Theresa dollars. These coins, dated 1780, are still minted. They are about the size of a five-shilling piece, are worth half-a-crown, and are the only coins acceptable here; the Arabs call them *riyals*.

This money was in canvas bags tied with string; the saddle-bags were unfastened. My companions were desperately poor and yet the coins were as safe in my saddle-bags as if they had been in a bank. I was five years with the Bedu and I never lost a single coin nor a round of ammunition, although this was even more valuable to them than money.

I lay in my sleeping-bag listening to the never-ending noises. Some people were still talking. They talked at intervals throughout the night as, woken by the cold, they squatted round the fire. Someone else was singing quietly to himself on the far side of the camp. The camels, uncomfortable on the rocky floor, shuffled and groaned. I heard a leopard cough somewhere on the slopes above us. Others heard it too and Musallim called out, 'Did you hear that? It is a leopard.' I found it difficult to sleep; my mind was too full of plans, too stimulated by my return. I thought how welcoming are Arabs, more so than any race I know.

We remained next day at Al Ain. In the afternoon I climbed the slopes above us. Sultan, Musallim, bin Turkia and his son, bin Anauf, came with me. We visited a Qarra encampment on a small terrace, immediately above a narrow gorge, choked with trees and creepers. A family were living in a shallow cave which undercut the limestone cliff. The floor was carpeted with goat-droppings. We sat talking with them for a while, sitting in the mouth of the cave. There was an old man, half blind, two sixteen-year-old boys, both of them with cock's-combs of hair, and a powerfully built man of middle age who carried a straight-bladed sword, a throwing-stick of heavy wood, and a small, deep, circular shield of wicker-work, covered with hide, which he used as a stool. One of the boys fetched us some sour milk in a dirty wooden bowl. Musallim warned me to look out for *dhafar*, leathery ticks, whose bites raise large painful lumps and sometimes cause fever, and which are common in these caves where goats are housed. I had slept in one such cave the year before when it threatened rain, and had been so badly bitten I had scratched for days.

The sun was setting and it was time to go back to camp. We were high on the mountain-side looking down on the plain, on Salala and the distant ocean. As we rose to go an old man approached. He mumbled a salutation and we replied. He stood and stared at me, wrinkling his eyes; he wore a short dirty loin-cloth and carried a stick – he was evidently too poor to own a dagger. Grey hair sprouted on his chest and eldritch locks fell round his emaciated face; a single tooth wobbled as he spoke. He looked at me for some time and then mumbled again, 'I came to see the Christian'. Sultan said to me, 'He is a Shahara'. I wondered what he saw as he peered at me with bleary eyes, this old man whose ancestors were tabled in Genesis. Perhaps dimly he foresaw the end. As we went down the hillside I asked my companions who he was. 'He is mad', one of them answered, and parodied 'I came to see the Christian', and they laughed. Yet I wondered fancifully if he had seen more clearly than they did, had sensed the threat which my presence implied – the approaching disintegration of his society and the destruction of his beliefs. Here especially it seemed that the evil that comes with sudden change would far outweigh the good. While I was with the Arabs I wished only to live as they lived and, now that I have left them, I would gladly think that nothing in their lives was altered by my coming. Regretfully, however, I realize that the maps I made helped others, with more material aims, to visit and corrupt a people whose spirit once lit the desert like a flame.

Next day we climbed to the top of the Kismim Pass and camped in a hollow in the downs. Some Al Kathir lived here between the Bait Qatan and Bait Saad sections of the Qarra, whom they resembled in mode of life and general appearance, although they spoke Arabic. Our camp was soon infested with them, anxious to sell butter or goats at fantastic prices, and to scrounge flour. Their sheikh was a particularly unpleasant old man. Avarice inflamed his eyes and raised the pitch of his voice, while he pawed at my possessions with eager, trembling fingers. We felt no desire to linger here, and in any case water was difficult to obtain.

To the south, grassy downs, green jungles, and shadowy gorges fell away to the plain of Jarbib and to the Indian Ocean which opened on to another world, whereas immediately to the north a landscape of black rocks and yellow sand sloped down to the Empty Quarter. I looked out over the desert. It stretched away unbroken for fifteen hundred miles to the orchards round Damascus and the red cliffs of Rum. A desert breeze blew round me. I thought of that ruined castle in distant Syria which Lawrence had visited. The Arabs believed that it had been built by a prince of the border as a desert palace for his queen, and declared that its clay had been kneaded with the juice of flowers. Lawrence was taken by his guides from room to crumbling room. Sniffing like dogs, they said, 'This is jasmine, this violet, this rose'; but at last one of them had called, 'Come and smell the very sweetest smell of all', and had led him to a gaping window where the empty wind of the desert went throbbing past. 'This', they told him, 'is the best: it has no taste.'

Early next morning we moved down to the pool of Aiyun, which lies beneath sheer-sided limestone cliffs two hundred feet in height, at the head of the Wadi Ghudun. This deep pool, which is fed by a small spring, is a hundred and fifty yards long and thirty yards across, and its still, green waters are fringed with rushes. Tamtaim declared that a monster serpent lived in the pool and that sometimes it seized a goat when the flocks came down to drink.

We watered our camels and filled our water-skins. The watercourse which gave access to the pool was soon packed with jostling camels, picking their way with clumsy deliberation among the boulders and snatching mouthfuls from any bushes they passed.

Many Englishmen have written about camels. When I open a book and see the familiar disparagement, the well-worn humour, I realize that the author's knowledge of them is slight, that he has never lived among the Bedu, who know the camel's worth: 'Ata Allah', or 'God's gift', they call her, and it is her patience that wins the Arab's heart. I have never seen a Bedu strike or ill-treat a camel. Always the camels' needs come first. It is not only that the Bedu's existence depends upon the welfare of his animals, but that he has a real affection for them. Often I have watched my companions fondling and kissing them whilst they murmured endearments. The year before, riding through the cultivations near Tarim, we had come across a villager thrashing a camel. Several of the Rashid who were with me jumped down at once and remonstrated angrily with the man, and then as we rode on they expressed their contempt for him.

A few days later as we were walking across the desert, with the camels unattended some thirty yards away, Sultan challenged another Arab to call his camel over to him. Camels are gregarious and hate separating from their fellows, but as soon as her owner called she swung out of the line and came over. I can remember another that was as attached to her owner as a dog might have been. At intervals throughout the night she came over, moaning softly, to sniff at him where he lay, before going back to graze. My companions told me that no one else could ride her unless he took with him a piece of her owner's clothing.

To Arabs, camels are beautiful, and they derive as great a pleasure from looking at a good camel as some Englishmen get from looking at a good horse. There is indeed a tremendous feeling of power, rhythm, and grace about these great beasts. I certainly know few sights finer than mounted Arabs travelling fast on well-bred camels, but this is rarely seen for they seldom travel faster than at a walk.

To talk intelligently to the Bedu about camels I tried to learn the different terms which they used, and these, numerous enough in any case, tended to vary among different tribes. They used several different words for the singular and the plural. They had different names for the different breeds and colours, for riding camels and herd camels, and a different term, which varied according to the animal's sex, for a camel in each year of its life until it was fully grown, and others for it as soon as it began to grow old. They had terms for a barren female, and for one in calf or in milk, which varied again depending on how long she had been in calf or in milk. I listed many of these words but found it impossibe to carry most of them in my head.

We had unsaddled beneath some acacia trees, where the wadi widened out. Soon, Arabs appeared from the pool staggering under filled water-skins, which they laid out in the shadow of the trees. The skins lay there in the thin shade, wobbling slightly like giant slugs, bloated and curiously obscene. Travelling with Bedu I learnt to use their things. It is, I am convinced, a mistake to introduce innovations from outside, however much better they may appear to be. The Arabs know their own gear – it has stood the test of time. The goat-skins in which they carry their water can be rolled up when they are empty, weigh nothing, and are easily stowed away. If they sweat they can be treated with butter; if they leak the holes can be plugged with thorns or with splinters of wood wrapped round with cloth. This looks precarious but it works surprisingly well. The water tastes and smells of goat, but in the desert untainted water is tasted only in dreams. Flour, rice, and dates are packed in other skins which are easily slung along the saddle and balance the weight of water on the other side. Butter is usually carried in lizard-skins, about eighteen inches long.

Musallim had gone out hunting along the cliffs, and he came in a little before sunset, carrying an ibex which he dumped down beside the fire. It was an old ram whose meat would taste much as it smelt, but it was meat. Musallim gave some to each party and then, tireless as ever, helped young bin Anauf to cook the rest of it. Later he heaped the steaming rice on to a single tray, and surrounded the tray with bowls of greasy gravy. The cooked meat was set apart. Sultan then divided it into seven equal portions. Tamtaim took seven twigs and named each twig after one of us. Musallim, whose back had been turned, then placed a twig on a heap of meat, saying as he did so, 'Here is for the best man.' This lot fell to bin Turkia. 'Here is for the worst', as he laid down another twig. This was for

Mabkhaut, which was not fair. 'This is for the man who won't get up in the morning.' It was mine and apposite, as the laughter reminded me, but the laughter was redoubled when Musallim called out, 'This is for the man who pokes the girls', and Tamtaim picked up the meat which had fallen to him. Bin Anauf grinned at the old man, and said, 'Evidently, uncle, you will have another son next year.' Musallim went on until each of us had drawn his share of the meat.

There is always trouble if meat is not divided by lot. Someone immediately says that he has been given more than his share, and tries to hand a piece to someone else. Then there is much arguing and swearing by God, with everyone insisting that he has been given too much, and finally a deadlock ensues which can only be settled by casting lots for the meat – as should have been done in the first place. I have never heard a man grumble that he has received less than his share. Such behaviour would be inconceivable to the Bedu, for they are careful never to appear greedy, and quick to notice anyone who is. I remember the story of a destitute Bedu boy, who told his mother that he liked dining when there was no moon, for then his companions could not see how much food he took. His mother said, 'Sit with them in the dark and cut at a piece of rope with your knife turned the wrong way round.' The boy did so that very night. There was no moon and it was very dark, but as he picked up the knife a dozen voices called out, 'You have got it the wrong way round!'

We squatted round the dish of rice over which Musallim had poured some gravy, each of us with his portion of meat in front of him, and we dipped our right hands in turn into the rice. We moulded the handful which we had taken in the palm of the hand until it had become a ball, and then put it neatly into our mouths with fingers and thumb. An Arab always feeds with his right hand and avoids if possible touching food with his left hand, for this is the unclean hand with which he washes after he has relieved himself. It is even bad manners to pass anyone anything with this hand or to accept anything with it.

After dinner we sat round and talked, the favourite occupation

Qarra tribesmen of Dhaufar.

Below: A cave dwelling in the Qarra mountains.

Overleaf: The northern slopes of the Qarra mountains.

Trilithons on the northern slopes of the Qarra mountains.

Below: The southern slopes.

Salim bin Kabina.

Two boys of the Bait Kathir.

Below: Sultan, a sheikh of the Bait Kathir.

Ghaf trees near Mughshin.

Below: A herdsboy of the Manahil; *right*: Manahil raiders encountered near Hulaiya.

The Empty Quarter: the steep side of a 600-foot dune.

The Wadi Umm al Hait (the Mother of Life) after twenty-five years of unbroken drought.

Below: Al Auf, the Rashid guide.

Overleaf: The Empty Quarter.

A camp in the Sands.

Below: Vegetation in the Sands after heavy rain: Tribulus (*Zahra*) and *Qassis*.

Bin Anauf, a fifteen-year-old boy of the Bait Kathir.

Overleaf: The Empty Quarter: bin Kabina, bringing camel fodder, by the crest of a great dune, on the lee side.

Cleaning out a well in the Sands.

Below: Preparing a meal.

of the Bedu. They are unflagging talkers. A man will tell the same story half a dozen times in a couple of months to the same people and they will sit and listen with apparent interest. They find it an almost unendurable hardship to keep silent. Yet that evening when someone started to recite poetry a hush fell over the camp, broken only by the sound of pounding as they crushed *saf* leaves which they had gathered in the wadi before plaiting the fibre into rope. One after the other they gathered round, silent except when they repeated the final line of each verse.

When moved, Arabs break easily into poetry. I have heard a lad spontaneously describe in verse some grazing which he had just found: he was giving natural expression to his feelings. But while they are very sensible of the beauty of their language, they are curiously blind to natural beauty. The colour of the sands, a sunset, the moon reflected in the sea: such things leave them unmoved. They are not even noticed. When we returned from Mughshin the year before, and had come out from the void of the desert on to the crest of the Qarra range and looked again on green trees and grass and the loveliness of the mountains, I turned to one of them and said, 'Isn't that beautiful!' He looked, and looked again, and then said uncomprehending, 'no – it is rotten bad grazing.' Yet their kinsmen in Hadhramaut have evolved an architecture which is simple, harmonious, and beautiful. But this architecture is doomed, for the Arabs' taste is easily corrupted. New and hideous buildings, planned by modern Arab architects, are already rising in these ancient cities. My companions when they saw them were deeply impressed. They turned to me and said, 'By God, that is a wonderful building!' It was useless to argue.

We travelled slowly northwards following the Ghudun, one of the five dry river-beds which run down from the coastal range to form the great trunk wadi of Umm al Hait. Gouged out from the limestone plateau the Ghudun begins abruptly as a canyon two hundred feet below the desert floor. Gradually it increases in size until finally it is four hundred feet in depth, and several hundred yards across. Great slabs of rock, fallen from the cliffs on either side, forced us to travel in the stream bed, where a jumble of polished boulders made awkward going for our camels. There was a little scattered vegetation among the screes below the cliffs – caper bushes, acacias, various leguminous plants, and small thickets of *saf*, a species of palmetto. Sometimes I climbed the cliffs with Musallim to look for ibex, and then I could see for miles across a flinty plain which sloped gradually down towards the inner desert and where the only signs of vegetation were a few leafless acacia bushes growing on pans of gravel and hard sand.

We passed two or three families of Bait Kathir. They had no tents but were camped under trees or in the shelter of rocks. Only the Arabs who live in the Sands use tents. We stopped for the night with Mabkhaut's family under two trees on a spit of sand. His wife was there and his two sons, bright-eyed, long-haired children, the elder about twelve years old. A young man, who Mabkhaut said was his cousin, was living with them. He had been bitten by a snake two months before, and his leg was very swollen and pus was running out from beneath his toes. I washed the wound and gave him some medicine. Mabkhaut slaughtered a goat, and his wife cooked the meat for us. She was a middle-aged woman, very thin, and troubled with a cough which shook her while she worked. She was wrapped in the dark-blue clothes which these women wear, and was unveiled. Mabkhaut owned five camels and about thirty goats. These Bedu keep no other animals, not even dogs or chickens. The Qarra, who own cattle, do not live in the desert. The Manahil have sheep, but I never saw any with the Rashid or Bait Kathir.

Lying on the sand around me was everything this family owned – a few pots, a drinking bowl, some water-skins, another goatskin half-filled with flour, a heap of sardines spread out on a torn shirt, an old rug, and a few rags with which they would cover themselves at night. There were also two camel-saddles, a leather bucket for drawing water, and a coil of rope. The cousin wore a dagger, and held an old single-shot ·450 rifle between his knees; he had eleven rounds of ammunition in his belt. Mabkhaut told me that this rifle belonged to him. He himself was at the time armed with one of the twelve service rifles which I had brought with me.

Next day we reached the well of Ma Shadid, two days after leaving Aiyun. The water was at the bottom of a natural hole in the limestone rock and the Arabs told me that it was forty-five feet below the surface. They reached it in the dark, clambering down seven shelves of rock with the help of ropes. The water flowed knee-deep and was said to come from Aiyun, for once a woman's wooden comb which had been lost there was recovered here.

In this southern desert, between Oman and the Hadhramaut, there is little water. In areas as large as an English county there are only single wells, and some of these will run dry after watering a few score camels. Yet this water has to suffice for all the human beings in the area and for their stock, not only in winter when it is cool but also in summer when the temperature often reaches 115 and sometimes 120 degrees in the shade – and there is no shade. But the country was not empty. I wished it had been. Every evening our unwanted guests – sometimes a dozen, sometimes more – turned up to make further inroads on our flour.

We rode across a sombre land. The rocks beneath our feet and the broken scattered fragments were dark with age, sepia-coloured. They looked as if they had been scorched by the sun and polished by the wind ever since they first emerged from beneath the sea. It was difficult to think that this stark land had ever been other than it was, that flowers and crops may once have flourished here. Now it was dead; the earth's bared bones lay round us, sand-scoured beneath a glaring sky.

The Arabs talked of death. They named men who had died in recent raids and pointed to low ridges where they had fought. I thought of the blood that had splashed on the ground and darkened for a while the colouring of the stones. Round us were the graves of the ancient dead: tumuli, grouped together on high places. Immensely old, they had grown into the desert floor; only their shapes indicated that they were once the work of men. On some of them were set upright slabs of rock, such as I had seen erected by the Danakil on similar burial mounds to scare away hyenas and to stop them from digging out the corpses. There were other

monuments of long-dead people flanking here and there the paths
and shallow watercourses which marked the mountain slopes.

I called out to Sultan that I was going over to look at some of
these monuments which I could see two hundred yards away on
our right, but he said, 'Don't bother about that lot. There are many
more beyond that ridge. Come, I will show you', and with his stick
he tapped his camel on the side of her neck to turn her aside from
the others. We reached the ridge and saw ahead of us a small plain
rimmed with crumbling grey cliffs a few feet high which drained
down to a tributary of the main valley on our right. Some *harmal*
bushes, shiny-leaved like laurels but only eighteen inches high,
marked a stony watercourse. Nothing else grew here. I could see
the monuments aligned with the watercourse, like stone flowerbeds
on a gravel lawn. They were trilithons in groups of from three to
fifteen, each one consisting of three stone slabs about two feet high,
standing on end and leaning against each other with their base
forming a triangle; a few were capped with a fourth and usually
round stone. They were in line a yard apart, each group surrounded
by an oval bed of small stones. On one side of each group, parallel
with it and about three yards away, was a line of fireplaces consisting
of piles of small stones. I had seen the Bedu grilling meat on similar
piles of stones which they had heated in a fire. There were also
some rocks arranged singly in line, probably as seats. Near the
trilithons were burial mounds, and also some circles about twelve
feet in diameter, bordered with large stones and filled-in with a
level floor of pebbles.

The trilithons were plentiful on the northern slopes of the
Dhaufar mountains, but were uncommon farther to the east or
west. I saw a few of them as far westward as the Saar country, and
others near Ghail ba Yamin, in the country of the Humum. I also
saw one set in the top reaches of the Wadi Andam in Oman. The
number in a group varied, five being the most frequent, but I
noticed groups of three, five, seven, nine, twelve, fifteen, and once
twenty-five. They were always aligned with a watercourse or path
but otherwise appeared to have no special orientation. A few of the
slabs bore inscriptions of a type called Tamudic, a script usually

found in north and central Arabia and dating from pre-Islamic times.

Bertram Thomas thought these trilithons marked the sites of graves, but I frequently found them erected above solid rock. I think they may have been commemorative, like the memorials which I had seen erected near a path by the Danakil in Abyssinia. It seems to me probable that the people who set them up placed their dead in the tumuli which were scattered on the hill-tops near by. Even today the Bait Kathir on the plateau seldom dig a grave, but wall-in a corpse against a rock or in a fissure in a cliff. Whatever may have been their purpose, these piles of uncut stones are among the few tangible monuments which the Arabs of the past have left behind them in Arabia. They seemed to me a fitting memorial to the ancestors of a people who, at their best, have cared little for material things.

I wandered about among the monuments, taking photographs and looking for inscriptions, while Sultan sat on a rock near the two couched camels. Eventually he called out, 'Come on, Umbarak.' This was the name by which they now called me. 'Get on your camel and let's catch up with our companions. This is no place to hang about; Shisur is not far away – a bad place for raiders. Come on – those things have no value. They are just bits of rock stuck up by the Early Ones. Come on man, mount, and let's be off.'

I mounted and we rode after the others. I could see them a couple of miles away, a cluster of tiny dots moving imperceptibly across Arabia. I thought, 'They could go on and on, until at last they come to Syria or Transjordan and they would probably not pass a village or even a palm-tree; and yet it is as far from here to Damascus as it is from the southern tip of India to the Himalayas.' I wondered idly how many Arabs there were in Arabia; between six and seven millions is, I believe, the generally accepted figure, and of these only about a quarter are Bedu. Yet only Bedu can live in the deserts that cover all but a small part of Arabia. The other Arabs have settled in the few places where it is possible to make a living from the soil. Except for some serfs and the rabble in a few of the larger towns, all these Arabs are tribesmen. Most of them live in the Yemen, that fertile corner of Arabia which the Romans called Arabia Felix; perhaps it was there that the Semitic race originated. They themselves divide their race into the *Arab al Araba*, or pure Arabs, who they say are descended from Qahtan or Joktan and originated in the Yemen, and the *Arab al Mustaraba*, or adopted Arabs, descended from Adnan, the offspring of Ishmael, who originated in the north. European experts have confirmed the existence of two races in Arabia, the round-headed southerners and the long-headed northerners; but both have been in Arabia since earliest times. Shut off from the outside world by the desert and the sea, the inhabitants of Arabia have kept their racial purity. The neighbouring countries, Egypt, Syria, and Iraq, have been highways for invading armies and migrations, but there is no record of any migration into the Arabian peninsula. Abyssinians, Persians, Egyptians, and Turks imposed their uneasy rule at intervals on the Yemen, Oman, the Hajaz, and even on the Najd. They held the larger towns and waged intermittent and often unsuccessful war against the tribes. Their mercenaries spawned in the garrison towns, but they never mixed their blood with that of the tribesmen. No race in the world prizes lineage so highly as the Arabs and none has kept its blood so pure. There is, of course, mixed blood in the towns, especially in the seaports, but this is only the dirty froth upon the desert's edge.

As I rode along I reflected that nowhere in the world was there such continuity as in the Arabian desert. Here Semitic nomads, resembling my companions, must have herded their flocks before the Pyramids were built or the Flood wiped out all trace of man in the Euphrates valley. Successive civilizations rose and fell around the desert's edge: the Minaeans, Sabaeans, and Himyarites in southern Arabia; Egypt of the Pharaohs; Sumeria, Babylonia, Assyria; the Hebrews, the Phoenicians; Greeks and Romans; the Persians; the Muslim Empire of the Arabs, and finally the Turks. They lasted a few hundred or a thousand years and vanished; new races were evolved and later disappeared; religions rose and fell; men changed, adapting themselves to a changing world; but in the desert the nomad tribes lived on, the pattern of their lives but little changed over this enormous span of time.

Then, in forty years, less than a man's lifetime, all was changed; their life disintegrated. Previously the great Bedu tribes of the Najd and the Syrian desert had dominated central and northern Arabia. All traffic between the oases, villages and towns, the pilgrim caravans, everyone in fact who moved about Arabia, had to pass through the desert, and the Bedu controlled the desert. They levied tolls on travellers or looted them at will; they extorted blackmail from villagers and cultivators and from the weaker desert tribes. Bedu raiders, as elusive as the bands of Norsemen who once harried the coasts of Europe, had only to regain the desert to be free from all pursuit, whether by Roman legionaries or Turkish mercenaries.

The ascendancy of the Bedu was, however, moral as well as physical. Valuing freedom far above ease or comfort, careless of suffering, taking indeed a fierce pride in the hardship of their lives, the Bedu forced an unwilling recognition of their superiority on the villagers and townsmen who hated and affected to despise them. In the Hajaz I had heard men, sitting full-fed round the coffee hearths of great halls, disparage the Bedu as uncouth and lawless savages and curse them as infidels who neither prayed nor fasted. They had spoken scornfully of their poverty, marvelling that any human beings could endure this desert life. Then inevitably they had spoken of the Bedu's courage and their unbelievable generosity, and they had told stories, many of them fantastically improbable, which they vowed were true, and had recited long passages of verse about the Bani Hilal. Listening to them I had realized that the hungry ragged men whom they had just been reviling had been transmuted into the legendary heroes of the past.

The Bedu themselves never doubted their superiority. Even today such tribes as the Mutair and the Ajman would not regard it as an honour to give a girl from their tents in marriage even to the king of Arabia. I remembered asking some Rashid, who had visited Riyadh, how they had addressed the king, and they answered in surprise, 'We called him Abd al Aziz, how else would we call him except by his name?' And when I said, 'I thought you might call him Your Majesty', they answered, 'We are Bedu. We have no king but God.'

After the First World War, cars, aeroplanes, and wireless gave government for the first time in history a mobility greater than that of the Bedu. The desert was no longer a refuge for raiders but an open plain where concealment was impossible. It was a strange coincidence that at the same time as the Bedu in the Syrian desert were being brought under control with the help of modern weapons, the greatest king in Arabian history should reign in central Arabia. Abd al Aziz Ibn Saud had already broken and brought to heel the most powerful tribes in the peninsula before he introduced a single car or aeroplane into his kingdom. The peace which he had imposed would normally have disappeared with his death, and the desert would have reverted to the state of anarchy necessary to Bedu society; but I knew that the mechanical innovations which he had introduced would enable his successors to maintain the control which he had established. The desert had been pacified, and raids and tribal warfare had been effectively prevented from the Jordan valley to the northern edge of the Empty Quarter. Only here, on the far side of this great barrier of sand, did the old way of life linger on, little affected as yet by the changes in the north.

The society in which the Bedu live is tribal. Everyone belongs to a tribe and all members of the same tribe are in some degree kinsmen, since they are descended from a common ancestor. The closer the relationship the stronger is the loyalty which a man feels for his fellow tribesmen, and this loyalty overrides personal feelings, except in extreme cases. In time of need a man instinctively supports his fellow tribesmen, just as they in like case support him. There is no security in the desert for an individual outside the framework of his tribe. This makes it possible for tribal law, which is based on consent, to work among the most individualistic race in the world, since in the last resort a man who refuses to accept a tribal decision can be ostracized. It is therefore a strange fact that tribal law can only work in conditions of anarchy and breaks down as soon as peace is imposed upon the desert, since under peaceful conditions a man who resents a judgement can refuse to be bound by it, and if necessary can leave his tribe and live by himself. There is no central authority inside the tribe which can enforce the judgement.

In northern and central Arabia, while the structure of tribal life was breaking down as a result of the peace which had been imposed on the tribes and of administrative interference from outside, the economy of Bedu life was also collapsing. Deprived of their inaccessibility, the tribes could no longer blackmail the government into paying them large subsidies for their good behaviour. They could no longer levy tolls on travellers, nor exact tribute from the villagers and cultivators. A man who had lost his animals from disease could no longer borrow a mount and ride forth with a raiding party to retrieve his fortune. But the most disastrous change of all was caused by the introduction of mechanical transport, which practically abolished the dependence of the townsmen and villagers on the camels which the Bedu breed. In the past the Bedu had always found a ready sale for their camels, especially the thoroughbreds, for which the Arab rulers and the richer merchants were prepared to pay large prices. Some tribes made money by carrying goods across the desert, and even where the carrying trade was in the hands of professional carriers the Bedu sold them camels and extorted tolls.

Money acquired by individual Bedu was soon distributed among their families and tribes. I knew, for instance, that the money I was paying to my party would be divided by them with others who had a share in the venture although they did not accompany us. My companions also frequently asked me for advances, explaining that they had been asked for a loan and that having money it would be unseemly if they refused.

The discovery of oil on the Persian Gulf has brought enormous wealth into Arabia. Partly as a result of this, and partly as a result of the war, prices in the towns have soared. In the desert the Bedu need very little to keep themselves alive. Their herds provide them with food and drink, but they have certain requirements which they cannot supply for themselves. They need cloth and cooking-pots, knives, ammunition, occasional loads of dates or grain, and such simple luxuries as a handful of coffee or a little tobacco. To get these things they visited markets in the villages or towns and sold a camel or a goat, a little butter, water-skins, rugs, or saddle-bags. Life in the desert ceased to be possible when the few, but entirely essential, commodities that the Bedu had hitherto been able to buy in exchange for the products of the desert became too expensive for them to afford, and when no one any longer required the things which they produced.

Bedu love money; even to handle it seems to give them a thrill. They talk of it incessantly. They will discuss the price of a head-cloth or a cartridge belt intermittently for days. To pass the time on the march a man will put up his camel for sale, and the others, although they know that he has no intention of selling her, enter into the spirit of the game and bargain noisily for hours. They are all obsessed by dreams of buried treasure. Frequently as we rode along my companions assured me that there was *dhahab* (gold) to be found here and *dhahab* to be found there – under enormous sand-dunes or great rocks or in the middle of a quicksand. In the Wadi Difin near Habarut they pointed out a tunnel twenty feet up in the face of a limestone cliff, inaccessible except with a rope from above. This tunnel, whose mouth was two feet by four feet, had been filled with a plug of clay which the Arabs had recently tried to remove, as they have a tradition of treasure buried there. They claimed to have penetrated about twenty feet along the twisting tunnel, but said that they had given up before they reached the end of the plug. There was a considerable pile of excavated earth at the foot of the cliff. Sometimes, finding their preoccupation with money tedious, I chided them for their avarice, and they answered: 'It is all very well for you; you have plenty; but for us a few *riyals* may make all the difference between starving and not starving.'

On the oil-fields the Bedu could find the money of which they dreamt. They could earn large sums by sitting in the shade and guarding a dump, or by doing work which was certainly easier than watering thirsty camels on a nearly dry well in the middle of summer. There was plenty of good food, abundant sweet water, and long hours for sleep. They had seldom had these things before, and now they were being paid into the bargain. Their love of freedom and the restlessness that was in their blood drew most of them back into the desert, but life there was becoming more and more difficult. Soon it might be altogether impossible.

Here in the south the Bedu were still unaffected by the economic changes in the north, but I knew that they could not long escape the consequences. It seemed to me tragic that they should become, as the result of circumstances beyond their control, a parasitic proletariat squatting around oil-fields in the fly-blown squalor of shanty towns in some of the most sterile country in the world. All that is best in the Arabs has come to them from the desert: their deep religious instinct, which has found expression in Islam; their sense of fellowship, which binds them as members of one faith; their pride of race; their generosity and sense of hospitality; their dignity and the regard which they have for the dignity of others as fellow human beings; their humour, their courage and patience, the language which they speak and their passionate love of poetry. But the Arabs are a race which produces its best only under conditions of extreme hardship and deteriorates progressively as living conditions become easier. Lawrence described the nomad life as 'the circulation which kept vigour in the Semitic body' and wrote 'there were few, if indeed there was a single northern Semite, whose ancestors had not at some dark age passed through the desert. The mark of nomadism, that most deep and biting social discipline, was on each of them in his degree'.

Now as I rode along, ignoring Sultan's repeated injuctions to catch up with the others, which I knew were prompted by his craving for conversation that I was in no mood to supply, I reflected on the Arab influence on world history. It seemed to me significant that it was the desert Arabs who had imposed their characteristics on the Arab race and not the more numerous inhabitants of the Yemen, with their traditions of an ancient civilization. It was the customs and standards of the desert which had been accepted by townsmen and villagers alike, and which were spread by the Arab conquest across North Africa and the Middle East, and by Islam across a great part of the world. The civilization of the Yemen had sunk into decay before the time of Muhammad, and the dialects of the south had already been superseded by northern Arabic as the classical language of Arabia. With the establishment of the new religion of Islam the importance of the south declined still further and the centre of power shifted north to Mecca. The northern Arabs had no traditions of civilization behind them. To arrange three stones as a fireplace on which to set a pot was the only architecture that many of them required. They lived in black tents in the desert, or in bare rooms devoid of furnishings in the villages and towns. They had no taste nor inclination for refinements. Most of them demanded only the bare necessities of life, enough food and drink to keep them alive, clothes to cover their nakedness, some form of shelter from the sun and wind, weapons, a few pots, rugs, water-skins, and their saddlery. It was a life which produced much that was noble, nothing that was gracious.

These desert Arabs were avaricious, rapacious, and predatory, born freebooters, contemptuous of all outsiders, and intolerant of restraint. In the seventh century, united for the first time in their history, they swept out of Arabia under the banners of Islam and carried all before them. They overran the richest provinces of the Roman Empire and the whole of the Persian Empire. A little over a century after the battle of the Yarmuk in AD 636, which decided the fate of Syria, their rule extended from the Pyrenees and the shores of the Atlantic to the Indus and the borders of China. They had established an empire greater in extent than the Roman Empire. They had emerged from the desert craving for plunder and united by a new faith. It would not have been surprising if they had proved to be another scourge similar to the hordes of Attila and Genghis Khan, which swept across the world leaving only devastation behind them. It is one of the miracles of history that they created a new civilization, uniting into one society the hitherto incompatible cultures of the Mediterranean and Persia. Arabic, which had been evolved as the dialect of nomad tribesmen in the deserts of Arabia, was soon spoken from Persia to the Pyrenees and, superseding Greek and Latin, developed into one of the great cultural languages of the world. As the Muslim faith and the Arabic language spread throughout the Empire, the distinction between the Arab conquerors and their subjects largely disappeared, and conquerors and conquered tended to become fellow Muslims in one community. This Muslim civilization was profoundly influenced by Greek thought, for the Arabs translated every available Greek work into their own language; but while this civilization assimilated all it could, it was not merely imitative, and it made its own contribution to the civilizations of the world in architecture, literature, philosophy, history, mathematics, astronomy, physics, chemistry, and medicine. Few of the great intellectual figures of this society were Arabs, and several of them were not even Muslims but were Jews and Christians, but the rulers of the state in which they flourished were Arabs, and it was Arabs who had founded and inspired this civilization. Without them neither the Alhambra nor the Taj Mahal would ever have been built.

Today sixty million people speak Arabic as their native tongue and most of them claim to be Arabs, although in fact few of them are of Arab descent. A seventh part of the human race professes Islam, the religion which Muhammad founded in Arabia in the seventh century. It is a religion which claims to regulate not only a Muslim's religious beliefs and the ritual of his religious observance, but also the structure of his society and every aspect of his daily life, even how he should wash after sexual intercourse. The customs and conventions which Islam imposed upon its adherents were those of Arabia. I knew that wherever I went among Muslims, whether it was in Nigeria or in China, I should find much that was familiar to me in the pattern of their lives. It seemed to me not altogether fanciful to suppose that if the civilizations of today were to disappear as completely as those of Babylon and Assyria, a school history book two thousand years hence might devote a few pages to the Arabs and not even mention the United States of America.

The others were unloading their camels on a patch of hard sand when we caught up with them. From afar off they had seen the wisps of greyish grass which distinguished this hollow from other hollows they had passed on their way across the flint-strewn plain, and had turned aside to stop. Luckily, camels had grazed here years before, and their bleached droppings gave us a little fuel; but not enough to cook a proper meal.

Tonight while I was warm in my sleeping-bag the others would shiver under the cold north wind. They were Bedu, and these empty spaces where there was neither shade nor shelter were their homelands. Any of them could have worked in the gardens around Salala; all of them would have scorned this easier life of lesser men. Among the Bedu only the broken are stranded among the cultivations on the desert's shore.

FIVE

The Approach to the Empty Quarter

~~~~~~

The Rashid meet us at Shisur well and we travel to
Mughshin on the edge of the Sands. An accident
deprives me of all but two of the Rashid.

We watered at Shisur, where the ruins of a crude stone
fort on a rocky mound mark the position of this famous
well, the only permanent water in the central steppes.
Shisur was a necessary watering-place for raiders and had been the
scene of many fierce fights. At the bottom of the large cave which
undercuts the mound there was a trickle of water in a deep fissure.
This water could only be reached with difficulty down a narrow
passage, between the rock wall and a bank of sand, thirty feet in
height, which half filled the cave. When we arrived at the well the
water was buried under drifted sand and had to be dug out. I offered
to help but the others said that I was too bulky for the job. Two
hours later they shouted that they were ready, and asked us to fetch
the camels. In turn they scrambled up the slope out of the dark
depths of the cave, the quaking water-skins heavy on their shoulders. Moisture ran down their bodies, plastering the loin-cloths to
their slender limbs; their hair, thick with sand, fell about their
strained faces. Lowering the water-skins to the ground, they loosed
jets of water into leather buckets, which they offered to the crowd-
ing camels, while they sang the age-old watering songs. Showers
of camel-droppings pattered on to the ground, and rolled down

the slope into the water, and small avalanches of sand, encrusted with urine, slipped down to add more bitterness to water that was already bitter. Each camel, as soon as she had been watered, was couched near by. Every now and again one of them rose jerkily to her feet, anxious to wander off, and her owner ran across the gravel stream-bed to bring her back, shouting her name, Farha (joy), Matara (rain), Ghazala (gazelle), Safra (the yellow one), or some other name which in battle might be his war-cry.

Suddenly the sentinel on the slope above gave the alarm. We seized our rifles, which were always at hand, and took up our position round the well. The camels were quickly collected behind the mound. In the distance we could see riders approaching. In this land all strangers are counted hostile until they declare themselves. We fired two shots over their heads. They came on steadily, waving their head-cloths, and one of them jumped off his camel and threw up sand into the air. We relaxed. As they drew near, someone said, 'They are Rashid – I can see bin Shuas's camel.' Bedu can always recognize camels much farther off than they can distinguish human beings. Meeting a stranger, they can tell which tribe he belongs to by numerous signs perceptible at once to their discerning eyes: whether he wears his cartridge-belt buckled tightly or sagging low in front, whether he wears his head-cloth loosely or more closely wound round his head; the stitchings on his shirt, the folds of his loin-cloth, the leather cover in which he carries his rifle, the pattern on his saddle-bags, the way he has folded his rug above them, even the way he walks, all these reveal his identity. But above all they can tell from a man's speech to which tribe he belongs.

The riders were close now. The Bait Kathir could identify them. 'That is bin Shuas.' 'That is Mahsin.' 'That is al Auf.' 'That is bin Kabina and Amair – and Saad and bin Mautlauq.' There were seven of them, all of them Rashid. We formed up in line to receive them. They halted their camels thirty yards away, couched them by tapping them on their necks with their sticks, got off, and came towards us. Bin Shuas and bin Mautlauq wore only loin-cloths; the others were dressed in head-cloths and shirts of varying shades of brown. I recognized the tattered shirt which bin Kabina wore as the one which I had given to him when we had parted in the Hadhramaut. Only he was unarmed, without rifle or dagger. The others carried their rifles on their shoulders. Bin Shuas and al Auf had their rifles inside covers made of undressed hide and decorated with tassels. When they were a few yards away Mahsin, whom I identified by his lame leg, called out 'Salam alaikum,' and we answered together 'Alaikum as salam.' Then one behind the other they passed along our line, greeting each of us with the triple nose-kiss, nose touching nose on the right side, left side, and again on the right. They then formed up facing us. Tamtaim said to me, 'Ask their news'; but I answered 'No, you do it. You are the oldest.' Tamtaim called out, 'Your news?' Mahsin answered, 'The news is good.' Again Tamtaim asked, 'Is anyone dead? Is anyone gone?' Back came the immediate answer, 'No! – don't say such a thing.' Question and answer were as invariable as the responses in the Litany. No matter what had really happened, they never changed. They might have fought with raiders; half their party might have been killed and be lying still unburied; their camels might have been looted; any affliction might have befallen them – starvation, drought, or sickness, and still at this first formal questioning they would answer, 'The news is good.' They now returned to the camels, unsaddled them, and, after hobbling their forelegs, turned them loose. We had meanwhile spread rugs for them, and Tamtaim shouted to bin Anauf to prepare coffee. As soon as this was ready Musallim set a dish of dates before them; then, standing, he poured out coffee and handed the cup to Mahsin and to the others in their order of importance. They drank, ate dates, and were again served with coffee. Now at last we should get the real news.

They were small men, none more than five feet six inches in height, and very lean. They had been weathered by life in the desert until only the essential flesh, bone, and skin remained. They sat before us, very restrained in their movements, and quiet and slow of speech, careful of their dignity in front of strangers. Only their dark, watchful eyes flickered to and fro, missing nothing. Mahsin sat with his crippled leg stiffly out in front of him. He was a compactly built man of middle age, with a square face. His thin lips were pinched, and there were deep lines round his mouth and nose. I knew that until he had been wounded two years ago he had been famed as a raider, and that he had killed many men. He was reputed to be very rich in camels. But it was Muhammad al Auf who interested me most, for the Rashid had talked much about him when I was with them the year before. They said he had never recovered his old light-hearted gaiety since his brother had been killed by the Saar. He had a fine face. Skin and flesh were moulded over strong bone, his eyes, set wide apart, were large and curiously flecked with gold, while his nose was straight and short and his mouth generous. He had a thin moustache and a few hairs on a dimpled chin. His hair, very long and wavy, was unbraided and fell round his shoulders. I thought he was about thirty-five years old. He gave me an immediate impression of controlled energy, of self-confidence and intelligence. Bin Kabina called out to me. 'How are you, Umbarak? Where have you been since you left us?' I thought he looked gaunt. He had grown an inch since I parted from him in Tarim. I was glad to see him again, for I had become much attached to him during the time he had been with me. I listened to the news. The Dahm had raided the Manahil, and the Manahil under bin Duailan, who was known as 'the Cat', had taken many camels off the Yam. The Saar had raided the Dawasir. They told us who had been killed and who had been wounded. There had been good rain two months before in the steppes, but the drought which had lasted for seven years near the Jiza was still unbroken. I asked about bin al Kamam and they told me that he had gone to the Yemen to seek a truce with the Dahm, and that the other two Rashid whom I had told Amair to fetch were far away in the Sands. I asked news of the other Rashid who had been with me, and they in turn asked where I had been and how my tribe had fared in my absence. We talked for a while and then dispersed.

Bin Kabina and I climbed to the ruined fort above the well and kept watch across the empty, shimmering landscape, while the others finished watering the camels and filling the water-skins. Bin Kabina asked me where I was going and I told him that I planned to cross the Sands, but pledged him to secrecy for I had not yet spoken to the others. He said, 'The Bait Kathir are no good in the Sands and won't go there, but the Rashid will come with us. It is lucky that Muhammad al Auf is here, for he is the best guide in the tribe and knows the eastern sands.' I asked him why Muhammad was nicknamed al Auf, which means the Bad, and he said, 'Because he isn't.' I said, 'You are looking thin and tired. Have you been ill?' and he answered, 'I nearly died since you went away. I was circumcised three months ago and they could not stop the bleeding. When it stopped they thought it was because I was dead. There were eight of us and we were circumcised by one of the sheikhs of the Bait Khawar in the valley of the Kidyut. One of us was a Manahil, a grown man with a beard, the others were Bait Khawar. They were all older than I was. Before the operation our families rubbed our bodies with butter and saffron so that they shone. We were circumcised in turn sitting on a rock. Everyone had come to watch and there was a large crowd.'

I asked him if he had been afraid, and he said, 'Of course I was. Everyone is afraid when they know that they are going to be hurt, but they don't admit it. I was most afraid that I should flinch. As I was the youngest I was done first. The old man tied my foreskin very tightly with a piece of string and then left it to die. By God it hurt! It was almost a relief when he cut it off, though his knife was blunt and he went on hacking away for what seemed ages. One of the others fainted.'

I interrupted to ask if they put anything on the wound. 'Yes,' he said, 'a mixture of salt, ashes, and powdered camel dung – it stung like fire.' He went on: 'We were operated on in the evening. I started to bleed during the night. I had been asleep and woke to feel a warm wetness on my thighs. The sheepskin on which I lay was soaked with blood. It was pitch dark and we could not see anything until my mother lit a fire. I had bled very little when they cut it off.' He added with pride, 'The people who were watching said that I showed no sign of pain while I was being done.' He told me that he had healed in three weeks, but that two of the others, one of them the Manahil with the beard, were still unhealed and very swollen when he left them two months later. When I asked why they waited till they were grown up to be operated on, he said that it was their custom, and added with a grin that some of the Mahra waited until the eve of their marriage. I wondered what effect it had on a boy to grow up anticipating this ordeal. Probably he was resigned, for he had no choice but to submit to it. Certainly during the operation the fear of lasting ridicule if he flinched gave him courage to endure, and his pride made him anxious to face the test. In southern Iraq I have seen fourteen- and fifteen-year-old boys thrusting each other aside, as they crowded forward, as eager to be circumcised as boys to buy sweets at the counter of a school shop in England; and in the Sudan I have met Arab boys who had circumcised themselves because their fathers had delayed giving permission for the operation. Yet among Arabs, circumcision is not a coveted sign conferring special privileges and marking the emergence of a boy into manhood, as it is among many primitive tribes such as the Masai.

Bin Kabina had undergone the normal circumcision, obligatory for all Muslims, although it is usually performed on a child about the age of seven. As I sat there talking to him I thought of the ceremony I had watched five months earlier in the distant Tihama. For a fortnight the young men who were to be circumcised had danced each evening and late into the night, waiting for the day when the old men would announce that the positions of the moon and stars were favourable. The initiates wore short, tight-sleeved red jackets and baggy white drawers, tight at the ankle, the only time in their lives when they wore drawers, which were women's dress. On the appointed day, riding on camels, they were paraded behind the musicians round the neighbouring villages, and then brought back just before sunset, followed by a large crowd, to their own village. Their friends helped them to take off their drawers, and then one after the other these young men, looking like girls with their flowing hair and delicate features, stepped forward in front of their tribe. Each of them stood, with legs apart and his hands gripping his long hair, staring motionless and unflinching at a dagger stuck in the ground in front of him, while a slave handled his penis until it was erect and then flayed the entire organ. When the slave stepped aside, his work at last completed, the lad sprang forward and, to the compelling rhythm of the drums, danced frenziedly before the eager, craning crowd, leaping and capering while the blood splashed down his legs.

This is the modified form of a rite far older than Islam. In the Hajaz mountains some of the tribes still performed 'the flaying circumcision', which was often postponed until a man was married and had children, and in which the skin was removed from the navel down to the inside of the legs. Ibn Saud forbade even the modified form of this circumcision, which he declared was a pagan custom, but the young men were prepared to risk the severest punishment rather than forgo the credit of submitting to this rite. On this particular occasion one of them had already been circumcised as a child, but he insisted on undergoing this second operation. Even after it was over their sufferings were not yet ended. Each morning they were held down over a small hole in the ground so that their mutilated parts dangled down, to kipper in the heat and smoke which came up from a fire below. Lads who had stood unmoved while they were circumcised screamed with the agony of this barbarous treatment. I described what I had seen to bin Kabina, who said, 'That is not circumcision – it is butchery.'

In the evening I gave bin Kabina the clothes which I had brought for him and the spare dagger which was in my saddle-bag. He buckled it on with pride. A stranger would have thought that he should have expressed his gratitude, but this was not customary among Arabs. He had accepted my gift and felt that there was no need for words. He would express his gratitude by other means.

We left Shisur on 9 November in the chill of dawn; the sun was resting on the desert's rim, a red ball without heat. We walked as usual till it grew warm, the camels striding in front of us, a moving mass of legs and necks. Then one by one, as the inclination took us, we climbed up their shoulders and settled in our seats for the long hours which lay ahead. The Arabs sang, 'the full-throated roaring of the tribes'; the shuffling camels quickened their pace, thrusting forward across the level ground, for we had left the hills behind us and were on the steppes which border on the Sands. We noticed the stale tracks of oryx, saw gazelle bounding stiff-legged across the plain, and flushed occasional hares from withered salt bushes in shallow watercourses.

Bin Shuas told us how they had carried Mahsin, who was his uncle, for three days tied on a camel, with the bone of his shattered thigh sticking through the skin, while they tried to outdistance the pursuers who followed in their tracks. Then bin Mautlauq spoke of the raid in which young Sahail was killed. He and fourteen companions had surprised a small herd of Saar camels. The herdsman had fired two shots at them before escaping on the fastest of his camels, and one of these shots had hit Sahail in the chest. Bakhit held his dying son in his arms as they rode back across the plain with the seven captured camels. It was late in the morning when Sahail was wounded, and he lived till nearly sunset, begging for water which they had not got. They rode all night to escape from inevitable pursuit. At sunrise they saw some goats, and a small Saar encampment under a tree in a shallow valley. A woman was churning butter in a skin, and a boy and a girl were milking the goats. Some small children sat under the tree. The boy saw them first and tried to escape but they cornered him against a low cliff. He was about fourteen years old, a little younger than Sahail, and he was unarmed. When they surrounded him he put his thumbs in his mouth as a sign of surrender, and asked for mercy. No one answered him. Bakhit slipped down off his camel, drew his dagger, and drove it into the boy's ribs. The boy collapsed at his feet, moaning, 'Oh my father! Oh my father!' and Bakhit stood over him till he died. He then climbed back into his saddle, his grief a little soothed by the murder which he had just committed. As bin Mautlauq spoke, staring across the level plain with his hot, rather bloodshot eyes, I pictured the scene with horrible distinctness. The small, long-haired figure, in white loin-cloth, crumpled on the ground, the spreading pool of blood, the avid clustering flies, the frantic wailing of the dark-clad women, the terrified children, the shrill insistent screaming of a small baby.

I rode along haunted by the thought of that murdered child, while around me the watchful Arabs formed and re-formed into chattering groups. There was not one of them whose life would not be forfeit if we were surprised by Saar raiders. Vindictive as this age-old law of a life for a life and a tooth for a tooth might be, I realized none the less that it alone prevented wholesale murder among a people who were subject to no outside authority, and who had little regard for human life; for no man lightly involves his whole family or tribe in a blood-feud. I remembered that, in 1935, Glubb, describing the Bedu of the north, had written: 'It was curious to think that even in the anarchical days of raging tribal chaos in ungoverned Arabia before the emergence of the Akhwan or the present establishment of law and order, there was probably less fear and apprehension abroad than there is today in peaceful England.' It was easy to be shocked by the Bedu's disregard for human life. After all, many people feel today that it is morally indefensible to hang a man, even if he has raped and killed a child, but I could not forget how easily we ourselves had taken to killing during the war. Some of the most civilized people I had known had been the most proficient.

The country grew more arid; every plant and bush was dead. Skeletons of trees, brittle powdery branches, fallen and half buried in the drifting sand, and deposits of silt left by ancient floods, but now as dry as ashes, marked the course of Umm al Hait, 'The Mother of Life', the great trunk wadi which leads down to Mughshin. Nothing stirred, not even a lizard, for here there had been twenty-five years of unbroken drought.

On the second day at sunset we saw the Sands stretching across our front, a shimmering rose-coloured wall, seemingly as intangible as a mirage. The Arabs, roused from the nodding torpor of weary, empty hours, pointed with their sticks, shouted, and broke into a sudden spate of talk. But I was content to look in silence upon that long-awaited vision, as excited as a mountaineer who sees above the Indian foothills the remote white challenge of the Himalayas.

We rode parallel with the Sands, since the hard gravel surface of the plain was easier for our camels than the soft steepness of the dunes. In the late afternoons we usually turned in to the Sands to camp. Large mimosa-like trees, which the Arabs called *ghaf*, grew here. Deep down, their questing roots had found water, and their branches were heavy with flowering, trailing fronds that fell to the clean sand and formed arbours in which we camped.

One night, near Mughshin, when sleeping on the open plain, I was awakened by a long-drawn howl. Again and again the uncanny sound quavered across the camp, sending shivers down my back. It came from a group of figures sitting twenty yards away. I called out, 'What is wrong?' and bin Kabina answered, 'Said is possessed by a *zar*.' I got up, walked round some camels, and joined them. By the light of the setting moon I could see the boy, one of the Bait Kathir, crouching over a small fire. His face and head were covered with a cloth, and he rocked himself to and fro as he howled. The others sat close to him, silent and intent. Suddenly they began to chant in two parts, while Said thrashed himself violently from side to side. More and more wildly he threw himself about, and once a corner of the cloth with which he covered his face fell into the embers and began to smoulder. Someone leant forward and put it out. Steadily the chanting rose and fell about the demented boy, who gradually became calmer. A man lit some incense in a bowl and held it under the boy's nose beneath the cloth. Suddenly he began to sing in a curious, strained, high-pitched voice. Line by line the others answered him. He stopped, grew violent again, and then calmed once more. A man leant forward and asked him questions and he answered, speaking like someone in his sleep. I could not understand the words, for they spoke Mahra. They gave him more incense and the spirit left him. A little later he lay down to sleep, but once again he was troubled. This time he sobbed bitterly and groaned as if in great pain. They gathered round him once more and chanted until he grew calm. Then he slept. In the morning he was all right.

The belief in possession by a *zar* or evil spirit is also widely held in the Sudan, Egypt, and Mecca, and is generally thought to have originated in Abyssinia or central Africa. It seems to me possible that it originated in southern Arabia. My companions told me that whenever they exorcized a *zar* they used the Mahra tongue, and I knew that the ancestors of the Mahra had originally colonized Abyssinia.

We reached Mughshin eight days after leaving Shisur. We were approaching the well and Mahsin was telling us once more about the battle in which he had been wounded. His stiff leg was stretched out in front of him. Suddenly, unaccountably, our camels panicked, scattering in great plunging bounds. I saw a man fall from his camel in front of me as I fought to keep my seat. When my camel was under control I looked back. Mahsin lay crumpled and motionless on the ground. We ran back to him. His damaged leg was twisted under him and he was moaning faintly. His head-cloth had fallen off and the close-cropped hair showed grey upon his skull. As I bent over him I realized that he was older than I had thought. We tried to straighten him but he screamed. I got morphia from my saddle-bags and gave him an injection, and then we carried him on a blanket to the trees. By the grace of God the well was close at hand. Perhaps our thirsty camels had smelt the water and this had started the stampede. We fashioned rough splints from branches and set his leg; there seemed little left but splintered bone. Bin Shuas crouched beside him, keeping the flies off his face, while others sat round discussing whether he would live or die. Occasionally a man would shake his head and say sorrowfully, 'Mahsin didn't deserve this.' Then they rose and set about their tasks, watering the camels and cooking food.

In the evening we discussed what we must do. They said that Mahsin could not be moved. He must stay here till he recovered or till he died, and the Rashid must remain with him. He had killed many men, especially from the Saar, and if his enemies heard that he was lying helpless here, they would come from afar to kill him. During the past days I had let the news leak out that I planned to cross the Empty Quarter. I knew from bin Kabina that I could count on the Rashid. Sultan and Musallim had both said they would come with me, and were insistent that I should take some of the Bait Kathir, for they were jealous of the Rashid. Now everything was changed. I was in the hands of the Bait Kathir and I wondered whether they would still be eager for this journey. Sultan soon suggested that we should travel eastwards, through the Sahma sands where I had been the year before, and perhaps visit the quicksands of Umm al Samim which he knew I was anxious to see. I went to bed disconsolate, certain that my plans were wrecked.

Next morning bin Kabina told me that the Rashid had agreed that he and Al Auf should go with me, but asked that I should lend the others two of my service rifles, and enough ammunition. I willingly agreed. Mahsin seemed better and drank a little milk. I promised him that I would remain with him till he was on the mend and I gave him another injection of morphia, for he was still in great pain. I then spoke to Sultan, hinting that as the Bait Kathir would not come with me across the Sands, I should send bin Kabina to find me more Rashid. He protested. 'Why do you speak like this, Umbarak? Listen to me! Have I not promised to take you across the Sands? I, Sultan. What do you want with the Rashid anyway. You know the Bait Kathir – old friends – your companions of last year. Did we fail you then? By God, Umbarak, why do you doubt us now?'

I remained at Mughshin for nine days. The extensive but shallow depression where the Umm al Hait ends against the Sands was well wooded with *ghaf* and tamarisk, and on the surrounding plains there were plenty of *arad* salt bushes, which are good food for camels as long as water is available. Near the well there was a dense grove of untended palms whose dates are collected in September by the Al Kathir tribes. Among the palms was a salt-encrusted ditch of very brackish water, three hundred yards long, and in the middle of it a small spring of fresher water just fit to drink.

Usually, Bedu lop tall trees to provide food for their camels, but the *ghaf* trees here were unmutilated, for Mughshin is a *hauta* where no tree may be cut. On my way to the Hadhramaut I had passed several of these *hautas*, probably once the sacred groves of some forgotten cult. We would ride down a wadi and camp under trees in no way remarkable from others which we had passed, but I would be warned not to damage them for this was a *hauta*. The Bedu believed that to ignore this prohibition would be to incur misfortune and possibly even death. Mughshin was distinguished from other *hautas* since hares might not be killed here. Even in the sands of Ghanim, where there was no *hauta*, the Bedu would not eat hares, although elsewhere they ate their meat with relish. The ban did not include gazelle. I remember being told in the Hajaz that hunting and cutting wood were both forbidden within the sanctuary around Mecca.

In the evening after we had fed we heard angry voices behind us where the Rashid sat around Mahsin. Bin Kabina and I went over to them, and soon everyone in the camp was there. Amair was shouting at bin Mautlauq, and while I watched he snatched his head-cloth from his head and threw it at his feet. Many people were talking and it was difficult to make out what the row was about. Among Bedu anyone, however young, can always express his opinion, and will probably do so even if the argument has got nothing to do with him. No Bedu would ever think of saying 'For God's sake mind your own business', for he would accept the fact that anything that concerned him concerned everyone else in the community. Eventually I gathered that some weeks earlier Amair had lost a camel, and bin Mautlauq had offered to look for it provided Amair promised him a reward of five *riyals* if he found it. Amair now maintained that bin Mautlauq had known all the time where the camel was, and he refused to hand over the money he had promised. Finally the matter was referred to Tamtaim, who was respected by the Rashid for his great age and shrewdness. He decided that Amair should pay the money provided that bin Maut-lauq swore on the tomb of al Jauhari, which was on the coast several days' journey to the west of Salala, that he had not known where the camel was when he had offered to look for it. Both of them accepted the judgement and were soon helping each other to mend a saddle. Disputes are generally settled among the Bedu by one side or the other swearing on oath on a saint's tomb to the truth of their statement, and it is for the arbitrators to decide which side shall be asked to take the oath. Few Bedu would swear falsely on one of these tombs, of which there are several along the coast and in the Hadhramaut.

During the days that I was at Mughshin my companions often asked me for medicines. Bedu suffer much from headaches and stomach trouble. Sometimes my aspirin worked, but if not the sufferer would get someone to brand him, usually on his heels, and would announce a little later that his headache was now gone, and that the old Bedu remedies were better than the Christian's pills. Bedu cauterize themselves and their camels for nearly every ill. Their bellies, chests, and backs are often criss-crossed with the ensuing scars. I had heard that many years ago a British cargo steamer was ship-wrecked on the southern coast of Arabia. A few survivors were picked up by some Junuba who, hoping no doubt for a reward, took them eventually to Muscat. Camel's milk and dates had given the Englishmen acute diarrhoea, and the Bedu, despite their protests, forcibly cauterized them. They eventually arrived at Muscat nearly killed by dysentery and this primitive treatment.

One of the Bait Kathir had an exposed nerve in a back tooth, which he asked me to remove. I hate taking out teeth, especially as they are usually nothing but blackened shells. This one was fairly sound, however, and I removed it without difficulty, the patient lying on the ground with his head firmly held between someone's knees. Musallim was suffering from severe constipation. I gave him a powerful dose of Epsom salts, but when this did not work at once, he resorted to the Bedu remedy of *hamrar*. He lay on the ground while a dozen of his friends knelt round him in a circle chanting. Old Tamtaim led the singing, which got faster and faster as the participants got more and more excited. At intervals one of the singers would lean forward and take up a mouthful of flesh from Musallim's stomach, making a curious bubbling noise as he did so. Musallim's bowels were loosed soon after this. I gave the credit to the Epsom salts, while they claimed it for the *hamrar*.

Gazelle were plentiful at Mughshin. Musallim and bin Shuas shot us meat each day, so we fed well; indeed, too well. I was worried about our rations, especially as I should now have to leave enough food with Mahsin and the Rashid. All Bedu are improvident, and my companions cooked lavish meals from our fast-dwindling supplies. I encouraged them to eat the rice which they preferred, since this would be of little use to me during the waterless journey which lay ahead. Bedu have no desire for variety in their meals and will happily eat the same food twice a day for months, judging it not by its quality but by its quantity. I tried once to vary the sameness of our food. Musallim had shot a gazelle and I cooked an elaborate and, I thought, excellent lunch; unfortunately, bin Turkia had gone off to look for a camel and did not come back till after dark, by which time the grilled meat was a congealed mess liberally sprinkled with sand. The others ate it, but declared unanimously that they preferred the boiled meat and soup which Musallim cooked.

After incessant discussions we decided that bin Kabina, al Auf, Sultan, Musallim, Mabkhaut, bin Turkia, young Said (the boy who had suffered from the evil spirit), and five other Bait Kathir should accompany me. I was anxious to take a smaller party, with only the best camels, but Sultan said that we could change the worst camels with the Bait Musan, whose herds were in the Sands a few days distant. He argued that it would be dangerous for us to be a small party on the far side of the Sands, where the Al bu Falah of Abu Dhabi and the bin Maktum of Dubai were at war, and also when we travelled back through the Duru country in Oman. He told me that the Duru, after hearing I had visited Mughshin last year, had vowed that they would allow no infidel to travel in their country. We settled to meet the main party again at Bai near the southern coast in two months' time.

On 24 November we spent a busy day re-dividing our rations, looking to water-skins, and watering the camels. I had bought bin Shuas' camel for bin Kabina to ride. I paid the equivalent of twenty-five pounds, which was a lot more than she was really worth, but she was a fine animal in excellent condition, and in milk. For myself I had selected a powerful, dark-coloured camel from Dhaufar, which belonged to Musallim and was one of the spares we had with us. She was a rough ride, but al Auf said she would go well in the Sands when once she was used to them. He himself was mounted on a magnificent but almost uncontrollable animal, riding her on a thin chain fastened to a ring in her nose. This camel was from Mahsin's herd, and our camel guards had found her grazing to the east of the well. Camel theft, as opposed to raiding, was almost unknown here, and these Bedu often left their animals free to roam for weeks on end. If a camel turned up at a well, anyone there would give her a drink. Most of our other camels were in poor condition.

I had a final look at Mahsin, who was much better; for several days he had refused food, but now he was eating again. Bin Shuas would be able to shoot meat for him, and one of the Rashid camels was in milk. Then we loaded up, and after saying good-bye to the others we set off into the sands. As I approached my camel to take her halter she kicked sideways at me, grazing the skin. Had the kick landed it would have broken my leg.

We camped a few miles away. At last I had started on my journey across the Empty Quarter.

SIX

On the Edge of the Empty Quarter

We water for the last time at Khaur bin Atarit in
Ghanim and travel to Ramlat al Ghafa.

After our evening meal I had a long talk with Muhammad al
Auf. He was the only one of our party who had been across
the Sands and knew what conditions were like on the other
side. He was quiet and reserved, and inspired me with confidence.
The Bait Kathir were jealous of him, and he was anxious not to
assume responsibility as guide until we had left the area which they
knew. Young Said, who was the son of the Bait Musan sheikh,
could take us as far as Ramlat al Ghafa. He knew these Sands, but
the rest of the Bait Kathir had only been on the edge of them when
travelling with me the year before.

I knew that Sultan and the others would join me at once if they
saw me talking to al Auf. He and I therefore told the others that
we were going to round up the grazing camels. Taking our rifles
we walked off into the desert, hunted round until we found the
camels, and then sat and talked. I asked al Auf when he had crossed
the eastern Sands. He said, 'Two years ago. I know them.' When
I pressed him for details of his journey he smiled and repeated, 'I
know them', and I felt sure he did. He said that if we could cross
the formidable Uruq al Shaiba, which he described as successive
mountains of sand, we should arrive at Dhafara, where in the palm
groves of Liwa there were wells and villages. I had vaguely heard
of Dhafara. To the southern Bedu it stood for the *ultima Thule:* 'as

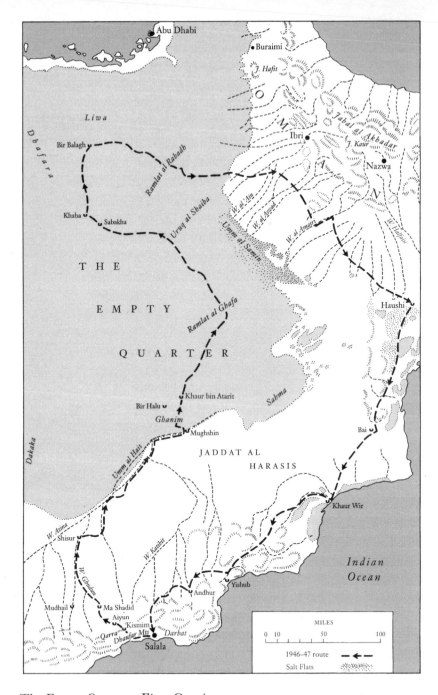

The Empty Quarter: First Crossing

far as Dhafara' they said, to imply the limits of the known world. Al Auf described Liwa to me as we sat there in the dark. It sounded very exciting, an oasis with palm groves and villages which extended for two days' camel journey. I knew that no European had ever been there, and that it must be bigger than Jabrin, which Cheesman had discovered in 1924. Al Auf reckoned that it would take us a month to get there and was worried about the Bait Kathir camels which were in poor condition. He said, 'They will never get across the Uruq al Shaiba.' I asked if there was no way round these sands, and he said, 'No, only if we went far to the west by Dakaka, where Thomas crossed. There the Sands are easy.' He told me that to the east the Uruq al Shaiba ran into the dangerous quicksands of Umm al Samim (the Mother of Poison). Bertram Thomas had heard of Umm al Samim, and believed that the legendary quicksands of the Bahr al Safi, which von Wrede the Bavarian traveller claimed to have discovered to the north of the Hadhramaut in 1843, would eventually be identified with it. There were fascinating problems to be solved in the desert ahead of us, but could we get there? I estimated that we should have to cross four hundred miles of desert before we reached Liwa. Once more we discussed camels, distances, food, and water. We were seriously short of food. We had started from Mughshin with two hundred pounds of flour, rice for two meals, one of which was eaten, a few handfuls of maize, and a little butter, coffee, sugar, and tea. This must last twelve of us for at least a month, which was half a pound of flour a day each, and nothing else. I thought bitterly of the food which the Arabs had squandered on the way to Mughshin. We should be very hungry. We could probably carry enough water for twenty days if we rationed ourselves to a quart a day for each person. Twenty waterless days was the very limit that camels would stand, travelling for long hours across heavy sands; and they would only do this if they found grazing. Should we find grazing? It is the continual problem which faces the Bedu. If we did not find it, the camels would collapse and that would be the end of us all. It is not hunger nor is it thirst that frightens the Bedu; they maintain that riding they can survive in cold weather for seven days without food or water. It is the possible collapse of their camels which haunts them. If this happens, death is certain. I asked al Auf again what he thought; would we find grazing? 'God knows,' he answered. 'There is grazing as far as Ramlat al Ghafa from rain two years ago; beyond that, who knows?' He smiled, and added, 'We will find something.' We rose and went back to the camp to sleep, but I lay awake for a long time. The journey ahead of us seemed very formidable and I was doubtful of the Bait Kathir.

In the morning we allowed the camels to feed for a while on the *ghaf* trees which grew round our camping place. Musallim had shot a gazelle the day before, and we had eaten only half the meat. He had placed the rest in a low bush to keep it out of the sand, and when we woke it was gone. Tracks showed that a fox had taken it. I was angry, for this was the last meat we were likely to have for very many days. Musallim followed the tracks, and unearthed most of the meat where the fox had buried it under another bush. We brushed the sand off it, thankful to have recovered it.

After we had saddled we rode northward to Ghanim. This country was familiar to me, from my visit of the year before. Isolated dunes, two or three hundred feet in height, rose in apparently haphazard confusion from the desert floor. These enormous piles of sand, produced by vagaries of the winds which blew there, conform to no known rule of sand formation. The Bedu call them *qaid*. I have only seen them in the south-eastern Sands and in modified form round Liwa. These *qaid* are known individually to the Bedu, for each dune has its own shape, which does not change perceptibly with the years; but all of them have certain features in common. Here in every case it was the northern face which was steep. On this side the sand fell away from beneath the summit in an unbroken wall, set at as steep an angle as the grains of sand would lie. Down this face small avalanches constantly subsided, each fall leaving a temporary, light-coloured smear upon the surface of the sand. On either side of this face sharp crested ridges swept down in undulating curves, and behind them were other alternating ridges and troughs, smaller and more involved as they became farther from the main face. The sand on the lower slopes at the back of the dune was firm, and rose and fell in broad sinuous trenches, or was dimpled with shallow hollows. The surface of the sand was marked with diminutive ripples, of which the ridges were built from the heavier and darker grains, while the hollows were filled with the smaller paler-coloured stuff. Continuously the wind shifted the sand, separating the heavier from the lighter grains, which are always of different colour. Only once did I notice sands where the large were paler than the small. Although they are the least numerous it is the large grains which give the prevailing hue to the landscape. Disturb the surface of the sand and the underlying paleness is immediately revealed. It is this blending of two colours which gives such depth and richness to the Sands: gold with silver, orange with cream, brick-red with white, burnt-brown with pink, yellow with grey – they have an infinite variety of shades and colours.

We reached the well of Khaur bin Atarit, discovered by some forgotten Bedu, but still bearing his name, on the evening of 27 November, four days after leaving Mughshin. The shallow well was in the hard, white gypsum floor that underlay the sands, and was on the north side of a high dune. It was drifted in, but using our hands, and the few basins and pots which we had with us, we dug it out before nightfall. The water tasted brackish, as I had expected, and I knew that the taste would grow worse the longer we kept the water in the skins. Surprisingly it was only mildly purgative, although it contained magnesium sulphate mixed with calcium and common salt. Next day Said and two others went to look for the Bait Musan at Bir Halu, 'the sweet well'. I knew from the year before that the name was misleading and that the water of Bir Halu tasted as foul as the water of Khaur bin Atarit.

I climbed to the summit of the dune and lay peacefully in the sun, four hundred feet above the well. A craving for privacy is something which Bedu will never understand; something which they will always instinctively mistrust. I have often been asked by Englishmen if I was never lonely in the desert, and I have wondered how many minutes I have spent by myself in the years that I have lived there. It is true that the worst loneliness is to be lonely in a crowd. I have been lonely at school, and in European towns where I knew nobody, but I have never been lonely among Arabs. I have arrived in their towns where I was unknown, and I have walked into the bazaar and greeted a shopkeeper. He has invited me to sit beside him in his shop and has sent for tea. Other people have come along and joined us. They have asked me who I was, where I came from, and innumerable questions which *we* should never ask a stranger. Then one of them has said, 'Come and lunch', and at lunch I have met other Arabs, and someone else has asked me to dinner. I have wondered sadly what Arabs brought up in this tradition have thought when they visited England; and I have hoped that they realized that we are as unfriendly to each other as we must appear to be to them.

I watched bin Kabina walking along the arête of sand which swept upwards to the summit where I sat. He carried the service rifle which I had lent him for this journey. He joined me and sat talking, while he stripped the bolt. Bedu love taking rifles to pieces. He told me that he was going to buy a rifle with the money I should give him, and I chaffed him, asking him if he had his eye on the rifle which he had borrowed when he came with me to the Hadhramaut. Then he asked me if I had met Thomas, the only other Englishman who had been with his tribe. I told him that I had, and later when he had stopped talking and gone to sleep I thought about the journey that Thomas had made. When he crossed this desert it offered the final and greatest prize of Arabian exploration. Doughty and other famous Arabian travellers had dreamt of this achievement, but the realization of the dream was reserved for Thomas and Philby, whose names will always be remembered together in connexion with the crossing of the Empty Quarter, as the names of Amundsen and Scott will be associated with the South Pole. Bertram Thomas proved that this desert was not impassable as was once supposed. His object was to cross the Empty Quarter, and naturally he crossed it by the easiest way, where the dunes were small and the wells, known to his Rashid guides, were frequent. Today this route would offer no real difficulty because the traveller would know what lay ahead of him. But

I knew that to minimize Thomas's achievement by saying that his route proved easy would be as unjustifiable as to depreciate the first ascent of a great mountain because it was climbed by the easiest face. Philby's route had obviously been far more difficult, and the four hundred miles between wells which he covered across the western Sands at the end of his journey must always remain an epic of desert travel. Before he started from Riyadh he had heard that Thomas had already crossed from Dhaufar to Qatar. Although he was bitterly disappointed, he continued, undeterred, with his plans and carried out a journey which the discerning will regard as the greater of the two. Yet Philby had certain advantages which were denied to Thomas. Once he had obtained Ibn Saud's permission to undertake the journey – and it was the king's delay in granting this permission that lost him the race – he had behind him the king's far-reaching authority. As a Muslim with the backing of the widely feared Ibn Jalawi, Governor of the Hasa, he could pass safely through the territory of the powerful Murra, whereas Thomas ran his greatest risk from this tribe, many of whom were extremely fanatical. Thomas had to make all his preparations himself. The Sultan of Muscat and his Wali in Salala were friendly, but their effective authority did not extend as far as the Qarra mountains. He discovered from experience which tribes could be of use to him, but as a Christian he was at first suspected and disliked. The measure of his achievement was that he won the confidence of these tribesmen and, with no authority behind him, persuaded them by patience and fair dealing to take him across the Sands.

The sun was getting low. Bin Kabina was still asleep. I touched him to wake him, and in one movement he was on his feet with his dagger drawn. I had forgotten that to touch a sleeping Bedu is usually to jerk him awake ready instinctively to fight for his life. I raced him down the dune face, floundering through the avalanching sand, and then we walked across to the well where the others had filled the water-skins ready for our departure in the morning. There were fourteen of these skins, but several of them were small. Said and the others had come back. They had found nobody at Bir Halu and told us that the Bait Musan and a family of Bait Imani had

been there and had left five days ago travelling north-east towards
Ramlat al Ghafa. They gave us the names of the individual Arabs
who had been there, and told us which camels they had with them.
All this they had read from the tracks which they found. Said looked
wretched and when I asked him what was wrong he confessed that
he had a severe pain in his stomach. I offered him some soda-mint
tablets but he scorned them; later I saw him drinking camel's urine
which Sultan recommended.

Musallim made porridge for our evening meal, the only meal
of the day. From now on we should be eating gritty lumps of
unleavened bread, smeared with a little butter. We assembled to
feed, and bin Kabina poured water over our outstretched hands.
This was the last time we should wash, even our hands, until we
reached the wells in Dhafara. Mabkhaut moved a rug for us to sit
on, and uncovered one of the large pale-green scorpions that are
plentiful in the Sands wherever there is any vegetation. I always
hoped I would not tread on one with my bare feet. In Abyssinia I
had once put on my trousers with a scorpion inside them, and knew
how painful their sting could be. I was also afraid of treading on a
snake when I fetched the camels after dark; there were plenty of
them about. Most of them were horned vipers, but there was also
a small burrowing snake, a diminutive boa, which was harmless. A
year before, one of these snakes had burrowed its way out of the
sand underneath one of the Rashid as he sat with us beside the fire.
He was known thereafter as 'the father of the snake' and was not
allowed to forget his momentary panic. But it was the spiders I
really loathed, and they were common in all but the most arid
places. They were as much as three inches across, with hairy, reddish legs, and pendulous bodies, and they scuttled about in the
firelight. I saw one now and tried to kill it but it escaped. A little
later bin Kabina tickled the back of my neck, and thinking it was
this spider I jumped convulsively and upset my tea. Laughingly the
others assured me that these spiders were harmless, which I already
knew, but this knowledge did not lessen the revulsion which I felt
for them.

A cold wind blew in gusts across the desert, charged with a fine spray of sand; the stars were very bright. We piled more wood upon the fire – long snake-like roots of tribulus and heliotrope which we had dragged out of the sand. I was still hungry. I knew that I should be hungry for weeks, perhaps months, but tonight there was plenty of water, so I told bin Kabina to make more coffee and tea. The others were busy in the firelight – sewing a buckle on a cartridge belt, patching a rent in a shirt, seeing to a saddle, cleaning a rifle, or plaiting a rope. Sultan was digging with the point of a dagger in the horny sole of his foot, looking for a thorn, and al Auf was shaping me a new camel-stick. These sticks are brittle and I had broken mine the day before. While he heated the *abal* root which he had selected, before bending its end to make a crook, he spoke of the fighting on the Trucial Coast. I gathered that the Al bu Falah could call on the tribes in time of need. Al Auf explained: 'The bin Maktum of Dibai would have to pay for our service; we owe them no loyalty. The Al bu Falah are different; if one of that family, even a child, gave me an order it would be awkward to refuse.' He added with a grin, 'Being a Bedu I expect I should, unless it suited me.' I gathered that the Al bu Falah had recently been successful in several raids. It was extraordinary how widely news travels in the desert. Al Auf had heard this news from two of his kinsmen when they had returned to the southern steppes with a rifle and three camels which they had captured. These men had travelled seven hundred miles across the Sands before they met him. He had then come four hundred miles to Mughshin, and now the Bait Kathir would carry the news down to Bai on the southern coast, a further two hundred miles, and from there others would take it up into Oman. Later my companions spoke of camels and grazing, and of how to cure mange, of the price of flour in Salala, of when the dhows might be expected to arrive there with dates, and of an old man who had died recently in Ghaidat on the Mahra coast. They agreed that he had been skilful in curing sickness with his spells, and cited cases. Musallim spoke of the festivities he had watched at a slave's wedding in Salala, and bin Turkia described the feasting and dancing at a recent circumcision ceremony among the Mahra. Said said, 'By God, Ali's son made a fuss when they cut him. He cried out like a woman.' The others laughed, and some of them exclaimed, 'God blacken his face!' I realized that this wretched boy's failure would soon be known far and wide among the Bedu. Musallim next told a long story about an oryx hunt, which I had heard at least three times before. They discussed the Dahm raids and bin al Kamam's mission to seek a truce. Then bin Kabina described the meals which he had eaten when he was with me in the Hadhramaut, probably the first time in his life that he had had enough to eat. During the months ahead we were to talk often of food, of meals which we had eaten and of others which we planned. At Mughshin my companions had spoken of women, for then they were full fed and eating meat. The Bedu are a vigorous race with strong passions, and their talk of sex is vivid and frank, but never obscene. Similarly their swearing is direct and purposeful – 'God's curse on you.' 'May God destroy your house.' 'Cursed of your two parents.' 'May raiders get you' – not the meaningless obscenities which pass for cursing among the gutter-bred Arabs of the towns. But we seldom spoke of sex, for starving men dream of food, not of women, and our bodies were generally too tired to lust.

Homosexuality is common among most Arabs, especially in the towns, but it is very rare among the Bedu, who of all Arabs have the most excuse for indulging in this practice, since they spend long months away from their women. Lawrence described in *Seven Pillars of Wisdom* how his escort made use of each other to slake their needs, but those men were villagers from the oasis, not Bedu. Glubb, who knows more about the Bedu than any other European has ever known, once told me that active homosexuality among them was almost unknown. I myself could not have lived as I did with my companions and been unaware of it had it existed among them; we lived too close together. Yet during all the time I was with them I saw no sign of it. Nor did they talk about it. They sometimes joked about goats but never about boys. Only twice in five years did I ever hear them mention the subject. Once when we were staying in a town on the Trucial Coast, bin Kabina pointed out two youths, one of whom was a slave, and said that they were sometimes used by the Sheikh's retainers. He evidently thought the practice both ridiculous and obscene. On the other occasion bin al Kamam described an execution which he had watched in Riyadh. The man, one of the Habab from the Hajaz, had been sentenced to death for raping a boy. None of my companions showed the slightest sympathy for him; instead they muttered, 'It was a just sentence. God blacken his face! He deserved to die.'

Bin al Kamam said: 'We had come across to Riyadh from the Wadi Dawasir – Said was with me and Muhammad bin Bakhit'; and when I looked at him in inquiry he said, 'No, you don't know Muhammad. You have never met him. He spends his time in the Dakaka sands.' He went on: 'It was Friday and we had gone into the town to buy provisions, for we planned to leave next day for the Hasa. We had camped a little way outside the town. It was just after the midday prayers and the market square was crowded. They brought the man out from prison, and as they led him through the crowd he chanted, over and over again, "There is no god but God, and Muhammad is the Prophet of God." He was quite unafraid. He was a young man, very good looking, and dressed in freshly-washed white clothes. He had darkened his eyelids with kohl and stained his palms with henna, as we do for a wedding. In the centre of the square they told him to kneel, and the executioner, a large slave, very black, dressed in a robe – which, by God, was worth a camel – drew his sword, and fastened back his long white shirt sleeve to bare his right arm. Then his assistant pricked the condemned man in the side, and as he stiffened, the executioner cut off his head with one blow. The head jumped among the crowd and the blood spouted an arm's length into the air as the body collapsed. They left it lying there till sunset for the crowd to look at.'

I asked bin al Kamam what his feelings were as he watched, and he said, 'It made me feel quite sick.'

In the morning we gave the camels another drink. Several of them, accustomed to clean-tasting water in Dhaufar, refused to touch this bitter stuff. We held their nostrils but they still refused, and finally we poured it down their throats by force. It was the last water we should find till we reached Dhafara. Some of the skins had leaked a little. We filled them up and plugged the tiny dribbling holes. The Arabs said their midday prayers, and then we loaded our camels and led them away between the golden dunes. We went on foot, for the full skins were heavy on their backs. It was 29 November. We travelled north-east towards Ramlat al Ghafa, where we hoped to find the Bait Musan and to change the weakest of our camels. The going was easy, along gravel flats splashed with outcrops of white gypsum and fringed with bright-green salt-bushes. We camped at sunset, but there was nothing for our camels to eat. One of them cast a nine-month-old calf. They carry their young for a year. I noticed that Salim bin Turkia took water for the ritual ablutions before he prayed. I protested, saying he should use sand, as is the custom when water is short, and added that we should not have enough to drink if it was used for washing. He said, 'It is better to pray than to drink.' I answered that he would not be doing either in a week's time if he wasted water. This incident worried me. It showed that some of the Bait Kathir had not begun to realize how narrow was our margin of safety. In the evening I warned them that Dhafara was twice as far from Khaur bin Atarit as was Salala. Sultan remarked gloomily, 'In that case neither we nor our camels will ever live to see it.'

The next afternoon we found a little parched herbage on the flank of a high dune. We let our camels graze for two hours and then continued until dark. Throughout the day my companions had gathered any plants they had seen, to feed their camels as they went along; it did not matter how high up on a dune a plant was growing, someone was sure to dismount, scramble up, and collect it. They always did this, however long or tiring the march might be. Where we camped, the dunes were very big whale-backed massifs, rising above white plains of powdery gypsum. There was no warmth in this sterile scene. It was bleak and cheerless and curiously arctic in appearance. Twice I woke during the night and each time I saw Sultan brooding over the fire. We did another long day's marching, ten hours without a stop; there was nothing to stop for among these life-less dunes. We had picked up the Bait Musan tracks and were follow-ing them. In the evening we found a little vegetation.

We started again soon after sunrise. As Sultan seemed gloomy and little inclined for conversation I rode beside al Auf. He sat his restive, half-tamed camel with easy mastery, unconsciously anticipating her fretful movements, a confident, commanding figure, typical of a people whom no hardship can daunt.

I asked him whether it rained more often in summer or in the winter, and he said: 'It seems to have changed since I was a boy. Then I remember we got more rain in the summer; now we expect it in the winter, but as you can see there is not much at any time. The trouble is that when it does fall it is usually very local, and the grazing is difficult to find.'

I asked how much rain was required to produce grazing, and he answered, 'It is no use if it does not go into the sand this far,' and he indicated his elbow.

'How long does it have to rain to do that?'

'A heavy shower is enough. That would produce grazing that was better than nothing, but it would die within the year unless there were more rain. If we get really good rain, a whole day and night of rain, the grazing will remain green for three and even four years.'

'Do you mean without any more rain?'

'Yes, without another drop. Not all the sands are the same; some are better than others. We divide all the sands into "red" and "white". We should call these sands "white". The "red" ones produce the best grazing. The "red" downs in Dakaka are the best of all. You ought to go and see them sometime, Umbarak, they are wonderful sands.'

After a pause he went on: 'We like winter rain best; it generally lasts longer. Summer storms, it is true, are often heavier, but the great heat at that time of year kills the seedlings, unless the rain has been heavy. However, praise be to God, rain is rain whenever it comes.' He pointed to some dead tribulus: 'Do you see that *zahra*? You would think it was quite dead, wouldn't you? but it's only got to rain and a month later it will be green and covered with flowers. It takes years of drought to kill these plants; you have seen how long their roots are. In a place where the plants really are dead, like the Umm al Hait, which we saw the other day, the vegetation comes up again from seeds when at last it does rain. It does not matter how long they have lain in the sand.'

I said: 'Take, for instance, these Bait Musan whose tracks we are following, how long will they be able to stay here without water?'

Al Auf answered: 'It depends on how good the grazing is. On good grazing they could remain here from the late autumn until the spring. Of course, when the weather gets hot they will have to move back to within reach of the wells.'

'So they may be here for six or seven months without any water? What do they eat?'

'Camel's milk is their food and drink. As long as there is plenty of milk the Bedu want nothing more.'

'Don't the camels ever get thirsty?'

He answered: 'If you loosed a camel that was dying of thirst on fresh green grazing, not only would she recover from her thirst, but she would be fat within two months. Sometimes a camel gets so fat that her hump splits, and then she dies.'

'How do you know where you will find grazing?'

'In the autumn while they are still on the wells the Arabs send out scouts to look for it. These scouts must be good men, accustomed to endure, and their camels must be the best. During the summer we may have seen clouds or lightning in the distance, or while we are searching the desert we may find tracks of oryx or *rim* all going in one direction and follow them. We may go back to look at the grazing we had been on the year before or other grazing we had found during the winter. If there's grazing in the desert we probably find it. We are Bedu; we know the desert.'

'How do you manage for grazing in the summer?'

'Yes, that is the difficulty. Often there is none round the wells and we have to take the camels long distances to water them.'

'How long will a camel last without water in summer?'

'Again it depends on the grazing. They will last longer in the wadis where they can get some shade from the trees. Under those conditions they would go for a week without a drink. In the Sands we try to water them every two or three days. Life is hard for the Bedu in the summer, Umbarak. Sometimes we are camped on wells which are so bitter that we can only drink the water mixed with milk. We water the camels and cannot drink the water ourselves. We splash it over us to cool us while we work, and our bodies get covered with sores. Watering the camels is hard work. They are thirsty and drink a lot, and the sun is hot. It is worse when the wind blows; then it is like a fire. Even when we stop to rest there is no shade on these wells in the sand. Only the Bedu could endure this life.'

Four hours later we came to large red dunes set close together. There were green plants growing there as the result of heavy rain which had fallen two years before. A little later we saw camels of the Bait Musan and a herdsboy who was tending them. We camped in a hollow and loosed our camels to revel among the juicy shrubs.

Larks were singing round our camping place. Butterflies flitted from plant to plant. Lizards scuttled about, and small black beetles walked laboriously across the sand. We had seen a hare that morning, and the tracks of gazelle. The sand around us was still marked where jerboas and other small rodents had scampered about during the night. I wondered how they got here, how they had located this small green island, in the enormous emptiness which surrounded it.

Sultan, Musallim, and several others had gone off with the herdsboy to the Bait Musan encampment. Al Auf was herding the camels. Several people were sleeping, their faces covered with their head-cloths. I climbed a slope above our camp and bin Kabina joined me. I was hungry; I had eaten only half my portion of ash-encrusted bread the night before. The brackish water which I had drunk at sunset had done little to lessen my nagging thirst. Yet the sky seemed bluer than it had been for days. The sand was a glowing carpet set about my feet. A raven croaked, circling round us, and bin Kabina shouted, 'Raven seek thy brother.' Then another raven flew over the shoulder of a nearby dune and he laughed, and explained to me that a single raven is unlucky, a bearer of ill-tidings. We sat there happily together, and he taught me the names of the plants which grow in the Sands. The tribulus was *zahra*; the helio-trope which grew on the hard sand in the hollows was *rimram*; and the tasselled sedge was *qassis*. The straggling bush under which we sat, its fragile branches bright with fluffy yellow balls, was *abal*, and was good food for a thirsty camel. He gave me the names of other plants and bushes: *harm*, the vivid green salt-bush; *birkan, ailqi, sadan*, and several others. He knew them all. Later when they were working out my collection in the museum in London they some-times thought that bin Kabina had given me different names for the same plant, but nearly always when they examined them care-fully they found that he was right.

He talked about his mother and his young brother Said, whom I had not met, and about his cousin whom he hoped to marry. The distant camels drifted in greedy haste from bush to bush. Then we saw Sultan and the others returning. As they drew near, bin Kabina said, 'Sultan will make trouble. He is frightened and does not wish to go on', and I knew that bin Kabina was right. They brought a bag of sour milk with them. We drank it thirstily and it was very good. Then Sultan called the others and they went off and sat in a circle apart from me. I told bin Kabina to fetch al Auf. Later Sultan asked me to join them. He said that they had discussed the situation and agreed that the Bait Musan camels were all in poor condition, that neither they nor our camels were capable of getting to Dhafara, that we must therefore return to the others on the southern coast, where if I wished we could hunt oryx in the Jaddat al Harasis. He added that our food was insufficient and that we had not enough water to go on, even if the camels had been in good condition. I then suggested that six of us should go on with the best of the camels, and that the other six should go back. But Sultan said that six would be too small a party, since the country on the other side of the Sands would be full of raiders as a result of the fighting between the rulers of Abu Dhabi and Dibai; to discourage me he said that the Bait Musan had told him that a party of Arabs, well mounted and with plenty of water, had tried to cross to Dhafara two years before, when the grazing was good, and that all of them had died in the Sands. He declared that we must either all go on or all go back. We argued for a long time but I knew that it was useless. His nerve had gone. He had always been the undisputed leader, with a reputation for daring. It was a reputation not easily acquired among the Bedu; but he had lived all his life in the mountains and on the steppes. In the Sands he was confused and bewildered, no longer self-reliant. He looked an old and broken man and I was sorry. He had helped me so often and I liked him. I asked al Auf if he would come with me, and he said: 'I thought we came here to go to Dhafara. If you wish to go on I will guide you.' I asked bin Kabina, and he answered that where I went he would go. I wondered if Musallim would come with us. The camel which I rode belonged to him; without it I did not see how I could go on. I knew that he was jealous of Sultan. I asked him, and he answered, 'I will come.' The others said nothing.

Once again we divided up the food. We took as our share fifty pounds of flour, some of the butter and coffee, what remained of the tea and sugar, and a few dried onions. We also took four skins of water, choosing the best skins that did not leak. Musallim told me that the Bait Musan possessed a bull camel in good condition, and suggested that we should buy it and take it with us as a spare. He also said that Mabkhaut bin Arbain was his friend and would come with us if he asked him to. I thought that Mabkhaut's camel looked thin, but al Auf replied that they knew about camels and that this one would stand much hard work. He was anxious for Mabkhaut to accompany us, for he said that it would be better if we had one more person with us and that Mabkhaut was the most reliable of the Bait Kathir. Musallim went off to see about this. Later Mabkhaut came over, carrying his saddlery, and joined us. In the evening bin Turkia asked if he too might come with us. He was a relation of Mabkhaut's and wished to share with him the dangers that were ahead of us. Unfortunately his camel was one of the worst, so reluctantly we refused. I promised him instead that I would take him and his young son bin Anauf with me to Mukalla, when I travelled there from Salala on my return from my present journey. We bought the bull, a large and very powerful black animal, after much haggling and for a fantastic price, paying the equivalent of fifty pounds, more than twice what it was worth. I felt more confident than I had felt for days. I had with me chosen companions all mounted on good camels. We had a spare camel with us which was used to the Sands. If our food ran out we could kill one of our animals and eat it. Water was short. We should have to be careful with this, and ration ourselves to a pint a day. Bin Kabina, Musallim, and Mabkhaut each carried one of the service rifles which belonged to me. Al Auf had a long-barrelled $\cdot$303 Martini, a weapon favoured by the Bedu. I carried a sporting model $\cdot$303. We divided the spare ammunition between us. There was more than a hundred rounds for each of us. Next day after we had left the others, I told my companions that they could have these weapons as presents, and promised al Auf that he could take the pick of my remaining rifles as soon as we returned to Salala. Nothing that I could have given them could have delighted them more. Service rifles in good condition were unprocurable among these tribes. Even ammunition was scarce. All tribesmen like to wear a dagger or carry a rifle, even in peaceful surroundings, as a mark of their manhood, as a sign of their independence, but in southern Arabia the safety of their herds, even their lives, may at any moment depend upon their rifles. Bin Kabina had already confided to me that he hoped to buy a rifle with the money I gave him. He no doubt had visualized himself as the proud owner of some ancient weapon, such as he had borrowed when he accompanied me to the Hadhramaut, a fighting-man at last, envied by his young brother. Now he owned the finest rifle in his tribe. I watched the disbelief slowly fading from his eyes.

The Bait Musan came to us at dusk, carrying bowls of camel's milk. The milk was soothing and cool after the bitter water, which rasped our throats. I sat with the Bait Kathir but there was constraint among us so I went and joined al Auf and bin Kabina who were mending a saddle. If they had not come to Shisur I should be turning back as Thomas had once turned back from Mughshin.

SEVEN

The First Crossing of the Empty Quarter

~~~

The departure of five Bait Kathir leaves me with a
party of only four. We are short of food and water.
We cross the Uruq al Shaiba and arrive at Khaba
well near Liwa Oasis.

The Bait Kathir helped us to load our camels. We said good-
bye, picked up our rifles, and set off, passing the bush where
bin Kabina and I had sat the day before. The plants he had
collected to show me still lay there, withered on the ground. It
seemed a long time ago.

The Rashid took the lead, their faded brown clothes harmoniz-
ing with the sands: al Auf, a lean, neat figure, very upright; bin
Kabina, more loosely built, striding beside him. The two Bait Kathir
followed close behind, with the spare camel tied to Musallim's
saddle. Their clothes, which had once been white, had become
neutral-coloured from long usage. Mabkhaut was the same build
as al Auf, whom he resembled in many ways, though he was a less
forceful character. In the distance he was distinguishable from him
only by the colour of his shirt. Musallim, compactly built, slightly
bow-legged, and physically tough, was of a different, coarser breed.
The least likeable of my companions, his personality had suffered
from too frequent sojourns in Salala and he tended to be
ingratiating.

After a short distance al Auf suggested that, as he did not know what we should find to the north, it would be wise to halt near by, with the Bait Imani, to allow our camels a further day's grazing. The Arabs, he added, would give us milk so that we need not touch our food and water. I answered that he was our guide and that from now on such decisions must rest with him.

Two hours later we saw a small boy, dressed in the remnants of a loin-cloth and with long hair falling down his back, herding camels. He led us to the Bait Imani camp, where three men sat round the embers of a fire. They rose as we approached. 'Salam alaikum', 'Alaikum as salam', and then, after we had exchanged the news, they handed us a bowl of milk, its surface crusted with brown sand. These Bait Imani belonged to the same section of the Rashid as al Auf and bin Kabina and were from three different families. Only one of them, a grizzled elderly man called Khuatim, wore a shirt over his loin-cloth, and all were bareheaded. They had no tent; their only possessions were saddles, ropes, bowls, empty goat-skins, and their rifles and daggers. The camping ground was churned and furrowed where the camels slept, and littered with camel droppings, hard and clean on the sand like dried dates. These men were cheerful and full of talk. The grazing was good; their camels, several in milk, would soon be fat. Life by their standards would be easy this year, but I thought of other years when the exhausted scouts rode back to the wells to speak through blackened, bleeding lips of desolation in the Sands, of emptiness such as I myself had seen on the way here from Ghanim; when the last withered plants were gone and walking skeletons of men and beasts sank down to die. Even tonight, when they considered themselves well off, these men would sleep naked on the freezing sand, covered only with their flimsy loin-cloths. I thought, too, of the bitter wells in the furnace heat of summer, when, hour by reeling hour, they watered thirsty, thrusting camels, until at last the wells ran dry and importunate camels moaned for water which was not there. I thought how desperately hard were the lives of the Bedu in this weary land, and how gallant and how enduring was their spirit. Now, listening to their talk and watching the little acts of courtesy which they instinctively performed, I knew by comparison how sadly I must fail, how selfish I must prove.

The Bait Imani talked of Mahsin and of the accident which had befallen him, asking endless questions. Then Khuatim shouted to the small herdsboy, his son, to fetch the yellow four-year-old and the old grey which was still in milk. When the boy had brought them, Khuatim told him to couch them and loosed the hobbles from our bull's forelegs. Already the bull was excited, threshing itself with its tail, grinding its teeth, or blowing a large pink air sac from its mouth and sucking it back with a slobbering sound. Clumsily it straddled the yellow camel, a comic figure of ill-directed lust, while Khuatim, kneeling beside it, tried to assist. Bin Kabina observed to me, 'Camels would never manage to mate without human help. They would never get it in the right place.' I was thankful that there were no more than these two camels to be served; there might have been a dozen to exhaust our bull.

The boy brought in the rest of the herd, thirty-five of them, at sunset. Khuatim washed his hands beneath a staling camel and scrubbed out the bowls with sand, for Bedu believe that a camel will go dry if milked with dirty hands or into a bowl which was soiled with food, especially meat or butter. He stroked a camel's udder, talking to her and encouraging her to let down her milk, and then standing on one leg, with his right foot resting on his left knee, he milked her into a bowl which he balanced on his right thigh. She gave about two quarts; several of the others, however, gave less than a quart. There were nine of these camels in milk. Al Auf milked Qamaiqam, bin Kabina's camel. She had given us a quart twice a day at Mughshin, but now from hard work and lack of food she only gave about a pint.

After milking, the Bait Imani couched their camels for the night, tying their knees to prevent them from rising. Al Auf told us to leave ours out to graze, adding that he would keep an eye on them. Our hosts brought us milk. We blew the froth aside and drank deep; they urged us to drink more, saying, 'You will find no milk in the sands ahead of you. Drink – drink. You are our guests. God brought you here – drink.' I drank again, knowing even as I did so that they would go hungry and thirsty that night, for they had nothing else, no other food and no water. Then while we crouched over the fire bin Kabina made coffee. The chill wind whispered among the shadowy dunes, and fingered us through our clothes and through the blankets which we wrapped about us. They talked till long after the moon had set, of camels and grazing, of journeys across the Sands, of raids and blood feuds and of the strange places and people they had seen when they had visited the Hadhramaut and Oman.

In the morning bin Kabina went with one of the Bait Imani to collect our camels, and when he came back I noticed he was no longer wearing a loin-cloth under his shirt. I asked him where it was and he said that he had given it away. I protested that he could not travel without one through the inhabited country beyond the Sands and in Oman, and that I had no other to give him. I said he must recover it and gave him some money for the man instead. He argued that he could not do this. 'What use will money be to him in the Sands. He wants a loin-cloth,' he grumbled, but at length he went off to do as I had told him.

Meanwhile the other Bait Imani had brought us bowls of milk which al Auf poured into a small goatskin. He said we could mix a little every day with our drinking water and that this would improve its taste, a custom which enables Arabs who live in the Sands to drink from wells which would otherwise be undrinkable. They call this mixture of sour milk and water *shanin*. When we had finished this milk a week later we found in the bottom of the skin a lump of butter, the size of a walnut and colourless as lard. Al Auf also poured a little milk into another skin which was sweating, explaining that this would make it waterproof.

Then, wishing our hosts the safe keeping of God, we turned away across the Sands. As he walked along, al Auf held out his hands, palms upwards, and recited verses from the Koran. The sand was still very cold beneath our feet. Usually, when they are in the Sands during the winter or summer, Arabs wear socks knitted from coarse black hair. None of us owned these socks and our heels were already cracking from the cold. Later these cracks became deeper and very painful. We walked for a couple of hours, and then rode till nearly sunset; encouraging our camels to snatch mouthfuls from any plants they passed. They would hasten towards each one with their lower lips flapping wildly.

At first the dunes were brick-red in colour, separate mountains of sand, rising above ash-white gypsum flats ringed with vivid green salt-bushes; those we passed in the afternoon were even higher – 500 to 550 feet in height and honey-coloured. There was little vegetation here.

Musallim rode the black bull and led his own camel, which carried the two largest water-skins. Going down a steep slope the female hesitated. The head-rope attached to the back of Musallim's saddle tightened and slowly pulled her over on to her side. I was some way behind and could see what was going to happen but there was no time to do anything. I shouted frantically at Musallim but he could not halt his mount on the slope. I prayed that the rope would break, and as I watched the camel collapse on top of the water-skins I thought, 'Now we will never get across the Sands'. Al Auf was already on the ground slashing at the taut rope with his dagger. As I jumped from my saddle I wondered if we should have even enough water left to get back to Ghanim. The fallen camel kicked out, and as the rope parted heaved herself to her knees. The water-skins which had fallen from her back still seemed to be full. Hardly daring to hope I bent over them, as al Auf said 'Praise be to God. They are all right,' and the others reiterated 'The praise be to God, the praise be to God!' We reloaded them on to the bull, which, bred in the sands, was accustomed to these slithering descents.

Later we came on some grazing and stopped for the night. We chose a hollow sheltered from the wind, unloaded the water-skins and saddle-bags, hobbled the camels, loosened the saddles on their backs and drove them off to graze.

At sunset al Auf doled out a pint of water mixed with milk to each person, our first drink of the day. As always, I had watched the sun getting lower, thinking 'Only one more hour till I can drink', while I tried to find a little saliva to moisten a mouth that felt like leather. Now I took my share of water without the milk and made it into tea, adding crushed cinnamon, cardamom, ginger, and cloves to the brew to disguise the taste.

Firewood could always be found, for there was no place in the Sands where rain had not fallen in the past, even if it was twenty or thirty years before. We could always uncover the long trailing roots of some dead shrub. These Arabs will not burn tribulus if they can find any other fuel, for *zahra*, 'the flower' as they call it, is venerated as the best of all food for their camels and has almost the sanctity of the date palm. I remember how I once threw a date-stone into the fire and old Tamtaim leant forward and picked it out.

Bin Kabina brewed coffee. He had stripped off his shirt and head-cloth, and I said, 'You couldn't take your shirt off if I had not rescued your loin-cloth for you.' He grinned, and said, 'What could I do? He asked for it,' and went over to help Musallim scoop flour out of a goatskin: four level mugfuls measured in a pint mug. This, about three pounds of flour, was our ration for the day and I reflected that there must be very few calories or vitamins in our diet. Yet no scratch festered or turned septic during the years I lived in the desert. Nor did I ever take precautions before drinking what water we found. Indeed, I have drunk unboiled water from wells, ditches, and drains all over the Middle East for twenty-five years without ill-effect. Given a chance, the human body – mine at any rate – seems to create its own resistance to infection.

When Musallim had made bread, he called to al Auf and Mab-khaut, who were herding the camels. It was getting dark. Though a faint memory of the vanished day still lingered in the west, the stars were showing, and the moon cast shadows on the colourless sand. We sat in a circle round a small dish, muttered 'In the name of God', and in turn dipped fragments of bread into the melted butter. When we had fed, bin Kabina took the small brass coffee-pot from the fire and served us with coffee, a few drops each. Then we crouched round the fire and talked.

I was happy in the company of these men who had chosen to come with me. I felt affection for them personally, and sympathy

with their way of life. But though the easy equality of our relationship satisfied me, I did not delude myself that I could be one of
them. They were Bedu and I was not; they were Muslims and I
was a Christian. Nevertheless, I was their companion and an inviol-
able bond united us, as sacred as the bond between host and guest,
transcending tribal and family loyalties. Because I was their companion on the road, they would fight in my defence even against
their brothers and they would expect me to do the same.

But I knew that for me the hardest test would be to live with
them in harmony and not to let my impatience master me; neither
to withdraw into myself, nor to become critical of standards and
ways of life different from my own. I knew from experience that
the conditions under which we lived would slowly wear me down,
mentally if not physically, and that I should be often provoked and
irritated by my companions. I also knew with equal certainty that
when this happened the fault would be mine, not theirs.

During the night a fox barked somewhere on the slopes above
us. At dawn al Auf untied the camels, which he had brought in for
the night, and turned them loose to graze. There would be no food
till sunset, but bin Kabina heated what was left of the coffee. After
we had travelled for an hour we came upon a patch of grazing
freshened by a recent shower. Faced with the choice of pushing on
or of feeding the camels al Auf decided to stop, and as we unloaded
them he told us to collect bundles of tribulus to carry with us. I
watched him scoop a hole in the sand to find out how deeply the
rain had penetrated, in this case about three feet; he invariably did
this wherever rain had fallen – if no plants had yet come up on
which to graze the camels while we waited, we went on, leaving
him behind to carry out his investigations. It was difficult to see
what practical use this information about future grazing in the heart
of the Empty Quarter could possibly be to him or to anyone else,
and yet I realized that it was this sort of knowledge which made
him such an exceptional guide. Later I lay on the sand and watched
an eagle circling overhead. It was hot. I took the temperature in
the shade of my body and found it was 84 degrees. It was difficult
to believe that it had been down to 43 degrees at dawn. Already

the sun had warmed the sand so that it burnt the soft skin round the sides of my feet.

At midday we went on, passing high, pale-coloured dunes, and others that were golden, and in the evening we wasted an hour skirting a great mountain of red sand, probably 650 feet in height. Beyond it we travelled along a salt-flat, which formed a corridor through the Sands. Looking back I fancied the great, red dune was a door which was slowly, silently closing behind us. I watched the narrowing gap between it and the dune on the other side of the corridor, and imagined that once it was shut we could never go back, whatever happened. The gap vanished and now I could see only a wall of sand. I turned back to the others and they were discussing the price of a coloured loin-cloth which Mabkhaut had bought in Salala before we started. Suddenly al Auf pointed to a camel's track and said, 'Those were made by my camel when I came this way on my way to Ghanim.'

Later Musallim and al Auf argued how far it was from Mughshin to Bai, where Tamtaim and the others were to wait for us. I asked al Auf if he had ever ridden from the Wadi al Amairi to Bai. He answered, 'Yes, six years ago.'

'How many days did it take?'

'I will tell you. We watered at al Ghaba in the Amairi. There were four of us, myself, Salim, Janazil of the Awamir, and Alaiwi of the Afar; it was in the middle of summer. We had been to Ibri to settle the feud between the Rashid and the Mahamid, started by the killing of Fahad's son.'

Musallim interrupted, 'That must have been before the Riqaishi was Governor of Ibri. I had been there myself the year before. Sahail was with me and we went there from . . .'

But al Auf went on, 'I was riding the three-year-old I had bought from bin Duailan.'

'The one the Manahil raided from the Yam?' Bin Kabina asked.

'Yes. I exchanged it later for the yellow six-year-old I got from bin Ham. Janazil rode a Batina camel. Do you remember her? She was the daughter of the famous grey which belonged to Harahaish of the Wahiba.'

Mabkhaut said, 'Yes, I saw her last year when he was in Salala, a tall animal; she was old when I saw her, past her prime but even then a real beauty.'

Al Auf went on, 'We spent the night with Rai of the Afar.'

Bin Kabina chimed in, 'I met him last year when he came to Habarut; he carried a rifle, "a father of ten shots", which he had taken from the Mahra he had killed in the Ghudun. Bin Mautlauq offered him the grey yearling, the daughter of Farha, and fifty *riyals* for this rifle, but he refused.'

Al Auf continued, 'Rai killed a goat for our dinner and told us . . .', but I interrupted: 'Yes, but how many days did it take you to get to Bai?' He looked at me in surprise and said, 'Am I not telling you?'

We stopped at sunset for the evening meal, and fed to our camels the tribulus we had brought with us. All the skins were sweating and we were worried about our water. There had been a regular and ominous drip from them throughout the day, a drop falling on to the sand every few yards as we rode along, like blood dripping from a wound that could not be staunched. There was nothing to do but to press on, and yet to push the camels too hard would be to founder them. They were already showing signs of thirst. Al Auf had decided to go on again after we had fed, and while Musallim and bin Kabina baked bread I asked him about his former journeys through these Sands. 'I have crossed them twice,' he said. 'The last time I came this way was two years ago. I was coming from Abu Dhabi.' I asked, 'Who was with you?' and he answered, 'I was alone.' Thinking that I must have misunderstood him, I repeated, 'Who were your companions?' 'God was my companion.' To have ridden alone through this appalling desolation was an incredible achievement. We were travelling through it now, but we carried our own world with us: a small world of five people, which yet provided each of us with companionship, with talk and laughter and the knowledge that others were there to share the hardship and the danger. I knew that if I travelled here alone the weight of this vast solitude would crush me utterly.

I also knew that al Auf had used no figure of speech when he said that God was his companion. To these Bedu, God is a reality, and the conviction of his presence gives them the courage to endure. For them to doubt his existence would be as inconceivable as for them to blaspheme. Most of them pray regularly, and many keep the fast of Ramadhan, which lasts for a whole month, during which time a man may not eat or drink from dawn till sunset. When this fast falls in summer – and the Arab months being lunar it is eleven days earlier each year – they make use of the exemption which allows travellers to observe the fast when they have finished their journey, and keep it in the winter. Several of the Arabs whom we had left at Mughshin were fasting to compensate for not having done so earlier in the year. I have heard townsmen and villagers in the Hadhramaut and the Hajaz disparage the Bedu, as being without religion. When I have protested, they have said, 'Even if they pray, their prayers are not acceptable to God, since they do not first perform the proper ablutions.'

These Bedu are not fanatical. Once I was travelling with a large party of Rashid, one of whom said to me, 'Why don't you become a Muslim and then you would really be one of us?' I answered, 'God protect me from the Devil!' They laughed. This invocation is one which Arabs invariably use in rejecting something shameful or indecent. I would not have dared to make it if other Arabs had asked me this question, but the man who had spoken would certainly have used it if I had suggested that he should become a Christian.

After the meal we rode for two hours along a salt-flat. The dunes on either side, colourless in the moonlight, seemed higher by night than by day. The lighted slopes looked very smooth, the shadows in their folds inky black. Soon I was shivering uncontrollably from the cold. The others roared out their songs into a silence, broken otherwise only by the crunch of salt beneath the camels' feet. The words were the words of the south, but the rhythm and intonation were the same as in the songs which I had heard other Bedu singing in the Syrian desert. At first sight the Bedu of southern Arabia had appeared to be very different from those of the north, but I now

realized that his difference was largely superficial and due to the
clothes which they wore. My companions would not have felt out
of place in an encampment of the Rualla, whereas a townsman from
Aden or Muscat would be conspicuous in Damascus.

Eventually we halted and I dismounted numbly. I would have
given much for a hot drink but I knew that I must wait eighteen
hours for that. We lit a small fire and warmed ourselves before we
slept, though I slept little. I was tired; for days I had ridden long
hours on a rough camel, my body racked by its uneven gait. I
suppose I was weak from hunger, for the food which we ate was a
starvation ration, even by Bedu standards. But my thirst troubled
me most; it was not bad enough really to distress me but I was
always conscious of it. Even when I was asleep I dreamt of racing
streams of ice-cold water, but it was difficult to get to sleep. Now
I lay there trying to estimate the distance we had covered and the
distance that still lay ahead. When I had asked al Auf how far it
was to the well, he had answered, 'It is not the distance but the
great dunes of the Uruq al Shaiba that may destroy us.' I worried
about the water which I had watched dripping away on to the sand,
and about the state of our camels. They were there, close beside
me in the dark. I sat up and looked at them. Mabkhaut stirred and
called out, 'What is it, Umbarak?' I mumbled an answer and lay
down again. Then I worried whether we had tied the mouth of the
skin properly when we had last drawn water and wondered what
would happen if one of us was sick or had an accident. It was easy
to banish these thoughts in daylight, less easy in the lonely darkness.
Then I thought of al Auf travelling here alone and felt ashamed.

The others were awake at the first light, anxious to push on
while it was still cold. The camels sniffed at the withered tribulus
but were too thirsty to eat it. In a few minutes we were ready. We
plodded along in silence. My eyes watered with the cold; the jagged
salt-crusts cut and stung my feet. The world was grey and dreary.
Then gradually the peaks ahead of us stood out against a paling sky;
almost imperceptibly they began to glow, borrowing the colours of
the sunrise which touched their crests.

A high unbroken dune-chain stretched across our front. It was not of uniform height, but, like a mountain range, consisted of peaks and connecting passes. Several of the summits appeared to be seven hundred feet above the salt-flat on which we stood. The southern face confronting us was very steep, which meant that this was the lee side to the prevailing winds. I wished we had to climb it from the opposite direction, for it is easy to take a camel down these precipices of sand but always difficult to find a way up them.

Al Auf told us to wait while he went to reconnoitre. I watched him walking away across the glistening salt-flat, his rifle on his shoulder and his head thrown back as he scanned the slopes above. He looked superbly confident, but as I viewed this wall of sand I despaired that we would ever get the camels up it. Mabkhaut evidently thought the same, for he said to Musallim, 'We will have to find a way round. No camel will ever climb that.' Musallim answered, 'It is al Auf's doing. He brought us here. We should have gone much farther to the west, nearer to Dakaka.' He had caught a cold and was snuffling, and his rather high-pitched voice was hoarse and edged with grievance. I knew that he was jealous of al Auf and always ready to disparage him, so unwisely I gibed, 'We should have got a long way if you had been our guide!' He swung round and answered angrily, 'You don't like the Bait Kathir. I know that you only like the Rashid. I defied my tribe to bring you here and you never recognize what I have done for you.'

For the past few days he had taken every opportunity of reminding me that I could not have come on from Ramlat al Ghafa without him. It was done in the hope of currying favour and of increasing his reward, but it only irritated me. Now I was tempted to seek relief in angry words, to welcome the silly, bitter squabble which would result. I kept silent with an effort and moved apart on the excuse of taking a photograph. I knew how easily, under conditions such as these, I could take a violent dislike to one member of the party and use him as my private scapegoat. I thought, 'I must not let myself dislike him. After all, I do owe him a great deal; but I wish to God he would not go on reminding me of it.'

I went over to a bank and sat down to wait for al Auf's return. The ground was still cold, although the sun was now well up, throwing a hard, clear light on the barrier of sand ahead of us. It seemed fantastic that this great rampart which shut out half the sky could be made of wind-blown sand. Now I could see al Auf, about half a mile away, moving along the salt-flat at the bottom of the dune. While I watched him he started to climb a ridge, like a mountaineer struggling upward through soft snow towards a pass over a high mountain. I even saw the tracks which he left behind him. He was the only moving thing in all that empty, silent landscape.

What were we going to do if we could not get the camels over it? I knew that we could not go any farther to the east, for al Auf had told me that the quicksands of Umm al Samim were in that direction. To the west the easier sands of Dakaka, where Thomas had crossed, were more than two hundred miles away. We had no margin, and could not afford to lengthen our journey. Our water was already dangerously short, and even more urgent than our own needs were those of the camels, which would collapse unless they were watered soon. We *must* get them over this monstrous dune, if necessary by unloading them and carrying the loads to the top. But what was on the other side? How many more of these dunes were there ahead of us? If we turned back now we might reach Mughshin, but I knew that once we crossed this dune the camels would be too tired and thirsty to get back even to Ghanim. Then I thought of Sultan and the others who had deserted us, and of their triumph if we gave up and returned defeated. Looking again at the dune ahead I noticed that al Auf was coming back. A shadow fell across the sand beside me. I glanced up and bin Kabina stood there. He smiled, said 'Salam alaikum', and sat down. Urgently I turned to him and asked, 'Will we ever get the camels over that?' He pushed the hair back from his forehead, looked thoughtfully at the slopes above us, and answered, 'It is very steep but al Auf will find a way. He is a Rashid; he is not like these Bait Kathir.' Unconcernedly he then took the bolt out of his rifle and began to clean it with the hem of his shirt, while he asked me if all the English used the same kind of rifle.

When al Auf approached we went over to the others.

Mabkhaut's camel had lain down; the rest of them stood where we had left them, which was a bad sign. Ordinarily they would have roamed off at once to look for food. Al Auf smiled at me as he came up but said nothing, and no one questioned him. Noticing that my camel's load was unbalanced he heaved up the saddle-bag from one side, and then picking up with his toes the camel-stick which he had dropped, he went over to his own camel, caught hold of its head-rope, said 'Come on', and led us forward.

It was now that he really showed his skill. He picked his way unerringly, choosing the inclines up which the camels could climb. Here on the lee side of this range a succession of great faces flowed down in unruffled sheets of sand, from the top to the very bottom of the dune. They were unscalable, for the sand was poised always on the verge of avalanching, but they were flanked by ridges where the sand was firmer and the inclines easier. It was possible to force a circuitous way up these slopes, but not all were practicable for camels, and from below it was difficult to judge their steepness. Very slowly, a foot at a time, we coaxed the unwilling beasts upward. Each time we stopped I looked up at the crests where the rising wind was blowing streamers of sand into the void, and wondered how we should ever reach the top. Suddenly we were there. Before slumping down on the sand I looked anxiously ahead of us. To my relief I saw that we were on the edge of rolling downs, where the going would be easy among shallow valleys and low, rounded hills. 'We have made it. We are on top of Uruq al Shaiba', I thought triumphantly. The fear of this great obstacle had lain like a shadow on my mind ever since al Auf had first warned me of it, the night we spoke together in the sands of Ghanim. Now the shadow had lifted and I was confident of success.

We rested for a while on the sand, not troubling to talk, until al Auf rose to his feet and said 'Come on'. Some small dunes built up by cross-winds ran in curves parallel with the main face across the back of these downs. Their steep faces were to the north and the camels slithered down them without difficulty. These downs were brick-red, splashed with deeper shades of colour; the under-lying sand, exposed where it had been churned up by our feet, showing red of a paler shade. But the most curious feature was a number of deep craters resembling giant hoof-prints. These were unlike normal crescent-dunes, since they did not rise above their surroundings, but formed hollows in the floor of hard undulating sand. The salt-flats far below us looked very white.

We mounted our camels. My companions had muffled their faces in their head-cloths and rode in silence, swaying to the camels' stride. The shadows on the sand were very blue, of the same tone as the sky; two ravens flew northward, croaking as they passed. I struggled to keep awake. The only sound was made by the slap of the camels' feet, like wavelets lapping on a beach.

To rest the camels we stopped for four hours in the late afternoon on a long gentle slope which stretched down to another salt-flat. There was no vegetation on it and no salt-bushes bordered the plain below us. Al Auf announced that we would go on again at sunset. While we were feeding I said to him cheerfully, 'Anyway, the worst should be over now that we are across the Uruq al Shaiba.' He looked at me for a moment and then answered, 'If we go well tonight we should reach them tomorrow.' I said, 'Reach what?' and he replied, 'The Uruq al Shaiba', adding, 'Did you think what we crossed today was the Uruq al Shaiba? That was only a dune. You will see them tomorrow.' For a moment, I thought he was joking, and then I realized that he was serious, that the worst of the journey which I had thought was behind us was still ahead.

It was midnight when at last al Auf said, 'Let's stop here. We will get some sleep and give the camels a rest. The Uruq al Shaiba are not far away now.' In my dreams that night they towered above us higher than the Himalayas.

Al Auf woke us again while it was still dark. As usual bin Kabina made coffee, and the sharp-tasting drops which he poured out stimulated but did not warm. The morning star had risen above the dunes. Formless things regained their shape in the first dim light of dawn. The grunting camels heaved themselves erect. We lingered for a moment more beside the fire; then al Auf said 'Come', and we moved forward. Beneath my feet the gritty sand was cold as frozen snow.

We were faced by a range as high as, perhaps even higher than, the range we had crossed the day before, but here the peaks were steeper and more pronounced, rising in many cases to great pinnacles, down which the flowing ridges swept like draperies. These sands, paler coloured than those we had crossed, were very soft, cascading round our feet as the camels struggled up the slopes. Remembering how little warning of imminent collapse the dying camels had given me twelve years before in the Danakil country, I wondered how much more these camels would stand, for they were trembling violently whenever they halted. When one refused to go on we heaved on her head-rope, pushed her from behind, and lifted the loads on either side as we manhandled the roaring animal upward. Sometimes one of them lay down and refused to rise, and then we had to unload her, and carry the water-skins and the saddle-bags ourselves. Not that the loads were heavy. We had only a few gallons of water left and some handfuls of flour.

We led the trembling, hesitating animals upward along great sweeping ridges where the knife-edged crests crumbled beneath our feet. Although it was killing work, my companions were always gentle and infinitely patient. The sun was scorching hot and I felt empty, sick, and dizzy. As I struggled up the slope, knee-deep in shifting sand, my heart thumped wildly and my thirst grew worse. I found it difficult to swallow; even my ears felt blocked, and yet I knew that it would be many intolerable hours before I could drink. I would stop to rest, dropping down on the scorching sand, and immediately it seemed I would hear the others shouting, 'Umbarak, Umbarak'; their voices sounded strained and hoarse.

It took us three hours to cross this range.

On the summit were no gently undulating downs such as we had met the day before. Instead, three smaller dune-chains rode upon its back, and beyond them the sand fell away to a salt-flat in another great empty trough between the mountains. The range on the far side seemed even higher than the one on which we stood, and behind it were others. I looked round, seeking instinctively for some escape. There was no limit to my vision. Somewhere in the ultimate distance the sands merged into the sky, but in that infinity of space I could see no living thing, not even a withered plant to give me hope. 'There is nowhere to go', I thought. 'We cannot go back and our camels will never get up another of these awful dunes. We really are finished.' The silence flowed over me, drowning the voices of my companions and the fidgeting of their camels.

We went down into the valley, and somehow – and I shall never know how the camels did it – we got up the other side. There, utterly exhausted, we collapsed. Al Auf gave us each a little water, enough to wet our months. He said, 'We need this if we are to go on.' The midday sun had drained the colour from the sands. Scattered banks of cumulus cloud threw shadows across the dunes and salt-flats, and added an illusion that we were high among Alpine peaks, with frozen lakes of blue and green in the valley, far below. Half asleep, I turned over, but the sand burnt through my shirt and woke me from my dreams.

Two hours later al Auf roused us. As he helped me load my camel, he said, 'Cheer up, Umbarak. This time we really are across the Uruq al Shaiba', and when I pointed to the ranges ahead of us, he answered, 'I can find a way through those; we need not cross them.' We went on till sunset, but we were going-with the grain of the country, following the valleys and no longer trying to climb the dunes. We should not have been able to cross another. There was a little fresh *qassis* on the slope where we halted. I hoped that this lucky find would give us an excuse to stop here for the night, but, after we had fed, al Auf went to fetch the camels, saying, 'We must go on again while it is cool if we are ever to reach Dhafara.'

We stopped long after midnight and started again at dawn, still exhausted from the strain and long hours of yesterday, but al Auf encouraged us by saying that the worst was over. The dunes were certainly lower than they had been, more uniform in height and more rounded, with fewer peaks. Four hours after we had started we came to rolling uplands of gold and silver sand, but still there was nothing for the camels to eat.

A hare jumped out from under a bush, and al Auf knocked it over with his stick. The others shouted 'God has given us meat.' For days we had talked of food; every conversation seemed to lead back to it. Since we had left Ghanim I had been always conscious of the dull ache of hunger, yet in the evening my throat was dry even after my drink, so that I found it difficult to swallow the dry bread Musallim set before us. All day we thought and talked about that hare, and by three o'clock in the afternoon could no longer resist stopping to cook it. Mabkhaut suggesed, 'Let's roast it in its skin in the embers of a fire. That will save our water – we haven't got much left.' Bin Kabina led the chorus of protest. 'No, by God! Don't even suggest such a thing'; and turning to me he said, 'We don't want Mabkhaut's charred meat. Soup. We want soup and extra bread. We will feed well today even if we go hungry and thirsty later. By God, I am hungry!' We agreed to make soup. We were across the Uruq al Shaiba and intended to celebrate our achievement with this gift from God. Unless our camels foundered we were safe; even if our water ran out we should live to reach a well.

Musallim made nearly double our usual quantity of bread while bin Kabina cooked the hare. He looked across at me and said, 'The smell of this meat makes me faint.' When it was ready he divided it into five portions. They were very small, for an Arabian hare is no larger than an English rabbit, and this one was not even fully grown. Al Auf named the lots and Mabkhaut drew them. Each of us took the small pile of meat which had fallen to him. Then bin Kabina said, 'God! I have forgotten to divide the liver', and the others said, 'Give it to Umbarak.' I protested, saying that they should divide it, but they swore by God that they would not eat it and that I was to have it. Eventually I took it, knowing that I ought not, but too greedy for this extra scrap of meat to care.

Our water was nearly finished and there was only enough flour for about another week. The starving camels were so thirsty that they had refused to eat some half-dried herbage which we had passed. We must water them in the next day or two or they would collapse. Al Auf said that it would take us three more days to reach Khaba well in Dhafara, but that there was a very brackish well not far away. He thought that the camels might drink its water.

That night after we had ridden for a little over an hour it grew suddenly dark. Thinking that a cloud must be covering the full moon, I looked over my shoulder and saw that there was an eclipse and that half the moon was already obscured. Bin Kabina noticed it at the same moment and broke into a chant which the others took up.

> God endures for ever.
> The life of man is short.
> The Pleiades are overhead.
> The moon's among the stars.

Otherwise they paid no attention to the eclipse (which was total), but looked around for a place to camp.

We started very early the next morning and rode without a stop for seven hours across easy rolling downs. The colour of these sands was vivid, varied, and unexpected: in places the colour of ground coffee, elsewhere brick-red, or purple, or a curious golden-green. There were small white gypsum-flats, fringed with *shanan*, a grey-green salt-bush, lying in hollows in the downs. We rested for two hours on sands the colour of dried blood and then led our camels on again.

Suddenly we were challenged by an Arab lying behind a bush on the crest of a dune. Our rifles were on our camels, for we had not expected to meet anyone here. Musallim was hidden behind mine. I watched him draw his rifle clear. But al Auf said, 'It is the voice of a Rashid', and walked forward. He spoke to the concealed Arab, who rose and came to meet him. They embraced and stood talking until we joined them. We greeted the man, and al Auf said, 'This is Hamad bin Hanna, a sheikh of the Rashid.' He was a heavily-built bearded man of middle age. His eyes were set close together and he had a long nose with a blunt end. He fetched his camel from behind the dune while we unloaded.

We made coffee for him and listened to his news. He told us that he had been looking for a stray camel when he crossed our tracks and had taken us for a raiding party from the south. Ibn Saud's tax-collectors were in Dhafara and the Rabadh, collecting tribute from the tribes; and there were Rashid, Awamir, Murra, and some Manahil to the north of us.

We had to avoid all contact with Arabs other than the Rashid, and if possible even with them, so that news of my presence would not get about among the tribes, for I had no desire to be arrested by Ibn Saud's tax-collectors and taken off to explain my presence here to Ibn Jalawi, the formidable Governor of the Hasa. Karab from the Hadhramaut had raided these sands the year before, so there was also a serious risk of our being mistaken for raiders, since the tracks of our camels would show that we had come from the southern steppes. This risk would be increased if it appeared that we were avoiding the Arabs, for honest travellers never pass an encampment without seeking news and food. It was going to be very difficult to escape detection. First we must water our camels and draw water for ourselves. Then we must lie up as close as possible to Liwa and send a party to the villages to buy us enough food for at least another month. Hamad told me that Liwa belonged to the Al bu Falah of Abu Dhabi. He said that they were still fighting Said bin Maktum of Dibai, and that, as there was a lot of raiding going on, the Arabs would be very much on the alert.

We started again in the late afternoon and travelled till sunset. Hamad came with us and said he would stay with us until we had got food from Liwa. Knowing where the Arabs were encamped he could help us to avoid them. Next day, after seven hours' travelling, we reached Khaur Sabakha on the edge of the Dhafara sands. We cleaned out the well and found brackish water at seven feet, so bitter that even the camels only drank a little before refusing it. They sniffed thirstily at the water with which al Auf tried to coax them from a leather bucket, but only dipped their lips into it. We covered their noses but still they would not drink. Yet al Auf said that Arabs themselves drank this water mixed with milk, and when I expressed my disbelief he added that if an Arab was really thirsty he would even kill a camel and drink the liquid in its stomach, or ram a stick down its throat and drink the vomit. We went on again till nearly sunset.

The next day when we halted in the afternoon al Auf told us we had reached Dhafara and that Khaba well was close. He said that he would fetch water in the morning. We finished what little was left in one of our skins. Next day we remained where we were. Hamad said that he would go for news and return the following day. Al Auf, who went with him, came back in the afternoon with two skins full of water which, although slightly brackish, was delicious after the filthy evil-smelling dregs we had drunk the night before.

It was 12 December, fourteen days since we had left Khaur bin Atarit in Ghanim.

In the evening, now that we needed no longer measure out each cup of water, bin Kabina made extra coffee, while Musallim increased our rations of flour by a mugful. This was wild extravagance, but we felt that the occasion called for celebration. Even so, the loaves he handed us were woefully inadequate to stay our hunger, now that our thirst was gone.

The moon was high above us when I lay down to sleep. The others still talked round the fire, but I closed my mind to the meaning of their words, content to hear only the murmur of their voices, to watch their outlines sharp against the sky, happily conscious that they were there and beyond them the camels to which we owed our lives.

For years the Empty Quarter had represented to me the final, unattainable challenge which the desert offered. Suddenly it had come within my reach. I remembered my excitement when Lean had casually offered me the chance to go there, the immediate determination to cross it, and then the doubts and fears, the frustrations, and the moments of despair. Now I had crossed it. To others my journey would have little importance. It would produce nothing except a rather inaccurate map which no one was ever likely to use. It was a personal experience, and the reward had been a drink of clean, nearly tasteless water. I was content with that.

Looking back on the journey I realized that there had been no high moment of achievement such as a mountaineer must feel when he stands upon his chosen summit. Over the past days new strains and anxieties had built up as others eased, for, after all, this crossing of the Empty Quarter was set in the framework of a longer journey, and already my mind was busy with the new problems which our return journey presented.

EIGHT

Return to Salala

To avoid crossing more sand we return over the
gravel plains of Oman, a long detour made difficult
by the distrust of the tribes and our lack of food.

We were across the Empty Quarter, but we still had to
return to Salala. We could not go back the way we had
come. The only possible route was through Oman.

I tried to work out our position on a map which showed Mughshin and Abu Dhabi but nothing else, except from hearsay. It was
difficult to plot our course with no firm surface larger than my
notebook on which to work. Bin Kabina held the map while the
others sat and watched, and all of them distracted me with questions. They could never follow a map unless it was orientated,
though curiously enough they could understand a photograph even
when they held it upside down. I estimated that we should have
between five hundred and six hundred miles to travel before we
could rejoin Tamtaim and the rest of the Bait Kathir on the
southern coast, and then a further two hundred miles to reach
Salala. I asked al Auf about water and he said, 'Don't worry about
that, there are plenty of wells ahead of us. It is food which is going
to be our trouble.' We went over to the saddle-bags and Musallim
measured out the flour. There were nine mugfuls left – about seven
pounds.

While we were doing this, Hamad came back, bringing with
him another Rashid, called Jadid. 'Another mouth to feed', I

thought as soon as I saw him. Bin Kabina made coffee for them, and we then discussed our plans. Hamad assured us that we should be able to buy plenty of food in Liwa, enlarging on what we should find there – flour and rice and dates and coffee and sugar – but he added that it would take us three, perhaps four, days to get there. I said wryly, 'We shall be as hungry as the camels', and al Auf grunted, 'Yes, but the sons of Adam cannot endure like camels.' Hamad, questioned by Mabkhaut and Mussalim, said that as long as we remained to the south of Liwa we should be outside the range of the fighting on the coast, and insisted that all the tribes in the south, whether they were Awamir, Manasir, or Bani Yas, were on good terms with the Rashid. He said, 'It will be different when you reach Oman. There the Duru are our enemies. There is no good in any of the Duru. You will have to be careful while you are among them for they are a treacherous race.' Al Auf laughed and quoted, 'He died of snake-bite', a well-known expression for Duru treachery.

He was tracing patterns on the sand with his camel-stick, smoothing them out and starting again. He looked up and said thoughtfully, 'The difficulty is Umbarak. No one must know he is here. If the Arabs hear that there is a Christian in the sands they will talk of nothing else, and the news will soon be all round the place. Then Ibn Saud's tax-collectors will hear of it and they will arrest us all and take us off to Ibn Jalawi in the Hasa. God preserve us from that. I know Ibn Jalawi. He is a tyrant, utterly without mercy. Anyway, we don't want the news about Umbarak to get ahead of us among the Duru. We shall never get through the country if it does. If we meet any Arabs we had better say that we are Rashid from the Hadhramaut, travelling to Abu Dhabi to fight for the Al bu Falah. Umbarak can be an Arab from Aden.'

Turning to me, he said, 'Keep quiet if we meet anyone. Just answer their salutations, and, what is more, from now on you must ride all the time. Any Arab who came across your monstrous foot-prints would certainly follow them to find out who on earth you were.' He got up to fetch the camel, saying, 'We had better be off.'

We went down to Khaba well. It was three miles away in a

bare hollow, among a jumble of small, white crescent-dunes. The water was ten feet below the surface, and it took us a long time to water the camels, for we had only one small leather bucket, and each camel drank ten to twelve gallons. Bin Kabina stood beside Qamaiqam and whenever she stopped he scratched between her hind legs and crooned endearments to encourage her to drink again. At last all of them were satisfied, blown out with the water which they had sucked up in long slow draughts. Al Auf dashed a few bucketfuls against their chests, and then started to fill the water-skins. The sun was very hot before we had finished. We mounted. My companions had wrapped themselves in their cloaks and muffled their faces in their head-cloths till only their eyes showed. I remembered a Bedu I had once seen in Syria. It was noon on a blazing midsummer day and he was trudging across the desert, travelling apparently from nowhere to nowhere, enveloped to his feet in a heavy sheepskin coat. Arabs argue that the extra clothes which they put on when it is hot keep the heat out; in fact, what they do is to stop the sweat from evaporating and thereby build up a cool layer of air next to the skin. I could never bear this clammy discomfort and preferred to lose moisture by letting the hot air dry my skin. But if I had done this in summer I should have died of heat-stroke.

Next day we had difficulty in avoiding several inquisitive Awamir, who at first took us for raiders and gave the alarm. Hamad got in touch with them and said that we were a party of Rashid going to Abu Dhabi. They then invited us to their encampment, saying that they would slaughter a camel for us. Hamad made excuses and this again aroused their suspicions, but when we camped Hamad, al Auf, and Mabkhaut went back to their encampment and spent the night there in order to reassure them. When they returned in the morning they brought us a goatskin full of milk. Three days after leaving Khaba we reached the Batin, and lay up in the dunes near Balagh well. Next morning Hamad, Jadid, and bin Kabina went to the settlements in Liwa to buy food. They took three camels with them, and I told bin Kabina to buy flour, sugar, tea, coffee, butter, dates, and rice if he could get any, and above all to bring back a goat. Our flour was finished, but that evening Musallim produced from his saddle-bags a few handfuls of maize, which we roasted and ate. It was to be the last food we had until the others returned from Liwa three days later. They were three interminable nights and days.

I had almost persuaded myself that I was conditioned to starvation, indifferent to it. After all, I had been hungry for weeks, and even when we had had flour I had had little inclination to eat the charred or sodden lumps which Musallim had cooked. I used to swallow my portion with even less satisfaction than that with which I eventually voided it. Certainly I thought and talked incessantly of food, but as a prisoner talks of freedom, for I realized that the joints of meat, the piles of rice, and the bowls of steaming gravy which tantalized me could have no reality outside my mind. I had never thought then that I should dream of the crusts which I was rejecting.

For the first day my hunger was only a more insistent feeling of familiar emptiness; something which, like a toothache, I could partly overcome by an effort of will. I woke in the grey dawn craving for food, but by lying on my stomach and pressing down I could achieve a semblance of relief. At least I was warm. Later, as the sun rose, the heat forced me out of my sleeping-bag. I threw my cloak over a bush and lay in the shade and tried to sleep again. I dozed and dreamt of food; I woke and thought of food. I tried to read, but it was difficult to concentrate. A moment's slackness and I was thinking once more of food. I filled myself with water, and the bitter water, which I did not want, made me feel sick. Eventually it was evening and we gathered round the fire, repeating, 'Tomorrow they will be back'; and thought of the supplies of food which bin Kabina would bring with him, and of the goat which we should eat. But the next day dragged out till sunset, and they did not come.

I faced another night, and the nights were worse than the days. Now I was cold and could not even sleep, except in snatches. I watched the stars; some of them – Orion, the Pleiades, and the Bear – I knew by name, others only by sight. Slowly they swung overhead and dipped down towards the west, while the bitter wind keened among the dunes. I remembered how I had once awakened with hunger during my first term at school and cried, remembering some chocolate cake which I had been too gorged to eat when my mother had taken me out to tea two days before. Now I was maddened by the thought of the crusts which I had given away in the Uruq al Shaiba. Why had I been such a fool? I could picture the colour and texture, even the shape, of the fragments which I had discarded.

In the morning I watched Mabkhaut turn the camels out to graze, and as they shuffled off, spared for a while from the toil which we imposed upon them, I found that I could only think of them as food. I was glad when they were out of sight. Al Auf came over and lay down near me, covering himself with his cloak; I don't think we spoke. I lay with my eyes shut, insisting to myself, 'If I were in London I would give anything to be here.' Then I thought of the jeeps and lorries with which the Locust Officers in the Najd were equipped. So vivid were my thoughts that I could hear the engines, smell the stink of petrol fumes. No, I would rather be here starving as I was than sitting in a chair, replete with food, listening to the wireless, and dependent upon cars to take me through Arabia. I clung desperately to this conviction. It seemed infinitely important. Even to doubt it was to admit defeat, to forswear everything to which I held.

I dozed and heard a camel roaring. I jerked awake, thinking, 'They have come at last', but it was only Mabkhaut moving our camels. The shadows lengthened among the sand-hills; the sun had set and we had given up hope when they returned. I saw at once that they had no goat with them. My dream of a large hot stew vanished. We exchanged the formal greetings and asked the formal questions about the news. Then we helped them with the only camel which was loaded. Bin Kabina said wearily, 'We got nothing. There is nothing to be had in Liwa. We have two packages of bad dates and a little wheat. They would not take our *riyals* – they wanted rupees. At last they took them at the same valuation as rupees. God's curse on them!' He had run a long palm-splinter into his foot and was limping. I tried to get it out but it was already too dark to see.

We opened a package of dates and ate. They were of poor quality and coated with sand, but there were plenty of them. Later we made porridge from the wheat, squeezing some dates into it to give it a flavour. After we had fed, al Auf said, 'If this is all we are going to have we shall soon be too weak to get on our camels.' We were a depressed and ill-tempered party that evening.

The past three days had been an ordeal, worse for the others than for me, since, but for me, they could have ridden to the nearest tents and fed. However, we had not suffered the final agony of doubt. We had known that the others would return and bring us food. We had thought of this food, talked of this food, dreamt of this food. A feast of rich and savoury meat, the reward of our endurance. Now all we had was this. Some wizened dates, coated with sand, and a mess of boiled grain. There was not even enough of it. We had to get back across Arabia, travelling secretly, and we had enough food for ten days if we were economical. I had eaten tonight, but I was starving. I wondered how much longer I should be able to face this fare. We *must* get more food. Al Auf said, 'We must get hold of a camel and eat that', and I thought of living for a month on sun-dried camel's meat and nothing else. Hamad suggested that we should lie up near Ibri in the Wadi el Ain, and send a party into Ibri to buy food. He said, 'It is one of the biggest towns in Oman. You will get everything you want there.' With difficulty I refrained from pointing out that he had said this of Liwa.

Musallim interrupted and said that we could not possibly go into the Duru country; the Duru had heard about my visit to Mughshin last year and had warned the Bait Kathir not to bring any Christians into their territory. Al Auf asked him impatiently where in that case he did propose to go. They started to wrangle. I joined in and reminded Musallim that we had always planned to return through the Duru country. Excitedly he turned towards me and, flogging the ground with his camel-stick to give emphasis to his words, shouted: 'Go through it? Yes, if we must, quickly and secretly, but through the uninhabited country near the sands. We never agreed to hang about in the Duru country, nor to go near Ibri. By God, it is madness! Don't you know that there is one of the Imam's governors there. He is the Riqaishi. Have you never heard of the Riqaishi? What do you suppose he will do if he hears there is a Christian in his country? He hates all infidels. I have been there. Listen, Umbarak, I know him. God help you, Umbarak, if he gets hold of you. Don't think that Oman is like the desert here. It is a settled country – villages and towns, and the Imam rules it all through his governors, and the worst of them all is the Riqaishi. The Duru, yes; Bedu like ourselves; our enemies, but we might smuggle you quickly through their land. But hang about there – no; and to go near Ibri would be madness. Do you hear? The first people who saw you, Umbarak, would go straight off and tell the Riqaishi.'

Al Auf asked him quietly, 'What do you want to do?' and Musallim stormed, 'God, I don't know. I only know I am not going near Ibri.' I asked him if he wanted to return to Salala by the way we had come, and added, 'It will be great fun, with worn-out camels and no food.' He shouted back that it would not be worse than going to Ibri. Exasperated by this stupidity, al Auf turned away muttering 'There is no god but God', while Musallim and I continued to wrangle until Mabkhaut and Hamad intervened to calm us.

Eventually we agreed that we must get food from Ibri and that meanwhile we would buy a camel from the Rashid who were ahead of us in the Rabadh, so that we should have an extra camel with us to eat if we were in trouble. Hamad said, 'You must conceal the fact that Umbarak is a Christian.' Mabkhaut suggested that I should pretend that I was a *saiyid* from the Hadhramaut, since no one would ever mistake me for a Bedu. I protested, 'That is no good; as a *saiyid* I should get involved in religious discussions. I should certainly be expected to pray, which I don't know how to do; they would probably even expect me to lead their prayers. A nice mess I should make of that.' The others laughed and agreed that this suggestion would not work. I said, 'While we are in the sands here I had better be an Aden townsman who has been living with the tribes and is now on his way to Abu Dhabi. When we get to Oman I will say I am a Syrian who has been visiting Riyadh and that I am now on my way to Salala.' Bin Kabina asked, 'What is a Syrian?' and I said, 'If you don't know what a Syrian is I don't suppose the Duru will either. Certainly they will never have seen one.'

I then asked him about Liwa. He said: 'There are palms, good ones, and quite a lot of them on the dunes above the salt-flats. The houses are of mats and palm fronds. I never saw a mud house. The villagers were all either Manasir or Bani Yas, an unfriendly lot. One slave noticed at once that the pads under my camel's saddle were made of coconut fibre and not of palm fibre. He called out, "This boy is from the south. He does not belong to the same party as the other two. He is probably with some raiders who are hiding somewhere and has come in to get food for them. They would all have come in if they were honest men." I told them that I was with two other Rashid, who had come north to fight for Al bu Falah, and that one of them had fever and that the other had remained to look after him.'

Mabkhaut exclaimed, 'They are devils, these slaves; they notice everything.'

Bin Kabina went on: 'By God, I would like to lift some of their camels, not that the ones I saw were worth taking. They are a wretched crowd, these villagers, not like the people at Salala. Their women refused even to grind our corn. Bad luck to them. I had to borrow a grindstone and do it myself after dark.'

I knew that this was a woman's job and that he would have been ashamed to be seen doing it. I asked what he had been given to eat, and he laughed and said, 'Bread, dates, and a stew made from skinks.' He was always sickened by lizard-meat. This started a discussion on what was lawful food. Arabs never distinguished between what is eatable and what is not, but always between food which is lawful and food which is forbidden. No Muslim may eat pork, blood, or the flesh of an animal which has not had its throat cut while it was still alive. Most of them will not eat meat slaughtered by anyone other than a Muslim, or by a boy who is still uncircumcised, although in Syria Muslims will eat meat killed by a Christian or a Druze. Otherwise the definition of what is lawful varies endlessly and in every place, and usually bears little relation to reason. I asked if a fox was lawful food, and Hamad explained to me that sand foxes were, but mountain foxes were not. They agreed that eagles were lawful, but ravens were forbidden, unless they were eaten as medicine to cure stomach-ache. Musallim said that the Duru ate the wild donkeys which lived in their country, and the others expressed incredulity and disgust. I said I would far rather eat a donkey than a wild cat, which al Auf had just declared was lawful meat. The differences which had arisen between us a short while ago were forgotten.

Among these people arguments frequently become impassioned, but usually the excitement dies away as quickly as it arises. Men who were screaming at each other, ready apparently to resort to violence, will sit happily together a short while later drinking coffee. As a rule Bedu do not nurse a grievance, but if they think that their personal honour has been slighted they immediately become vindictive, bent on vengeance. Strike a Bedu and he will kill you either then or later. It is easy for strangers to give offence without meaning to do so. I once put my hand on the back of bin Kabina's neck and he turned on me and asked furiously if I took him for a slave. I had no idea that I had done anything wrong.

In the morning our camp was enveloped in thick mist. I could just make out an *abal* bush less than twenty yards from where I lay; beyond it was a drifting whiteness, dank as sea fog. Suddenly, somewhere, a camel roared, indicating that a human being had approached it. I felt for my rifle and glanced round to see if anyone was missing. Bin Kabina was puffing at a smoking pile of sticks; Musallim was piling lumps of dates on a tray; Hamad and Jadid were praying; and I realized it must be Mabkhaut and al Auf with the camels. I got up. The cloak which had covered my sleeping-bag was drenched. Each night for the past week we had had this soaking dew, the result of the northerly winds which carried the moisture inland from the Persian Gulf. I had noticed that in the southern Sands dew and morning mist coincided with a southerly wind off the Arabian Sea. I do not think that much dew falls in the Empty

Quarter itself, but nearer the coast the dew must freshen the herbage. I was always astounded when al Auf maintained that dew burnt
it up.

Hamad now volunteered to accompany us as far as Ibri, an offer
which we gladly accepted since he knew the Sands and the present
distribution of the tribes. He said that we had better keep along
the southern edge of Liwa, where the country was at present empty.
Normally the salt-flats south of Liwa were filled with camel herds
belonging to the Manasir, but recently they had been raided by a
force from Dibai and had suffered losses. Now most of the Manasir
were assembled farther to the west. Hamad explained to me that
the Manasir pastured their camels on salt-bushes, which made them
very thirsty, so that they had to be watered three or even four times
a day. In consequence they were tied to the neighbourhood of
the wells. Salt-bushes were little affected by drought and provided
abundant and permanent grazing on the flats around Liwa. Our
own camels would not eat these bushes, and bin Kabina asked if
we should find anything for them on our route. He said, 'The
wretched animals don't deserve any more starvation. It has made
me miserable to watch their suffering.' Hamad assured him that
we should find enough for them during the next few days and
plenty as soon as we reached Rabadh. We therefore agreed to his
suggestion.

We ate some dates, and Jadid then went back while the rest of
us set off in an easterly direction, the mist still thick about us. I
hoped we should not stumble on some Arab encampment. The
mist did not lift for another two hours.

The dunes ran from west to east so that we were travelling
easily. They consisted of great massifs similar to the *qaid* which I
had seen in Ghanim, but there they were linked together to form
parallel dune chains about three hundred feet in height, the broad
valleys between them being covered with bright-green salt-bushes.
We passed several palm groves and a few small settlements of
dilapidated huts made, as bin Kabina had described, from matting
and palm fronds. They were all abandoned.

At midday, while we were eating more of our revolting dates, two Arabs accompanied by a saluki appeared on a distant dune. They stood and watched us, so al Auf went over to them. They shouted to him not to come any nearer, and when he called back that he wanted 'the news' they answered that they had none and wanted none of his and threatened that they would shoot if he came any closer. They watched us for a while and then made off.

We travelled slowly to rest our camels and reached the Rabadh sands five days after leaving Balagh. Sometimes we saw camels. It did not seem to matter how far off they were; my companions were apparently always able to distinguish if they were in milk. They would say, 'There are camels', and point to some dots on a dune a mile or more away. After a further scrutiny they would agree that one or more were in milk. We would then ride over to them, for travellers in the desert may milk any camels they encounter. These camels were feeding on salt-bushes and gushes of liquid green excrement poured constantly down their hocks. Al Auf told me that camels which fed on salt-bushes always scoured like this, but that it did them no harm provided they had plenty of water. Certainly most of these looked in excellent condition.

Once we passed a dozen camels tended by a woman with two small children. Al Auf said, 'Let's get a drink', and we rode over to them. He jumped from his camel, greeted the woman, a wizened old thing bundled up in black cloth turned green with age, took the bowl which she handed him, and went towards the camels. She shrilled at her sons, 'Hurry! Hurry! Fetch the red one. Fetch the two-year-old. God take you, child! Hurry! Fetch the red one. Fetch the two-year-old. Welcome! Welcome! Welcome to the guests!' Al Auf handed us the bowl and in turn we squatted down to drink, for no Arab drinks standing, while the old woman asked us where we were going. We answered that we were going to fight for the Al bu Falah and she exclaimed, 'God give you victory!'

On another occasion we came upon a small encampment of Manasir. Hamad insisted that we must go over to them, or we should arouse their suspicions since they had already seen us. We were on foot at the time and I suggested that they should leave the camels to graze and that I should herd them until they returned. After some argument they agreed. I knew that they wanted milk, and I should have liked a drink myself, but it seemed stupid to run the risk of detection. When they returned, bin Kabina grinned whenever he looked at me, so I asked him what the joke was. He said, 'The Manasir gave us milk but insisted that we should fetch you, saying, "Why do you leave your companion without milk?" Al Auf explained that you were our slave, but they still insisted that we should fetch you.' I knew that among Bedu even a slave is considered as a travelling companion, entitled to the same treatment as the rest of the party. Bin Kabina went on, 'Finally al Auf said, "Oh! he is half-witted. Leave him where he is", and the Manasir insisted no more.' Mabkhaut said, 'True, they said no more, but they looked at us a bit oddly.'

Next morning while we were leading our camels down a steep dune face I was suddenly conscious of a low vibrant hum, which grew in volume until it sounded as though an aeroplane were flying low over our heads. The frightened camels plunged about, tugging at their head-ropes and looking back at the slope above us. The sound ceased when we reached the bottom. This was 'the singing of the sands'. The Arabs describe it as roaring, which is perhaps a more descriptive word. During the five years that I was in these parts I only heard it half a dozen times. It is caused, I think, by one layer of sand slipping over another. Once I was standing on a dune-crest and the sound started as soon as I stepped on to the steep face. I found on this occasion that I could start it or stop it at will by stepping on or off this slip-face.

Near Rabadh, Musallim suddenly jumped off his camel, pushed his arm into a shallow burrow, and pulled out a hare. I asked him how he knew it was there, and he said that he had seen its track going in and none coming out. The afternoon dragged on until we reached the expanse of small contiguous dunes which give these sands the name of Rabadh. There was adequate grazing, so we stopped on their edge. We decided to eat the rest of our flour, and Musallim conjured three onions and some spices out of his saddle-bags. We sat round in a hungry circle watching bin Kabina cooking the hare, and offering advice. Anticipation mounted, for it was more than a month since we had eaten meat, except for the hare that al Auf had killed near the Uruq al Shaiba. We sampled the soup and decided to let it stew just a little longer. Then bin Kabina looked up and groaned, 'God! Guests!'

Coming across the sands towards us were three Arabs. Hamad said, 'They are Bakhit, and Umbarak, and Salim, the children of Mia', and to me, 'They are Rashid.' We greeted them, asked the news, made coffee for them, and then Musallim and bin Kabina dished up the hare and the bread and set it before them, saying with every appearance of sincerity that they were our guests, that God had brought them, that today was a blessed day, and a number of similar remarks. They asked us to join them but we refused, repeating that they were our guests. I hoped that I did not look as murderous as I felt while I joined the others in assuring them that God had brought them on this auspicious occasion. When they had finished, bin Kabina put a sticky lump of dates in a dish and called us over to feed.

Feeling thoroughly ill-tempered I lay down to sleep, but this was impossible. The others, excited by this meeting with their fellow-tribesmen, talked incessantly within a few yards of my head. I wondered irritably why Bedu must always shout. Gradually I relaxed. I tried the old spell of asking myself, 'Would I really wish to be anywhere else?' and having decided that I would not, I felt better. I pondered on this desert hospitality, and compared it with our own. I remembered other encampments where I had slept, small tents on which I had happened in the Syrian desert and where I had spent the night. Gaunt men in rags and hungry-looking children had greeted me, and bade me welcome with the sonorous phrases of the desert. Later they had set a great dish before me, rice heaped round a sheep which they had slaughtered, over which my host poured liquid golden butter until it flowed down on to the sand; and when I had protested, saying, 'Enough! Enough!', had answered that I was a hundred times welcome. Their lavish hospitality had always made me uncomfortable, for I had known that as a result of it they would go hungry for days. Yet when I left them they had almost convinced me that I had done them a kindness by staying with them.

My thoughts were interrupted by the raised voices of my companions. Bin Kabina was protesting passionately. I could see him gesticulating against the sky. I listened and, as I had expected, they were talking about money, the rights and wrongs of some ancient dispute about a few shillings which concerned none of them. I wondered if any other race was as avaricious as the Arabs, with such an intense love of money, and then I thought of bin Kabina giving away his only loin-cloth in Ramlat al Ghafa and wondered who, other than a Bedu, would have done that. It is characteristic of Bedu to do things by extremes, to be either wildly generous or unbelievably mean, very patient or almost hysterically excitable, to be incredibly brave or to panic for no apparent reason. Ascetic by nature, they derive satisfaction from the bare simplicity of their lives and scorn the amenities which others would judge essential. Although, on the rare occasions that offer, they eat enormously, I have never met a Bedu who was greedy. Continent for months on end, not one of them, even the most austere, would regard celibacy as a virtue. They want sons, and consider that women are provided by God for the satisfaction of men. Deliberately to refrain from using them would be not only unnatural but also ridiculous, and Bedu are very susceptible to ridicule. Yet an Arab will use his sister's name as his battle-cry, and Glubb has suggested that the medieval conception of chivalry came to Europe from the Arabs at the time of the Crusades. Bedu set great store by human dignity, and most of them would prefer to watch a man die rather than see him humiliated. Always reserved in front of strangers and accustomed on formal occasions to sit for hours motionless and in silence, they are a garrulous, lighthearted race. But, at the instigation of religious zealots, they can become uncompromisingly puritanical, quick to frown on all amusement, regarding song and music as a sin and laughter as unseemly. Probably no other people, either as a race or as individuals, combine so many conflicting qualities in such an extreme degree.

I was dimly conscious of their voices until nearly dawn.

In the morning Bakhit pressed us to come to his tent, saying, 'I will give you fat and meat', the conventional way of saying that he would kill a camel for us. We were tempted, for we were very hungry, but Hamad said that it would be wiser not to go there, for the sands in which Bakhit was camped were full of Arabs. We told Bakhit that we wished to buy a camel, and he said he would fetch one and meet us next day at an abandoned well farther to the east. He met us there a little before sunset. He had with him an old camel, a *hazmia*, black-coated and in good condition, which had been bred in the sands. There were long strips of skin hanging from the soles of her feet. Al Auf said she would not be able to travel far on the gravel plains in the Duru country, but Mabkhaut answered that we could take her along with us until her feet wore through and then kill her. We bought her after a little haggling.

The next morning we saw some tents, and Hamad said, 'I don't know who they are', so we bore off to the right in order to pass wide of them; but a man came out from among them and ran across the sand towards us, shouting, 'Stop! Stop!' As he came near, Hamad said, 'It is all right. He is Salim, old Muhammad's son.' We greeted him and he said, 'Why do you pass by my tent? Come, I will give you fat and meat.' I protested instinctively, but he silenced me by saying, 'If you do not come to my tent I shall divorce my wife.' This was the divorce oath, which he was bound to obey if we refused. He took my camel's rein and led her towards the tents. An old man came forward and greeted us. He had a long white beard, kindly eyes, and a gentle voice. He walked very upright, as do all the Bedu. Hamad said, 'This is old Muhammad.' The two tents were very small, less than three yards long and four feet high, and were half-filled with saddles and other gear. An old woman, a younger woman, and three children, one of them a small naked child with a running nose and his thumb in his mouth, watched us as we unloaded. The women were dressed in dark-blue robes, and were unveiled. The younger one was very pretty. Salim called to al Auf and together they went off across the dunes. They came back later with a young camel, which they slaughtered behind the tents.

Meanwhile the old man had made coffee and set out dates for us to eat. Hamad said, 'He is the Christian.' The old man asked, 'Is he the Christian who travelled last year with bin al Kamam and the Rashid to the Hadhramaut?' and after Hamad had assented he turned to me and said, 'A thousand welcomes.' It had not taken long for this news to arrive, although here we were near the Persian Gulf, far from the Hadhramaut; but I was not surprised. I knew how interested Bedu always are in 'the news', how concerned to get the latest information about their kinsmen, about raids and tribal movements and grazing. I knew from experience how far they would go out of their way to ask for news. I had realized that it was the chance of getting this as much as the craving for milk that had tantalized my companions during the past days when we had seen and avoided distant tents. They hated travelling through inhabited country without knowing exactly what was happening around them.

'What is "the news"?' It is the question which follows every encounter in the desert even between strangers. Given a chance the Bedu will gossip for hours, as they had done last night, and nothing is too trivial for them to recount. There is no reticence in the desert. If a man distinguishes himself he knows that his fame will be widespread; if he disgraces himself he knows that the story of his shame will inevitably be heard in every encampment. It is this fear of public opinion which enforces at all times the rigid conventions of the desert. The consciousness that they are always before an audience makes many of their actions theatrical. Glubb once told me of a Bedu sheikh who was known as 'The Host of the Wolves', because whenever he heard a wolf howl round his tent he ordered his son to take a goat out in the desert, saying he would have no one call on him for dinner in vain.

It was late in the afternoon when Salim spread a rug in front of us, and placed on it a large tray covered with rice. He lifted joints of meat from the cauldron and put them on this, ladled soup over the rice, and finally tipped a dishful of butter over it. He then poured water over our outstretched hands. Old Muhammad invited us to eat, but refused our invitation to join us. He stood and watched us, saying, 'Eat! Eat! You are hungry. You are tired. You have come a long way. Eat!' He shouted to Salim to bring more butter, although we protested that there was enough already, and taking the dish from Salim's hand poured it over the rice. Gorged at last, we licked our fingers and rose together muttering 'God requite you.' We washed, using water. There was no need here to clean our fingers with sand, for the well was near by. Salim then handed us coffee and the bitter drops were welcome and clean-tasting after the greasy rice and cold lumps of fat which we had eaten. He and his father urged us to remain with them at least for another day to rest ourselves and our camels, and we willingly agreed. They brought us milk at sunset and we drank till we could drink no more. As each of us handed back the bowl from which he had drunk, he said, 'God bless her!', a blessing on the camel who had given the milk. Bakhit and Umbarak turned up next morning, saying that they had expected to find us here. Bakhit was anxious to accompany us to Ibri, where he wished to buy rice and coffee with the money we had given him for the camel. He was afraid to go alone because of the enmity between the Rashid and the Duru.

All the tribes between the Hadhramaut and Oman belong to one or other of two rival factions, known today as Ghafari and Hanawi. The names themselves date back only as far as a civil war in Oman at the beginning of the eighteenth century, but the division between the tribes which these names denote is very ancient and probably originated in the difference between tribes of Adnan and Qahtan origin. The Duru were Ghafaris, while the Rashid, who were descended from Qahtan, were Hanawis. To travel safely among the Duru we needed a *rabia* or companion, who could frank us through their territory. He could be either from the Duru or from some other tribe entitled by tribal custom to give his travelling companions protection among the Duru while they were in his company. A *rabia* took an oath: 'You are my companions and your safety, both of your blood and of your possessions, is in my face.' Members of the same party were responsible for each other's safety, and were expected to fight if necessary in each other's defence, even against their own tribes or families. If one of the party was killed, all the party were involved in the ensuing blood-feud. No tribe would be likely to attack a party which was accompanied by a tribesman from a powerful tribe to which they were allied, but a *rabia* could belong to a small and insignificant tribe and still give protection. The question of how and where each tribe could give protection was complicated. It often amused my companions to argue hypothetical cases as we rode along, and their arguments sometimes became so involved that I was reminded of lawyers disputing. Our present difficulty was that we should have to penetrate into the Duru territory without a *rabia* and hope to find one when we arrived there. At present the Rashid and the Duru were not at war, but there was no love lost between them.

Three days later we camped on the eastern edge of the Sands among some scattered thorn-bushes, and the following day we rode for seven hours across a flat plain, whose gravel surface was overspread with fragments of limestone. Ahead of us a yellow haze hung like a dirty curtain across the horizon. We camped in the evening in a sandy watercourse, among some *ghaf* trees. There was a large package of dates in the fork of one of these, left there by its owner in perfect confidence that no one would touch it. At sunset we saw some goats in the distance; but no one came near us. During the night a wolf howled round our camp; it was one of the eeriest sounds I have ever heard.

At dawn I saw a great mountain to the east and Hamad told me that it was Jabal Kaur near Ibri. Later the haze thickened again and hid it from our sight. As we approached the Wadi al Ain, Hamad suggested that he and al Auf had better ride on ahead, in case there was anyone on the well, so that they could give them warning of our approach; otherwise they would certainly shoot at us. They trotted off towards the belt of trees which stretched across our front. A little later, when we arrived near the well, we saw a group of Arabs arguing with Hamad; al Auf came to us and told us to stop where we were as there was trouble. Hurriedly he explained that when they had reached the well they spoke to two Duru who were watering camels, and that these men had been friendly, but that some other Duru, with camels loaded with dates

A woman of the Harasis.

Previous page: Salim bin Ghabaisha.

The girl from the Saar, drawing water at Manwakh well.

One of the bin Maaruf Saar, the wolves of the desert.

A Saar family on the move.

Overleaf: In the Hadramaut: Shibam, from the wells.

Shibam: a mosque and houses.

Overleaf: The Empty Quarter: descending a great dune.

A Saar encampment.

Below: The author's party loading up in the Sands.

Sulaim, the *rabia* from the Mahra.

Overleaf: Dhiby well.

Rashid: Amair and (*right*) bin al Mamam.

Below: Salim bin Mautlauq and (*right*) Muhammad bin Kalut, bin Kabina's half-brother.

The author during the second crossing of the Empty Quarter.

Below: Bin Ghabaisha pouring cofee; *right*: A Rashid boy milking a camel.

from Ibri, had arrived shortly afterwards and they had declared that no Rashid might use their well. Al Auf then went back to the group round the well, while we waited anxiously to see what was going to happen. Half an hour later he and Hamad came over to us with a young man who greeted us and then told us to unload our camels and make ourselves comfortable; he said that when he had finished watering he would take us to his encampment. The caravan from Ibri watered their animals. One of them unexpectedly gave Hamad a small package of dates; they were very large and very sweet, but I was sick of dates and never wanted to see another. They moved off up the wadi and we then went over to the well, which had clean water at a depth of twenty feet.

In the afternoon the young herdsman, whose name was Ali, led us to his encampment two miles away. Here the Wadi al Ain, the largest of the three great wadis which run down from the Oman mountains into the desert to the west, consisted not of a single dry river-bed, but of several smaller watercourses separated by banks of gravel and drifts of sand. The trees and shrubs that grew here were parched with drought but, even so, they made a pleasant change after the bare gravel plain which we had just crossed.

There were no tents or huts at Ali's encampment. He and his family were living under two large acacias on which they hung their household utensils. They had evidently been here for a long time, since the two brushwood pens in which they put their goats at night were thickly carpeted with droppings. There were two women, both of them veiled, a half-witted boy of fourteen, and three small children. We unsaddled a short distance away from this encampment, in a grove of *ghaf* trees which had been lopped and mutilated to provide grazing for the goats and camels. Ali slaughtered a goat for us, and in the evening brought over a good meal of meat, bread, and dates. He was accompanied by a slave who was spending the night here. Ali agreed to take some of my party to Ibri, although the slave disconcerted us by saying that there had been trouble there a few days earlier between the townsfolk and a party of Rashid. Ali asked me if I was going to Ibri, but I said that I had been suffering from fever and would remain here to rest. Al Auf had told him already that I was from Syria, that I had recently been at Riyadh, and that I was now on my way to Salala. We agreed that bin Kabina and Musallim should remain with me while the others went to Ibri. Ali promised that when he returned from Ibri he would come with us to the Wadi al Amairi, where he could find us another *rabia* to take us through the rest of the Duru country.

The party going to Ibri left in the morning; Ali said that they would be back in five days' time. In the afternoon his father, who was called Staiyun, arrived with a nephew called Muhammad. Staiyun was a kindly, simple old man with a wrinkled face and humorous eyes. He was not likely to ask disconcerting questions, but I was not so sure about Muhammad, who was well dressed, in a clean white shirt, with an expensive woollen head-cloth, and a silver-hilted dagger. He had recently been in Muscat and was obviously a great deal more sophisticated than his uncle. However, he seemed friendly. Staiyun said that it would be better if Muhammad went with us to the Wadi al Amairi instead of his son, but I would rather have had the credulous Ali. It was not going to be easy to live at close quarters with Muhammad for several days and maintain my disguise, since he would soon notice that I did not pray. I was relieved when he said he was going to his own encampment. He promised to come back as soon as Staiyun sent for him. Staiyun confirmed that some Rashid had had trouble at Ibri, but said that they had paid compensation and that all was now well.

They were pleasant, lazy days. Staiyun fed us on bread, dates, and milk and spent most of his time with us. The more I saw of the old man the more I liked him. I asked him about Umm al Samim, and he told me that the three wadis, al Ain, al Aswad, and al Amairi, ended in these quicksands. As far as I could make out they were about fifty miles to the west of us. He confirmed the stories I had already heard that raiding parties had been swallowed up in them, and said that he himself had seen a flock of goats disappear when the ground had suddenly broken up around them; after struggling for a while they had sunk beneath the surface. I determined that I would come back and visit Umm al Samim and that I would try to penetrate into the mountains which were ruled by the Imam. It was interesting to collect from old Staiyun the information I should require to enable me to do this journey: about the tribes and their alliances, the different sheikhs and their rivalries, the Imam's government and where and how it worked, and about wells and the distances that lay between them. But for the present I should be satisfied if I arrived at Bai without mishap and without delay; already I was worried, for five days and then six had passed and still there was no news of my companions.

Staiyun was anxious about his son as a result of the recent trouble in Ibri, and he urged me to go there. He said that if they were in difficulties I could intervene with Muhammad al Riqaishi, the Governor, or even go and see the Imam in Nazwa on their behalf. On the seventh day I decided that I must go in the morning with Staiyun to Ibri. There I should stand revealed as a Christian, and from what I had heard of the Riqaishi and the Imam this would not be pleasant; nor would my intervention help my companions if they were in trouble, but there was nothing else for me to do. It was a great relief when they arrived at sunset. All was well. They pretended that the way was farther than they had expected, but I knew that they had dallied in Ibri enjoying themselves, and I did not blame them.

Next day Hamad and Bakhit returned to their homes, and after Staiyun had fetched Muhammad the rest of us camped on the far side of the wadi. It took us eight hours to reach the Wadi al Aswad and two more long days to reach the Amairi. It was difficult to get the observations which I required for my mapping, and impossible to take photographs while Muhammad was with us. He inquired from the others why I did not pray, and they said that Syrians were evidently lax about their religion.

The Amairi was another large wadi with many trees and bushes. Muhammad took us to the encampment of a man called Rai, who belonged to the small tribe of the Afar, and arranged with him that he should take us to the Wahiba country. The Wahiba are Hanawis and are enemies of the Duru, and none of the Duru could escort us into their country. But the Afar are accepted as *rabia* by both the Duru and the Wahiba. Muhammad went back next day, but we remained for four days, since we had a long way still ahead of us and Rai said that there would be little grazing for the camels once we left the Amairi. Here there had been recent rain and the trees were in leaf. There were many Duru in the wadi, with herds of camels, flocks of sheep and goats, and numerous donkeys. That night I told Rai who I was, since Musallim said that there was no necessity to keep my identity a secret from him. He looked at me and said, 'You would not have got here if the Duru had known who you were', and he warned me to tell no one else. From our camp I could see the long range of Jabal al Akhadar, the Green Mountain, which lies behind Muscat. It rises to ten thousand feet and was still unexplored. I could see other and nearer mountains, none of which were marked on my map. What was shown was guesswork. The Wadi al Ain, for instance, was marked as flowing into the sea near Abu Dhabi. I was more than ever determined to come back and explore this country properly.

I suggested that we should slaughter the *hazmia*, as her soles were wearing thin and she was beginning to go lame, but the others said that there was too many people here and we should have to give all her meat away.

We set off once more. Each interminable, empty day ended at sunset and started again at dawn. The others ate dates before we started, but I could no longer face their sticky sweetness, and I fasted till the evening meal. Hour after hour my camel shuffled forward, moving, it seemed, always up a slight incline towards an indeterminable horizon, and nowhere in all that glaring emptiness of gravel plain and colourless sky was there anything upon which my eyes could focus. I would notice some dots, think that perhaps they were far-off camels, only to realize a few strides farther on that they were stones immediately beneath our feet. I marvelled how Rai kept his direction, especially when the sun was overhead. I knew that camels will never walk straight; my own animal edged off the whole time to the right towards her homeland and I had to tap her back with my stick, a constant source of irritation. Rai and the others talked continuously and seemingly paid no attention to where they were going, and yet when at intervals I checked our course with my compass it never varied more than a few degrees. We reached the well at Haushi near the southern coast six days after leaving the Amairi. For the past two days it had been grievous to watch the limping agony of the *hazmia*. There was nothing here for the camels to eat but the shoots of leafless thornbushes growing in occasional watercourses. The *hazmia* could not even feed. She was accustomed to the grazing of the Sands, and her tender gums could not chew this woody fare. She was becoming thin. Al Auf eyed her and said, 'When we do kill her she won't be worth eating.' We murdered her the evening we got to Haushi. We cut the meat into strips and hung it on bushes to dry, and put the marrow bones into the sac of her stomach, which we tied up with a strip of her skin and buried in the sands, lighting a fire on top of it. Next day when we uncovered it there was a blood-streaked mess floating among the empty bones, which Mabkhaut poured into an empty goatskin. Bedu yearn hungrily for fats, but I dreamt of fruit, of bunches of grapes, and whiteheart cherries. We had hidden our-selves away among sand-dunes but two Wahiba found us there. They were, however, delightful old men, courteous and welcoming, who had not come looking for meat but seeking news and entertain-ment. They fetched us milk and then spent the night with us. We fed at sunset, eating till we could eat no more. The meat smelt rank and was very tough, the soup was greasy and of a curious flavour, but it was a wonderful meal after all these hungry weeks. Replete at last, I lay on the sand while the old men mumbled reminiscences through toothless gums and the nearby camels bel-ched and chewed the cud.

We spent the next day there drying the meat, and then set off westwards for Bai.

Once more we rode across an empty land, but now it was not only empty, it was dead. Shallow depressions in the limestone floor held sloughs of glutinous black mud, crusted with scabs of salt and sand, like putrescent patches on a carcase rotting in the sun. We rode for seven and eight and nine hours a day, without a stop, and it was dreary work. Conversation died with the passing hours and boredom mounted within me like a dull ache of pain. We muffled our faces against the parching wind, screwed up our eyes against the glare which stabbed into our heads. The flies we had brought with us from our butchers' work at Haushi clustered black upon our backs and heads. If I made a sudden movement they were thick about my face in a noisy questing cloud. I rode along, my body swaying backwards and forwards, backwards and forwards, to the camel's stride, a ceaseless strain upon my back which from long practice I no longer felt. I watched the sun's slow progress and longed for evening. As the sun sank into the haze it became an orange disc without heat or brilliance. I looked at it through my field-glasses and saw the sun-spots like black holes in its surface. It disappeared while still a span above the horizon, vanishing in a yellow sky that was without a cloud.

We reached Bai five days after leaving Haushi. Seeing camels in the distance, Mabkhaut said, 'That is bin Turkia's camel and there is bin Anauf's.' We approached a ridge and suddenly a small figure showed up upon it. It was bin Anauf. 'They come! They come!' he screamed, and raced down the slope. Old Tamtaim appeared, hobbling towards us. I slid stiffly from my camel and greeted them. The old man flung his arms about me, with tears running down his face, too moved to be coherent. Bitter had been his wrath when the Bait Kathir returned from Ramlat al Ghafia. He said they had brought black shame upon his tribe by deserting me. We led our camels over to their camping place and there exchanged the formal greetings and 'the news'. It was 31 January. I had parted from them at Mughshin on 24 November. It seemed like two years.

Only Tamtaim, bin Turkia, and his son were here. The others were near the coast, where there was better grazing. Bin Turkia said he would take the news to them next day. We slept little that night. We talked and talked, and brewed coffee and yet more coffee, while we told them of our doings. They were Bedu, and no mere outline would suffice either them or my companions; what they wanted was a detailed account of all that we had seen and done, the people we had spoken to, what they had said, what we had said to them, what we had eaten and when and where. My companions seemed to have forgotten nothing, however trivial. It was long past midnight when I lay down to sleep and they were still talking. Next day the others arrived and with them were many Harasis who had come to see the Christian. Some women also turned up. All of them were masked with visor-like pieces of stiff black cloth, and one of them was dressed in white, which was unusual. There was much coming and going and much talk; only Sultan sat apart and brooded. My anxieties and difficulties were now over, but we still had far to go before we reached Salala.

We rode across the flatness of the Jaddat al Harasis, long marches of eight and even ten hours a day. We were like a small army, for many Harasis and Mahra travelled with us, going to Salala to visit the Sultan of Muscat, who had recently arrived there. I was as glad now to be back in this friendly crowd as I had been to escape from it at Mughshin. I delighted in the surging rhythm of this mass of camels, the slapping shuffle of their feet, the shouted talk, and the songs which stirred the blood of men and beasts so that they drove forward with quickened pace. And there was life here. Gazelle grazed among the flat-topped acacia bushes, and once I saw a distant herd of oryx looking very white against the dark gravel of the plain. There were lizards, about eighteen inches in length, which scuttled across the ground. They had disc-shaped tails, and in consequence the Arabs called them 'The Father of the Dollar'. I asked if they ate them, but they declared that they were unlawful; I knew that they would eat other lizards which resembled them except for their tails. But, anyway, there was no need now for us to eat lizard-meat. Every day we fed on gazelles, and twice Musallim shot an oryx.

We watered at Khaur Wir: I wondered how much more foul water could taste and still be considered drinkable. We watered again six days later at Yisbub, where the water was fresh and maiden-hair fern grew in the damp rock above the pool. We went on again and reached Andhur, where I had been the previous year, and camped near the palm grove. Then we climbed up on to the Qarra mountains and looked upon the sea. It was nineteen days since we had left Bai. We descended the mountain in the afternoon and camped under great fig-trees beside the pools of Darbat. There were mallard and pintail and widgeon and coots on these pools, and that night Musallim shot a striped hyena. It was one of three which ran chuckling round our camp in the moonlight.

We had sent word into Salala, and next morning the Wali rode out to meet us accompanied by a crowd of townsfolk and Bedu. There were many Rashid with him, some of them old friends, others I had not yet met, among these bin Kalut who had accompanied Bertram Thomas. With him were the Rashid we had left at Mughshin, who told us that Mahsin had recovered and was in Salala.

The Wali feasted us in a tent beside the sea, and in the afternoon we went to the RAF camp. My companions insisted on a triumphal entry, so we rode into the camp firing off our rifles, while ahead of us some Bait Kathir danced and sang, brandishing their daggers.

NINE

From Salala to Mukalla

A leisurely journey with the Rashid to Mukalla
completes my survey of this part of Arabia.

I stayed at Salala for a week. I was busy writing up my notes, sorting out my collections, and arranging to travel with the Rashid to Mukalla.

I had come to Dhaufar determined to cross the Empty Quarter. I had succeeded and for me the venture needed no justification. I realized, however, that from the point of view of the Locust Research Centre my return journey through Oman was far more important than my crossing of the sands. To them the only justification for this crossing would be that it had enabled me to enter Oman. Had I tried to go there from the south the Duru would certainly have identified me with the Christian who had travelled the year before with the Bait Kathir and would have held me up. Coming from the north my rather unconvincing disguise passed muster because no one expected me to be European.

My own observations, and the inquiries I had made while crossing the Empty Quarter, had convinced me that there were few years when it did not rain somewhere in this area. The rain was usually slight, a few scattered showers; but little rain was needed to produce vegetation in the sands, and where it rained locusts could breed. I had seen a few locusts during the journey, some of them yellow, which showed that they were ready to breed. I had made notes of their colour, numbers, and direction of flight, and often bin Kabina and the others had secured me specimens, chasing and swatting them with their head-cloths. I had collected specimens of the plants that grew in the sands, and had compiled information about their distribution, and about recent rainfall. All this was useful, confirming what was already known or suspected as a result of my first journey to Mughshin, but I doubted that by itself it would have justified the expense of this second expedition. However, from Oman I had brought back the information which the Locust Research Centre required. Dr Uvarov had thought that the river-beds which drained the western slopes of the ten-thousand-foot Jabal al Akhadar might carry down sufficient water to the sands to produce permanent vegetation there, and that in consequence the mouths of the great wadis might be outbreak centres for the desert locusts. I had found out that floods were rare in the lower reaches of the wadis, and that when they occurred they dispersed in the sterile salt-flats of the Umm al Samim, where nothing grows.

I enjoyed the days I spent at Salala. It was a pleasant change talking English instead of the constant effort of talking Arabic; to have a hot bath and to eat well-cooked food; even to sit at ease on a chair with my legs stretched out, instead of sitting on the ground with them tucked under me. But the pleasure of doing these things was enormously enhanced for me by the knowledge that I was going back into the desert; that this was only an interlude and not the end of my journey.

The Sultan, Saiyid Said bin Timur, whom I met for the first time, was very kind to me and gave me every assistance in arranging the next stage. He assured me that the restrictions which had been imposed on the RAF did not apply to me, and that I could go anywhere and talk to anyone while I was in Salala. This made it much easier to make my arrangements.

I now planned to travel to Mukalla in the Eastern Aden Protectorate and to map the country along the watershed between the wadis which ran northwards to the sands and those which ran southwards to the sea. A map of this area, together with the one which I had made the year before during my journey to the

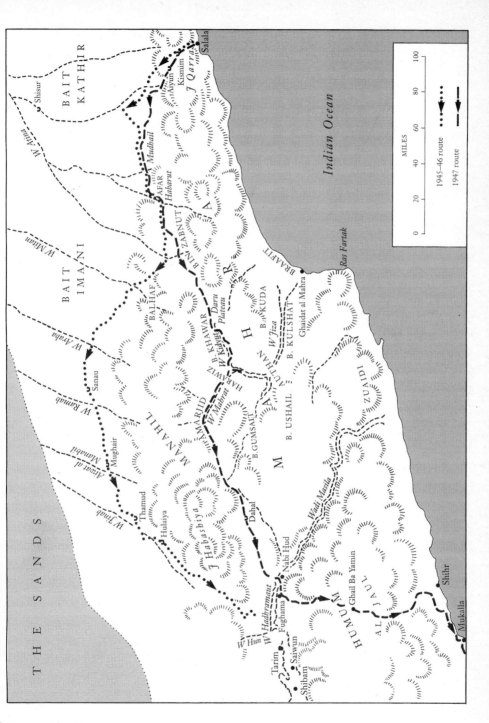

The Mahra Country

Hadhramaut, would establish the outline of the unknown country to the west of Dhaufar.

I arranged with bin Kalut that he and a party of Rashid should go with me to Mukalla. We agreed that I should pay for fifteen men, as I had done the previous year, but that the Rashid should settle among themselves how many actually accompanied me. A large force of Dahm had raided the Rashid and Manahil two months before, capturing many camels, and my companions were afraid that we might encounter other raiding parties near the Hadhramaut. Bin Kalut undertook to find the necessary *rabias* from the tribes whose territory we should pass. I meanwhile paid off the Bait Kathir, except for Mabkhaut, bin Turkia, and his son bin Anauf. Musallim could not come with us because we should be travelling through Mahra country and, having killed one of them, he had a blood-feud with that tribe. Al Auf, bin Kabina, and the three Bait Kathir were to come, in addition to the party which bin Kalut was collecting.

On 3 March bin Kalut and about sixty Rashid turned up in the RAF camp. The airmen moved about among them taking photographs and watching them loading their camels. These airmen were my fellow countrymen, and I was proud to be of their race. I knew the essential decency which was the bed-rock of their character, their humour, stubbornness, and self-reliance. I knew that if called upon they could adapt themselves to any kind of life, in the desert, in the jungle, in mountains, or on the sea, and that in many respects no race in the world was their equal. But the things which interested them bored me. They belonged to an age of machines; they were fascinated by cars and aeroplanes, and found their relaxation in the cinema and the wireless. I knew that I stood apart from them and would never find contentment among them, whereas I could find it among these Bedu, although I should never be one of them.

A large number of Bait Kathir and other tribesmen camped with us that night at Al Ain. Musallim was among them, having come to see us off. Rather apprehensively I asked bin Kalut how many of these people were going with us to Mukalla. He reassured me by saying that there would be only thirty Rashid, as well as my own party and *rabias* from the Bait Khawar, Mahra, and Manahil. We then divided up the flour, rice, sugar, tea, and coffee, which I had provided, and also the three camel-loads of Omani dates given to me by the Sultan. I hoped that we should have plenty of food even if we travelled slowly and took two months to reach Mukalla. I was tired of being hungry.

Bin Kalut was a striking person. Short, thick-set, and immensely powerful, his body was heavy with old age, so that he moved with difficulty, and rose to his feet only with a laboured effort and after many grunted invocations of the Almighty. His speech, movements, and gestures were very deliberate. He had a broad rugged face and a jutting nose, steady eyes, a wide mouth, and a heavy grey beard, and he was completely bald. He seldom spoke, but I noticed that when he did no one argued. His son Muhammad, who was half-brother, through his mother, to Salim bin Kabina, was with him; a young man, heavily-built like his father, amiable but rather ineffective. There were many Rashid here who had been with me the year before. Musallim bin al Kamam was among them; a lean middle-aged man with a quick receptive mind and a relentless spirit which drove him so that he was the most widely travelled of the Rashid, and the most intelligent. I had liked him greatly when we had been together, and had found him an amusing companion, quick to tell me anything that he thought might interest me. He was very self-controlled and I never heard him raise his voice. Unfortunately he could not travel with me now. A year before, he had concluded a two-year truce with the Dahm which this last raid had violated. Now he was going to demand the return of the Rashid camels that had been lifted.

Until recently, the Saar who live on the plateau to the north of the Hadhramaut had been the main enemy of the Rashid, the Bait Kathir, and the Manahil, but during recent years the Dahm and Abida from the Yemen had taken their place as the most formidable raiders in the southern desert. These two tribes were not Bedu but villagers living in the Yemen foothills. It was an inversion of the usual role that the Bedu raided the settled tribes, and bin al Kamam and others of the Rashid assured me that the Yemen authorities in the Jauf supplied these raiders with the arms and ammunition which gave them their superiority over the desert tribes. There seemed to be little doubt that the Yemen government encouraged these raids in order to embarrass the Aden government by increasing the chaos in the desert north of the Hadhramaut.

In 1945 a large force of Manahil under the leadership of bin Duailan, who was nicknamed al Bis or 'The Cat', had set out to raid the Dahm. Unfortunately they had not reached the Dahm villages, but instead had attacked an encampment of the Yam, had killed several of that tribe and lifted a large number of their camels. The Yam were Bedu, owing allegiance to Ibn Saud, and their home-lands were near Najran. When they were attacked they were grazing their herds in the desert on the Yemen border. This was not the first time that the Yam had suffered from raiders from the Eastern Aden Protectorate, who had intended to attack the Dahm, but had been diverted by the prospect of easier loot encountered on the way. When I was in Jidda in the summer of 1945 the British Ambassador had questioned me about these raids and had told me that Ibn Saud had threatened to loose his tribes on the Hadhramaut if they continued.

Bin al Kamam's proposal to go to the Dahm and demand the return of the Rashid camels was opposed by many of the tribe who wanted war. After dinner an argument about this started among the Arabs who were sitting with me. The discussion, like most Bedu discussions, quickly became heated and the raised voices drew other people over to us. More than a hundred tribesmen from the Rashid, Bait Kathir, Mahra, and Manahil were camped around us that night, and soon they were all collected round our fire. They belonged to tribes which had suffered from Dahm raids. The moon was nearly full, so that I could see them clearly as they sat there, crowded together with their rifles in their hands. Behind them the cliffs were white in the moonlight, and above were the wooded slopes of the Qarra mountains. All around us were the couched camels and the dying light of many fires. Bin Kabina and bin Anauf moved round pouring out coffee for each man in turn. I could sense the expect-

ancy which is always present when Bedu contemplate a raid. I knew
that many of them were already picturing the looted camels which
would make them rich.

Bin al Kamam argued that the Dahm were tribesmen and would
be bound to return camels taken during a truce. He spoke slowly,
poking at the ground with his camel-stick. There were mutters of
'Yes, by God!' and 'True! True!' Someone interrupted him, saying
that the Dahm were faithless, worse even than the Saar. Another
man spoke, trying by raising his voice to hold the attention of the
crowd, but his words were lost in the growing din. Suddenly an
excited Rashid, whose name I did not know, sprang to his feet,
hurled his head-cloth on the ground, and shouted, '*Ba Rashud*, if
twenty men will come with me I will go and fetch the two camels
they have taken from me. What is more, by God, I will bring back
a hundred Dahm camels as well!' He turned on bin al Kamam and
asked furiously, 'What is the good of your negotiations? You made
a truce for the Rashid, and the Dahm immediately broke it. The
only result of your truce was that we were caught unprepared. How
many camels have the Rashid lost? The Dahm are utterly faithless.
God's curse on them! Our rifles should be our answer to this raid.
Let the rifles speak. Listen to me, you people. Get together and
raid. God almighty, are the Rashid women thus to be harried by
the Dahm? It would be a disgrace to negotiate now.'

Everyone was shouting, and I could hardly make out a word.
Old one-eyed Abdullah was arguing furiously with a group of
Mahra, while he hammered the ground with his stick. Bin Mautlauq
was shouting for war, abetted by a handsome boy in a blue loin-
cloth. Bin Kabina had stopped pouring out coffee and was gesticulating with the pot. Occasionally one man commanded attention for
a while, and then the strained silence was broken only by a single
urgent voice, but inevitably someone else joined in and the two
voices rose, the one against the other, until both were lost in the
returning noise. I noticed a little man sitting opposite me who was
insistent that the tribes should unite and inflict a really crushing
defeat on the Dahm. His clothes were stained and torn, but he
wore a large silver-hilted dagger set with cornelians and a belt filled

with cartridges, and he held a brass-bound Martini rifle between his knees. He had very bright eyes, and all his movements were jerky. He looked rather like an assertive sparrow, but I noticed that the others listened carefully to everything he said. I asked bin Kabina who he was, and he answered, 'Don't you know him? He is bin Duailan, "The Cat".' I looked at him again with interest, for bin Duailan was the most famous raider in southern Arabia. Eight months later he was to die on the Yemen border, surrounded by the men he had killed in his last and most desperate fight, which plunged the desert into war. Bin al Kamam made a joke which I could not catch, and everyone nearby laughed; and then bin Kalut, who had been sitting silent and unmoved, spoke in his deep voice. 'Let bin al Kamam go to the Dahm and demand the return of the Rashid camels. If they hand them over the Rashid will keep the truce. If they refuse we will collect a force and raid them after we have taken Umbarak to Mukalla.' The decision seemed to have been made as far as the Rashid were concerned.

Next day we crossed the Kismim pass and camped once more by the pool of Aiyun. Bin Kabina was accompanied by the boy I had noticed the night before. They were about the same age. This boy was dressed only in a length of blue cloth, which he wore wrapped round his waist with one tasselled end thrown over his right shoulder, and his dark hair fell like a mane about his shoulders. He had a face of classic beauty, pensive and rather sad in repose, but which lit up when he smiled, like a pool touched by the sun. Antinous must have looked like this, I thought, when Hadrian first saw him in the Phrygian woods. The boy moved with effortless grace, walking as women walk who have carried vessels on their heads since childhood. A stranger might have thought that his smooth, pliant body would never bear the rigours of desert life, but I knew how deceptively enduring were these Bedu boys who looked like girls. He told me that his name was Salim bin Ghabaisha and he asked me to take him with us. Bin Kabina urged me to let him join us, saying that he was the best shot in the tribe and that he was as good a hunter as Musallim, so that if he was with us we should feed every day on meat, for there were many ibex and gazelle in the country ahead of us. He added, 'He is my friend. Let him come with us for my sake. The two of us will go with you wherever you want. We will always be your men.' I told bin Ghabaisha that he could come, and later when we camped I gave him one of my spare rifles to use until we reached Mukalla. Next morning he went off at dawn to hunt for ibex and he came back in the evening carrying across his shoulders a large ram which he had shot. I met few good hunters among the Bedu – only an occasional one of them possessed the necessary enthusiasm – but bin Ghabaisha was one of these, and Musallim bin Tafl was another.

After dinner bin Kabina got up from beside me, saying that he was going to fetch his camel. Suddenly someone called out, 'Bin Kabina has fallen down.' I looked round and saw him lying on the sand. He was unconscious when I reached him. His pulse was very feeble and his body cold; he was breathing hoarsely. I carried him to the fire and piled blankets on him to warm him. I then tried to pour a little brandy down his throat but he could not swallow. Gradually his breathing became easier and his body a little warmer, but he did not recover consciousness. I sat beside him hour after hour wondering miserably if he was going to die. I remembered how I had first met him in the Wadi Mitan, how he had come to Shisur to join me, how he had unhesitatingly remained with me at Ramlat al Ghafa when the Bait Kathir had deserted me. I remembered his happiness when I gave him his rifle, and I knew that whenever I thought of the past months I should be thinking of him, for he had shared everything with me, even my doubts and difficulties. I remembered with bitter regret how I had sometimes vented my ill-temper on him to ease the strain under which I lived, and how he had always been good-tempered and very patient. The others crowded round and discussed the chances of his dying, until I could scarcely bear it; and then someone asked where we were going tomorrow and I said that there would be no tomorrow if bin Kabina died. Hours later as I lay beside him I felt him relax and knew that he was sleeping and was no longer unconscious. He woke at dawn and at first could hear but could not speak, and signed to me that his chest was hurting. By midday he could speak and in the evening he was all right again. The Rashid gathered round him, changing incantations and firing off their rifles; and then sprinkled flour, coffee, and sugar in the stream-bed to appease the spirits which they had exorcized. Later they slaughtered a goat, sprinkled him with its blood, and declared him cured. I have often wondered what was wrong with him and can only think it was some kind of fit.

Next day we travelled slowly to Mudhail, where a trickle of water seeped out from beneath a low cliff, but the trunks of fifty dead palms proved that this water had been more abundant in the past. We camped under some low cliffs where an overhang gave us a little shade. Here I picked up a small, well-burnished, neolithic axe-head, similar to one I had been given by a Kathir who had told me that he had found it on the Jarbib plain. Both the axes were made of jade, which is unknown in Arabia.

There were two Muslim tombs in the valley, fifteen feet square and seven feet high, crowned with plaster-covered domes. My companions could tell me nothing of these tombs except that someone called Sheikh Saad was buried there, and this was confirmed by a well-executed Arabic inscription on the stele of one of the three graves inside the tombs, but unfortunately his father's name was obliterated. One section of the Bait al Sheikh, a religious tribe, is called the Bait Sheikh Saad. Near the tombs was a small graveyard, no longer in use because of the Bedu belief that the ancient dead would not tolerate intrusion. There were many trilithon monuments in the valley and tumuli on the nearby hills.

My companions had already told me about buildings and 'writings' at Mudhail. I had hoped I might discover another Petra, and had at any rate expected to find something older and more interesting than these Islamic tombs. The civilizations of southern Arabia had been situated farther to the west, but for fifteen hundred years they had depended for their prosperity on frankincense gathered on the mountains of Dhaufar. I knew that the best frankincense was collected on the northern slopes of this mountain and that the gum from the other side of the mountain was of poor quality. Near Aiyun I had seen a grove of brittle bushes with small crumpled leaves which the Arabs told me produced frankincense, but there seemed to be few of these groves. I saw only this one.

It seems strange that there are so few ruins on the northern side of the mountain, considering the great length of time during which this region was of vital importance to the successive civilizations of southern Arabia. I had expected to find the remains of forts or block-houses which had been made to defend these priceless groves against attack from the desert. But apart from crude tumble-down *sangars* of indeterminate age above many of the wells, it was only at Andhur that I found the ruins of a well-constructed building. This, which was on a ridge above the palm grove, seemed to have been a storehouse rather than a fort. The walls were built of cut stones set in mortar, and were half buried in rubble. Along the top of the low outer wall were some mortar-lined stone troughs, about five feet in length and two feet in width and depth, similar to others which I had seen among the ruins near Salala. I had already been told of the buildings at Mudhail and the ruins at Andhur before I visited them; I never heard of any others.

On my way back from the tombs I saw a young man sitting under the cliff near our camping-place. I noticed that his wrists were shackled with a short length of heavy chain. I greeted him, but he did not reply, though he turned his head and looked at me. He had a striking face, but there was no intelligence in his eyes. His hair was long and matted, and the rag that he wore did not cover him. He stood up, stretched his arms above his head, yawned, and then walked away muttering to himself. I asked bin Kabina who he was and he told me that he was Salim bin Ghabaisha's brother, and that he had lost his reason three years earlier; before this happened he had been one of the friendliest boys in the tribe. I asked why he was shackled, and bin Kabina answered that two years ago he had killed a boy who had been his special friend by smashing in his skull with a rock while he slept. The dead boy's family had accepted blood-money.

Bin Ghabaisha returned later carrying a buck which he had shot. Bin Kabina told him that his brother had turned up, and without a word he went off to find him, taking a dish of dates.

Later he came back depressed and unhappy. He took me aside and said: 'Have you no medicine, Umbarak, that will cure my brother? I beseech you if you have to give it to me. I loved my brother. We used to be inseparable. We did everything together; we went everywhere together. I was like his shadow. Now he hardly knows me. He wanders round like an animal and is less responsive to me than a camel. Give me medicine to cure him, Umbarak, and all that I have is yours.' I told him sadly, 'I have no medicine that will do your brother any good. Lies are no use to you. Only God can cure him.' He answered resignedly, 'The praise be to God.'

We travelled slowly, for I was in no hurry to reach Mukalla. After the slogging effort of the past months it was sheer enjoyment to dawdle along, on the watch, almost from the moment when we started, for somewhere to stop again. We would choose a spot in the cool shadow of a cliff, or else under some trees, where the tracery of branches threw a net of shade across the sand. There we would remain for the rest of the day or move on again in the evening, as the fancy took us. We had plenty of food and water, and there was acacia to feed our camels. Almost daily bin Ghabaisha shot ibex or gazelle, and then bin Kabina cooked the meals of which he and I had dreamt when we had starved together in the sands.

The intimacy which had characterized our small party on that journey was impossible in these crowded camps. I was especially sorry that I never really got to know bin Duailan, the famous Cat, as he fed with another group. Sometimes he came over to us, bearing a battered brass coffee-pot. He would carefully unwrap from a dirty rag a small cracked cup, dark with stains, and serve us with coffee, explaining to me with a twinkle that he was the only person in camp who knew how to make it properly. He would then squat down and sooner or later lead the conversation round to rifles, expressing the hope that I would give him a service .303. How, he would ask, could a man raid effectively armed only with an old single-shot Martini? I would counter by saying that he at least seemed to have managed very successfully.

We remained for three days at Habarut, where families of Mahra watered their camels at the shallow wells beside the tangled palm groves. At dawn, on our first day there, I heard one Rashid ask another, as they washed before they prayed, 'Is he dead yet?' and the other answered, 'No, not yet, but he soon will be.' Startled, I sat up and asked, 'Who is dying?' and one of them said, 'The old Afar who is travelling with us. He fell down when he got up to pray. He is over there.' I knew the man; he came from the east, from somewhere near the Wadi al Amairi, and had attached himself to us two days before, for the food and protection which we afforded him whilst he travelled in our company. The night before, bin Kabina had told me that this man was sick, and had shown me where he lay behind a rock, a desiccated bundle of skin and bones, shivering under the goatskin which he had wrapped about his head and shoulders. I had given him some tablets, and he had clasped my hand and murmured a blessing, grateful for this light attention in an indifferent world. Now he lay where he had fallen, and no one heeded him. I could not feel his pulse. I called to bin Kabina, and together we lifted him on to a rug and covered him with blankets; the others took no notice, being either busy with their prayers or frankly indifferent. We then lit a fire beside him and I poured some brandy down his throat. He spluttered and recovered consciousness. I gave him more brandy and soon he was a little tipsy from the forbidden spirits. Three days later he parted from us, quite recovered.

This incident impressed upon me the Bedu's indifference to human life. The man was sick and if God ordered it he would die. He was a stranger who came from a tribe unrelated to theirs. None of them felt an interest because he was a human being like themselves. His death would in no way affect them. Yet their code demanded that, however unwanted he might be, they should fight in his defence if he were attacked whilst with them.

There was a constant passage of visitors to our camping place while we were at Habarut. A woman came over to us and I recognized her as Nura, whom I had met the year before. Her three small children were with her; only the eldest one, aged about nine, wore any clothes. She told me that they were camped four miles away, and that the children had insisted on coming to see me again when they heard I was here. I gave the children dates and sugar to eat, while I talked to Nura. She was unveiled, and like most of the women in this part of Arabia was dressed in dark blue. She had a strong, square, weather-beaten face, and wore a silver ring through her right nostril. I thought she was surprisingly old to have three small children. She talked in a rather husky voice, telling me how she was going down to Ghaidat al Mahra on the coast to get a load of sardines. As bin Ghabaisha had shot an ibex we had meat and soup for lunch. The children fed with us, but Nura was given a dish by herself. Arabs will not feed with women. Later, however, she returned and, sitting a little back from the circle, was given coffee and tea which she drank with the rest of us.

The general belief among the English people that Arab women are kept shut up is true of many of the women in the towns, but not among the tribes. Not only is it impossible for a man to shut up his wife when he is living under a tree, or in a tent which is always open on one side, but he requires her to work, to fetch water and firewood, and to herd the goats. If a woman thinks she is being neglected or ill-treated by her husband she can easily run away to her father or brother. Her husband has then to follow her and try to persuade her to come back. Her family will certainly take her part, insisting that she has been monstrously ill-treated. In the end the husband will probably have to give her a present before he can induce her to return. Wives cannot divorce their husbands, but the husband may agree to divorce his wife if she has refused to live with him, on condition that he recovers the two or three camels which he gave as the bride-price. If, however, he divorces her of his own accord he does not get back these camels.

In the evening someone mentioned Nura. I asked if her husband was dead, and al Auf said, 'She has no husband. The children are bastards.' When I expressed my surprise he said that bin Alia, who was one of our party, was also 'a son of unlawfulness'. I asked if there was any slur attached to being a bastard, and bin Kabina said, 'No. It is not the child's fault,' and added jokingly, 'Next time, Umbarak, you see a girl that pleases you, sit down next to her in the dark, push your camel-stick through the sand until it is underneath her, and then turn it over until the crook presses against her. If she gets up, gives you an indignant look, and marches off, you will know that you are wasting your time. If she stays where she is, you can meet her next day when she is herding the goats.' I said, 'If it is as easy as all that there must be plenty of bastards,' and someone answered, 'Not among the Rashid, but the Humum near Mukalla have a whole section composed entirely of bastards.'

I knew that elsewhere in the Arab world a girl who is immoral, or indeed in many places even if she is only suspected of immorality, will be killed by her relatives in order to protect the family honour. An Englishman told me of a tragic case that occurred on the Lower Euphrates while he was serving there as a Political Officer after the First World War. An Arab boy and his sister, who were orphans, lived in a tent outside his house and were close friends of his. One day his servants rushed into his house and told him that the boy had stabbed his sister and that she was calling for the Englishman. He went to their tent where the girl was lying fatally wounded. She said, 'I am dying and I have a last request to make of you.' He asked her what it was, and she said, 'Grant it before I ask you.' The Englishman hesitated, and the girl became so upset that he granted her request. She said, 'Tell my brother that I was innocent and that I never did anything to shame him. I swear this as I die. But you have promised me my request and you are not to punish him, for I know that I was talked about and by our custom he did right to kill me.' Later, when the Englishman told the tribal sheikhs what had happened, they all said, 'But of course the boy was right to kill her. She brought shame upon her family because she was talked about.' I told my companions this story, and they shook their heads, and old bin Kalut said it was barbarous to kill a girl even if she had been immoral, and that among them such things would never happen.

From Habarut we climbed up on to the Daru plateau, a featureless gravel plain which drains to the sea. We came across some crude shelters with walls of rock and roofs of branches overlaid with earth and supported on pillars of piled stones. But they were all empty,

since seven rainless years had driven the Bait Khawar down into
the valley of the Kidyut, which starts here as a deep sheer-sided
canyon. I climbed down into this with some of my companions,
while the others took the camels round by an easier route. A small
spring trickled out from among the limestone slabs which had fallen
from the precipices above. Some Mahra were watering camels and
filling goatskins. One of their women had stained her face green,
and another had blue and green stripes painted down her nose and
chin, and across her cheeks. The effect was not only weird but
repulsive. I was on the point of suggesting to bin Kabina that both
of them would be more alluring if they were veiled, when a small
boy about ten years old darted over to us. He was Said, bin Kabina's
brother. He had large sparkling eyes, very white teeth, and a face
as fresh as a half-opened flower. He was trying desperately to be
dignified, but could not hide his excitement. He assured me at once
that he was coming with us, and pointed to the camel which I had
given to bin Kabina the year before, saying, 'There is my mount.'
I asked him where his rifle was and he waved his stick and said that
this would have to do unless I gave him one. Suddenly we heard
many voices shouting on the cliff above us. A party of Bait Khawar
were refusing passage to our camels, saying that the Christian might
not pass through their valley. A scuffle had started, and it looked
as if there might be a fight, until our *rabia* drove his tribesmen
back, and the camels came lurching down the steep path to join us
in the valley-bottom. Said said scornfully, 'They are only Bait
Khawar,' and went on to tell me how he had heard that we should
pass this way and had ridden for two days to meet us. I asked him
who would look after his mother and sister if he came with us to
Mukalla, and he assured me that they were with his uncle and that
they would be all right without him. I decided to let him come and
he trotted happily off to tell bin Kabina.

A large, vociferous, but badly-armed crowd of Bait Khawar had
collected and they insisted that I could not pass down the valley
unless I paid them money. I refused, saying that I had a *rabia* and
was entitled to pass, but they went on shouting that I must give
them money if I wished to see their valley. I knew that there would

be no end to our troubles if I once paid blackmail. I have never done so and had no intention of doing so now. In the Western Aden Protectorate European travellers are constantly held up, since the tribes have learnt that they can extort money from them. Our *rabia*, an old man with tired faded eyes and a straggling white beard, said furiously that he would take me through the valley if I wished to go in defiance of his whole tribe, since they had no right to stop us. However, the gathering broke up without reaching an agreement. Many of the Bait Khawar who had been defying us a few minutes earlier came over to our camping place to chat with us and give us their news.

That evening we discussed what we should do. The general opinion was that the Bait Khawar were bluffing, since they were defying tribal custom and had no reason for their behaviour except avarice, but bin Kalut, al Auf, and bin Duailan and others asked me how much it would matter if we followed the path along the top of the cliffs. This was the route we had indeed originally planned to take, but the Rashid had wished to travel down the valley, where they thought that there would be better grazing for their camels. Bin Kalut pointed out that if some fool did shoot at us and hit anyone it would start a war between tribes who were traditionally allied. I willingly agreed to take the top road, which indeed suited me better, since, for the purpose of mapping, I should overlook the valley and the country on both sides of it. In any case, the last thing I wished to do was to cause trouble among the tribes. I knew that my freedom of movement in the desert depended on my reputation for harming no one.

We descended into the valley again where it joins the Mahrat to form the Jiza. There were palm groves and small settlements, with a little cultivation in all these valleys. The Jiza bends in a great arc, draining the greater part of the Mahra country, before it finally enters the sea near Ghaidat, the largest of the Mahra villages. All this country was completely unmapped, but I was now able to fix its general outlines. My companions wished to travel due west to the Masila, which is the name of the lower reaches of the Wadi al Hadhramaut, but the Gumsait Mahra refused to let us pass. They collected in our camp in the evening and explained that they were prepared to take me through their country, provided that I hired their camels and sent the Rashid who were with me back to their homes. The Mahra are Ghafaris, and are usually on terms of armed neutrality with the Rashid and Bait Kathir. Since we had no *rabia* from their section their attitude seemed to me reasonable, but I had no intention of parting with the Rashid. Sulaim, our Mahra *rabia*, belonged to the Amarjid, and he said that he could frank us through the Mahra tribes along the upper Mahrat as far as the watershed, beyond which lay the country of the Manahil. This route suited me better than the other, since by following it I should be able to fix the watershed as far as the Masila.

We were held up again in the Mahrat, this time by the Amarjid, who had probably heard that we had been turned back by the Gumsait. They, too, offered to take me on provided I sent back the Rashid. I eventually agreed to engage five of them to accompany us for two days. A little later one of them came back and said that, as they had no animals here with which to feast us, they would forgo the payment of these men. I then gave them an equivalent sum as a present and everyone was satisfied.

Fifteen years earlier, watching the coronation of Haile Selassie as King of Kings of Ethiopia, I had been fascinated by the continuity, however tenuous, which linked that ceremony with Solomon and Sheba. Now watching these half-naked, indigo-smeared figures, sitting beneath the dying palms in the Wadi Jiza, discussing our movements in a language which had once been spoken by Minaeans, Sabaeans, and Himyarites, I realized that here was a link with the past even older and more authentic, for scholars believe that the Mahra are descended from the ancient Habasha, who colonized Ethiopia as long ago as the first millennium BC and gave their name to the Abyssinians. I myself had discovered the year before a mountain called Jabal Habashiya which was only fifty miles to the west of our present camp.

Three days later we crossed the watershed between the wadis flowing to the north and to the south, a flat rocky plateau about a quarter of a mile across. To the south the country was very broken and there were many deep gorges, while to the north a number of broad valleys, whose beds were of gravel and hard sand, started abruptly from the foot of the escarpment. I watched an eagle chasing a gazelle and a little later saw two ibex. These were very common both here and on the cliffs above the Mahrat.

We arrived at Dahal well three days later. The water, which stank of sulphur, was at the end of a tunnel through the limestone rock and was difficult to reach. While we were watering the camels bin Duailan told us that a wolf had killed two small boys a few months earlier. Their father had left them at the well with a load of sardines which he had brought up from the coast, saying that he would come back next day. During the night the wolf drove them off the sardines, some of which it ate. When some Manahil turned up in the morning the children told them what had happened, but as these Manahil were going down to the coast they left the children at the well, confident that their father would shortly return. The father did not arrive until the following day, and then he found both his sons dead and partly eaten.

In the afternoon a small party of Manahil turned up with some goats. They warned us that two hundred and fifty Dahm were raiding the country ahead of us, and had killed seven Manahil in one place and seven or eight Awamir elsewhere. They said that they themselves intended to seek refuge among the Mahra. Beyond Dahal the land was empty; everyone had fled, either across the watershed or down into the valley of the Masila, which it took us three more days to reach. The country was very broken, and the only possible route for our camels was along the bottom of deep canyons, which cut the limestone plateau into blocks. We pushed scouts out ahead when we were travelling, and posted sentries whenever we stopped, for we were well aware what would happen to us if we were trapped by the Dahm in the bottom of one of these sheer-sided gorges.

When we reached the shrine of Nabi Hud in the Masila, we found many Manahil collected there with their camels, sheep, and goats. They told us that one party of raiders, believed to be seventy strong, had surprised an encampment of six Manahil in the nearby

Wadi Hun. One of them had escaped, but no one knew what happened to the others. They also said that another and much larger force was raiding in the steppes to the north. Eighty Manahil had gone off up the Wadi Hun in pursuit.

We decided to move up the valley of the Masila to the village of Fughama, where we were told that bin Tanas, the Manahil Sheikh, was collecting his fighting-men. Bin Duailan went on ahead to tell him that we were coming, and that we would join him in an attack upon the Dahm if he could find out where they were. I had been uncertain whether the Rashid would agree to this, since they were still nominally at peace with the Dahm, but they said at once that, acting under my orders, they would consider themselves to be *askar*, or soldiers, not bound by tribal custom.

At Fughama there were only women and children and one old man, who told us that bin Tanas was farther up the valley, and that bin Duailan had gone on to find him. We camped near the village, among some tamarisk shrubs beside a stream fifteen feet wide, flowing under a high silt bank. Soon after sunset a man arrived who said that raiders had entered the Masila above Nabi Hud. A little later we heard three shots in rapid succession down the valley. We had already saddled our camels and posted sentries, and bin Kalut now told the Rashid to put out the fires. We sat in the dark beside our camels. Bin Kabina, his brother Said, and bin Ghabaisha were close beside me. Bin Ghabaisha was busy filling his cartridge belt from the spare ammunition in my saddle-bags. I whispered to them not to get separated from me if we were attacked. It was very dark and very quiet. I could hear the belching of the camels as they brought up the cud, the grinding of their teeth as they chewed it. A large bird, probably an owl, flew about over our heads. Al Auf had taken five other Rashid down the valley to scout. He came back and said that they could hear no movement in the valley. As he was convinced that the Dahm would not come on through unknown country in the dark, he told us to leave the camels saddled and sentries posted, and to be on the watch at dawn. I crawled into my sleeping-bag. Bin Kabina said, 'God help you if you are caught in that. You will be knifed before you can get out of it,' but I bet him that I would be out of it before he could even draw his dagger.

It was cold and cheerless at dawn. I told bin Kabina and bin Anauf to make coffee and tea, for we had not eaten the night before. Al Auf had gone down the valley again while it was still dark. Later he came back and told us that he had seen no sign of the raiders. Shortly afterwards bin Tanas and bin Duailan arrived with about thirty other Manahil. The Dahm had evidently turned north. Later the pursuit party arrived and confirmed this. They had come back, since they were too few to take on the Dahm, who were more than two hundred strong. Bin Duailan urged us to join the Manahil in pursuit even if it took us to the Yemen, but the Rashid refused, saying their camels were tired. I was glad of this, for if they had agreed it would have been difficult for me to refuse. I could imagine the protests which would arrive in Aden from the Yemen government if I entered their country with a raiding party.

We stayed there for another day, in case there was any more news of the raiders, and on 14 April we started for Mukalla, the journey's end that I had no desire to reach. Dawdling away the days, we mounted through narrow, twisting gorges, among piles of fallen rock, to the large village and palm groves of Ghail ba Yamin. We crossed the stony blackened table land, known to the Arabs as al Jaul, descended to the coast near Shihr, and arrived at Mukalla on 1 May.

Sheppard, who was the Resident in Mukalla, arranged for the Arabs who were with me to stay in the Beduin Legion camp on the outskirts of the town. I left them there and went down to the Residency to get a bath and to change into the clothes which had arrived from Salala. Later, having washed, shaved off my beard, and put on European clothes, I went back to the camp. My party was in a large building. As I approached, bin Anauf called out, 'There is a Christian coming.' Realizing that he had not recognized me, I went to the door and stood there looking uncertain. Bin Turkia spoke to me and I answered in English. Someone said, 'Bring him in'; another person told them to make coffee, and someone else asked, 'Do the Christians drink coffee?' They spread a rug for me and signed to me to sit down. Bin Kabina, bin Ghabaisha, al Auf,

Mabhkaut, and old bin Kalut were all there looking at me. Suddenly bin Kabina said, 'By God, it is Umbarak!' and seized me by the shoulders with playful violence. I had not realized I looked so different. I said, 'How would you like me to travel with you dressed like this?' and they said, 'No one would go with you like that. You look like a Christian.'

Perhaps the next four days eased the final parting. Until the Rashid left, some of them were nearly always with me. They made themselves free of the Residency, sitting or sleeping in my room throughout the day, eager to accompany me wherever I went, for none of them had been here before. It was the largest town most of them had ever seen. They strolled with me through the streets hand in hand, as is usual with Arab friends, but I was slightly uncomfortable, having reacquired my inhibitions with my trousers. In any case I sensed that the old familiarity between us was impaired. I was most conscious of the change when I visited their camp, where I was received as a visitor. By shaving off my beard, changing my clothes, moving into a house, and using the gadgets which our civilization provided, I had estranged myself from them. I thought ruefully that the effect on me would have been much the same if one of them, after adapting himself to English ways and living with me in London, had suddenly appeared in Arab clothes and insisted on eating with his fingers.

On his last evening in Mukalla, bin Kabina showed me what he had bought – a load of grain, two pounds of coffee-beans, two cooking-pots, three water-skins, a length of rope, a ball of string, two packing needles, a dozen boxes of matches, four yards of dark blue cloth for his mother, a loin-cloth for himself, and a penknife. I had watched him wandering about the bazaar, inspecting the bales of cloth, the coats, shirts, rugs, and blankets which were displayed in the successive stalls. Now that he had both the opportunity and the money I had hoped he would buy himself some protection against the cold. I shrank from the thought of him lying naked on the sands during the winter nights, and I knew that it might be years before he visited a town again. When I suggested that he should have bought some blankets, he said, 'Camels are what I want. They are what matter. I can buy three more with the money which you have given me. With Qamaiqam, and the camel I bought in Salala, and the one you gave me last year I shall have six. Now I am rich. I am used to hardship. Cold won't hurt me. I am a Bedu.'

TEN

Preparations for a Second Crossing

I return to Arabia with the intention of crossing the
Western Sands. Starting from the Hadhramaut I
make a journey through the country of the Saar
while waiting for my Rashid companions to arrive.
After they have joined me we make ready at
Manwakh well.

From Mukalla I went to the Hajaz, and travelled there for
three months, going as far as Najran in the country of the
Yam, on the north-western edge of the Empty Quarter. Then
I returned to London.

In deserts, however arid, I have never felt homesick for green
fields and woods in spring, but now that I was in England I longed
with an ache that was almost physical to be back in Arabia. The
Locust Control Centre offered me a new job supervising the
destruction of locusts in the Hajaz, with a good salary, all expenses
paid, and the prospect of permanent employment. But it was not
enough. I wanted the wide emptiness of the sands, the fascination
of unknown country, and the company of the Rashid.

The Western Sands offered the challenge which I required in
order to find a purpose for another journey. To cross them would
be to complete the exploration of the Empty Quarter. Two years
earlier I had thought of doing this journey. King Ibn Saud had
however emphatically refused permission when our Ambassador
had asked for it – and, in any case, it had been too late in the season
to go there when I reached the Hadhramaut from Dhaufar. Now

I made up my mind to make this crossing. I should be defying the King, but I hoped that I should be able to water at some well on the far side of the sands and then slip away unobserved. I was certain that some of the Rashid would accompany me, and with them I should have the freedom of the desert. I therefore wired to Sheppard at Mukalla asking him to send a messenger to bin Kabina at Habarut telling him, bin al Kamam, and bin Ghabaisha to meet me in the Hadhramaut at the time of the new moon in November. If I kept the party small I could pay for the journey with the money I had saved. The future could take care of itself.

I arrived in Mukalla on 3 November and, after staying for a few days with Sheppard and collecting the rifles and ammunition which I had left with him the year before, I went up to Saiwun where I stayed with Watts, the Political Officer. Watts was having trouble with the Manahil. Some of them, led by my old friend bin Duailan, 'The Cat', had recently surprised two government posts in the Hadhramaut and captured a large number of rifles and much ammunition. One Bedu legionary had been killed. Since bin Duailan refused to hand back the rifles, Watts had forbidden any of the Manahil to come into the towns.

As there was no news of bin Kabina and the others, I decided to travel for a fortnight in the Saar country before I started on my journey across the Sands, in order to link up the traverses which I had made in southern Arabia, between the Halfain and the Hadhramaut, with Philby's work in 1936 along the Yemen border. The Saar, a large and powerful tribe, have been aptly described as 'the wolves of the desert'. They were hated and feared by all the south Arabian desert tribes, whom they harried unmercifully, raiding as far eastward as Mughshin and the Jaddat al Harasis, and northwards to the Yam, the Dawasir, and the Murra. Boscawen had hunted oryx in their country in 1931, and Ingrams paid a cursory visit to the edge of their territory in 1934; otherwise no Englishman had been there.

Watts found in Shibam two Saar who said they would take me into their country. They had two camels with them, both of which were bulls, for the Saar, like the Humum, own large numbers of bull camels which they hire for carrying goods to towns in the Hadhramaut. One of them, called Salim, was a lively little man in a blue loin-cloth. The other was tall and was called Ahmad. He was dressed in a white shirt, rather short for him, and his dour appearance belied a friendly spirit. Both were armed with Martini rifles.

We went up to Raidat al Saar, a shallow valley about two hundred yards across, running through a barren limestone plateau. On the low cliffs which enclosed it were stone buildings and watch-towers, many of them empty. Ahmad told me that their inhabitants had died in the great famine in 1943. The terraced valley was green with crops of sorghum and beans, planted on floods in July; and there were clumps of date palms and many *ilb* trees. Raidat is the heart of the Saar country, but lacks permanent water. The inhabitants had recently tried to dig a well but had abandoned it when they failed to find water at sixty feet. In the Saar country there are only two permanent wells, one at Manwakh about 180 feet deep, and the other at Zamakh, which they told me was 240 feet deep.

The Saar, many of whom were collected in the Raidat to harvest the crops, had heard of me as a result of my wanderings in southern Arabia and welcomed me with great friendliness. I found them a pleasant, virile people, without the corroding avarice of the Bait Kathir. Other tribes call them treacherous, but this is probably a slander inspired by dislike. However, their reputation for godlessness is well merited in Arab eyes, since they neither fast nor pray, saying that the prophet Muhammad gave their forefathers a dispensation from both. Like all the southern Bedu, they are a small, lightly-built race. A few wore rags round their heads but most of them were bareheaded; they were dressed only in loin-cloths, many of which were dyed with indigo. All the men and most of the boys wore daggers and nearly everyone carried a rifle.

Leaving the Raidat we passed the grave of a woman saint known as Walia Riqaiya. This place was a sanctuary whose limits, about a hundred yards round the tomb, were marked by cairns of whitened stones. Salim and Ahmad walked round the grave, kissed their right hands after touching all three of the upright stones, and then rubbed dust on their foreheads. We left some coffee-beans in a stone shelter beside the tomb. There are many shrines in this country, and it is the custom for any passer-by who can do so to leave an offering of coffee. Other travellers who are weary can then use this offering, and the necessary utensils are kept inside the shrine. The Saar generally flavour their coffee strongly with ginger. When they serve it they fill the cup, which is usually large and made of local earthenware, but the man to whom the cup is handed is expected to take only a few sips and then hand it back to the server, who fills it up again and hands it to the next person.

We visited the well at Manwakh, in the Aiwat al Saar which drains to the sands and of which the Raidat is a tributary. I was glad to have a look at this well, knowing that I must start my journey across the Empty Quarter either from it or from Zamakh. We found some Saar watering camels and goats. The water was fresh and I noticed that they mixed rock-salt in it before watering their camels. They raised the water by hand, the long ropes of palmetto fibre running over pulleys attached to a wooden scaffolding round the well. The southern Bedu do not use camels to draw the well-ropes, as is done on the deep wells in the Najd, although villagers in the Hadhramaut use camels and oxen to raise the trip-buckets from which they water their cultivations. After they had finished watering they took their ropes, pulleys, and leather watering-troughs away with them. There was a very lovely girl working with the others on the well. Her hair was braided, except where it was cut in a fringe across her forehead, and fell in a curtain of small plaits round her neck. She wore various silver ornaments and several necklaces, some of large cornelians, others of small white beads. Round her waist she had half a dozen silver chains, and above them her sleeveless blue tunic gaped open to show small firm breasts. She was very fair. When she saw I was trying to take a photograph of her she screwed up her face and stuck out her tongue at me. Salim, thinking to help me, had told her not to move and explained what I was doing. During the following days both he and Ahmad chaffed me whenever I was silent, saying that I was thinking of the girl at Manwakh, which was frequently true.

The Saar told me some Rashid were camped near by. We went over to them next day and found one-eyed Abdullah, Muhammad, who was bin Kalut's son, and some Awamir and Mahra sheikhs. When I was close they fired shots low over my head, their usual greeting for sheikhs or other distinguished people. About forty Saar were with them, discussing the renewal of a truce with the Rashid. Muhammad told me that bin Kabina had received my letter at Habarut and that he had ridden down to Ghaidat on the coast to find someone to translate it. I knew that it was at least a hundred miles from Habarut to Ghaidat and realized this extra distance would account for his not having arrived yet. However, it was good to know that he was on the way. Muhammad also told me that bin al Kamam was still in the Yemen, negotiating with the Dahm for the return of the Rashid camels, and that bin Ghabaisha was in Dhaufar. Taking me aside he asked where I was going and I told him, but begged him to keep it secret since I knew that it would be dangerous if the tribes learnt of my movements in advance. He volunteered to come with me and I accepted his offer, as it seemed unlikely that I should be able to get hold of either bin al Kamam or bin Ghabaisha. We agreed to meet in the Raidat at the time of the next new moon. He could not come with me now, as the discussions with the Saar would go on for some days. He told me news had just arrived that the Manahil had again raided the Yam. It had been a big raid of a hundred and forty men and they had killed ten Yam and lifted a hundred and fifty camels. Nine of the Manahil had been killed, including bin Duailan, who had led the raid. Later I was to hear the story of his death from the man who killed him.

This was very bad news, for it meant that there were almost certain to be large-scale retaliatory raids by the Yam, and probably by the Dawasir, several of whom had recently been killed in a raid by the Saar. If we crossed the Sands we should have to water in the Dawasir country near Sulaiyil, and I knew from the inquiries I had made at Najran, a few months earlier, that the Yam pastured their herds during the winter in the sands to the south of Sulaiyil. We could not possibly find a *rabia* from either of these tribes, and both tribes would now consider themselves at war with my companions.

The news here was all of raids and rumours of raids. Muhammad and Abdullah were worried about a force of a hundred and fifty Abida from the Yemen which had passed eastwards along the edge of the Sands a fortnight earlier. They had heard that the leader of this raid was Murzuk, a renegade Saar who lived with the Abida. I knew that Murzuk had a formidable reputation as a raider and a bitter hatred for the Mishqas, the collective name for the tribes who live to the east of the Saar. The desert was more disturbed than it had been for years.

Muhammad pressed me to spend the night with them, but I was anxious to get back to the Hadhramaut now that I knew that bin Kabina had received my message. Two days later we were near Tamis well, which belongs to the Awamir. This was dangerous border country. Ahmad went on ahead to scout as we approached the well. A little later he came back and signalled to us to be quiet and to stay where we were. When he got up to us he told us that a large party of Manahil were coming up the main valley. I went with him to look. He warned me to keep well out of sight, since he said the Manahil hated the Saar, and that after their attacks on the government posts in the Hadhramaut they might well feel that they were at war with the Christians. He added that, anyway, they were raiders who had suffered losses and would be in a savage mood. Peering cautiously between some rocks I saw about twenty men just disappearing round a corner a quarter of a mile away. They were driving some camels with them and were riding in silence with their rifles in their hands. They were naked except for their dark-blue loin-cloths. If they had been ten minutes later they would have found us on the well. We remained where we were till late in the afternoon, and then after Ahmad had looked to see that there was no one about, we went up to fill our water-skins. There were fresh tracks everywhere. Ali said he had seen about forty mounted men with about thirty captured camels, and explained that the main party would have split up into several groups after the raid in order to make pursuit more difficult.

There was excellent water at fifteen feet in a hole in the rock. A loopholed *sangar* overlooked it from the cliff immediately above. Although it was getting late we went on again after filling our water-skins, so as not to camp near the well, always a dangerous thing to do in disturbed country. We found a shallow cave and stopped there, since the weather was cloudy and looked like rain. After dinner, as we were making tea and chatting quietly, a voice suddenly said 'Salam alaikum'. We grabbed our rifles, which were beside us, unable owing to the firelight to see into the darkness. I answered, and Amair dropped off his camel and came forward to greet us. He told me that he had come with bin Kabina from Habarut and that bin Kabina had foundered his camel and had stopped with Muhammad to await my return. He explained that bin Kabina had ridden to Ghaidat, and then, after he had found out what was in the letter, had ridden back to tell his mother and young Said where he was going. I realized that he must have ridden nine hundred miles and I was not surprised that his camel had collapsed.

I asked Amair for news of bin Ghabaisha and he said that he was with his father at Mudhail. Later I asked him if he thought that bin Ghabaisha would fly to Mukalla from Salala if I could arrange it, but he said, 'No, he is only a boy. If you were with him he might go in an aeroplane but he won't go by himself with the Christians.'

On our way back to Saiwun we passed the palm groves at Quff, the original homeland of the Awamir, although most of this tribe, like their allies the Rashid, now live in the Sands. Thirteen days after leaving Shibam, we camped once more on the plateau above the Hadhramaut. We had travelled 225 miles. For the last three days the sky had been overcast, and that night we saw continuous flickers of lightning far away to the north. Amair watched with intent eyes, and several times exclaimed, 'God willing, we will have a year of plenty.'

Next morning we scrambled down the high cliffs into the Hadhramaut itself. Below us we could see the Sultan's palace at Saiwun, massive and very white above the dark wall of palms. Other buildings, too, with crenellated towers, and minarets, and glistening domes, stood among green fields and gardens filled with fruit-trees.

I always felt imprisoned in the Hadhramaut; I should have been interested to see it ten years earlier, before Ingrams had established law and order; for it was very old, a fragment from a vanished world that had survived in this remote valley. But now the spoiling hand of progress was on the land. Already some of the richer and more ostentatious *saiyids* in Tarim and Saiwun had built themselves houses which were as hideous as they were incongruous, furnished at great cost with modern 'conveniences'. The year before in Tarim I had experienced how embarrassing it could be to use a lavatory which, intended only for display, was not connected with anything. These houses were much admired and would, I knew, be assiduously copied. Soon this new style would oust the local architecture, which, although harmonious and beautiful, was suddenly no longer fashionable, simply because it had lasted unchanged for centuries. I had been told that the late Shah of Persia divided everything in his realm into *moderne* and *démodé* and gave orders for the *démodé* to be replaced. The same process would happen here. Walking through Saiwun, the largest town in the Hadhramaut with about twenty thousand inhabitants, I felt that it would not be long before there were cinemas, and wirelesses blaring at street corners.

Watts was on leave in Aden but I stayed with Johnson, his assistant. Despite Amair's scepticism, I sent a telegram to the Air Officer Commanding at Aden. I asked whether the CO at Salala could get hold of bin Ghabaisha through the Wali, and if he was successful – whether bin Ghabaisha could be flown to Riyan and then sent up to Saiwun by car. A week later I got a reply: 'Bin Ghabaisha contacted Stop Leaving by air for Riyan tomorrow.'

Two days later Johnson was entertaining the Saiwun and Tarim football teams to tea in his house. I had watched with sardonic amusement as they had rushed about kicking a football to cries of 'Well played!' and 'Pass! Pass!' I was busy handing cakes to the Tarim centre-forward when I heard a well-known voice saying 'Salam alaikum' and in walked bin Ghabaisha. He was wearing his dagger and carried a camel-stick. He had nothing else with him.

He sat down beside me, and I asked him where he had come from.

'We were near Mudhail, in the wadi where you stopped on your way to Mukalla,' he said. 'I and my brother were herding our camels when one of the Wali's slaves arrived. You remember him, Abdullah, the young one who went with you to Jabal Qarra. The slave said that you had arrived, and that the Wali had sent for me; so I told my brother to take the camels back in the evening and to tell my father I had gone to Salala. When I got there I went in to see the Wali in the palace; he said to me, "Umbarak is in the Hadhramaut and has sent for you; an aeroplane is going there tomorrow. Will you go there in it?"'

I interrupted to ask what his answer had been.

He replied: 'I said, "Why would I not go in an aeroplane?" The Wali then sent me to the Christians' camp. The Christians gave me food – horrid stuff; I did not like it, I slept there and next afternoon the aeroplane arrived.'

I asked: 'Had you ever seen an aeroplane before?' and he answered, 'Yes, on my way back from Mukalla last year; it was very high up but it made more noise than this one. When I got into the aeroplane the Christians tried to tie me with a rope. I would not let them.'

I asked him how he had liked flying.

He said: 'It was all right when we flew over the ground. I could see the wadis and hills – I knew where I was. By God, Umbarak, once I saw men and camels, very small like ants! I was frightened when we flew over the sea. When it got dark I thought the Christians had lost their way. They all began to chatter and wave their arms about. When we arrived at Riyan an Arab interpreter said that I was to go to Aden in the morning. The man was a fool, so I went to one of the Christians who had driven the aeroplane. I told him you were in the Hadhramaut. At first none of them could understand me, but at last they said *"Aiwah! Aiwah!* Umbarak – Hadhramaut," and hit me on the back and then gave me tea and bread. They had put milk in the tea and I would not drink it. This morning they mounted me on a lorry and now I am here.'

He asked me where I was going, and I told him that I planned to cross the Empty Quarter to the Wadi Dawasir and to go from there to the Trucial Coast. All he said was, 'I have not got a rifle,' so I took him into my room and told him to choose one of the five rifles there. When he had chosen one I told him it was a present.

We spent two days in Shibam, the most interesting of these towns. Built on the edge of the dry river-bed, on a low mound in the middle of the valley, it had a population of about seven thousand. The town is surrounded by a high wall, but this is dwarfed by the close-packed houses, which rise inside it to seven or eight storeys. Whenever I was in the silent alleyways under the sheer walls of these houses I felt as if I were at the bottom of a well. Here Amair and bin Ghabaisha arranged with the Saar for camels to take us to the Raidat and bought such things as we still required. I had brought flour, rice, sugar, tea, and coffee from Mukalla, and we now purchased dried shark-meat, butter, spices, saddle-bags, ropes, and water-skins. I bought the water-skins myself, and among them I was palmed off with several sheepskins which invariably sweat when filled with water. This would not have happened if Amair or bin Ghabaisha had been with me, but they were busy elsewhere.

We left Shibam on 17 December and went up to Raidat. Ali bin Sulaiman of the Hatim section of the Saar who was with us was to be extremely helpful. The land was filled with rumours and alarms. Abdullah bin Nura, usually known by his family name of bin Maiqal, had recently arrived at Manwakh with the bin Maaruf Saar. Although these bin Maaruf belong to the Hatim section of the Saar, they no longer lived upon the Saar plateau but in the sands and steppes to the north, and for a dozen years had acknowledged Ibn Saud as their overlord and paid him tribute through the Amir at Najran. They were grazing their herds in the desert south of Najran when word reached them that the Yam and Dawasir were massing, having been authorized by Ibn Saud to attack the Saar and other Hadhramaut tribes in retaliation for the recent raids in which some of them had been implicated. They therefore fled southward to seek refuge among their kinsmen.

We now heard that advance parties of the Yam had already

entered the Karab country to the west of us, lifting several hundred camels and killing any Arabs whom they met. Some Saar women with whom we spoke had seen them and described their clothes, saying that they wore trousers 'like women'. This was convincing proof that they were from the north. The Saar had evacuated the country between Al Abr and Zamakh, and it seemed probable that they would also abandon Manwakh and withdraw into the broken country along the middle Makhia. It was important for me to reach this well before they deserted it if I was to find guides and camels for my journey across the Sands.

I left the Raidat at once and arrived at Manwakh late in the evening of 28 December. There was no one near the well. As we had had a long day we decided to camp near by. At sunset six bin Maaruf came past. They were all young men and rode magnificent camels. They were worried by some camel-tracks which they had found farther up the valley. These they had been unable to identify, and they feared they might be tracks of Yam scouts, for Bedu push scouts out far ahead to locate an encampment and then after an all-night march fall on it at dawn. They told us that bin Maiqal was two hours away, and advised us not to camp where we were. We did not wish to arrive at the Saar encampment in the dark, so we decided to move into a side valley and spent the night there. I sent Amair to tell Muhammad and bin Kabina that we had arrived. Having camped, I think we all wished we had gone on after all, for the low rocky bluffs and empty plain looked menacing in the dying light and made us feel very lonely. We cooked a quick meal and then put out the fire; Ali advised us not to talk. In the night one of our camels suddenly got to its feet. I had been lightly asleep and in a second was awake. The others crouched about me, their rifles pointing into the darkness. Ali said, 'It is only the camel,' and seizing its head-rope jerked at it until the grumbling animal subsided once more upon its knees. We lay down again, tense after this alarm.

In the sharp cold of the winter morning we rode to the Saar camp, passing herds of fat milch camels, which the herdsboys had just driven out to pasture. Small, black, goat-hair tents were scattered about the valley. Naked infants romped round them, and dark-clad women sat churning butter or moved about getting sticks or herding goats. I noticed with anxiety that several familes had already struck their tents and loaded their camels. The small children were seated in camel-litters, the first I had seen in southern Arabia, though I was familiar with them in the north. I hoped these preparations did not mean that the Saar were leaving Manwakh.

As we approached, the bin Maaruf formed up to receive us and greeted us by firing low over our heads, before sweeping down on us, yelling and brandishing their daggers. We got off our camels to greet their sheikhs and some Karab, Manahil, and Mahra who were with them. A little apart from the others was a group of four or five so-called *saiyids*. They had come up here from the Hadhramaut, hoping no doubt to profit from the credulity of the Saar, who would unhesitatingly accept their improbable claims that they were descended from the Prophet. Their pallid, indoor faces seemed to me as out of place in this gathering of weathered tribesmen as did their clothes, which were of the Indonesian style fashionable in the towns of the Hadhramaut.

Bin Kabina had led the wild rush which welcomed us and I was glad indeed to see him. He looked well, but his shirt was in ribbons. There were, however, new clothes for him in my saddle-bags.

After we had drunk coffee and exchanged our news we chose a camping place near by, where low-growing bushes and a bank of drifted sand gave us a little shelter from the cold north wind. We were still unloading when a dozen Saar came racing across the low dunes; their camels, travelling at about eighteen miles an hour, were urged on by the wild yells of their riders, who rode them with effortless mastery. The camels swept forward across the undulating ground with raking, pounding strides, their necks stretched out low in front of them as they surged up to the crests, and swept down into the hollows. But there was nothing ungainly about these great beasts, which moved as gracefully as galloping horses. The lads who rode them were among the finest in the tribe, lithe, hard-bodied, and alert. They were the scouts who went out at dawn to scour the desert, alert for the tracks of strangers. Hearing shots, they had supposed that the camp was being attacked and had ridden back to help.

At first sight these bin Maaruf were very different from the other Saar. They wore long white shirts, cut with pointed sleeves which reached to the ground, and head-cloths and head-ropes of northern fashion. They were distinguished too by the herds of she-camels which they kept for breeding and for milk. All their camels were in excellent condition, for they had been on rich grazing near Najran.

We required nine camels, and next day my Rashid wandered round the encampments making inquiries. We knew that we should have to pay high prices, for we could get them nowhere else and we were in a hurry. We each of us needed a riding camel, as Muhammad, bin Kabina, and Amair had decided to leave theirs, which were in poor condition, with some Manahil who were here on a visit. I decided to buy four baggage camels since we should have a very long way to go before we reached the Trucial Coast. Bin Ghabaisha, who was a good judge, soon found himself a black *hazmia* for the equivalent of fifteen pounds. We chaffed him about his choice, for there is a prejudice against riding these black camels, but he said that she was a fine animal – which she was – and that he needed her for work and not for display. Whenever anyone approached her she flipped her tail up and down in a ridiculous manner, a sign that she had recently been served successfully.

Bin Kabina bought a young grey with a very long stride. She was six months gone in calf, but this would not matter since camels carry their young for a year. Gradually we collected the number we needed. I bought a small thoroughbred from Oman, a very willing animal but with an irritatingly short stride.

We also needed saddles and head-ropes. The woollen head-ropes were difficult to come by. A *saiyid* had an old one which he sold to bin Ghabaisha for the equivalent of ten shillings. It was worth less than a shilling. The same man sold my Rashid various other things, overcharging them in each case. It happened that two days later he got conjunctivitis and came to me scarcely able to see, as I sat with a crowd of Arabs. Brusquely he demanded medicine.

I told him I should be delighted to treat him but would require five shillings for each eye. He turned to the crowd and said, 'Does the Christian not know I am a *saiyid*, a descendant of Muhammad?' I said I was aware of this, but it did not alter my charges for treating him. He went away muttering angrily, but the pain drove him back. I took his money and was able to cure his eyes. This is the only time I have ever charged for doctoring anyone.

We needed a guide. Ali told me that bin Daisan, a middle-aged man from the bin Maaruf, knew these Western Sands better than anyone else. We spent several evenings in bin Daisan's tent trying to persuade him to come with us. I offered him money and a rifle, but avarice fought a losing battle in his mind with the caution that comes with middle age. Each night, by the time we left him, he would have agreed to come with us, but in the morning we would get a message saying that his family refused to agree.

Everyone assured us that we should certainly be killed by the Yam or the Dawasir as soon as we met them on the far side of the Sands. They told us that three large parties of Yam were even then raiding round Al Abr and had killed two Saar a few days ago. They said contemptuously that my Rashid were too young and inexperienced to know what lay ahead of us. Young they certainly were, for Muhammad was perhaps twenty-five years old, Amair twenty, and bin Kabina and bin Ghabaisha seventeen, yet they refused to be intimidated or to desert me. Muhammad suggested one evening that instead of crossing to the Wadi Dawasir we should cross the Sands farther to the east through Dakaka, but when I told him that Thomas and Philby had already been there and that it was the Western Sands that I wished to explore, he said, 'Don't worry. We will go with you wherever you want to go, whatever the Saar may say.' However, we agreed that we must get hold of a Saar to come with us so as to have protection from that tribe. Many of the Saar, who hate the Rashid, were talking almost openly of following us when we left and killing us in the Sands. Not only were there bitter scores to settle between these two tribes, but they knew that I had a lot of money with me, as well as our rifles, ammunition, and camels. Our Manahil friends warned us against going without a Saar *rabia*, and yet where were we to get one? Two young Karab had volunteered to come with us, but they neither knew these sands nor would their presence protect us from the Saar.

Ali and I went back again to bin Daisan, and at last, after I had offered him more money, he agreed to accompany us. We arranged to water our camels and fill our water-skins next day and to leave the day after that. Next morning as we were getting ready, a Mahra arrived from Shagham well, in the nearby Makhia, with news of bin Murzuk and the Abida raiders. They had looted the Rashid and Manahil and captured many camels and killed two Rashid herdsmen. The Mahra told us that the Abida had themselves been surprised while watering in the dark on Thamud well, and that five of them had been killed, but that the pursuit party, which was small, had been driven off. He had seen and spoken with the Abida at Shagham two days before; they had two very badly wounded men with them, and were consequently moving slowly on their way back to their own country, angry at their losses. He advised us to wait for a few days before we started. Though I was almost superstitiously unwilling to put off our departure, now that bin Daisan had at last made up his mind to go with us, I realized that there was nothing else to do. Everyone assured me that the raiders under bin Murzuk would follow us and kill us without mercy, if they, or any other Abida who were behind them, crossed our tracks.

The pursuit party had used as their battle-cry *Murzuk ya talabta* (Death to Murzuk), a battle-cry obviously invented for the occasion, and this for some reason convinced the Rashid that the pursuers had been from their own tribe, and neither Manahil nor Mahra. They were desperately anxious for every scrap of information about the raid, and especially about one of the pursuers who had been killed in the fight at Thamud. The Mahra repeated to them the description of this man, as he had heard it from the Abida, and he also described his rifle which he had seen. Muhammad and the others said, 'It is Salim bin Mautlauq; without a doubt it is Salim,' but they were puzzled by the description of the rifle, which they said belonged to no one in their tribe. For weeks they were to discuss this question, hoping against hope that it was not Salim bin Mautlauq who had been killed. We did not hear what had happened until a year later on the Trucial Coast.

About twenty-five Rashid and a few Mahra had followed the Abida and found them watering their camels at Thamud. They knew that water was short and that, as the Abida numbered about a hundred and fifty, they would be all night watering their animals. They had crept towards the well. It was a cloudy night and they had got close before they were challenged. They fired a volley and then rushed the Abida using their daggers. Hopelessly out-numbered, they were soon driven back. When they collected again, where they had left their camels, they found that Salim was missing. A Mahra said that he had been killed near the well and produced his rifle. He explained that he had picked it up, leaving his own rifle which was no good. Saud, Salim's brother, said at once that he was going back and the others went with him. When they reached the well there was no one there and no sign of Salim. At dawn they followed the tracks which he had made as he had crawled away. They found him a mile away, unconscious, shot through the chest and neck. When he recovered consciousness he told them that a fatally wounded Abida had called out, 'Is there not one of them dead that I may look on him before I die?' and that someone had then seized him by the legs and dragged him over to the dying man, round whom many people were collected; the dying man had cursed him, and then someone had shot him again. When he came to, there was no one there and he had crawled off into the dark trying to get to the place where the Rashid had left their camels. He recovered from his wounds a few months afterwards.

Two days later we went to the well at Manwakh, bin Daisan having assured us again the night before that he was coming with us. We arranged with him to leave next day and he said he would meet us on the well. We travelled there with a family that was camped near us. They said we could use their gear for watering. The man rode a camel loaded with great coils of rope, with pulleys, well-buckets, rolled up water-skins, and a large watering-trough fashioned from skins stretched over a framework of wooden hoops. His son rode bareback on one of seven camels, and a woman and two small children drove a herd of goats. Others, too, were going down to the water. It was six miles away and we took two hours to get there. When we arrived there was already a crowd round the well mouth. Men and women drew on the ropes together, singing as they pulled, hand over hand. On each rope, as one bucket jerked up from the dark depths, slopping water down the glistening walls, another descended empty. Each clammy, dripping leather bucket was seized as it reached the scaffolding, and hastily tipped into a trough, round which moaning camels jostled in haste to quench their thirst. Rows of bulging black skins lay upon the sand, guarded from the trampling feet of men and beasts by shrill-voiced children. Camels were watered, couched, and later driven away; others arrived, breaking into a shuffling trot as they approached; colts frisked, stiff-legged, around their dams; men shouted with harsh voices to watchful, darting herdsboys; goats bleated, camels roared, the singing at the well-head rose and fell, the sun climbed higher, and the dark stain of spilt water spread farther across the ground.

Abdullah bin Nura and several elders arrived. They told us that they would not allow bin Daisan or anyone else from the bin Maaruf to go with us, and advised us to give up our plan to cross the Sands, as the Yam would certainly kill us if we did. I had half expected bin Daisan to let me down. We answered little and went apart to talk it over. Ali suggested that two young Saar from his own section of the Hatim might go with us if I gave each of them a rifle and fifty cartridges. They had never crossed the Sands but had watered at the Hassi near Sulaiyil and were confident that they could find the well once we had arrived on the other side. He said that if they were with us we should be safe from the Saar. I asked the Rashid what they thought, and Muhammad answered, 'We are your men. We will go where you go. It is for you to decide.' I told bin Kabina to make coffee while I thought it over, and we went and sat beneath the cliff, where we had unloaded our camels. It seemed crazy to try to cross the Empty Quarter without a guide. It was about four hundred waterless miles, which would take at least sixteen days, and bin Daisan had told me that the dunes were very high and difficult. I remembered how hard had been the journey which we had done the year before, and how little margin we had to spare, even when guided by al Auf. I asked the Rashid if they thought we could get across without a guide, and Muhammad said, 'We live in the Sands. We can take you across without a guide. The danger will be from the Yam after we have got to the other side.' I told Ali that we would go, and asked him to fetch the two Saar, and he said he would bring them in the evening.

Unlike my companions, I was far more concerned with the physical difficulties of crossing the Empty Quarter, especially without a guide, than worried by what would happen to us if we ran into Arabs on the far side. I did not think that they would take us for raiders, since we would be leading four laden camels. I knew that our clothes and saddling would show them that we came from the south and belonged to the hated Mishqas, but I hoped to be able to get speech with any Arabs we might meet before they opened fire; and if they belonged to Ibn Saud I though they might hesitate to kill us once they discovered I was a European, for fear of the King's anger. I knew that if they were from the Yemen we should be doomed. Looking back on the journey I realize how hopelessly I under-estimated the danger and how very slight were our chances of survival.

It was midday by now and there was still a crowd of people on the well, which had run dry. We therefore decided to stop to fill our water-skins during the night, and to water our camels at dawn before the Arabs arrived. We could camp in a little gully out of sight. Manwakh was one of the only two wells which were regarded as having permanent water in the Saar country, an area larger than Yorkshire. Yet now it had run dry after watering a couple of hundred camels, even though there had been a good rain six months earlier in the year. I wondered how the Saar managed for water in the summer and in years of drought.

In the evening Ali came to our camping place with the two men who had agreed to go with us to the Hassi. They were called Salih and Sadr and were about the same age as Muhammad. Salih had a large wart on his right eyebrow, wore his hair in plaits, and was dressed in a white shirt with long, pointed sleeves; whereas Sadr, the smaller of the two, wore his hair short and was dressed in a worn-out shirt, patched with so many different colours that it looked like a dervish *jibba*. They told us that they had been to the Hassi from Najran the year before and were certain that they would be able to find this well as soon as we reached the Aradh, a limestone escarpment running down into the sands from Sulaiyil; they said it would be impossible for us to miss it. In the evening they went back to their tents, but assured us that they would be with us at dawn.

After we had fed, the others took the water-skins over to the well to fill them ready for the morning start. Ordinarily I would have helped them, but now I was drained of energy, so I just lay beside the loads on the cold yielding sand and stared up at the stars. Later bin Kabina came and sat beside me. He did not speak and I was glad to have him there.

Sadr had told us that Ibn Saud had a post at the Hassi, and it therefore seemed unlikely that we should be able to water there and slip away again unobserved. I wondered what the King would say when he heard that I had crossed the desert without his permission, and whether he would identify me as the Englishman to whom he had refused permission to do the journey two years before. I only hoped that if we succeeded his anger would be tempered by some admiration for our achievement.

ELEVEN

The Second Crossing of the Empty Quarter

It was a bleak morning with a cold wind blowing from the north-east. The sun rose in a dusty sky but gave no warmth. Bin Kabina set out dates and fragments of bread, left over from the previous night, before calling to us to come and eat. I refused, having no desire for food, and remained where I was, crouching behind a rock, trying to find shelter from the cutting wind and eddies of driven sand. I had slept little the night before, trying to assess the dangers and difficulties which lay ahead. Later, in grey borderlands of sleep, I had struggled knee-deep in shifting sand with nightmares of disaster. Now, in the cold dawn, I questioned my right to take these men who trusted me to what the Saar vowed was certain death. They were already moving about their tasks preparatory to setting off, and only an order from me would stop them. But I was drifting forward, slack-willed, upon a movement which I had started, half-hoping that Salih and Sadr would fail to come and that then we could not start.

Some Saar were already at the well, which would soon be surrounded by Arabs impatient to water their animals. We drove ours down there and filled the troughs, but they would only sniff at the ice-cold water instead of drinking, and drink they must if they

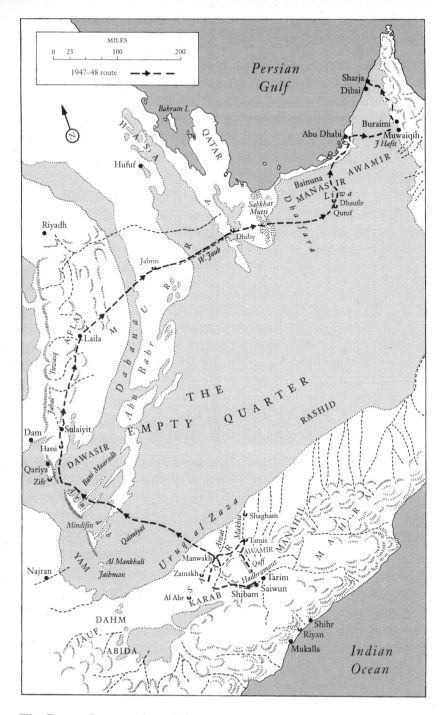

The Empty Quarter: Second Crossing

were to survive for sixteen waterless days, struggling heavily-loaded through the sands. Bin Kabina and I went back to sort the loads, while the others couched each roaring camel in turn, and, after tying her knees to prevent her from getting up, battled to hold her weaving neck, so that they could pour down her throat the water she did not want. Bin Kabina set aside the rice and the extra flour to give to Ali. We were taking with us two hundred pounds of flour, which was as much as we could carry, a forty-pound package of dates, ten pounds of dried shark-meat, and butter, sugar, tea, coffee, salt, dried onions, and some spices. There were also two thousand Maria Theresa dollars, which weighed very heavily, three hundred rounds of spare ammunition, my small box of medicines, and about fifty gallons of water in fourteen small skins. I knew already that several of these skins sweated badly, but had not been able to get others from the Saar. Even so, I reckoned that if we rationed ourselves to a quart each for every day and to a quart for cooking and coffee, we should be all right, even if we lost half our water from evaporation and leakage. This water was sweet, very different from the filthy stuff we had carried with us the year before. While we were busy dividing our stores into loads of suitable weight, Salih and Sadr arrived and I was glad to see that both their camels were powerful animals in good condition. We had decided the night before that we would load the spare camels heavily, at the risk of foundering them before we reached the Hassi, so as to save our mounts. I hoped that the two Saar would be able to slip away unobserved from that well, even if the rest of us were detained, and it was therefore important that their camels should be spared as much as possible. They must carry only the lightest loads, if they carried anything at all. I gave them the rifles which I had promised, and fifty rounds of ammunition each. Their friends who had come with them examined these weapons critically, but could find nothing wrong. I had already presented Muhammad and Amair each with a rifle and a hundred rounds of ammunition. Bin Ghabaisha had the rifle I had given him in Saiwun, bin Kabina the one I had given him the year before, and I had my sporting ·303, so we were a well-armed party.

The others returned from the well and we loaded the camels. The sun was warmer now and I felt more cheerful, reassured by the good spirits of my companions, who laughed and joked as they worked. Before leaving, we climbed the rocky hill near the well, and Sadr's uncle, a scrawny old man in a loin-cloth, showed us once more the direction to follow, pointing with both his arms. With his wild hair, gaunt face, and outstretched arms he looked, I thought, like a prophet predicting doom. I was almost surprised when he said in an ordinary voice that we could not go wrong, as we should have the Aradh escarpment on our left when we reached the Jilida. Standing behind him I took a bearing with my compass. As we climbed down the hill Ali told me that there had been another fight between the Yam and the Karab near al Abr two days before, and that the bin Maaruf had now decided to abandon Manwakh and to move tomorrow to the Makhia. He said that this was why there were already so many Arabs filling their skins at the well.

We were leaving only just in time. The camels lurched to their feet as we took hold of the head-ropes, and, after each of the Rashid had tied a spare camel behind his own, we moved off on foot. The Saar on the well stopped work to watch us go and I wondered what they were saying. Ali came with us a short distance, and then, after embracing each of us in turn, went back. We had started on our journey, and holding out our hands we said together, 'I commit myself to God.'

Two hours later Sadr pointed to the tracks of five camels that had been ridden ahead of us the day before. At first we wondered if they were Yam, but after some discussion Sadr and Salih were convinced that they were Karab and therefore friendly. Muhammad asked me to judge which was the best camel. I pointed at random to a set of tracks and they all laughed and said I had picked out the one which was indubitably the worst. They then started to argue which really was the best. Although they had not seen these camels they could visualize them perfectly. Amair, bin Ghabaisha, and Sadr favoured one camel, Muhammad, bin Kabina, and Salih another. I knew nothing about Sadr and Salih's qualifications, but felt sure that Amair and bin Ghabaisha were right since they were better judges of a camel than Muhammad or bin Kabina. Not all Bedu can guide or track, and Muhammad was surprisingly bad at both. He was widely respected as the son of bin Kalut and was inclined to be self-important in consequence, but really he was the least efficient of my Rashid companions. Bin Ghabaisha was probably the most competent, and the others tended to rely on his judgement, as I did myself. He was certainly the best rider and the best shot, and always graceful in everything he did. He had a quick smile and a gentle manner, but I already suspected that he could be both reckless and ruthless, and I was not surprised when within two years he had become one of the most daring outlaws on the Trucial Coast with half a dozen blood-feuds on his hands. Amair was equally ruthless, but he had none of bin Ghabaisha's charm. He had a thin mouth, hard unsmiling eyes, and a calculating spirit without warmth. I did not like him, but knew that he was competent and reliable. Travelling alone among these Bedu I was completely at their mercy. They could at any times have murdered me, dumped my body in a sand-drift, and gone off with my possessions. Yet so absolute was my faith in them that the thought that they might betray me never crossed my mind.

We travelled through low limestone hills until nearly sunset, and camped in a cleft on their northern side. The Rashid did not trust the Saar whom we had left at Manwakh, so Amair went back along our tracks to keep watch until it was dark, while bin Ghabaisha lay hidden on the cliff above us watching the plain to the north, which was a highway for raiders going east or west. We started again at dawn, after an uneasy watchful night, and soon after sunrise came upon a broad, beaten track, where Murzuk and the Abida had passed two days before.

Bin Kabina and Amair stayed behind to try to identify some of the looted stock by reading the confusion in the sand. We had gone on a couple of miles when they caught up with us, laughing as they chased each other across the plain. They appeared to be in the best of spirits, and I was surprised when bin Kabina told me that he had recognized the tracks of two of his six camels among the spoil. He had left these two animals with his uncle on the steppes. Luckily,

Qamaiqam, the splendid camel on which he had crossed the Empty Quarter the year before, and the other three were with his brother at Habarut. He told us which animals they had been able to identify, but said that there had been so many animals that it was only possible to pick out a few that had travelled on the outskirts of the herd. As I listened I thought once again how precarious was the existence of the Bedu. Their way of life naturally made them fatalists; so much was beyond their control. It was impossible for them to provide for a morrow when everything depended on a chance fall of rain or when raiders, sickness, or any one of a hundred chance happenings might at any time leave them destitute, or end their lives. They did what they could, and no people were more self-reliant, but if things went wrong they accepted their fate without bitterness, and with dignity as the will of God.

We rode across gravel steppes which merged imperceptibly into the sands of the Uruq al Zaza. By midday the north-east wind was blowing in tearing gusts, bitter cold but welcome, as it would wipe out our tracks and secure us from pursuit. We pressed on until night, hoping in vain to find grazing, and then groped about in the dark feeling for firewood. Here it was dangerous to light a fire after dark, but we were too cold and hungry to be cautious. We found a small hollow, lit a fire, and sat gratefully round the flames. At dawn we ate some dates, drank a few drops of coffee, and started off as the sun rose.

It was another cold grey day, but there was no wind. We went on foot for the first hour or two, and then each of us, as he felt inclined, pulled down his camel's head, put a foot on her neck, and was lifted up to within easy reach of the saddle. Muhammad was usually the first to mount and I the last, for the longer I walked the shorter time I should have to ride. The others varied their positions, riding astride or kneeling in the saddle, but I could only ride astride, and as the hours crawled by the saddle edge bit deeper into my thighs.

For the next two days we crossed hard, flat, drab-coloured sands, without grazing, and, consequently, had no reason to stop until evening. On the second day, just after we had unloaded, we

saw a bull oryx walking straight towards us. To him we were in
the eye of the setting sun and he probably mistook us for others
of his kind. As only about three Englishmen have shot an Arabian
oryx, I whispered to bin Ghabaisha to let me shoot, while the oryx
came steadily on. Now he was only a quarter of a mile away, now
three hundred yards, and still he came on. The size of a small
donkey – I could see his long straight horns, two feet or more in
length, his pure white body, and the dark markings on his legs and
face. He stopped suspiciously less than two hundred yards away.
Bin Kabina whispered to me to shoot. Slowly I pressed the trigger.
The oryx spun round and galloped off. Muhammad muttered disgustedly, 'A clean miss,' and bin Kabina said loudly, 'If you had let
bin Ghabaisha shoot we should have had meat for supper'; all I
could say was 'Damn and blast!'

I little realized at the time that by missing the oryx I probably
saved our lives. A year later bin al Kamam joined us on the Trucial
Coast. He told us that he had been at Main in the Jauf, when news
arrived that the Christian and some Rashid were at Manwakh,
preparing to cross the Sands. The Governor of the Jauf, Saif al
Islam al Hussain, one of the Imam Yahya's sons, sent off two parties
of Dahm to kill us. The larger party of twenty occupied some wells
on the desert's edge, which they thought we might visit, while the
other party of fifteen went into the Sands to pick up our tracks.
Bin al Kamam said that he and his companion had been imprisoned
to prevent them from escaping and giving us warning. He had
been certain that the Dahm would intercept and kill us, and when
eventually he saw them riding back across the plain towards the
town he was waiting to hear that we were dead. Suddenly he realized
that they were riding in silence, instead of singing their war-songs,
and that they must have failed to find us. The smaller party reported
that they had picked up our tracks, which were two days old; they
had followed us for two days, but as we were travelling very fast
they had been afraid that they would run out of water before they
could overtake us. They said that at our camping places they had
seen marks in the sand where we had put down our bags of gold.
If I had shot the oryx we should have delayed for a day to dry its

meat, and the Dahm would probably have caught up with us. We thought at the time that we were far enough into the Empty Quarter to be safe, and we were not keeping a good look-out. If our pursuers had been from the Yam they would certainly have overtaken us, but the Dahm are afraid of the Sands.

For the next three days we rode across sands where there were only occasional *abal* bushes and a few dry tufts of *ailqi* or *qassis*, the remains of vegetation which had grown after rain four years before. We were now in the Qaimiyat, where parallel dune chains ran from north-east to south-west. These dunes were only about a hundred and fifty feet high, but their steep inclines faced towards us, and the successive floundering ascents exhausted our camels, as they had eaten practically nothing for six days. When we left Manwakh they were very fat, and this gave them reserves on which to draw, but their very fatness distressed them in this heavy sand. They were fresh from pasturage and their backs were soft and unaccustomed to the saddle. Now they were heavily-loaded and doing very long marches. We knew that under such conditions they were certain to develop saddle swellings, which would turn all too easily into ulcers. We would gladly have rested them for a day if we could have found grazing and if our water supply had allowed it. The sheepskins, which I had bought in ignorance, sweated very badly, but we had already finished the water that was in them. Even the goatskins had not been long enough in use to become watertight and we were making constant but ineffectual efforts to check the alarming drip. We passed fresh tracks of oryx and of *rim*, the large white gazelle which is found in the Sands, and knew that if we followed these tracks they would lead us to fresh grazing, but we could not afford to lengthen our journey.

In the afternoon of the sixth day the dune chains turned into gentle downs, but we had already climbed over sixteen of them that day and on one of them a baggage camel collapsed, only moving again when we unloaded her. Bin Kabina's camel went lame in the shoulder, and all the others showed signs of exhaustion. I knew that it would be another ten days before we reached the Hassi and I began to wonder if we should get there.

Next morning we came on the fresh tracks of a pelican which had walked in a straight line across the sand. I tried to remember what it said in the Bible about a pelican in the wilderness. Amair told me that five years earlier he had seen several very large white birds near Mughshin, and that they had left tracks like these. While he was describing these birds we topped a rise and saw that the rolling sands ahead of us were green with *qassis*, growing in tasselled tufts a foot high. We unloaded and turned our camels loose. I knew that this grazing was going to make all the difference to our chance of reaching the Hassi, since it would not only satisfy the camels' hunger but would also alleviate their thirst.

We camped on a floor of hard sand in the shelter of a small dune. Two twisted *abal* bushes, one of them with a broken branch drooping to the ground, three clumps of *qassis*, beside which I had placed my saddle-bags, a pile of camel-droppings, and a low bank of sand, marked with a tracery of lizards' tracks, combined with our scattered possessions to become our home. There were similar places all around us, but, because bin Ghabaisha happened to call out 'Stop over there' and we had gone where he had directed, this particular spot acquired a temporary significance. This camping place was memorable because of the grazing, but I always thought each one distinctive at the time. The curious shape of some sticks beside the fire, a sprinkle of white on golden sand where bin Kabina had spilt flour, a rope lying where a camel had jerked it as she rose, such trifles seemed to distinguish each camp from others, but in fact the differences were too insignificant and the memory of them soon blurred. All but a few tended to become just one of a thousand others.

Bin Kabina and bin Ghabaisha were preparing food, and they called out to us, where we lay idly in the sun, that they were going to make porridge flavoured with sugar and butter. Porridge was wasteful of water, but now, contentedly watching the camels ripping succulent mouthfuls from the rich feeding around them, we cheerfully condoned the extravagance. After the meal, bin Ghabaisha and Sadr went off to hunt, but came back empty-handed at sunset, saying they had seen a herd of twenty oryx and many *rim*, but could not get near them. We decided to leave the camels out to graze during the night, feeling that here we were safe from attack. In the morning 'the Red One', the best of our baggage camels, had strayed and it took Amair two hours to find her and bring her back. No camel will ever remain contentedly in one place, however good the grazing, but, even though hobbled, will wander farther afield looking for something better. 'The Red One' was particularly bad at straying, and the others usually followed along behind her. Bin Kabina's camel and Amair's had become inseparable, while mine showed a preference for the *mirri*, an ugly grey, which we had bought in the Raidat because she was in milk. At first she refused to give us any, although her calf had already been weaned, but Amair sewed up her anus, saying he would not undo it until she let down her milk. After that she gave us about a quart a day.

These Bedu allow a camel to suckle her calf without interference for about six weeks; they then cover her udder with a bag, only allowing the calf to drink before they milk her in the morning and evening. They wean it after nine months. A camel will remain in milk for as long as four years provided she is not served by a bull. She may have as many as a dozen calves and has a working-life of about twenty years. These Arabs keep a piece of skin from a calf which has been slaughtered or has died before it was weaned, and allow the camel to smell it before they milk her; otherwise she would not let down her milk.

It was a crisp morning with a gentle breeze. A few white cumulus clouds deepened the blueness of a sky no longer tinged with yellow. Muhammad looked critically at the camels as Amair and bin Ghabaisha drove them towards us, and remarked, 'They look better now. God willing they will be able to reach the Hassi. Anyway, we may find more grazing. It looks as if there is a lot in the Sands this year, but it is very scattered.' It only took us ten minutes to load, and as we moved off I thought how pleasant it was to be free from the burden of possessions.

We walked across the red downs, and half an hour later came to the end of the grazing. Sadr told me that we had been camped on its eastern edge and that it only extended for four or five miles to the west. We could easily have missed it. A little later, finding some broken ostrich eggs, bin Kabina and Amair argued whether ostriches were lawful food, a purely academic point since ostriches had been extinct in southern Arabia for more than fifty years, although a few survived until recently in the Wadi Sirham in northern Arabia. When I was in Syria a Bedu told me that the Rualla had shot one there just before the war; it may well have been the last of them. My companions stopped to show me what their tracks looked like, saying that their grandfathers had known these birds. I had seen plenty of the tracks of the African ostrich, a larger bird than the Arabian, in the Sudan, and the copies which Amair made in the sand were correct. It is sad to think that the Arabian oryx and *rim* are also doomed as soon as cars penetrate into the southern desert. Unfortunately oryx prefer the hard, flat sands and gravel plains to the heavy dunes. Since they differ from the four species to be found in Africa, it means that yet another kind of animal will soon be extinct. In Saudi Arabia during the last few years even gazelle have become rare. Hunting-parties scour the plains in cars, returning with lorry-loads of gazelle which they have run down and butchered.

Every mile or so I checked our course with my compass; it was difficult to hold everything – the compass, notebook, pencil, camel-stick, and head-rope, especially when the camel fidgeted. I had dropped my stick for the second time when bin Kabina, who jumped down from his camel to pick it up, said as he handed it back to me, 'Really, Umbarak, this is too much. If I were you I should divorce her as soon as you get back.' The Bedu have a saying that whenever a man drops his stick his wife is being unfaithful.

We went on till evening without finding pasturage. When we camped we could see the dark plain of the Jilida six miles away. Bin Daisan had told me that the Jilida linked up with the plain of Abu Bahr, which in turn merged into the plains running down from the Hasa to Jabrin. He had also told me that when we reached the Jilida we should be half-way to the Hassi, but that the big and difficult sands would still lie ahead of us. He had explained that the

Aradh escarpment, which ran south from the Hassi, would then be about fifty miles to the west.

Next day we travelled across the Jilida plain. Its surface was of coarse sand and fine gravel, covered in places with small angular pebbles, highly polished by the wind. They were of many kinds: I recognized pieces of porphyry, granite, rhyolite, jasper, and limestone. There were occasional ridges, some of them twenty feet in height, of the quartz conglomerate that underlies the gravel surface of the plain, but these were easily avoided. We travelled fast until midday, when we came on grazing and stopped for two hours. I wandered off to a distant ridge, glad to be alone for a while, and sat watching formless shadows dapple an umber-coloured plain where nothing else moved. It was very still, with the silence which we have driven from our world. Then bin Kabina shouted to me and I went back. Coffee was ready. Muhammad said, 'We thought you were going after those oryx'; and when I asked, 'Which oryx?' he stared at me in amazement. I looked where he pointed and saw them at once, eighteen white dots on the dark plain. Bin Kabina said, 'If they had been Arabs you would have sat there, without seeing them, until they came and cut your throat.' Bedu are always observant; even when they are engrossed in an argument their dark, restless eyes notice everything, and their minds record it. They never daydream.

We found no more grazing and camped at last on flat empty sands beyond the Jilida. We passed much oryx spoor, and saw twenty-eight of them during the day. In the afternoon bin Ghabaisha and I stalked three which we saw ahead of us. As we were getting near them I heard someone calling. Looking round I saw Salih hastening towards us. I thought, 'They have seen Arabs and don't want me to shoot.' When he came up he said, 'Look out or you will give them your wind.' I whispered furiously, 'I hunted animals before you were born. It is you who will frighten them by making such a beastly noise.' Whereupon he merely added to my exasperation by maintaining that oryx did not mind the sound of voices, an inexplicable belief held by some of the Bedu, which probably explains why so few of them succeed in shooting one. I had to take a long shot. I saw that I had hit the one I had fired at, but they all galloped off. We hurried forward and found bloodstains on the ground. When the camels arrived we followed the oryx, but they were going to the south-east and after a while the others refused to go on, saying that we could not afford to lengthen our march by going in the wrong direction. This was so obviously true that I was forced to agree.

Two days later we reached the Bani Maradh. Looking at the mountainous dunes which stretched across our front, I realized that our real difficulties were only now beginning. Fortunately the prevailing winds were different from those in the sands to the south of the Jilida, and in consequence the easier slopes faced south. Even so they imposed a severe strain on our tired camels; they had had only one full meal in the eleven days since we had left Manwakh. If these southern faces had been steep, as in the Uruq al Shaiba the year before, we should never have got over them. Each dune was three to four hundred feet in height, and the highest peaks were built up round deep crescent-shaped hollows. It took us an hour or more to cross each range. Their northern faces fell away in unbroken walls of sand into successive valleys, two miles or more across, which ran down from the Aradh escarpment, and continued until they disappeared from sight twenty miles or more to the east. So far the sands we had passed on this journey had been dreary and uninteresting. Now for the first time the dunes were a lovely golden-red and, although I was tired, hungry, and thirsty, their shapes gave me great pleasure.

Once across the Bani Maradh we were on the southern edge of the *had* pastures on which the Bedu graze their camels, but ours were too thirsty to eat this plant. At midday we came upon tracks, less than a week old, of Arabs and camels, and from now on two of us scouted continuously ahead. We were uncomfortably aware that our own tracks would show any Arab that we had come from the south. A very strong north wind added to our discomfort by filling our eyes and ears with sand, without, however, hiding our tracks, which remained clearly visible in the valley-bottoms where the ground was covered with a mosaic of highly polished limestone fragments.

About four o'clock we decided to stop, so that we could cook a meal and put out the fire before dark. Salih remained to keep watch behind us, and we turned eastwards along the top of the next dune instead of crossing it. Half an hour later we unloaded in a hollow in the downs where our camels could graze without showing themselves upon a skyline. Sadr and bin Ghabaisha stood guard while Muhammad herded the camels, and the rest of us gathered wood and baked bread. The sky was overcast and I could see that it was raining heavily to the west.

When it grew dark we couched the camels, and waited for Salih to come. He arrived an hour later, to report that no one was following us. We fed; everything was cold from the long wait – the coffee, the bread, and the watery gravy from shark-meat. It was still blowing strongly, and now it had begun to rain. We dared not light a fire and sat talking in whispers. I had just decided to get into my sleeping-bag when bin Ghabaisha signed to us to be quiet and pointed to the camels. They had stopped chewing, and all of them were staring in one direction. Our rifles were already in our hands, during these days we never put them down, and we slid quietly to the ground, crawling to the edge of the small basin in which we had camped. It was too dark to see anything, but the camels still watched something, although now they were looking farther to our right. I lay there motionless, straining to see what they saw. Shadows formed and re-formed but I could be sure of nothing. Bin Kabina lay beside me. I touched him inquiringly but he made a sign that he too could see nothing. The cold rain which had soaked through my shirt ran down my flanks, and pattered on my bare legs. The camels started to chew the cud again and were no longer watching. I thought uneasily, 'They are working round behind us.' Amair and bin Ghabaisha evidently thought the same, for they moved farther round to watch the night behind us. Hours later I crawled to my saddle-bags to fetch a blanket, which I shared with bin Kabina. The rest of the night passed very slowly, and nothing happened.

In the morning bin Ghabaisha found the tracks of a wolf that had circled our camp. Muhammad said disgustedly, 'God! Fancy spending the whole night sitting in the rain staring my eyes out trying to see a wolf!', and bin Ghabaisha answered, 'Better be cold and wet than wake up with a dagger in your ribs.'

Wet, cold, and tired, we started early on a cloudy, sunless morning. Later the sun came through and it was very hot, and my thirst grew worse and worse. We passed more fortnight-old tracks of Arabs and their herds. Ahead of us Sadr and bin Ghabaisha scanned each slope and hollow before they signed to come on. The rest of us dragged the trembling camels up the slopes, and held them back as they ploughed down the far side of each dune in cascades of sand. It was weary work and all the time I felt that we were being watched. The dunes were now about five hundred feet high and at the western end of each valley we could at last see the dark wall of the Aradh. We stopped after nine hours when the camels could go no farther, again cooking a quick meal before sunset, and eating it in the dark after Sadr, who had been watching our tracks, had joined us. For the first time on this journey there was a heavy dew. We slept fitfully, jerking to wakefulness whenever a camel stirred. It was fine and clear when we started again at sunrise. Two hours later one of the baggage camels lay down and refused to move, until, at Amair's suggestion, we poured a little water down her nostrils, which revived her. We reached the Aradh at one o'clock and camped two hours later in a shallow watercourse on the limestone plateau. We were across the Sands.

The valleys when I woke at dawn were filled with eddying mist, above which the silhouettes of the dunes ran eastwards, like fantastic mountains towards the rising sun. The sky glowed softly with the colours of the opal. The world was very still, held in a fragile bowl of silence. Standing at last on this far threshold of the Sands I looked back, almost regretfully, the way we had come.

We reached the Hassi three days later, after travelling northward across a gravel plain scattered with pieces of limestone. The precipitous western edge of the Aradh was on our left. Beneath it were the three shallow wells of Zifr, and thirty miles to the north of them was the deep, brackish well of Qariya, among the ruins of a Sabaean city.

According to Sadr the well mounds of Mankhali, believed by the Bedu to be the wells of the Bani Ad, lay at the southern end of the Aradh; and their lost city of Ad under the sands of Jaihman, a further day's journey to the south. Muhammad was, however, convinced that this city, one of the two mentioned in the Koran as having been destroyed by God for arrogance, was buried in the sands to the north of Habarut. He reminded me of the many clearly defined tracks which converge on these sands, and which the Rashid maintain once led to that city. Sadr pointed beyond the sands of Bani Ramh to some peaks visible far to the west, which were, he said, in the foothills of the Hajaz, and I told them how I had visited that country two years before. When I told them that I had ridden through it on a donkey they scoffed at me and we argued happily as we went along.

On the second day after leaving the Sands we camped in the stream bed of the Hanu, that runs down to Qariya; and next morning, as we rode along the track to the Hassi, we came unexpectedly on eight mounted Yam, whose rifles were slung under their saddles, while ours were in our hands. We were only a few yards from them. I saw bin Ghabaisha slip his safety-catch forward. There was an old man opposite me, and though his face was muffled in his head-cloth I could see the hatred in his eyes. No one moved or spoke. The silence was heavy between us. At last I said 'Salam alaikum,' and he replied. A boy whispered to him, 'Are they Mishqas?' and he snarled back without taking his eyes off us, 'Don't you know the tribes? Don't you know the foe?' Muhammad said that we came in peace, that we were Rashid from the eastern sands on our way to visit Ibn Saud, adding that our main party was close behind and advising them to be careful when they met them. We then rode on. I wondered uneasily what we should have done with them if we had surprised them in the Sands. Perhaps if we had taken their rifles and their camels we could have let them live. Twenty minutes later we were at the Hassi. It was sixteen days since we had left Manwakh.

Having watered our camels and filled our skins, we learnt from some women that Ibn Saud's guardian on the well had just gone off with his son to look for a strayed camel. Sadr and Salih were anxious to seize this opportunity and slip away before he returned. We loaded their camels, which were still in good condition, with all the food and water that they could carry, and as the women had told us that the Yam had all moved westwards a week ago and that the sands to the south were empty, we hoped that they would be all right. To avoid arousing suspicion we told the women that they were going to fetch one of our camels which had collapsed two days earlier. We whispered our farewells, embraced them, and they left us. They arrived safely at Manwakh, as I later heard from bin al Kamam when I met him on the Trucial Coast.

There was nothing for us now to do but to go to Sulaiyil and hope for the best. Our camels were in need of rest; we had very little food and no guide. Even if we had been able to slip away, a pursuit party would certainly be sent after us. The guardian of the well, a Yam, returned next day and made no attempt to conceal his dislike of us. When he learnt that I was a Christian he refused to drink the coffee we offered him, saying that I was an infidel and that my companions, as Muslims who had sold themselves into the service of an infidel for gold, were even worse. Virtually under arrest, we went with him to Sulaiyil, where we arrived two days later.

The oasis extended for about two miles along the Wadi Dawasir, and the settlement itself consisted of five small villages. On our way to the village where the Amir lived we passed fields of wheat and lucerne, watered from trip-buckets raised from the wells by animals descending ramps. There were palms to the west of the village. The Yam led us down narrow, twisting lanes. Some men called out asking who we were, and he answered scornfully, 'An infidel and his servants.' We stopped at the Amir's house, flat-roofed and made of mud, like all the others.

Rather to my surprise, the Amir, who was a young slave, received us graciously. He showed us to an empty house with a courtyard on the outskirts of the village and, after saying that we should of course feed with him, told us that we must remain at Sulaiyil until he heard from Ibn Saud. He and one of his retainers, a Murra who knew the Rashid, and two young wireless operators were the only friendly people. Everyone else was fanatical and unpleasant. The elders spat on the ground whenever we passed, and the children followed me round chanting derisively, '*Al Nasrani, al Nasrani*,' the name by which these Arabs know a Christian. In the evening we bought lucerne, but only Muhammad's camel would eat it. When after supper we gave the Amir an account of our journey, he said: 'You do not realize how lucky you have been to get here. I should not have thought that you would have had a chance. The sands you came through were filled with Arabs until a week ago, when most of them moved westward across the Aradh to better grazing. If a single Arab had seen you, the hue-and-cry would have been out, for they would have known at once that you are from the south. Didn't you know that Ibn Saud has given permission to his tribes to raid the Mishqas and to kill any of them they meet, in revenge for the recent raids on the Yam and the Sawasir? They are wildly excited here at having permission to raid after years of enforced peace. Many parties have gone off and others are getting ready to go. Any of them would have killed you out of hand if they had met you; nothing could have saved you if they had found that one of you was a Christian. These tribes are the last of the *Akhwan*. Even in this village, where they are under control, you can see how they hate you as an infidel.' He looked at me, shook his head, and said again, 'By God, you were lucky!'

I knew he was right and realized how badly I had misjudged our chances. This realization increased the responsibility I felt towards my companions, who had appreciated the true risks and yet had come with me.

Two days later the Amir came to our room to tell me he had received orders by wireless from Ibn Saud to detain the Englishman and to imprison his companions. He removed our rifles and daggers, told me to remain where I was, leaving the Murra as a guard, and ordered Muhammad and Amair to follow him. He said that bin Kabina and bin Ghabaisha, who were herding the camels, could wait till the evening. When I protested at being separated from my companions, and asked that we should be treated alike, he said he must obey the King's orders, but allowed me to send a telegram to Ibn Saud.

After several efforts I composed a telegram saying that we had been travelling in the Empty Quarter and had come to the Hassi for water. I asked for his forgiveness, adding that if he wished to punish anyone I was solely to blame, since my companions, who had no knowledge of this country, had gone where I wished and that it was I who had guided them.

In the evening, I saw bin Kabina and bin Ghabaisha coming towards the village with the camels. They looked very cheerful, laughing and joking together. The Murra allowed me to meet them and tell them what had happened. Seeing me, some children called out, 'Now the King will cut off the Christian's head and the heads of his companions.' I was so distressed that I could hardly speak. They had trusted me and I wondered unhappily whether they were now going to suffer for it. I felt worse about them than I did about the others, for they were so much younger. They asked a few questions, and then bin Kabina put his hand on my shoulder and said, 'Don't worry, Umbarak; if God wills, all will be well.'

At sunset the Amir did his best to cheer us up with a meal in his house, but it was an unhappy evening. Hours later when I was half asleep the door was thrown open. A large black slave came in swinging a pair of fetters, and ordered me to get up and go with him at once, as the Amir of the Wadi had arrived. I followed through silent streets to the Amir of Sulaiyil's house.

The room was packed with people. An elderly bearded man in a brown gold-embroidered cloak returned my formal greeting, bidding me sit opposite him. His clerk, a shifty-looking, self-important slave whom I disliked on sight, was bullying Amair. 'Don't lie,' he shouted after every answer. 'You only know how to lie.' Eventually the Amir asked me where we came from and why. I explained that I had come from the Hadhramaut, that I had been exploring and shooting oryx in the Empty Quarter and, having run out of water, had come to the Hassi. I told him that the Rashid, who were with me, knew neither the country nor where we were going. He asked me how in that case we had found the Hassi, and I said that Philby had marked it on the map, and that the two Saar who had been with us had known where it was, having visited it from Najran. I said they had gone back when we reached this well. I insisted that I alone was to blame for having come here, and accepted all responsibility.

Later, after coffee and tea had been handed round, the Amir of the Wadi said I must go with him to Dam, and that one of my companions could come with me. I asked for bin Kabina. Eventually the two of us climbed into the back of the Amir's truck, the slave who had fetched me from my room got in with us, still holding the fetters. After the Amir, his clerk, and the driver had mounted in front, we drove off to the west. It was very cold, the car lurched and bumped, and bin Kabina was car-sick. He had told me as we waited to get into the car that all four of them had been put in the stocks, when suddenly a messenger arrived and asked which was bin Kabina. I said the Amir had given permission for one of them to accompany me and that I had asked for him. He replied, 'You should have asked for Muhammad. He is the eldest.'

At last we arrived at another village and stopped in front of a large castle. The slave informed us that we were at Dam. We followed the Amir inside, and he gave orders for tea and coffee to be made, and a fire to be lit where we could warm ourselves. He told me that he had seen my telegram to the King, and said, 'Don't worry. I am sure that all will be well.' Then he bade us good night and left the room.

The slave came in again with some quilts for our bedding. He asked if we wanted more coffee and when we refused helped himself and went out. The fire died down and the room grew very dark. The wind banged a loose shutter throughout the night.

TWELVE

From Sulaiyil to Abu Dhabi

~~~

After our release we plan to travel eastwards to the
Trucial Coast. We visit Laila where we are refused
a guide, but make our own way to Abu Dhabi.

W e were in a small bare room at the top of the castle.
We had been given bread and tea at dawn, but since
then no one had come near us. It was now nearly eleven
o'clock. Bin Kabina, silent and depressed, had covered himself again
with his blanket and I wondered if he was asleep. Every now and
again I could hear a wheel creaking on a well, but on looking out
of the window could see nothing but a drab plain, where the wind
spun eddies of dust among leafless bushes. In the distance I could
just make out the dark wall of the Aradh.

The night had seemed very long, for I had not slept. I had been
haunted by the memory of three boys whom I had seen a few
months earlier sitting outside a village in the Tihama. Each of them
nursed in his lap a bundle of stained wrappings which concealed
the suppurating stump of his right hand. Their hands had been cut
off simply because they had been circumcised in a manner which
the King had forbidden. I could not forget the twitching face and
pain-filled eyes of one gentle, delicate-looking youth. I had been
told that when the Amir's slave hesitated to execute this savage
punishment he held out his hand, saying, 'Cut. I am not afraid.' I
had lain there in the dark, dreading that some such punishment

might be inflicted on bin Kabina and my other companions as a warning to others not to bring foreigners into Saudi Arabia without permission, and that if I was taken away to Jidda I should never know their fate.

However, these forebodings were dispelled when the door opened and the Amir came in. Smiling, he said cheerfully, 'I told you it would be all right. Abdullah Philby spoke to the King on your behalf, and the King has given orders that you are to be released and allowed to go on your way.' Philby, who is a Muslim, had lived in Riyadh for many years and was a regular attendant at the King's court. I had seen him recently in London, and had told him that I planned this journey. He came to meet me at Laila a few days later, and then he told me what had happened.

The Amir now asked where I proposed to go, so that he could inform the King. I told him that I would like to go to Laila and to cross from there to the Trucial Coast. He said that the car was waiting and would take me back to Sulaiyil.

We drove down the Wadi Dawasir, passing through the gap which separates the Aradh from the main Tubaiq range to the north. The cliffs of the Aradh were here about eight hundred feet high. We went to the Amir of Sulaiyil's house where the others were waiting for us, having spent a cold night in the stocks. Bin Ghabaisha said, 'By God! if I had realized that they were going to do this to me they would never have caught me, when I had a rifle in my hand and a camel under me'; but they were as relieved as I was that nothing more had happened to them. We arranged to go to Laila next day. We had little food left, but agreed that it would be better to buy what we needed there than tire our camels by carrying it.

Two Yam dined with the Amir that night and, after we had fed, one of them told us how he had killed bin Duailan. The lamp smoked and gave little light, and the room was filled with weird shadows; the embers glowed on the coffee hearth and wisps of smoke were bitter in our nostrils. Outside, a rising wind pressed at the badly-fitting door. I watched the man as he told his story, speaking slowly and with many pauses. He was leaning forward and occasionally stroked his pointed black beard with a thin small hand. His face was framed in the white folds of his head-cloth, which was topped with a simple black head-rope. He had great dignity, and was unmistakably a desert Arab, passionate, yet austere.

'It was late in the morning,' he said. 'Three of my relatives had unsaddled at my tent, and we were drinking coffee, while my son was skinning the goat we had killed for them. Suddenly we heard the sound of firing to the south, very many shots. We gave the alarm and ran to fetch our camels. While we were mounting, a small herdsboy rushed up, shouting out that my uncle's camp was being attacked by Mishqas, many, many Mishqas. He cried to me to hurry, saying that they had already killed Salim, and Jabr, who was my nephew, and that they were taking all the camels. Twelve of us gathered from the surrounding tents, and we rode to their help. As we got near my uncle's tents we saw five Mishqas – God's curse on all Mishqas! – jump on their camels and ride off. They were dressed only in dark loin-cloths. They had been looting the tents and one of them carried a rug. The women were wailing round the body of my nephew – God have mercy on him – and as we galloped past they shouted that the main body of Mishqas was already gone, taking all the camels, and they cried on us for vengeance. We galloped after the few we could see, and we were gaining on them when they reached some low dunes covered with bushes. They stopped there and fired on us. The plain was as bare as this floor, and we could only get near them from the north, where there were other dunes. They had already killed one of us. We could not see them. Do you understand? We got off our camels and ran towards them through the dunes. There was much firing. We killed three of them, and they had killed another of us and wounded two more. Then we killed another, and knew that there was only one left. He was somewhere among the big dunes, and every time one of us moved he fired, and he never missed. He had killed four of us, and still we could not see him, though we knew where he was. I realized that he was very close, with only the crest of a dune between us. I and my cousin crawled slowly up it towards him. Then my cousin lifted his head to look as we neared the top of the dune, and fell back dead beside me, shot through the forehead. I saw the barrel of a rifle jerking. By God, it was less than eight paces from where I lay! I realized that the rifle had jammed. I drew my dagger and leapt on the man before he could get to his feet. I drove my dagger into his neck and killed him. He was a little man and was armed with an English rifle.'

He stopped speaking and fetched a rifle from the corner and held it out to me, saying, 'This was the rifle; and he also had a pair of field-glasses hung round his neck. Later someone recognized him and told us that he was bin Duailan, "The Cat".'

I said that he had travelled with me the year before and that I had given him the field-glasses. The Yam said, 'Yes, we have heard of you as the Christian who travels with the Mishqas, and we thought that you had probably given him this rifle.' But I replied, 'No, he captured that from a government post in the Hadhramaut quite recently.'

After a pause, he said, 'By God, he was a man! He knew how to fight. I thought he would kill us all.' He told us that in this raid the Mishqas had killed fourteen Yam and captured a hundred and thirty camels, and that nine Mishqas had been killed. He added, 'Now that the King has given us permission to raid them, we shall, if God wills, recover our camels and capture many others and, by God, we shall kill every Mishqas we see. By God, you were lucky that we did not find you before you got here!'

We left Sulaiyil next morning, 29 January. Laila was a hundred and sixty miles away, and Abu Dhabi on the Trucial Coast was at least six hundred miles beyond that, twice as far from here as Manwakh, from where we had started our journey. It took us eight days to reach Laila. Our camels were tired, and Muhammad's camel and three of the baggage camels had large saddle-swellings. The Amir at Sulaiyil warned us that we should find no grazing other than acacias until near Laila, where there had been a little rain in the autumn.

The first afternoon we overtook two Yam and a Dahm driving a couple of hundred white sheep and black goats to Laila for sale. We camped with them and bought a goat for our evening meal, which they shared with us. They were friendly, and curious about our journey across the sands. The Dahm had a blood-feud with his own tribe and was living among the Yam. He told me that he had been in Najran in the summer when a Christian had come there from Abha and stayed for two days with bin Madhi, the Amir. He was amused when I told him that I was this Christian. He said he had seen me in the distance in the market-place, but that I was then wearing different clothes. This was true, as at that time I was dressed as a Saudi. When we left them they explained how to find the next well. There was a clearly-marked track to Laila, and this route, surveyed by Philby, was shown on the map I had with me.

The following afternoon, seeing dark clouds banking up in the west, I asked Muhammad, without thinking, if it would rain, and he answered immediately, 'Only God knows.' I should have realized that this would be his answer. No Bedu would ever express an opinion about the weather, since to do so would be to claim know-ledge that belongs to God. I told him that in England wise men could foretell the weather, but this was almost blasphemy and he exclaimed, 'I seek refuge in God from the Devil.'

The last two days before we reached Laila were bitterly cold, with a strong north-easterly wind. We rode across a stony plateau which sloped gently to the east. There was little vegetation until we were near the town, when the ground was suddenly covered with a small white flower called *rahath*. We stopped early, so that the camels could have a good feed, and started late next morning. It was a pleasure to look round at sunset and see our camels lying down fully fed, instead of roaming about in their perpetual hungry quest for food. This was only the second time they had had enough to eat since we had left Manwakh. Little did I know that it was going to take us another forty days to reach Abu Dhabi and that in all that time our camels would only get one more proper meal. After dark we saw the lights of a car in the distance. Later we heard its engine racing and realized that it was stuck in the sand. Resenting all cars, especially in Arabia, I was rather pleased that it was in trouble!

The following afternoon we rode into Laila, a small dun-coloured town of flat-roofed mud buildings, with a population of about four thousand. We halted outside the Amir's house, where we were told by a slave to unload our camels, and were then shown into a long dark room, bare of furnishings except for the rugs which covered the earthen benches round the walls. We greeted the Amir, a sour-faced, elderly man called Fahad, who was wrapped in a gold-embroidered cloak. He called for coffee and tea and then informed me in as few words as possible that Abdullah Philby had arrived yesterday by car from Riyadh, and not finding me here had gone off to look for me.

For the next two hours we sat in silence, which did not, however, prevent the Amir from making it quite clear how greatly he resented my presence. He left the room at sunset, and I went out into the courtyard to stretch my legs. I was looking at some saker falcons, which were sitting hooded on their blocks, when I heard the call to prayer. Everyone else hurried off to the mosque, except some small boys who now crowded round and reviled me for being an infidel and for not praying. One little urchin explained at length that I was unclean. I was tired, irritated by their ill manners, and wished they would go away.

Philby arrived about an hour later. He was an old friend of mine and I was delighted to see him. His car had stuck in the sands while he was looking for us, and I realized that it was his lights which we had seen the night before. He said: 'I happened to call on the King just after the telegram arrived informing him that you and your party had turned up in Sulaiyil. He was absolutely furious. Asked me if I knew who you were; then said he would make an example of you that would stop other unauthorized Europeans from entering his country. I tried to put in a word for you, but he wouldn't even let me open my mouth. I was worried what might happen to you and decided the best thing to do was to write him a letter. I gave it to him in the morning, saying as I did so that it was a man's duty to intercede for his friends. He was quite different from the night before; said at once that he would send off an order for your release.'

The Amir had pitched a tent for Philby in the space outside

his house, and we went there after dinner and talked till nearly dawn.

I grumbled about my churlish reception by the Amir that afternoon. Philby was sympathetic, but told me that I ought to realize that as a Christian I was anathema to these strict Wahabis. He pointed out that, after all, it was only this rigid adherence to their principles in a fast changing world that still preserved in a few remote areas the qualities which we both admired in the Arabs. To illustrate the length to which their puritanism sometimes led them, he told me that once he was sitting with Ibn Saud on the palace roof in Riyadh when they heard someone singing in the distance. Genuinely shocked, the King exclaimed, 'God protect me! Who is that singing?' and sent an attendant to fetch the culprit. The man came back with a Bedu boy who had been driving camels into the town. Sternly the King asked the boy if he did not realize that to sing was to succumb to the temptings of the devil, and ordered him to be flogged.

As Philby was anxious to visit Qariya to investigate the ruins which no European had yet seen, he left next day, but we remained for a further twenty-four hours in Laila, during which time the Amir left us without food. I did not see him again. I remained reading in the seclusion of the tent, interrupted by children peeping in, making rude remarks, and running away. My Rashid tried to buy supplies for our journey, but were cursed and spat at for bringing an infidel into the town. The shopkeepers said that they would only accept our money after it had been publicly washed. This nicety did not, however, prevent them from charging us exorbitant prices when eventually I got hold of some flour, rice, dates, and butter through the Amir's son. Muhammad asked the Amir to find us a guide to take us to Jabrin, but he answered, 'I will encourage no man to travel with an infidel.' The villagers had already declared that none of them would go with us, expressing the hope that we should die of thirst in the desert. They said that this was sure to happen, as no rain had fallen in the country between Laila and Jabrin and consequently we should encounter no Bedu to direct us. Some of them horrified my companions by asking why they had not murdered me in the desert and gone off with my possessions. Bin Kabina kept muttering, 'They are dogs and sons of dogs. They say you are an infidel, but you are a hundred times better than such Muslims as these.'

Laila had been one of the strongholds of the Akhwan, a militant, religious brotherhood dedicated to the purification and the unification of Islam. This movement had aimed at breaking up the tribes and settling the Bedu round the wells and in the oases, since these fanatics regarded nomadic life as incompatible with strict conformity with Islam, which in their eyes entailed the scrupulous observance of fasts, prayers, and ablutions. Ibn Saud had risen to power on this movement, but later, when the Akhwan rebelled against him, accusing him of religious laxity because he forbade them to raid into the neighbouring states, he broke their power at the battle of Sabila in 1928. Here in Laila, and in the Wadi Dawasir, the old fanaticism had survived.

The hatred which I encountered was a disturbing experience. It was ugly, as is all hatred, and to me, accustomed to religious tolerance, it seemed senseless; but I wondered if it were not preferable to the new hatred based on distinctions of colour, nationality, and class which our civilization has engendered and which are convulsing the more sophisticated parts of the Middle East. In the early days of Islam, while their faith was still unchallenged, the Arabs were remarkably tolerant about religion. But to the people of Laila I was an intruder from an alien civilization, which they identified with Christianity. They knew that the Christian had subjugated most of the Muslim world, and that contact with their civilization had everywhere destroyed or profoundly modified the beliefs, institutions, and culture they cherished. Naturally they did not realize how little sympathy I had with the innovations and inventions with which they associated me, nor how much sympathy I had with the way of life they sought to preserve.

In the evening we discussed what we should do. Jabrin was about a hundred and fifty miles away, but I was confident that I could get there by following Philby's route, which was shown on an otherwise blank map. I realized, however, that if I failed to find this oasis we should be lost in the empty waterless desert to the south of the Hasa. I suggested to the others that I should guide them, but they were naturally doubtful of my ability to find a place which I had never seen, and which was eight days' journey away.

I said, 'We don't need a guide, I can find the way.'

Bin Ghabaisha asked, 'How can you do that? You have never seen the country.'

I explained: 'Abdullah Philby marked Jabrin on the map. I can find it with my compass.'

Muhammad was sceptical: 'There are no landmarks. The way is across open plains like the Jaddat al Harasis; it is different from the journey we have just made. Then we did not need a guide. We knew the Aradh was on our left. We had only to strike it to arrive at the Hassi. The Saar knew the actual place of the well. Now we need a guide.'

I suggested that we should probably meet some Bedu on the way, but Amair said doubtfully, 'They say here that the country is empty. There has been no rain.'

I went on, 'Believe me, I can find Jabrin. By God, I don't want to die of thirst in the desert any more than you do!'

Bin Kabina asked, 'How many days will it take?'

I answered, 'Eight'; and he said: 'That is what they say here.'

Eventually they agreed that I should guide them. Bin Ghabaisha said, 'It is obvious we shall not find a guide here and God forbid we should remain in Laila. We must put ourselves in Umbarak's hands.'

I asked if we should find Arabs at Jabrin, and Muhammad said, 'We are bound to find Murra there. There are always some of them there. Don't worry about that, Umbarak. You just get us to Jabrin. Do that and we shall be thankful.'

I sincerely hoped we should find Arabs at Jabrin. By then we should need more food, and, what was far more important, we should need a guide to show us the water-holes on our way to Abu Dhabi, four hundred miles farther on. Without a guide we should be stranded at Jabrin with worn-out camels, in the northern wastes of the Empty Quarter. It was not a pleasant thought.

That evening Muhammad tried to give me some money. He said, 'Abdullah Philby gave us this before he left. Here is a fifth of it, your share; we are travelling companions and should share all things alike.'

We left Laila on 7 February. We carried six skins full of water, and had with us ninety pounds of flour, fifteen pounds of rice, thirty pounds of dates, and some butter, sugar, tea, and coffee. The Amir's son pretended that he had difficulty in buying even this small quantity of food. As we were unlikely to get anything but dates from the Murra at Jabrin, I knew that we were going to be very hungry before we reached Abu Dhabi. I reckoned that it would take us at least a month to get there. We therefore decided to ration ourselves to three pounds of flour between the five of us for our one evening meal. We could use the rice only when we were on a well and had plenty of water. We would eat the dates for breakfast, or rather they would, for by now I could no longer even stand the sight of dates. As we led our camels out of the town, some Arabs shouted to us not to come back if we failed to find the way.

My diary shows that it took us eight days to reach Jabrin, and records our marching hours, which were not really long, since only twice did we do eight hours in a day. But my recollection is of riding interminably through a glaring haze-bound wilderness, which seemed to be without beginning and without end. The weariness of our camels added to my own, making it barely tolerable, especially when their bodies jerked in flinching protest as they trod with their worn soles upon the flints which strewed alike the hollows and the ridges. Sometimes we found a path, and its smooth surface afforded them temporary relief, but I dared not follow it if it deviated from my compass course, for there were no landmarks in this desert which I could recognize to warn me if I was going wrong. I knew that I should only have to be eight or ten miles out to miss Jabrin, not much after a hundred and fifty miles. Was Jabrin shown accurately on the map? Though Cheesman and Philby were meticulously accurate in their work, both of them had fixed Jabrin after a long journey. I could not recall what method they had used. If they had fixed its position by compass-traverse a ten-mile error was possible.

In the evening we camped wherever we could find a few bushes to give us fuel. We would turn the camels loose to search for food and I would watch them hobbling away, heading back instinctively towards their homelands in the south; and as they got farther and farther away, adding yet more miles to the miles they had already covered that day, I would think wearily, 'Now one of us will have to go and get them.' If I started to do so, the others would jump up, saying, 'We will get them, Umbarak'; but sometimes I would insist and, accompanied by one of them, would set off irritably in pursuit. To spare the camels, we were carrying little water, and during these days I was always thirsty and also hungry, for being thirsty I found it difficult to swallow the heavy, unappetizing bread which bin Kabina cooked. The weather was very cold, and on most nights we could see lightning and sometimes hear thunder, and I hoped it would not rain, for we would have no sort of shelter.

On previous journeys it had needed a conscious effort on my part to understand what my companions said; but now, although I still spoke Arabic haltingly, for I am a bad linguist, I could no longer withdraw into the sanctuary of my own mind, beyond reach of their disputes. I could follow their talk too easily. For one entire day bin Kabina and Muhammad argued about the money I had given them two years before at Tarim. On the ground that the camel which bin Kabina had ridden belonged to him, Muhammad had kept two-thirds of the money which I had intended for bin Kabina. Remembering how destitute bin Kabina had been at the time, I thought this mean and said so. The argument went on and on, angry shouted interruptions checking but not halting an endless flow of repetition. It only came to an end when we stopped for the night. They then sat contentedly together baking bread. Throughout another day, bin Kabina and Amair wrangled continuously about the respective merits of their grandfathers. Bin Kabina said maliciously, 'Anyway, my grandfather never farted in public,' and the discomfited Amair blushed for this appalling solecism on the part of a grandfather who had been dead for twenty years. When next day they started to quarrel once more about their grandfathers, I protested. They looked at me in surprise and said, 'But it passes the time,' which I suppose was true.

Two days before we reached Jabrin we crossed the Dahana sands, here about fifteen miles wide. This belt of crescent dunes links the sands of the Empty Quarter with the great Nafud sands in northern Arabia. Rain had fallen two months earlier and had penetrated three feet into the Sands, which were touched with a bloom of newly sprung seedlings. To me the unexpected hint of spring in the drab monotony of those days was very welcome. On the eighth morning we climbed a final ridge. I had calculated that if we were ever to see Jabrin we should see it now; and there it lay, straight in front of us, the splashes of the palm-groves dark on the khaki plain. I sat down on a tumulus to rest, for I was very tired, while the others broke into excited talk. Later, we went down into the plain and found a well near a grove of acacias.

We watered the camels and turned them loose. They would no doubt find something, although even the acacias were leafless from the long drought. Only twice during the past eight days had I noticed anything which I thought they could eat, but I suppose they must have found something more during those shuffling quests which took them so far afield. Bin Kabina may have noticed the compassion in my eyes, for he said, 'Their patience is very wonderful. What other creature is as patient as a camel? That is the quality which above all else endears them to us Arabs.'

The well was shallow and the water sweet. My companions stripped off their shirts and poured buckets of water over each other, but I shrank from this bitter washing in the cold wind despite their gibes and encouragement. 'Come on, Umbarak,' called out bin Ghabaisha, and denied that it was cold, although I could hear him gasp each time Amair threw water over him. He still wore his loin-cloth, but the water moulded it to him like draperies on a statue; all Arabs dislike uncovering themselves in public, but here this modesty seemed exaggerated. I contrasted it with the behaviour of other Bedu with whom I had bathed in the Euphrates, who had chased each other naked along the river bank.

Later, Muhammad and Amair went off to look for the Murra. We had been in the territory of this tribe since we had crossed the Dahana, and Muhammad was still confident that we should find some of them in this oasis. The Murra, one of the great tribes of the Najd, number between five and ten thousand persons and live in an area as large as France. They guided Philby across the Empty Quarter, but their knowledge of it is limited to parts of the central and Western Sand, and they do not range anything like as widely as the Rashid, who may be met with from the borders of the Yemen to Oman, and from Dhaufar to Riyadh, the Hasa, and the Trucial Coast.

The Murra have a great reputation in Saudi Arabia as trackers, and are widely employed by the government for tracking down criminals and identifying them from their footprints. The Murra who was friendly to us in Sulaiyil was so employed.

While the others were away we cooked a large meal of rice against their return, and then, while we lay idly round the fire, bin Kabina and bin Ghabaisha tried to teach me a game, rather like draughts, which they played with camel-droppings in the sand, but either their explanations were too involved or the game was too complicated, for I never understood it.

When the others came back at sunset they told us that they had found neither Arabs nor fresh tracks. They asked me how much farther I could guide them. Between here and Abu Dhabi, my map showed only a single well called Dhiby, which Thomas had located at the end of his great journey across the Sands. It was about a hundred and fifty miles away in a depression to the south of the Qatar peninsula. Sixty miles to the east of it were the salt-flats of the Sabkhat Mutti, which, starting on the coast, run southward into the desert. Al Auf had once told me that camels were sometimes inextricably bogged in the Sabkhat Mutti after rain, but that they would never be engulfed as in the Umm al Samim.

I told the others that I could take them as far as Sabkhat Mutti, but that I neither knew whether I could find Dhiby well nor whether its water would be drinkable. I vaguely remembered Hamad telling me the year before, when we were in Dhafara, that all the water near the Sabkhat Mutti was brackish. However, Muhammad said that if I could guide as far as the Sabkhat Mutti he could then guide us to Abu Dhabi. I was doubtful about this, but we had to go on, since we should starve if we stayed where we were. The others reassured me by saying that we were certain to encounter some of the Murra before we got to the Sabkhat Mutti.

We decided to fill the ten water-skins which we had with us. This would mean that our baggage camels would again be heavily loaded, but we were quite prepared to sacrifice them in order to save our riding camels and ourselves. Three of them and Muhammad's mount had developed deep, evil-smelling ulcers on their humps and withers, where the saddle-swellings had burst and the skin sloughed away. Amair cut off lumps of mortifying fat and flesh, which he said it was better to remove. They paid little heed to this operation, so I hoped it did not hurt them too much. My companions were always prepared to endure discomfort and even hardship to save their camels, but inevitably the hardness of their lives made them callous to all pain. Desert people can be as callous about their own sufferings as they are about the sufferings of others and of animals. I remember I once hired a camel in Tibesti. Its owner was to come with me on foot, but as we started I noticed that he was limping. I asked him what was the matter and he showed me his bare feet. He had worn through the soles on a recent journey to Kufra and was now walking on the raw flesh. The mere thought of his pain made me feel sick, and yet, because he needed the money, he proposed to walk across the mountains. But if Arabs are callous they are never deliberately cruel. It would have been inconceivable to my companions that anyone could derive pleasure from inflicting pain. Although, to avenge a death, any of them would have knifed an unarmed herdsboy, not one of them would ever have tortured him. Many of the RAF stationed at Aden believed that they would be castrated by Arabs if they came down in the desert, but I am convinced that no Arab tribesman would do this; the very idea would revolt him. Once when I was telling my companions about the Danakil, I mentioned that they castrated the men they had killed. They were really shocked, and Amair said disgustedly, 'They must be animals; no human being would do a thing like that.'

The next day we crossed some salt-flats to the far side of the Jabrin depression, where we found a few bushes which had been touched to life by a shower of rain, and there we stopped to let our camels feed. I was again surprised how local were many of these showers, wetting only a few score acres. In the afternoon we rode across a gravel plain marked with many tracks. Towards evening a grey haze from the north came down, blotting out the emptiness that lay beyond.

After dinner Muhammad insisted that we must have more to eat. I suggested facetiously that he should go off and buy some flour, and also a goat while he was about it, but he grumbled that they could none of them go on unless they had more food. I maintained that our supplies would barely last us, and that it would be idiotic to increase our rations, and asked him what we should do when our flour was finished. He said, 'God will provide!', but I, not having Elija's faith, doubted this. We argued angrily, and finally I got up, telling them that they had better finish the flour that evening and then we should know exactly where we were, and went off to bed in a temper, thinking indignantly, 'I am just as hungry as they are but less improvident.' Next day we ate the same ration as before and nothing more was said about it.

We travelled for eight and a half hours until we reached the western edge of the Jaub depression, which I hoped would lead us to Dhiby. It was a burning hot day. For the past ten days clouds had banked up each evening and there had been distant thunder and lightning; now it rained almost continuously for three days and intermittently for the next four, often with thunderstorms, especially at night.

They were miserable days. It was maddening to ride along drenched to the skin and watch the driving rain soak into the sand, for although I was bitterly cold I was also thirsty. We had no idea where we should find more water, and were again rationing ourselves to a pint a day. We had nothing with us, except a few small pots, in which to catch the rain, not that we could afford the time to stop. My companions were worried about the camels, and warned me that we might wake up any morning and find some of them dead, killed in their weakened state by the ulcers which were eating into them. Each morning I looked anxiously to see if they were still alive.

One night there was a terrific storm, which started soon after dark and revolved around us until dawn. On that bare plain there was no sort of shelter. We could only lie cowering on the ground while the lightning slashed through the darkness of driven clouds, and the thunder crashed about our ears. I had placed my rug and sheepskin over my sleeping-bag. On other nights these had kept me fairly dry, but tonight the weight of water was too great to be turned aside. It flowed over me like an icy torrent. Sometimes the rain stopped and I peered out to see, silhouetted against the night by the almost continuous flashes of lightning, the dark shapes where the others lay beneath their coverings, like grave-mounds on a wet seashore; and the group of sodden animals, squatting tail to storm. Then I would hear the muffled drumming of the rain as it came down once more. I was certain that some of our camels would die that night, but in the morning they were still alive.

At dawn there was no wood dry enough to light a fire. We exchanged once more the sodden misery of the night for the cold, dripping discomfort of the day, as we forced the unwilling camels forward into the wind and stinging rain. Nothing grew here but occasional matted growths of salt-bush, whose juicy green foliage gave an irritating illusion of fertility to depressions which were really more sterile than the surrounding sands. That evening the starving camels, finding nothing else, ate these bushes and suffered next day from the inevitable diarrhoea. We tied their tails sideways to our saddlery to prevent them from flicking messily over our clothes. There was no food in their stomachs, but this loss of liquid would entail immediate thirst. Luckily we came on a well, a shallow hole in hard sand, discernible from a distance only by the carpet of camel-droppings that surrounded it. We tasted the water, but it was too brackish to drink; the thirsty camels, however, drank as if they could never have enough. While we watered them a gleam of pale sunlight flooded across the wet plain, like slow, sad music. Then it started to rain again. Bin Kabina coaxed a fire to burn, and cooked a large meal of rice in water from the well, but it tasted horrible and most of it remained uneaten.

Next day was fine and sunny and our spirit rose as the sun dried our clothes and warmed our bodies. My companions sang as we rode across sands which looked as if they had been uncovered by an outgoing tide. They were Bedu and it had rained, not scattered showers, but downpours which might well have covered all the desert. 'God's bounty' they called it, and rejoiced at the prospect of rich grazing that would last for years. As I rode across these interminable naked sands it seemed incredible that in three months' time they would be covered with flowering shrubs. Eskimos enduring the cold and the darkness of the arctic winter can count the days till the sun appears, but here in southern Arabia the Bedu have no certainty of spring. Often there is no rain, and even if there is, it may fall at any time of the year. Generally the bitter winters turn to blazing summers over a parched and lifeless land. Bin Kabina told me now that he only remembered three springs in his life. Occasional springtimes such as these were all the Bedu ever knew of the gentleness of life. A few years' relief from the anxiety of want was the most they ever hoped for. It seemed to me pathetically little and yet I knew that magnificently it was enough.

As we rode along, the others spoke of years when it had rained, and bin Kabina told me that never in his life had he known such rain as this. Then inevitably they spoke of the great flood in Dhaufar of sixty years ago. I had myself seen palm-trunks which had been jammed by this flood eighteen feet up among the rocks in the cliffs of the Wadi Aidam, where the valley was more than a thousand yards wide. We speculated as to how many days it must have rained to produce this flood, which had occurred in summer when it was warm. I wondered how long a man could survive such rain in winter before he died of exposure. It rained again in the evening and continued to do so intermittently for the next three days.

On the afternoon of the eighth day since we had left Jabrin I reckoned that we must be near Dhiby well, and my calculation was confirmed by the bearings which I took on two rocky peaks in a low escarpment to the north of us. An hour later, after again checking our position, I said that we were near the well. Bin Ghabaisha went on to look for it and found it a quarter of a mile away in a hollow in the sands. He came back and said, 'By God, Umbarak, you *are* a guide!', but my justifiable satisfaction was spoilt when the water proved too brackish to drink. The camels, however, were thirsty and drank it greedily.

Near the well there was a little fresh *qassis* which I hoped foretold that we were on the edge of grazing, but the next day we marched twenty-eight miles and found nothing all day. It rained again throughout the night. I was too cold and wet to sleep, too worried about what we should do. We had decided to go on to the Sabkhat Mutti, still hoping to find Arabs, but as we had found no trace of any so far I saw no reason why we should. My map marked only Abu Dhabi about two hundred and fifty miles farther on and our water was nearly finished.

We woke to a grey, lowering day, heavy with massed clouds, threatening rain. With cold, numbed fingers we loaded our camels and then walked dispiritedly beside them trying to bring some warmth into our bodies, while our long shirts flapped damply round our legs. I felt sure that the camels could not survive another day. Then unbelievably we came on grazing. It covered only a few square miles, and we walked straight into it. The camels hardly moved. They just ate and ate. We stood and watched them and bin Ghabaisha said to me, 'This grazing has saved our lives.'

Next day we crossed the Sabkhat Mutti. We decided we must make a detour and cross these salt-flats near their head, otherwise the camels might become inextricably bogged, especially after the recent heavy rain. They would only have to sink in as far as their knees to be lost. Camels are always bad on greasy surfaces, so we fastened knotted cords under their feet to stop them from slipping. Here the salt-flats were divided into three arms by crescent-patterned drifts of sterile white sand. The flats themselves were covered with a crust of dirty salt which threw up a glare into our faces and, even through half-closed eyes, stabbed deep into my

Desolation in the Sands: travelling eastwards from Jabrin.

Below: Bad days in the Wadi Jaub.

Crescent dunes near the Sabkhat Muti.

Below: Sand massifs near the Liwa oasis.

A settlement in the Liwa oasis.

The sea journey to Bahrain: setting the mainsail in the dhow.

Below: Wind-towers on a house beside the creek at Dibai.

Falconers of Zayid bin Sultan.

Overleaf: A Kuwaiti boom returning from Zanzibar.

A mounted falconer.

Below: Peregrines on their blocks.

Omanis: the Imam's representative; *below*: one of the Junuba.

Some of the sheikh's retainers at Abu Dhabi.

Below: The Omani-type of camel saddle.

Omanis: A boy of the Wahiba and (*right*) Al Jabari of the Awamir.

Below: One of the Wahiba and (*right*) Huaishil, a sheikh of the Duru.

A settlement in the Liwa oasis.

Right: Omani thoroughbreds: a camel of the Wahiba and a camel from the Batina.

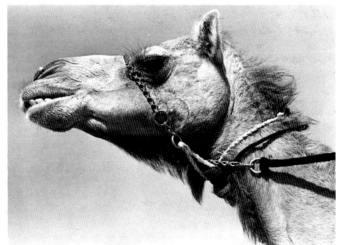

Bin Kabina riding a thoroughbred Wahiba camel.

Below: In the Oman Mountains: travelling northwards to Muwaiqih.

Overleaf: The Oman Mountains: Jabal Kaur, and Jabal al Akhadar on the extreme right.

Bin Kabina and bin Ghabaisha in Oman.

skull. The camels broke through this crust and floundered forward through liquid black mud. It took us five unpleasant, anxious hours to get across.

On the far side we camped among undulating, utterly lifeless white sands, where even the salt-bushes were dead and their stumps punctured our naked feet like needles. It was eleven days since we had left Jabrin. In the evening we had a long and anxious discussion. Muhammad had at last to admit that he knew nothing about this country, and my map was a blank as far as Abu Dhabi, which was still two hundred miles away. We had only a few gallons of water left. We should never get there unless we found water, and none of us had any idea if there were any wells along the coast. Muhammad said that we should probably find Bedu. He had been saying this since we left Laila, and we had come three hundred and fifty miles without meeting any. Finally, in desperation, I suggested that we should try to find the Liwa oasis, which I reckoned was only about a hundred miles away. I had not yet been there, but bin Kabina had visited three of the settlements from Balagh well when he fetched food for us the year before. He agreed that he would recognize the shape of the dunes at Liwa if I could guide us there. Unfortunately I did not have with me the compass-traverse which I had then made. Liwa was written in large letters across the map, but it was marked from hearsay, for no European other than myself had been near there. I puzzled over this map. Each time I fixed a bearing, some reason or other made me think I was wrong. The others sat round and watched me as I worked in the failing light. We all knew that if I went wrong and we missed Liwa we should be heading back into the Empty Quarter. It was a frightening thought; but to look for Liwa seemed to be our only chance.

Next morning, after travelling for twelve miles across flat white sands, we came to a succession of dune-chains, each of which, when approached from the west, showed up in turn as a wavy silver-blue wall, three to four feet high, running out of sight to north and south along the top of an orange-red slope a mile wide. Their farther sides fell away into a jumble of hollows. They gradually became larger and more complicated and developed into high but uniform dune-ranges and swelling downs, full of crescent-shaped hollows and deep pot-holes. The steeper sides of many of these hollows showed marks where water from the recent heavy rain had flowed down, and in some places the crust formed by the rain had been pitted by hailstones. Here we found grazing and noticed the tracks of hares, fennec foxes, honey badgers, and monitor lizards. On 28 February we found a filled-in well at the bottom of a deep hollow. Bin Kabina climbed to a summit and shouted down to us, 'I can see the sands of Liwa.' We climbed up to join him, and I saw the great mountains of golden sand where we had been the year before. We were safe now, but no one commented on the fact. Muhammad merely said, 'Those dunes are rather like those in Ghanim.'

Next day we found a shallow well where the water was drinkable though brackish. It was fifteen days since we had left Jabrin, and we had perhaps two gallons of water left in the skins.

We arrived at Balagh on 4 March, passing the hollow where bin Kabina and I had camped and starved for three days on our last journey. It was a still, hot afternoon. Next morning we found a small Manasir encampment on the edge of Liwa, and persuaded a man to guide us to Abu Dhabi. He told us that two months earlier a raiding party from Dibai, three hundred strong, had surprised an encampment not far away and killed fifty-two Manasir, losing five themselves, but that since then peace had been made between the Sheikhs of Abu Dhabi and Dibai. We had heard about this raid when we were in Laila.

We were now on the western edge of Liwa, which our guide said extended eastward for three days' journey. I should have liked to explore this famous oasis, but our camels were exhausted and we ourselves were worn out. Our food was nearly finished and it was difficult to buy anything here but dates. I knew that we must go direct to Abu Dhabi, and could only hope that perhaps I should be able to come back later. We passed through the settlements of Qutuf and Dhaufir. Palms were planted along the salt-flats, close under high steep-sided dunes, and in hollows in the sands. The groves were fenced in, and other fences were built along the dune-tops, to try to control the movement of the sands, which in a few places had partly buried the trees. They were carefully spaced, and evidently well tended. There was no other cultivation, probably because of the salt on the surface of the ground. Water was abundant at a depth of between seven and twenty feet. It was scarcely brackish, tasting only a little flat.

The Arabs here were Bani Yas. They lived in rectangular cabins made from palm fronds, built for the sake of coolness on the downs above the palm groves, two or three cabins being enclosed by a high fence and inhabited by one family. They owned some camels and a few donkeys and goats, and in the summer many of them went to Abu Dhabi to join the pearling fleet as divers.

We left Liwa on 7 March. Abu Dhabi was still a hundred and fifty miles away, but now we had a guide. We were very tired, and were no longer sustained by the struggle to survive, so each day's march became a plodding weariness during which we were inclined to quarrel over trifles. It rained at intervals during these days, sometimes heavily.

We reached the coast and followed it eastward through desolate country. There were limestone ridges, drifts of white sand, and stretches of gravel dotted with tussocks of woody grass and shrivelled plants. Salt-flats ran far out to sea, but yellow haze made it impossible to distinguish where the salt-flats ended and the sea began. The scene was colourless, without tones or contrast. We descended to the salt-flats, and led our slithering camels across this greasy surface to the creek which separates Abu Dhabi from the mainland. We waded through the sea, rested for a while outside the stone fort which guards the ford, and then went on to the town, arriving there early in the afternoon. It was 14 March. We had left Manwakh on 6 January.

A large castle dominated the small dilapidated town which stretched along the shore. There were a few palms, and near them was a well where we watered our camels while some Arabs eyed us curiously, wondering who we were. Then we went over to the castle and sat outside the walls, waiting for the Sheikhs to wake from their afternoon slumbers.

THIRTEEN

The Trucial Coast

From Abu Dhabi we go to Buraimi where we stay
for a month with Zayid bin Sultan, and then travel
to Sharja. From Dibai I sail by dhow to Bahrain.

The castle gates were shut and barred and no one was about.
We unloaded our camels and lay down to sleep in the
shadow of the wall. Near us some small cannon were half
buried in the sand. The ground around was dirty, covered with
the refuse of sedentary humanity. The Arabs who had watched us
watering had disappeared. Kites wheeled against a yellow sky above
a clump of tattered palms, and two dogs copulated near the wall.

In the evening a young Arab came out from a postern gate,
walked a little way across the sand, squatted down, and urinated.
When he had finished, Muhammad called to him and asked if the
Sheikhs were 'sitting' – an Arab expression for giving audience.
The boy answered, 'No, not yet,' and Muhammad told him to tell
them that an Englishman had arrived from the Hadhramaut and
was waiting to see them. The boy asked, 'Where is the Englishman?'
and Muhammad pointed to me and said, 'That's him.'

Half an hour later a grey-bearded Arab came out, asked us a
few questions, and went back into the castle. He came out again a
little later and invited us in. He led us up some stairs to a small,
carpeted room where Shakhbut, the ruler of Abu Dhabi, and his
brothers Hiza and Khalid were sitting. They were dressed in Saudi

fashion, in long white shirts, gold-embroidered cloaks, and white head-cloths, which fell round their faces and were held in place with black woollen head-ropes. Shakhbut's dagger was ornamented with gold. They rose as we came in, and after we had greeted them and shaken hands, Shakhbut invited us to be seated. He was a pale, slightly-built man, with small, regular features, a carefully-trimmed black beard, and large dark eyes. He was courteous, even friendly, but aloof. He spoke softly, moved slowly and deliberately, and seemed to impose a rigid restraint on a naturally excitable temper. I suspected that he mistrusted all men, and for this he had reason, since of the fourteen previous rulers of Abu Dhabi only two had died peacefully in power. Eight of them had been murdered and four had been driven out by rebellion instigated by their families. Hiza was very different from Shakhbut. He was large and jovial, with a thick black beard covering half his chest, whereas Khalid was chiefly remarkable for a loose front tooth which he poked at with his tongue.

Shakhbut called for coffee, and it was produced by an attendant in a saffron-coloured shirt. After we had drunk it and eaten a few dates, Shakhbut asked about our journey. Later I mentioned that I visited the outskirts of Liwa the year before. Hiza said, 'We heard rumours from some Awamir that a Christian had been there, but we disbelieved them. We could not believe that a European could have come and gone without being seen. Bedu news, as you know, is often unreliable. We thought they must have been talking of Thomas, who crossed the Sands sixteen years ago.'

Shakhbut then discussed the war in Palestine and ended with a diatribe against the Jews. Bin Kabina was obviously puzzled and whispered to me, 'Who are the Jews? Are they Arabs?'

Later the Sheikhs escorted us to a large dilapidated house near the market. We climbed up a rickety staircase to a bare room, carpeted ready for our arrival. Shakhbut ordered two of his attendants to look after us, and then said that he would leave us now as we must be tired, but would come and see us in the morning. When I asked him about our camels, he said they would be taken into the desert where there was grazing and brought back when we required them; but, he added, that would not be for many days, for we had come a long way and now we must rest here in comfort. He smiled at me and said, 'This is your home for as long as you will stay with us.'

When it was dark, servants arrived carrying a large tray heaped with rice and mutton, and many small dishes filled with dates and various kinds of sweetmeats. After we had fed they sat among us with easy informality and talked. In Arab households servants count as part of the family. There is no social distinction between them and their masters.

Merchants from the market-place and Bedu who were visiting the town came in to hear our news. A hurricane-lamp smoked through a broken glass but gave some light. It was cosy and very friendly, and pleasing to feel that for a while we had no further need of travelling, that we could eat and sleep at will. I wondered why people ever cluttered up their rooms with furniture, for this bare simplicity seemed to me infinitely preferable.

I remembered how, two years before, I had ridden in to Taif at sunset on a donkey, with two Arab companions and three half-naked Yemeni pilgrims who had joined company with us. We had come a long way across the mountains from the borders of the Yemen. We found a room in a lodging for pilgrims – an empty cubicle, one of several opening on to a courtyard. The others were all occupied. We swept it out, furnished it with our rugs, and borrowed a lamp. One of the Yemenis fetched us food from the market – grilled meat, rice, and flaps of bread; sour milk, water melons, and sweet black grapes. When we had fed, our neighbours came in and entertained us with their talk. I had everything that I could want – food, shelter, and good company after long days upon the road. In the morning I called upon the king's grandson, who was acting as Governor of Taif. I looked forward to the civilized comfort of Arab hospitality, but, thinking to please, he arranged for me to stay in the new 'hotel', where the rooms were filled with furniture in the Victorian style. On the walls were framed prints of Scottish lochs and Swiss chalets; there was electric light, fans, and tinned food served by a Sudanese suffraigi. My two companions were housed elsewhere. Some Egyptians were staying in the hotel, townsmen from Cairo with whom I had nothing in common; I could not even understand their speech. I was lonely, bored, and uncomfortable and I marvelled that Arabs should wish to ape our ways.

We stayed for twenty days at Abu Dhabi, a small town of about two thousand inhabitants. Each morning the Sheikhs visited us, walking slowly across from the castle – Shakhbut, a stately figure in a black cloak, a little ahead of his brothers, followed by a throng of armed retainers. We talked for an hour or more, drinking coffee and eating sweets, and, after they had left us, we visited the market, where we sat cross-legged in the small shops, gossiping and drinking more coffee; or we wandered along the beach and watched the dhows being caulked and treated with shark-oil to prepare them for the pearling season, the children bathing in the surf, and the fishermen landing their catch. Once they brought in a young dugong or sea-cow which they had caught in their nets. It was about four feet long, a pathetically helpless-looking creature, hideously ugly. They said its meat was good eating, and that its skin made sandals.

We had many visitors who made themselves at home in our room, often remaining overnight. They just rolled up in their cloaks and went to sleep among us on the floor. One of them was a Rashid called Bakhit al Dahaimi. He had enlisted two years before among the Sheikh's retainers and won a reputation as a fighter during the war with Dibai. I had already heard of his doings when I was on the southern coast. He was a lightly built man of about thirty, of average height, with a sallow face and close-set eyes. He wore a yellow shirt and a brown head-cloth. He stayed with us for three days. My Rashid were very impressed by him and frequently quoted what he had said, but I disliked him on sight. Hearing that I was going to Buraimi he announced that he would travel with us, but I arranged with Shakhbut that he should be sent on ahead to give Zayid bin Sultan, Shakhbut's brother at Buraimi, word of our coming. Al Dahaimi was to make trouble for me in the future.

I was anxious to penetrate into Oman and to visit the places which Staiyun had described to me the year before while we waited in the Wadi al Ain for the others to come back from Ibri. I believed that my best chance of getting there would be from Buraimi, and I hoped that Zayid would be able to help me. It was too late in the season to attempt a journey into Oman that year, and anyway I needed a rest. My mind was taut with the strain of living too long among Arabs. But I could at least go up to Buraimi, and make some discreet inquiries about Oman.

I left Abu Dhabi with my four Rashid, and a guide provided by Shakhbut on 2 April. Buraimi was about a hundred miles away, and it took us four days to get there. We had plenty of food and were no longer tired, and there was good grazing. Hiza had lent me a splendid camel to ride. These Al bu Falah sheikhs owned many thoroughbreds from Oman. The Arabs in Abu Dhabi had been inclined to disparage our animals, contrasting them with those owned by their sheikhs, until bin Ghabaisha was provoked to say, 'Your Sheikh's camels are admittedly wonderful animals, pictures of beauty. I am a Bedu, I can appreciate them; but there is not one of them that would do the journey ours have just done,' and his listeners were silent, for there was truth in what the indignant boy said.

The Batina camels from the Oman coast are famed throughout Arabia for their speed and comfort; but they are accustomed to being hand-fed on dates and are useless when food and water are short. The Wahiba in the interior of Oman own a famous breed, the *Banat Farha*, or 'The Daughters of Joy', and the Duru own the equally famous *Banat al Hamra*, or 'The Daughters of the Red one'. These are hardier than the Batina camels, but the Rashid said that none of them would survive for long in the Empty Quarter.

The evening before we reached Buraimi I was lying contentedly on the ground watching bin Kabina roasting some toadstools that he had found while herding the camels. They were creamy-tasting and delicious. There were also truffles here which were even better. Bin Ghabaisha tickled my foot, and, instinctively kicking out and catching him in the solar plexus, I knocked him out. Anxiously I bent over him, but bin Kabina said, 'He is all right. He is only knocked out'; and a few seconds later bin Ghabaisha sat up. He said reproachfully, 'Why do you try to kill your brother?' and when I protested he laughed and said, 'Don't be silly; of course I realize it was an accident.' I asked bin Kabina, 'What would you have done if I really had killed bin Ghabaisha?' and he answered at once, 'I should have killed you.' When I protested that it would have been an accident, he said grimly, 'That would have made no difference.' He was joking, and yet I knew that Bedu demand a life for a life whether the killing was intentional or accidental. Sometimes when their temper has cooled they may agree to accept blood-money, especially if the killing was accidental, but their immediate reaction is to exact vengeance. In Abu Dhabi we had met a Rashid lad who had been shot through the hand while raiding the Bani Kitab. Muhammad told him, 'As soon as Umbarak has gone off to his country we will avenge you. We will catch a boy of your own age from the Bani Kitab, hold his hand over a rifle, and blow it off.'

Next morning we approached Muwaiqih, one of eight small villages in the Buraimi oasis. It was here that Zayid lived. As we came out of the red dunes on to a gravel plain I could see his fort, a large square enclosure, of which the mud walls were ten feet high. To the right of the fort, behind a crumbling wall half buried in drifts of sand, was a garden of dusty, ragged palm-trees, and beyond the palms the isolated hog's back of Jabal Hafit about ten miles away and five thousand feet high. Faintly in the distance over the fort I could see the pale-blue outlines of the Oman mountains.

Some thirty Arabs were sitting under a thorn-tree in front of the fort. Our guide pointed and said to me, 'The Sheikh is sitting.' We couched our camels about thirty yards away and walked over, carrying our rifles and camel-sticks. I greeted them and exchanged the news with Zayid. He was a powerfully built man of about thirty with a brown beard. He had a strong, intelligent face, with steady, observant eyes, and his manner was quiet but masterful. He was dressed, very simply, in a beige-coloured shirt of Omani cloth, and a waistcoat which he wore unbuttoned. He was distinguished from his companions by his black head-rope, and the way in which he wore his head-cloth, falling about his shoulders instead of twisted round his head in the local manner. He wore a dagger and cartridge-belt; his rifle lay on the sand beside him.

I had been looking forward to meeting him, for he had a great reputation among the Bedu. They liked him for his easy informal ways and his friendliness, and they respected his force of character, his shrewdness, and his physical strength. They said admiringly, 'Zayid is a Bedu. He knows about camels, can ride like one of us, can shoot, and knows how to fight.'

A servant brought rugs for us to sit on; Zayid had been sitting on the bare sand. The servant then produced the inevitable coffee and dates. Zayid asked me questions about my journey, about the distances and the wells we had used, about Jabrin, and the Saudis we had met in Laila and Sulaiyil. He was well informed about the desert, and especially interested when I told him that I had been through the Duru country the year before, and expressed his surprise that the Duru had allowed me to pass. I told him that I had pretended to be a Syrian merchant, and he said laughingly, 'I should have known at once that you weren't.' He mentioned that an Englishman called Bird was staying in Buraimi in another of the villages, trying to persuade the tribes to let a Company look for oil. I gathered that he was having little success.

I had met Dick Bird three years before when he was a Political Officer in Bahrain. He was interested in and sympathetically disposed towards the Arabs, and we later became friends. But I realized that if, in the eyes of the local tribesmen, I became identified with an oil company, it would greatly lessen my chances of getting into Oman, and I therefore decided to stay with Zayid, and not with Bird, while I was in Buraimi.

Late in the afternoon a servant announced that lunch was ready, and we went into the fort. We passed through a wicket into a porch where armed men were sitting on a low earthen bench. A few months earlier they had been at war. They stood up as we came in. Beyond the porch was a sandy courtyard in which there was a tame gazelle and a bull camel that was rutting and dangerous. Zayid showed us into a large bare room on the left of the porch, lit by two small windows at ground-level opening on the yard. Our saddle-bags had been brought in, and carpets laid on the earthen floor. Zayid fed with us – a large meal of meat and rice, with side dishes of dates and curds, and bowls of sour milk.

I stayed with Zayid for nearly a month.

In the mornings, after we had breakfasted on tea and bread, a servant would come in and tell us that the Sheikh was 'sitting'. We would go out and join him. Sometimes Zayid would be on the bench in the porch, but more often under a tree outside the fort. He would call for coffee and we would sit there chatting till lunch-time, though we were frequently interrupted. Visitors would arrive, Bedu from the Sands or from Saudi Arabia, tribesmen from Oman, or perhaps a messenger from Shakhbut in Abu Dhabi. Everyone rose as they approached, and then Zayid would invite them to be seated and listen to their news. As they approached I tried to guess where they came from, noting the way they wore their clothes and saddled their camels. Sometimes they were Rashid or Awamir, and then, sitting beside my companions, they asked news of their kinsmen in the south. They were different from the Bani Yas and Manasir who comprised most of Zayid's retainers, hardier and more refined.

Perhaps an Arab would get up from the circle, sit down immediately in front of Zayid, hit the ground a wallop with his stick to attract attention, and interrupting us as we spoke together, would say: 'Now Zayid, what about those camels which were taken from me?' Zayid, who might be in the middle of a sentence, would stop and listen to the man's complaint. Most of the complaints were about camels. Frequently the complainant averred that some notorious outlaw, who might well be sitting with us, had taken his animals. Zayid had many of these outlaws in his entourage, since it suited him better to have them with him than in some rival sheikh's fort. Bin Ghabaisha, who sat beside me with his rifle between his knees – he was never parted from it – was soon to be numbered among them. I watched him listening with interest as each case was heard. Both sides argued noisily and with frequent interruptions, as was their wont. Zayid had no desire to offend the outlaw, nor to lose his reputation for justice. It was a proof of his skill that he usually satisfied both sides by his judgement.

I remember on one occasion a woman had run away from her husband, and her brothers were anxious that he should divorce her. The husband said that he would only do so if her family returned the full bride-price. This, they argued, was unfair as she had lived with him for years. Zayid consulted some of the greybeards who sat with us, and declared that the family should return half the bride-price. On another occasion a Manasir had shot his sister; we had heard the shot while we were sitting in our room. We soon learnt that she had been seduced by one of Zayid's Bani Yas retainers. Everyone, except my Rashid, thought that her brother had done right. Bin Kabina said to me, 'Poor little girl! It was a brutal thing to kill her.' Next day Zayid sentenced the man who had seduced her to be flogged.

Visiting Bedu would come up and ask for a present before they left, many of them having apparently come for no other purpose. I was interested to see that they were as importunate to Zayid as they were to me. I recalled that some of the Rashid on the southern coast thought it worth while to ride fourteen hundred miles to Riyadh and back in the expectation of getting something from Ibn Saud. A year later bin Kabina and bin Ghabaisha went to Muscat from Buraimi in the middle of the summer. Their camels were already worn out, and I had hoped that they would rest them against my return. In Muscat they each collected ten shillings from the Sultan. It is true that they had hoped to lift some camels on the way back to Buraimi but by then they were too well known and the alarm was out; even so, they did not seem to think that their five-hundred-mile journey had been in vain.

Zayid, as Shakhbut's representative, controlled six of the villages in Buraimi. The other two acknowledged the Sultan of Muscat as their nominal overlord, as did the tribes who lived in and around the mountains northwards from Ibri to the Musandam peninsula, although in fact this area was independent tribal territory. Ibri itself and the interior of Oman to the south of this town was ruled by the Imam. His authority was strong in the mountains and in all the towns, but was weak among the large and powerful Bedu tribes of the Duru and Wahiba who live on the steppes bordering on the Sands. Ibn Saud had undisputed control over the Murra beyond the Sabkhat Mutti, and his officials sometimes collected taxes from the Bedu who lived in Dhafara. But recently they had been driven out of Liwa by the Bani Yas, who acknowledged Sakhbut as their overlord. It was eighty years since Saudi forces, known in those days as Wahabis, had occupied the Buraimi. Now the only Saudis here were a few merchants engaged chiefly in the slave-trade, which still flourished in the two villages not controlled by Zayid.

Each of the Trucial Sheikhs had a band of armed retainers recruited from the tribes, but only Shakhbut had any authority among the tribes themselves, and he maintained this authority by diplomacy, not by force. There was no regular force anywhere on the Trucial Coast nor in Buraimi which could be used to support the authority of the Sheikhs. The Trucial Oman Scouts had not yet been raised, and although the RAF had an aerodrome at Sharja it was only a staging-post on the route to India.

Zayid was often busy during these days helping Bird with his interminable discussions with tribal sheikhs from the surrounding country. Bird used to come over to Muwaiqih in his car – Zayid also had a car and these were the only two nearer than Dibai on the coast. Bird was friendly but suspicious, wondering if I was working for some rival company. I kept away from him when visiting tribesmen were about. Anyway, I was averse to all oil companies, dreading the changes and disintegration of society which they inevitably caused.

The Iraq Petroleum Company had signed agreements with the Sultan of Muscat and with the Trucial Sheikhs, covering the area round Buraimi, and Bird was now trying to persuade the tribes to accept these agreements. It was not easy, since Zayid had no authority south of Buraimi, and the Sultan, whose authority there was at this time purely nominal, had no effective representative in the area. Each sheikh, excited by avarice, was noisily asserting his independence, while each of his tribesmen fancied that he could get special terms for himself by refusing to acknowledge any authority other than his own. None of this helped my chances of getting into Oman, which seemed slight enough at the best of times.

The interior of Oman had remained one of the least known of the inhabited places of the East, even less well-known than Tibet. It was first visited by Wellsted in 1835, and he was followed two years later by the French botanist Aucher Eloy. Colonel Miles made two long journeys through the country in 1876 and 1885, while he was British Consul in Muscat, and in 1901 Sir Percy Cox travelled southward from Buraimi to Nazwa and then on to Muscat.

Oman is largely inhabited by the Ibadhis, a sect of the Kharijites who separated themselves from the rest of Islam at the time of Ali, the fourth Caliph, and have been noted ever since for their condemnation of others. The Ibadhis have always maintained that their Imam or religious leader should be elected. The Al bu Said dynasty which ruled Oman from 1744, and to which the present Sultan of Muscat belongs, succeeded, however, in establishing an hereditary succession, but its neglect of the elective principle had always been resented by its subjects. The growth of Omani sea power between 1784 and 1856, overseas conquests, of which Zanzibar was the most important, and especially the removal of the capital from Rustaq to Muscat on the coast, weakened the hold of the Al bu Said rulers over the interior of the country, while foreign treaties and outside interference added to the fanatical resentment of the tribesmen. In 1913 the tribes, both Ghafari and Hanawi, rebelled and elected Salim bin Rashid al Kharusi as their Imam. The Sultan of Muscat rapidly lost all control over the interior and by 1915 the Imam was threatening Muscat. His forces, however, suffered a serious defeat when they attacked a British force outside Matrah. The Imam was murdered in 1920, and Muhammad bin Abdullah al Khalili was then elected. In the same year the treaty of Sib was signed between the Sultan and the Omani sheikhs, not between the Sultan and the Imam. By this treaty the Sultan agreed not to interfere in the internal affairs of Oman.

The present Imam, Muhammad bin Abdullah, was now an old man, a fanatical reactionary and bitterly hostile to the Sultan and to all Europeans. The interior of Oman was consequently more difficult for a European to penetrate in 1948 than it had been when Wellsted went there more than a hundred years before; for both Wellsted and his three successors had travelled under the protection of Sultans of Muscat who were recognized by the tribes in the interior.

I told Zayid of my plans and he promised to help me when I came back in the autumn. He warned me, however, to speak of them to no one else. I did not even tell my Rashid, for I had learnt that the most effective way to spread a story was to tell it to one or two Arabs under a pledge of secrecy. Zayid offered to send me down to the coast in his car, but I said I would go by camel. This would postpone a little longer my parting with my companions. He then said that he would lend me Ghazala, 'the gazelle', and this delighted me, for she was the most renowned camel in Oman, and may well have been the finest in all Arabia. Muhammad said to me, 'Any Bedu would give much to say that he had ridden Ghazala.'

We left Muwaiqih on 1 May, accompanied by four of Zayid's retainers, for we should pass through Bani Kitab territory and this tribe was at war with Rashid. We rode northwards along the edge of the Sands, parallel with the mountains. It was attractive country. Many watercourses ran down from the foothills and ended in the Sands. They were filled with *ghaf* and acacias which gave food to our camels, and to us shelter from the sun. Already the weather was hot. We dawdled along, for I was reluctant to arrive at Sharja. Bin Ghabaisha and I hunted wild ass, and shot two of them. They looked very different from the graceful, spirited animals I had seen in the Danakil country, and they were later identified as feral donkeys by the British Museum. They were difficult to skin, for our daggers were blunt. It was midday and the sun was very hot, there was no shade on the stony plain where we had found these donkeys, and we had no water with us.

While I had been at Muwaiqih I had hunted tahr on Jabal Hafit, camping for a week under the mountain with bin Kabina and bin Ghabaisha and two of Zayid's Arabs. The Arabian tahr had never previously been seen by a European, although they had been named from two skins bought in Muscat by Dr Jayakar in 1892. They resembled goats and had very thick short horns. It was exhausting work hunting them, for the mountains rose four thousand feet above our camp, and the slopes were everywhere steep and usually sheer, without water or vegetation. The tahr fed at night round the foot of the mountain, but the only ones we saw were near the top. The Arabs shot two females and we picked up the skull of a male. We had made ourselves sandals from green hide, without which we could never have climbed these cruel limestone rocks.

We arrived at Sharja on 10 May. We skirted the aerodrome, passing piles of empty tins, broken bottles, coils of rusting wire, and fluttering bits of paper. A generator thumped in the distance, and a jeep roared down a track, leaving a stink of petrol fumes behind it. We approached a small Arab town on an open beach; it was as drab and tumble-down as Abu Dhabi, but infinitely more squalid, for it was littered with discarded rubbish which had been mass-produced elsewhere. To me the sun-blistered skeleton of a car seemed infinitely more horrible than the carcass of a camel which we passed a little farther on.

I stayed with Noel Jackson, the Political Officer on the Trucial Coast, and in the peaceful comfort of his rooms forgot for a while the resentment which I had felt that morning. Later he took me round to the RAF mess. Listening to their talk while a wireless blared in a corner and the barman served drinks, I realized that these officers could have as little understanding of Bedu life as bin Kabina or bin Ghabaisha had of theirs. I could now move without effort from one world to the other as easily as I could change my clothes, but I appreciated that I was in danger of belonging to neither. When I was among my own people, a shadowy figure was always at my side watching them with critical, intolerant eyes.

I said good-bye to my companions at Sharja, hoping to be with them again in four months' time. I then went to Dibai and stayed with Edward Henderson. We had been together in Syria during the war. He was now working for the Iraq Petroleum Company, making preparations for the development which was expected there, but of which there was mercifully as yet no sign. He lived in a large

Arab house overlooking the creek which divided the town, the largest on the Trucial Coast with about twenty-five thousand inhabitants. Many native craft were anchored in the creek or were careened on the mud along the waterfront. There were *booms* from Kuwait, *sambuks* from Sur, *jaulbauts*, and even a large stately *baghila* with a high carved stern on which I could make out the Christian monogram IHS on one of the embossed panels. This work must have been copied originally from some Portuguese galleon. I wondered how many times it had been copied since, exactly to the last scroll and flourish. Commander Alan Villiers, who had sailed in a *boom* from Zanzibar to Kuwait, believed that there were only two or three of these *baghilas* still in existence. To the English all these vessels were dhows, a name no longer remembered by the Arabs. Once, however, dhows were the warships of this coast, carrying as many as four hundred men and forty to fifty guns. Miles saw the last of them at Bahrain, 'painted with two tiers of ports'.

Naked children romped in the shallows, and rowing-boats patrolled the creek to pick up passengers from the mouths of alleys between high coral houses, surmounted with square wind-turrets and pleasingly decorated with plaster moulding. Behind the diversity of houses which lined the waterfront were the *suqs*, covered passageways, where merchants sat in the gloom, cross-legged in narrow alcoves among their piled merchandise. The *suqs* were crowded with many races – pallid Arab townsmen; armed Bedu, quick-eyed and imperious; Negro slaves; Baluchis, Persians, and Indians. Among them I noticed a group of Kashgai tribesmen in their distinctive felt caps, and some Somalis off a *sambuk* from Aden. Here life moved in time with the past. These people still valued leisure and courtesy and conversation. They did not live their lives at second hand, dependent on cinemas and wireless. I would willingly have consorted with them, but I now wore European clothes. As I wandered through the town I knew that they regarded me as an intruder; I myself felt that I was little better than a tourist.

I could have gone to Bahrain by aeroplane from Sharja but I preferred to go there by dhow. The journey should have taken four days but lasted eleven. The *naukhada*, or skipper, was an old man, nearly blind, who spent most of his time asleep on the poop. The mate, an energetic Negro, described what he saw and the *naukhada* told him where to go. Once he woke the old man in the middle of the night to consult him. The *naukhada* gave his orders, but when the mate said 'Nonsense, Uncle!', he went grumbling back to sleep. The first night it blew a gale. The seas broke over the ship and I was very sick. We had to shelter under the Persian coast, and there we remained for three days, since the wind, when it moderated, was against us. While waiting for the wind to shift, we were joined by seven other dhows, great ocean-going *booms*, sailing back from Zanzibar to Kuwait. Their *naukhadas* rowed over to visit us, and we fed them on rice and dates and a large fish which we had just harpooned. They drank tea, smoked in turn from a hubble-bubble, and described their voyage, but I found it difficult to follow their talk, for I did not know the terms they used. Then the wind changed and we sailed for Bahrain. It was thrilling to watch these great dhows surging along beside us through the breaking seas. They were the last trading vessels in the world that made long voyages entirely by sail. Soon they too would disappear.

When we were almost within sight of Bahrain the wind dropped. For four days we lay, rolling slightly on an oily sea. The brief spring was past. The sky was without a cloud, and the damp heat wrapped itself round me like a wet towel. An occasional cat's-paw of wind ruffled the surface of the sea, but died away as I watched. The brackish water in the rusty iron tank was warm as tepid tea. I was sick of rice and dates flavoured with rancid butter. The crew, who, like all Arabs, had an enviable capacity for sleeping when there was nothing else to do, rigged themselves an awning and slept interminably, and I reread H. A. L. Fisher's *History of Europe*, the only book I had with me.

I was sailing on this dhow because I wanted to have some experience of the Arab as a sailor. Once they had been a great sea-going race, sailing their dhows round the coast of India to the East Indies and perhaps even farther. The Trucial Coast which we had just left had been known and dreaded as the Pirate Coast; in the early nineteenth century Juasimi pirates had fought our frigates on level terms on these very waters. But there was a deeper reason that had prompted me to make this journey. I had done it to escape a little longer from the machines which dominated our world. The experience would last longer than the few days I spent on the journey. All my life I had hated machines. I could remember how bitterly at school I had resented reading the news that someone had flown across the Atlantic or travelled through the Sahara in a car. I had realized even then that the speed and ease of mechanical transport must rob the world of all diversity.

For me, exploration was a personal venture. I did not go to the Arabian desert to collect plants nor to make a map; such things were incidental. At heart I knew that to write or even to talk of my travels was to tarnish the achievement. I went there to find peace in the hardship of desert travel and the company of desert peoples. I set myself a goal on these journeys, and, although the goal itself was unimportant, its attainment had to be worth every effort and sacrifice. Scott had gone to the South Pole in order to stand for a few minutes on one particular and almost inaccessible spot on the earth's surface. He and his companions died on their way back, but even as they were dying he never doubted that the journey had been worth while. Everyone knew that there was nothing to be found on the top of Everest, but even in this materialistic age few people asked, 'What point is there in climbing Everest? What good will it do anyone when they get there?' They recognized that even today there are experiences that do not need to be justified in terms of material profit.

No, it is not the goal but the way there that matters, and the harder the way the more worth while the journey. Who, after all, would dispute that it is more satisfying to climb to the top of a mountain than to go there in a funicular railway? Perhaps this was one reason why I resented modern inventions; they made the road too easy. I felt instinctively that it was better to fail on Everest without oxygen than to attain the summit with its use. If climbers used oxygen, why should they not have their supplies dropped to them from aeroplanes, or landed by helicopter? Yet to refuse mechanical aids as unsporting reduced exploration to the level of a sport, like big-game shooting in Kenya when the hunter is allowed to drive up to within sight of the animal but must get out of the car to shoot it. I would not myself have wished to cross the Empty Quarter in a car. Luckily this was impossible when I did my journeys, for to have done the journey on a camel when I could have done it in a car would have turned the venture into a stunt.

At last a puff of wind stirred the water and did not immediately die away. The mate shouted to the sleeping crew. They trimmed the sail, stamping and singing as they hauled. The breeze freshened.

We arrived at Bahrain on 28 May, the old blind *naukhada* taking his boat into the crowded roadstead under full sail. She smashed through the choppy waves and brought up within twenty yards of a dhow that had lain beside us under the Persian shore a week before.

FOURTEEN

A Holiday in Buraimi

～

I return to Buraimi, visit the Liwa oasis,
and go hawking with Zayid

I returned to Dibai from England at the end of October. Musallim bin al Kamam was waiting for me at Henderson's house, having come there to join me from the Yemen, where he had renewed the truce between the Rashid and the Dahm for another two years. He told me how the Imam of the Yemen's son had sent two parties of Dahm to intercept us when we crossed the Sands to Sulaiyil. He said, 'When I reached Najran I heard that you had been imprisoned in Sulaiyil. Bin Madhi, the Amir with whom you once stayed in Najran, declared that you had been lucky to get there, as the Yam would certainly have killed you if they had found you in the Sands.' I asked about the fight with the Abida at Thamud, and he told me how Salim bin Mautlauq had been wounded but had later recovered. He then asked me if I remembered Muhammad, Salim bin Mautlauq's brother, and told me that he had been savaged by a bull camel which had bitten off his knee-cap when he tried to shoot it, after it had attacked and killed an old man and a small boy as they sat round the fire in the evening. He also told me that Awadh had died of tuberculosis. Awadh had travelled with me to Tarim and also to Mukalla, and had been a charming man and a skilled hunter who had shot more than forty oryx. I was delighted to have bin al Kamam with me, for I had found him amusing and accommodating when he had travelled with me to

Tarim. He was exceptionally intelligent, level-headed, and reliable; he had travelled widely, was a good guide, skilled in negotiations, and had considerable authority among the desert tribes.

We left Dibai for Abu Dhabi on 27 October, going there by launch. I had meant to leave for Buraimi on the 31st but it poured with rain during the night and we woke to find most of the island under water. Shakhbut advised us to remain at Abu Dhabi for at least another day, to give the salt-flats, which we had to cross, a chance to dry. So bin al Kamam and I left on 1 November, riding borrowed camels, and arrived at Muwaiqih four days later. Zayid was there and put us in the room that I had been in before. He said, 'Bin Kabina, bin Ghabaisha, and Amair spent last night in an Awamir encampment on the edge of the Sands. They will turn up as soon as they hear that you are here. Muhammad has gone to Dakaka. They've been having a fine time while you were away, lifting camels from everybody.'

It was late at night when they arrived. Bin al Kamam and I had lain down to sleep, when someone hammered at our door and bin Kabina and the other two came in. Bin Kabina said, 'We only just heard that you had arrived. We were off in the morning to raid the Bani Kitab.' We relit the fire, bin al Kamam made coffee, and the others fetched their saddle-bags. They asked bin al Kamam about their families and friends, and pressed him for every detail of recent happenings in the south, discussing them at length. Later they told us of their own doings. They had spent the summer harrying the Bani Kitab and other tribes, and serving as soldiers of fortune with the local sheikhs. They had each collected half a dozen camels. As I listened to their talk I thought how well their adventures illustrated the chronic insecurity of these parts, where jealous and often hostile sheikhs relied on the uncertain support of the Bedu to maintain their position. These sheikhs competed for the support of the tribesmen by the lavishness of their hospitality and the scale of their gifts. Not one of them was prepared to acknowledge a paramount power, nor were any of them able to enforce their authority over the Bedu; none would even try, lest by doing so they should alienate Bedu support in time of need. In consequence the country was full of outlaws, who feared no punishment other than the blood-feud and the retaliation of hostile tribesmen. Knowing perfectly well that each sheikh would rather have their friendship than incur their enmity, the outlaws travelled quite openly among the villages which they had robbed, assured of hospitality commensurate with the strength and nearness of their own tribe and the reputation which they personally had acquired. If an exasperated ruler did detain them, they knew they could count on an immediate demand for their release by some other sheikh, who, anxious to court their favour, would claim that they were under his protection.

At present the politics of the area were dominated by the bitter enmity between the Al bu Falah of Abu Dhabi and the bin Maktum of Dibai. The truce between these two families which had recently put an end to several years of intermittent fighting had, I knew, in no way lessened this enmity. Beneath these recent hatreds and jealousies lay the age-old feud between the tribes of Yemen and Nizar origin, largely identified today with the factions of Hanawi and Ghafari. This feud had torn Oman for centuries, and here in the north had always prevented the establishment of an effective government.

Next morning bin Kabina appealed to me to secure the release of a young *saiyid*, called Ahmad bin Saiyid Muhammad who came from Qasm in the Hadhramaut, and was now imprisoned with a companion in Hamasa, one of the two villages at Buraimi which did not belong to Zayid. He said that both of them had been sold to Ali al Murri, a well-known slave-dealer, who had recently arrived from the Hasa. He added that the *saiyid* had been beaten to make him more amenable. I gathered that he and his companion had been shipwrecked on their way back from Singapore and that they had been picked up by a dhow and landed on the Trucial Coast, where they had been kidnapped and brought to Hamasa. Bin Kabina said: 'It is terrible that a descendant of the Prophet should be sold as a slave. You must secure his release. Do you remember the *saiyid* who gave us lunch in Qasm, the first time we went to the Hadhramaut? Well, he is this boy's uncle. They know quite well he is not a slave, otherwise they wouldn't have sold the two of them for 230 rupees.' I knew that many of the slaves who were sold in Hamasa were in fact Baluchis, Persians, or Arabs who had been kidnapped, but I also knew that the usual price slave-traders paid for one of them was 1,000–1,500 rupees, and for a young Negro even more. An Arab or Persian girl was, however, more valuable than a Negress and would fetch as much as 3,000 rupees. The ridiculously low price which Ali al Murri had paid for the *saiyid* and his companion showed that he expected to have great difficulty in disposing of them.

A few days later the Sheikh of Hamasa visited Zayid. I advised him to release these two men, saying that I knew their families in the Hadhramaut and that one of them was a *saiyid*. He grumbled that he would lose a lot of money if he let them go, but I assured him that it would pay him to do so. I heard later that they had been released and that they had gone to Sharjar, where the Political Officer had arranged to send them to the Hadhramaut.

I was anxious to explore Liwa before I started on my journey into Oman. Zayid advised me to take an old Rashid called bin Tahi as my guide. He said: 'You will like him. He is a pleasant old man. He has settled down and become respectable in the last few years, but he was a notorious outlaw when he was younger. He must have lifted camels from pretty well every tribe in southern Arabia, and knows every corner and water-hole in the desert. Your lads know him; everyone does.' Later I asked bin Kabina about bin Tahi and he said, 'Yes, that is a splendid idea. Let's take bin Tahi. He is a wonderful old man. He can guide us wherever we want to go. He is camped at present near the southern end of Jabal Hafit. I was staying with him only ten days ago.'

Bin Tahi had a grey beard and straggling grey hair, a strong square face, and a humorous expression, but he was younger than I had expected. He was heavily-built and obviously very powerful. He looked hard and enduring despite his grey hairs. He agreed at once to come with us.

We left Muwaiqih on 14 November and spent about a month travelling through Liwa as far as Dhafara, where we had been the year before. It was a pleasant journey. The sands were like a garden. There were matted clumps of tribulus, three feet high, their dark green fronds covered with bright yellow flowers, bunches of *karia*, a species of heliotrope, that was rated high as camel-food by the Bedu, and *qassis*, as well as numerous other plants which the camels scorned in the plenty that surrounded them.

We had a saluki with us, which I had borrowed from Zayid; but he was still too young to catch a full-grown hare, although he managed to catch an occasional leveret. My companions said disgustedly that he was not worth his keep. They had expected great things of him. But they played with him, and allowed him to lie on their blankets and drink from our dishes, for, although dogs are unclean to Muslims, the Bedu do not count a saluki as a dog. A middle-aged Rashid called Salih and his son were travelling with us as far as Dhafara, and this boy was more successful than the saluki in catching hares. He hunted for them while he was herding the camels, and often came back to camp with three or four which he had pulled out of the shallow burrows where they had taken refuge from the many eagles quartering in the sands. Once while we were riding along we saw a tawny eagle kill a full-grown fox. We drove the bird off its kill, and as the skin was still undamaged I kept it and later gave it to the Museum in London.

At Lahamma well we found many day-old tracks of men and camels. My companions said that they were made by Ali al Murri and the caravan of forty-eight slaves which he was taking to the Hasa. It seemed that the enormous wealth which was pouring into Saudi Arabia from the American oil company had greatly increased both the demand for slaves and the price paid for them. They said that Ali made a large profit not only from the slaves, but also from the camels which he bought in Buraimi.

One day when we had stopped at a shallow well, bin Kabina said to me, 'It was here that we had a fight with some Bani Kitab while you were away. We had raided them and taken twelve camels. It was the middle of summer and very hot. We were watering the camels, which were very thirsty for we had driven them hard, when we saw our pursuers. There were eight of them. We were six, for there were two Awamir with us. Do you see that high dune over there? Look! We left the camels here at the well and started to run up it from this side, knowing that the Bani Kitab were climbing it from the other side. By God! I thought my heart would burst. I got to the top and as I got there one of the Bani Kitab came in sight a few yards below. I fired at him and he fell down and rolled out of sight. The rest of them ran back to their camels, taking the wounded man with them. We fired many shots at them but were too blown to shoot straight. We knew they would not follow us any farther now that they had a wounded man to look after.'

Two days later we were camped near a well with the uninviting name of Faswat at Ajuz, or 'the Hag's Cunt'. In the morning Salih and his son went on ahead, while the others drove the camels off to water them at the well, out of sight from where I was sitting among our scattered kit writing up my diary. It was early in the morning and still chilly. Suddenly I heard a shot and shouts of 'Raiders! Raiders!' Salih and his son raced back over the dunes, shouting as they came towards me. I could make out no words. Immediately afterwards the others arrived from the well. They were naked except for their loin-cloths, cartridge-belts, and daggers. They must have left their clothes lying beside the well where they had stripped to dig it out. Bin Kabina slid from his camel and couched mine. 'Quick, Umbarak! Jump on her.' I turned to get my saddle-bags but bin Kabina urged me, 'Hurry! Hurry!' so I just grabbed a blanket, threw it over the saddle, and mounted. The others were already off. I had no idea whether we were running away or what we were doing. I shouted at bin Kabina to ask him, but like the others he was too excited to be coherent. Anyway, I was finding it difficult to stay on my camel, which had started to gallop, wrenching every joint in my body. I was riding on the bare framework of a saddle, my camel swerving up and down through a maze of small crescent dunes. I got her under control, and the others slowed theirs to a fast trot. Salih said, 'There are four of them, with eight stolen camels. Without a doubt they are Bani Kitab who have been raiding the Rashid in Dhafara.'

Five minutes later we picked up their tracks. They were travelling fast, but handicapped by the looted animals they were driving. Bin al Kamam said grimly, 'They cannot get away'; and bin Ghabaisha called out, 'We will kill the lot. God's curse on the Bani Kitab.' Bin Tahi was waving his stick and shouting, 'If I had a rifle you would see how bin Tahi fights.' The old man was armed only with a dagger. Salih told his son to go back and guard the stuff we had left lying on the sand. The boy refused, anxious to share the excitement of the chase, but his father insisted. 'Do as you are told. Go back! Go back at once!' and at last the boy halted his camel and sat watching us until we disappeared. Bin al Kamam said to me, 'They will head back to the north. You and I and bin Tahi will follow their tracks. The others will try to cut them off.' Bin Kabina called out, 'Don't miss, Umbarak!' as he swung off to the left with bin Ghabaisha, Amair, and Salih.

Two hours later bin Tahi said, 'They are getting tired. Do you notice how that camel is stumbling.' I hoped the others were not far away. Bin Tahi had no rifle and I knew that bin al Kamam's old Martini usually jammed after a shot or two. Then the tracks which we were following turned sharply to the east and bin al Kamam said, 'They have seen our companions. I hope to God they have seen them.' A little later we saw the raiders. They were about a mile away, four mounted figures driving a bunch of camels in front of them. We had left the small crescent dunes behind us and were riding across rolling downs of firm red sand dotted with tribulus. We urged our camels forward and gained rapidly on them. They drove their camels into a hollow and did not reappear on the farther slopes. Bin Tahi said, 'They have stopped. Get off and get up there where you can cover them with your rifles, and then I will go forward and find out who they are.'

Bin al Kamam and I couched our camels in a hollow, hurriedly tying their knees to stop them from rising, and then climbed a dune to get above the raiders. We crawled to the dune-crest, and I peeped round a clump of tribulus. Three camels were couched in a hollow two hundred yards away. I could see two men lying behind a small dune. A third man, still mounted, was driving off the captured camels and was about four hundred yards away. I could not see the fourth man and wondered if he could see me. Bin al Kamam was a few yards to my right. He signed to bin Tahi, who rode forward shouting. I could make out odd words. 'Rashid . . . Awamir . . . friends . . . otherwise enemies.' The raiders shouted back, and bin al Kamam said 'They are friends. They are from the Manahil.' The man whom I had been unable to see got up from behind a bush, went forward and spoke to bin Tahi, who then rode back to us. He said, 'It is Jumaan.' I knew that Jumaan bin Duailan was the brother of 'The Cat' whom the Yam had killed the year before, and that he was the worst outlaw in these parts. I had seen him in the spring at Zayid's fort, a small man like his brother, with the same quick, restless eyes. We went over to them, greeted them, and exchanged the news. They had taken the camels from the Manasir. The Manahil were allies of the Rashid, and the Manasir were no concern of ours, but bin al Kamam whispered to me, 'Offer them twenty-five *riyals* to return the camels. Zayid will be pleased if you recover them.' Jumaan, however, refused the offer, knowing that we would not take them by force. They said good-bye, mounted their camels, and rode off. Later, when I was back at Muwaiqih telling Zayid about this pursuit, he said, 'By God, Umbarak, you could have had the pick of my camels if you had killed Jumaan. He is the most troublesome of all these brigands.'

The others arrived an hour later, having missed the raiders when they changed their direction. We chaffed them for deserting us. They were disappointed that the raiders had not been Bani Kitab, for there was blood between them and the Rashid. They had counted on getting their camels and also the looted stock which would by tribal custom have belonged to them. Bin Kabina said regretfully, 'I thought I should get two camels'; but I teased him. 'You would have got nothing. We should have killed them and divided the camels between us long before you turned up.'

We camped where we were, and Amair, bin Ghabaisha, and Salih went back with the camels to get our things, returning next morning.

We sat round the fire and talked, too cold for sleep. I asked bin al Kamam how Arabs divided camels taken in a raid, and he said, 'We divide the spoil into the required number of shares; a good camel may be worth two or even three of the others. We then cast lots and each person chooses his share in the order in which he has drawn his lot. We divide the spoil equally between us, except that the leader of the raid or a big sheikh may sometimes be given an extra share. Among the Omani tribes a man may ask to keep whatever he himself captures and take no share in the division, but he will only do that if he has a fast camel.'

I asked about the division of captured rifles and he answered, 'The weapons of a man who has been killed belong to the man who has killed him. But the weapons of those who have surrendered are divided with the rest of the spoil. Only if a man has escaped from the rest of the raiders can the man who captures him claim his weapons and camel in addition to his share of the booty.'

We were now on the edge of Liwa. We rode westward through palm groves and small settlements similar to those I had seen in the spring at Dhaufir and Qutuf. I was glad that we were travelling slowly, for I had broken a rib wrestling with bin Tahi, and the stabbing pain in my side hurt most while I was riding. Salih and his son parted from us when we reached the edge of Dhafara, and bin Kabina went with them. He promised to rejoin me in Muwaiqih, but now he wished to collect some camels that he had left in Dhafara. The rest of us rode northward until we were nearly at the coast, and then turned back to Muwaiqih. We arrived there on 14 December.

We were hungry before we arrived at Zayid's fort and were looking forward to eating meat that evening. We had not bothered to take a spare camel on this short journey, and, being anxious not to tire our riding camels, had taken little food with us. For the last two days we had been living on milk. There was plenty of this as the sands here were full of camels. Just before dinner four Bani Yas visitors were brought into our room to share the meal with us. As we sat down to feed, each leant forward and took a leg of meat off the dish before us and put it on the mat in front of him before starting to eat the rice. The rest of us were left to share the head and some other scraps. I was struck once more by how uncouth and selfish were these Bani Yas and Manasir who lived on the fringe of the desert, compared with the Bedu from the interior.

After dinner the room filled up with Zayid's retainers, several of whom had falcons on their wrists. I have been told that in England it takes fifty days to train a wild falcon, but here the Arabs had them ready in a fortnight to three weeks. This is because they were never separated from them. A man who was training a falcon carried it about everywhere with him. He even fed with it sitting on his left wrist, and slept with it perched on its block beside his head. Always he was stroking it, speaking to it, hooding and unhooding it.

The room was packed with people, some disputing over the ownership of a camel, others recounting a raid or reciting poetry. The air was thick with smoke from the coffee hearth and from guttering lamps, and heavy with the pungent reek of locally grown tobacco. Yet a tiercel, blinking in the lamplight, sat undisturbed on the leather cuff which protected my neighbour's left hand. I asked him how long he had had it, and he said, 'A week. He is a fine bird. You will see, Zayid will prefer him to the other ones,' and he stroked the bird's head. All the birds in the room were peregrines, which the Arabs call *shahin*. I asked my neighbour if they used the *hurr*, or saker falcon, such as I had seen in the courtyard of the Amir's house at Laila. He said, 'Yes, if we can get them, but they are difficult to come by, and expensive. They are worth twice as much as a *shahin*, which you can get for a hundred rupees.' I knew that this was about eight pounds. He went on, 'In the Najd they prefer the *hurr*, since they have better eyesight than the *shahin*, and, as you know, the Najd is all open gravel plains. I myself would rather have a *shahin*. They are swifter, bolder, and more persevering.' He held up his falcon for me to admire and called its name, 'Dhib! Dhib!' which means 'wolf'.

I asked him how he had got the falcon, and he said, 'Zayid sent me with a message to Shakhbut and on my way to Abu Dhabi I saw a *shahin* on the salt-flats. Next day I went back there with a friend. We took a tame pigeon with us. I had tied a length of string to its leg and fastened the other end to a stone. Then we sat and waited and at last when we saw the *shahin* I threw the pigeon into the air and hurried away. As soon as it had taken the pigeon we returned and drove it from its kill. We quickly dug a shallow pit down-wind of the dead pigeon and about as far away as that wall opposite us. I got into this hole and my friend covered me over with some salt-bushes and then walked off. When the *shahin* came back to the pigeon I slowly pulled it towards me with the string. Do you understand? Good. When it was within reach I caught it by the leg.'

I asked him why it did not see his hand, and he said, 'It is easy. A *shahin* always faces up-wind, and anyway it was busy tearing at the pigeon.'

A little later Zayid came in, everyone rose, and after we had settled down again and Zayid had been served with coffee, one of the Bani Yas said, 'Zayid, I saw two *hubara* near bu Samr this morning,' and someone else said, 'I saw three last week.' *Hubara* are MacQueen's bustard, a bird the size of a hen turkey; they arrive in Arabia from Persia, Iraq, and Syria at the beginning of the winter and most of them leave in the spring, although a few breed there. Zayid had told me that his men had found three nests the year before. Now he asked about falcons, and someone said, 'Hiza is sending up two more which they caught last week. They should arrive tomorrow.' Falcons are caught at this time of the year on the coast while they are on passage, and Zayid needed a few more before he went hawking. He said, 'Good – we will get away in four days' time if God wills,' and then, turning to me, 'You must come with me.' I willingly agreed, having always wanted to go hawking.

In the morning Zayid was busy checking saddle-bags, ropes, and water-skins, giving orders about the food to be bought in the local market, and the camels to be fetched from the pasturages, and inspecting his falcons. He said that one of them looked off-colour and was to be given a purge of sugar, while another was thin and was to be fed on an egg mixed with milk. He watched a falcon being trained to the lure. It had only been taken ten days ago, but everyone agreed that it would be ready to go with us.

Later, three Arabs arrived with the two birds which Hiza had sent. One of them still had its eyes sealed. A piece of cotton had been threaded through its lower lids and tied at the top of its head, drawing them up so that the bird could not see. As it had begun to feed, Zayid told the men who carried it to remove the thread. The other, a tiercel, had a broken flight feather which Zayid now mended with a splint made from two slivers of gazelle horn. He then branded both birds on the bill with his mark.

Four days later, Zayid said, 'We will get away this evening. I expect we shall be away for about a month. We will hunt in the Sands to the south-west of here where there is plenty of grazing and lots of wells. The Bedu say that there are bustard there.'

Later that afternoon we rode away from the fort, past the palm-trees. Zayid had sent the baggage camels on ahead with orders to camp on the edge of the Sands, and now we trotted across the gravel plain, accompanied by twenty-five of Zayid's Bedu retainers, some of whom carried falcons on their wrists. They sang a *tagrud*, a marching song to which Bedu trot their camels. They were in high spirits, for they had been looking forward to the beginning of the hawking season as people in Scotland once looked forward to grouse shooting on the Twelfth.

We reached camp as the sun was setting. The dunes were already dark against a flaming sky where cirrus clouds floated like burning vapour. The slaves had collected bushes and piled them into wind-breaks behind which large fires were blazing. We soon gathered round them to warm ourselves, for the evening air was chill. We sipped coffee, while the rhythmic ringing of the brass coffee-mortar invited everyone to draw near. A Bedu family had already joined us, and soon their camels drifted across the darkening sand towards us, followed by ragged long-haired boys. A couple of goats had been slaughtered and cut up, and large cauldrons of rice were simmering on the fires. A little later the herdsboys came into the firelight. One of them was carrying a bowl of milk, capped with foam, which he handed to Zayid before sitting down in our circle to wait for dinner. They told us that they had found the fresh tracks of five bustard round the well, and tracks, two days old, of others in the Sands near by. Zayid turned to me and said, 'God willing we will eat bustard tomorrow.'

We were astir early next morning. Someone fetched the camels and couched them beside the fires, round which we huddled in our cloaks, for it was still bitterly cold. Zayid called out to ask if I would care to ride Ghazala and I eagerly accepted. Bin al Kamam said to me as he tightened the girth and adjusted the saddle-bags and sheepskin, 'You have never ridden a camel like this,' but I told him that I had ridden her on my way to Sharja in the spring. Then as the sun rose we picked up our rifles and camel-sticks and prepared to mount. The falconers lifted the eight peregrines from the blocks on which they had been perched, looking wet and bedraggled from the drenching dew, and called to the three salukis. We stood behind our mounts. Zayid looked round to see that I was ready, and then placed his knee in the saddle. Instantly his camel rose, lifting him into the saddle, and we were off across the sands. We expected to find the bustard on the flats between the dunes rather than in the dunes themselves. We walked our camels while we scanned the ground for their tracks. I had expected that we would be quiet, but I might have known from experience that no Bedu can ever keep silent. Everyone carried on a noisy conversation and anyone who got left behind and trotted to catch up broke automatically into song. Suddenly an Arab on the left of the line signalled to us that he had found fresh tracks, and as we turned our camels towards him a bustard rose about four hundred yards away, the white bands on its wings showing up clearly against the red sand. A falconer unhooded his bird and raised it in the air; then it was off flying a few feet above the ground; the bustard was climbing now but the peregrine was fast overhauling it; now they were faint specks not easily picked up again once they had been lost sight of; then some-one shouted, 'It's down!' and we were racing across the sands.

As we slithered down the dune-faces and climbed out of the hollows and then galloped across the flats, I realized what an excep-tional camel I was riding. I was fully occupied staying in the saddle, but the falconers who rode beside me carried their falcons on their wrists, held by the jesses.

We came upon the peregrine in a hollow, plucking at the lifeless bustard. One of the men slipped off his camel, slit open the bustard's head and gave its brains to the falcon. He then heaped sand over the corpse to hide it, and lifted the puzzled-looking falcon back on to his wrist. We had all dismounted. Zayid pointed to some oily splashes on the ground and said, 'Do you see that muck? The *hubara* squirts it at its attacker. If it gets into the *shahin*'s eyes it blinds it temporarily. Anyway, if it gets on to its feathers it makes a filthy mess of them, and you cannot use the bird again that day.' I asked how many bustard a peregrine could take in a day, and he said, 'A good bird might take eight or nine, but they will take seven on the wing to every four they take on the ground. Do you see where they have fought?' and he pointed to a trail of feathers for twenty-five yards across the sand. 'You can see what a battle they have had. Sometimes a *hubara* manages to stun a *shahin* with a blow of its wings.'

We went on again, and flushed a bustard from a hollow in the sands. It landed as soon as the peregrine overtook it. The peregrine stooped at it twice, and then landing beside it jumped at it, trying to seize it with its talons. The bustard spread out its tail and struck at the falcon with its wings. The salukis, which, whenever they saw a falcon loosed, raced along behind it, now arrived and helped the falcon to kill it. The falcon then drove the dogs off, and when we arrived they were lying down beside the dead bustard at which the falcon ripped and tore.

We killed two more bustard and several hares before Zayid stopped for lunch. I have been told that wild peregrines will not take hares or rabbits, yet Arabs find it easier to enter a newly-trained peregrine to hares than to bustard. Generally one of the salukis caught the hare, but during the next three weeks I frequently saw a peregrine bind to a hare which the dogs were coursing.

While we were baking bread and roasting two of the bustards by burying them in their feathers in the hot ashes, a raven circled round croaking. Zayid said, 'Let's see if a *shahin* will kill it. I had one last year which killed a raven,' but the peregrine which he loosed only made a few ineffective stoops, easily countered by the raven turning on its back. We went on again as soon as we had fed, and a little later put up a bustard within fifty yards of us, but the peregrine which Zayid had unhooded refused to fly. Zayid looked up and, pointing to four eagles high above us, said, 'It is afraid of them.' Shortly afterwards we put up another bustard and this time the peregrine took off. Almost immediately it dashed back to Zayid and thumped against his chest as an eagle swooped down at it with a loud swishing noise, rather like a shell going through the air. I was surprised that the eagle had gone for the peregrine and ignored the bustard. Stroking the frightened bird, Zayid said, 'That was a near thing – it was lucky it did not get her. Well, we shall have to go on – it is no use hanging about here with those eagles overhead.'

Late in the afternoon we saw eight bustard flying up a valley between the sands. We watched them alight, and rode slowly and, for once, in silence towards the spot, after having tied up the dogs. One of the falcons was unhooded and evidently saw the bustard on the ground, but when loosed failed to find them, although it flew backwards and forwards low over the ground. It was then brought back to the lure. Two bustard rose together a couple of hundred yards ahead of us as we moved forward. Another falcon was loosed, overhauled one of them, drove it to the ground, and killed it. We remained where we were while its owner went over and collected it. The remaining bustard lay very close, but one by one we tracked them down and flushed them. The salukis were untied as we flushed the last bustard. Each time it landed, the dogs arrived and it took to the air again, until at last it seemed determined to outfly the peregrine. Round they flew in a great circle, the falcon swooping and the bustard dodging it. The bustard seemed to be flying quite slowly with unhurried beats of its great wings, yet the peregrine was evidently flying its fastest. As they passed directly over our heads the peregrine made one last swoop, missed, shot up into the air, and then swung down to us.

We rode singing into camp long after dark, tired and bitterly cold, but well content with our opening day. As we sat round the fires and went over the kills again and later as I lay awake under the blazing stars and listened to the restless moaning of the camel herds, I was glad that we were hawking in the traditional way and not from cars as they do nowadays in the Najd.

We returned to Muwaiqih a month later. Bin Kabina had arrived from Dhafara and was waiting for me, but neither bin Ghabaisha nor Amair was anxious to travel any farther. They wished instead to remain at Buraimi and continue raiding camels from the Bani Kitab. I therefore engaged two Awamir instead. Mahalhal, a young man with an indolent manner, had a pleasant, open face, lightly marked by smallpox. Al Jabari was older. He was lean and tall, and his hair, reaching well below his shoulders, and his beard gave him a rather Biblical appearance. Sometime or other he had lost a front tooth.

We tried to keep our objective secret, but everybody was busy prying and speculating about where I was going and what was the purpose of my journey. Plenty of people intrigued to thwart me; some because they hated me as a Christian, others because I refused to take them with me, and not a few because they were blood-enemies of my companions. Rashid, son of the Sheikh of Dibai, hating all the Al bu Falah and bitterly jealous of Zayid's repute among the tribes, saw an opportunity of humiliating his rival by hurting his guest. Suspecting that I intended to visit Oman he sent messengers to the Al bu Shams, the Duru, and even to the Imam, warning them that I intended to travel in their lands and attributing many motives to my journey, all evil. In consequence the Sheikh of the Al bu Shams, to the south of Buraimi, sent Zayid a message forbidding me to enter any of the Ghafari territory; we also heard that the Duru were determined to prevent my passage. Bakhit al Dahaimi, whom I had met in Abu Dhabi in the spring, claimed the right to be of our party, but I had always disliked him and refused. He vowed angrily that none of his tribe should go with me, and when my companions ignored his noisy threats he became vindictive and promised to settle with us in the Sands. We pretended indifference and told everyone that we were returning to the Hadhramaut across the central Sands. Several people said to me, however, 'In that case why have you not bought sand camels? All the camels you have bought are mountain camels. Clearly you are going to Oman.' Zayid secretly sent off one of his retainers, a Mahra called Hamaid, to find Salim bin Habarut, a sheikh of the powerful Junuba tribe, and to persuade him to meet us in the Sands on the edge of the Duru country at Qasaiwara well. He said: 'Salim should be able to take you through the Duru and get you to Izz, for both the Junuba and the Duru are Ghafaris. I will give you a letter to Yasir who lives at Izz. He is the most important of the Junuba; he stayed with me here last year. I did him well then, and I think he will probably help you. You may be able to get into Oman, but God knows how you will get out again.'

FIFTEEN

The Quicksands of Umm al Samim

I plan to complete my travels in Southern Arabia by
exploring Oman. I travel with the Rashid through
the Duru country, find the quicksands, and reach
the southern coast.

The six of us left Muwaiqih on 28 January 1949 with two
spare camels to carry food and water. For the first two days
we travelled in a westerly direction to avoid the Al bu Shams
who were camped along the eastern edge of the Sands and to
convince anyone who saw us pass that we were heading not for
Oman but for the Hadhramaut.

On 6 February we arrived at Qasaiwara and there picked up the
tracks of Hamaid and Salim, who were camping near by. Hamaid,
whom I already knew, was small, dark, and dressed in white, whereas
Salim was middle-aged, of medium height, and dressed in brown.
Although they were of Bedu origin, both of them had lived for years
in villages on the fringe of the desert and it was immediately apparent
that this less-exacting life had softened them. I instinctively felt I
should not want either of them with me if I were crossing the Empty
Quarter. However, I hoped that in Oman they would be useful to us.
My companions inevitably mistrusted them as Ghafaris.

When I first entered the sands I was bewildered by the utter
unfamiliarity of my surroundings and frightened by the feeling that
I had only to be separated from my companions to be completely
lost in the maze of dunes. Now, like any Rashid, I regarded the

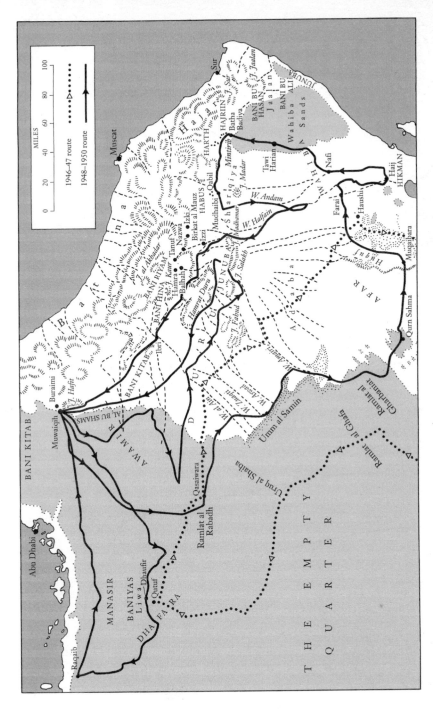

Oman: The Interior

Sands as a place of refuge, somewhere where our enemies could not follow us, and I disliked the idea of leaving the shelter they afforded. Nevertheless, it was essential to leave them now and turn eastwards across the Duru plains to avoid finding ourselves on the wrong side of the Umm al Samim quicksands.

Von Wrede was the first European to mention quicksands in the southern Arabian desert. He claimed that in 1843 he had found a dangerous quicksand known as Bahr al Safi in the Sands north of the Hadhramaut. Bertram Thomas was sceptical of von Wrede's claim to have discovered the Bahr al Safi and thought that it would eventually be identified with Umm al Samim, of which he had heard from his guides. I myself had travelled through the Sands where von Wrede claimed to have seen his quicksands, and I was convinced that they did not exist there. Many Bedu whom I questioned had heard of the Bahr al Safi. Some identified it with Umm al Samim, others with Sabkhat Mutti, and yet others thought it was somewhere in the Najd; not one suggested that it was to be found in the Sands north of the Hadhramaut. To me it seemed probable that the legend of the Bahr al Safi had grown out of Bedu stories of Umm al Samim. I was determined on this journey to fix the position of these quicksands, which I was certain were here – 750 miles east of the Hadhramaut.

After some discussion we decided to water again at the nearest well in the Wadi al Ain before going southwards along the eastern side of Umm al Samim. I was against visiting these wells, fearing trouble with the Duru, but Salim was confident that he could pass us through their country and, as the Rashid were anxious to spare their camels a long waterless march, I was overruled.

We arrived at the Wadi al Ain after three days and found a little sweet water near the surface. Some Duru were camped near by. We would have preferred to go on after filling our water-skins without attracting the attention of the Duru, but the weather was bitterly cold, blowing a northerly gale, and several of our camels were staling blood. We were afraid that we should lose them if we went on before the wind dropped; here at least there were a few bushes to give them a little shelter.

Early next morning we saw a party of about twenty mounted men approaching, two riders on each camel. They dismounted two hundred yards away where a low bank gave some protection from the wind. They were obviously a pursuit party and we realized that we were in for trouble. Bin al Kamam turned to Salim and asked 'Who are they?' and Salim answered 'God destroy them! It is Sulaiman bin Kharas and others of the Duru sheikhs.' He watched them for a while and then said, 'Come, Hamaid, we had better go and find out what they want.'

The Duru rose to greet them and they all sat down in a circle. Soon we heard raised voices. I suggested that we should go over to them, but bin al Kamam said, 'No, stay here. Leave it to Salim and Hamaid; they are Ghafaris.' Meanwhile more Duru arrived, among them Staiyun and his son Ali, both of whom came over to us. Bin Kabina started to make coffee and someone placed a dish of dates for them to eat in the shelter of our baggage, but even there the wind soon filled the dish with sand.

Old Staiyun said, 'The sheikhs are determined to stop any Christian from travelling in our country, but you stayed with me two years ago and are my friend. I and my son will now take you wherever you wish to go, regardless of what the sheikhs may say.' I thanked him and asked if he had realized who I was when I stayed with him. 'No,' he answered, 'we often wondered who you were and where you came from, but it never occurred to us that you were a Christian.' After he had drunk coffee, he said, 'Come. Let us go over to the sheikhs.' We picked up our rifles and followed him. I greeted the Duru, who now numbered about forty, and followed by my companions, walked down their line, shaking hands with each of them in turn. Then, after we had exchanged 'the news', we sat down opposite them, Staiyun and Ali sitting beside me. Salim and bin Kharas went on with their argument. Salim said furiously, 'The Junuba are accepted as *rabia* by the Duru. By what right do you stop us?' Bin Kharas shouted back, 'The customs of the tribes do not apply to Christians.' He was a thickset man with angry bloodshot eyes, dominant and aggressive. Old Staiyun now joined in: 'Why do you make all this trouble, bin Kharas? There is no harm in the man. He is known among the tribes and well spoken of. I know him; you don't. He stayed with me for ten days and did me no harm. On the contrary he helped me. He is my friend.' Hamaid interposed: 'Umbarak is Zayid's friend. He has lived among the tribes for years; he is not like other Christians, he is our friend.' But bin Kharas shouted, 'Then take him back to Zayid. We don't want him here. Take him back at least to Qasaiwara and don't bring him this way again or we will kill him.' Old Staiyun leant forward and said angrily, 'You have no right to talk like this. God Almighty! I myself will take him through our country in defiance of you and all the other sheikhs. You can't stop me.' I looked at the Rashid. Apparently unconcerned, they sat in silence, their eyes moving from speaker to speaker. Bin Tahi poked holes in the ground with his stick; otherwise they hardly moved. They were facing their enemies and very conscious of their dignity. Everyone else started to argue, and five of Staiyun's relations got up and joined us. Bin Kharas, however, silenced the others, and then declared loudly, 'We will have no infidel in our land. God's curse on you, Salim, for bringing him here,' and several of those sitting near him voiced their approval of his words. The argument went on and on. More Duru rode up, dismounted, and joined the crowd. Everyone had something to say, and they said it at length and usually several times over. Salim had thrown his head-cloth on the ground as a gesture of defiance, and was now bareheaded in the cutting wind that was blowing clouds of sand into our eyes. Eventually two men who were sitting with bin Kharas took him aside. When they came back he muttered ungraciously, 'All right, you may take the Christian southwards along the edge of Umm al Samim until you are out of our country, but you may not water at any of our wells.' At once the crowd broke up, for all were anxious to get back to the shelter of their encampments. Only Staiyun and Ali stayed with us. As we watched Sulaiman and the others ride away, bin al Kamam said, 'You cannot trust the Duru. Too many people who travel with them die of snake-bite.' I remembered how al Auf had used this same expression when I first entered the Duru country two years before. I wondered how we should get back through their country. Unless we could return through the mountains there was no way round it.

Next morning the wind had dropped. We filled all our waterskins, for Staiyun, who offered to come with us, thought that we might meet with further opposition when we tried to water in the Amairi. I asked him to take us along the edge of Umm al Samim so that I could see the quicksands. He said, 'All right, but there is really nothing to see.'

We travelled across interminable gravel strewn with limestone fragments and bare of vegetation, until at last we came to the shallow watercourse of the Zuaqti, defined by a sprinkling of herbs shrivelled by years of drought. Beyond, a tawny plain merged into a dusty sky, and nothing, neither stick nor stone, broke its drab monotony. Staiyun turned to me: 'There you are. That is Umm al Samim.'

I remembered my excitement two years before when al Auf had first spoken to me of these quicksands as we sat in the dark discussing our route across the Sands. Now I was looking on them, the first European to do so. The ground, of white gypsum powder, was covered with a sand-sprinkled crust of salt, through which protruded occasional dead twigs of *arad* salt-bush. These scattered bushes marked the firm land; farther out, only a slight darkening of the surface indicated the bog below. I took a few steps forward and Staiyun put his hand on my arm, saying, 'Don't go any nearer – it is dangerous.' I wondered how dangerous it really was, but when I questioned him he assured me that several people, including an Awamir raiding party, had perished in these sands, and he told me once again how he had himself watched a flock of goats disappear beneath the surface.

We watered in the Amairi and the few Duru who were there did not interfere with us. In order to link up my present compass-traverse with that which I had made three years earlier in the Sahma sands to the east of Mughshin, I was anxious to visit the Gharbaniat sands to the west of Umm al Samim. Some Duru had told us that these sands were full of oryx; but in any case the Rashid were happy at the idea of visiting them, since they expected to find grazing for their camels there. However, Hamaid refused to agree, saying that he and Salim had come to Qasaiwara not to wander about in waterless sands which offered nothing but hardship, but to take me to Yasir at Izz. Salim had already made trouble. A few days earlier he had suddenly demanded extra money, declaring that he would go no farther with us unless I gave it to him. We had paid no attention but, loading our camels, had started off without him. He had said no more at the time, but I suspected that he had instigated this new trouble. I was tempted to get rid of him for I disliked him, but the Rashid warned me that, if I did, he, knowing our plans, would thwart us when we tried to enter Oman. I agreed and eventually bin al Kamam took him aside with Hamaid and finally persuaded them to come with us.

Staiyun left from here to return to his encampment, but first he found an Afar to act as our guide until we reached the Wahiba country. This man offered to take us across the southern tip of Umm al Samim. We all disliked the idea of setting foot on it, but he assured us he knew a safe path which would save a long detour, an important consideration as the next well was far away. We started at dawn. For three hours we moved forward a few feet at a time across the greasy surface, trying to hold up the slipping, slithering camels, so that they should not fall down and split themselves. Often our weight broke through the surface crust of salt, and then we waded through black clinging mud which stung the cuts and scratches on our legs. Incessantly the half-bogged camels tried to stop, but we dragged and beat them forward, fearful lest, if they ceased to move, they would sink in too deep to get out again. Uneasily, I remembered stories of vehicles which had sunk out of sight in similar quicksands in the Qatara depression during the war. The others, too, were obviously nervous and bin Kabina voiced our thoughts when he said, 'I hope to God the whole surface doesn't break up; I don't want to drown in this muck.' It seemed a very long time before we reached the safety of a limestone ridge which marked the firm ground on the far side. From there we saw the Sands: wide-sweeping, warm-coloured dunes dotted with grazing for our camels.

In the evening we discussed where we should go to look for oryx and, as we could not agree, I suggested jokingly that someone should read the sands. Bin Kabina answered, 'None of us knows how to do it,' but bin Tahi said, 'How do you know that? I am an expert at it. My readings always come true. Look, I will show you.' He smoothed the sand in front of him and with two fingers made a row of dots which he marked off in spans with his hand. Muttering to himself and occasionally stroking his beard, he counted whether there was an odd or an even number of dots in each span. Then he made some marks in the sand, wiped out the row of dots and started again, still muttering. On various occasions I had watched Arabs reading the sands, and the method which bin Tahi now used seemed identical with theirs. The others watched intently. Finally he announced, 'There are oryx to the south near Sahma.' As this pronouncement confirmed the view which he had previously expressed, bin Kabina, who wanted to go to the west, immediately asked, 'How did you work that out?' The others were equally scepti- cal and soon forced the old man to confess that he knew as little about divining as they did. 'Well, anyway, I made you think I did,' he chuckled. Bin al Kamam then asked, 'Where do you want to go, Umbarak?' and I said, 'Let's go to the south. Who knows, perhaps bin Tahi will prove to be right after all.' And to this the others agreed.

We rode southwards for fifty miles to the edge of Sahma, but though we found fresh tracks we saw no oryx. Near Qurn Sahma we passed an Afar boy whose camels had been stolen by Jumaan, the same man whom we had chased a few weeks earlier near Liwa. The boy, mounted on a half-grown colt, was following his tracks and was already short of water. We advised him to return and collect a proper pursuit party. When he refused, we gave him water and wished him luck, feeling, however, that he would stand little chance if he caught up with Jumaan, for he had only three rounds in his belt and his rifle was an ancient and obviously unreliable weapon.

We arrived nine days later at Farai on the edge of the Wahiba country after watering at Muqaibara, a little-used well on the northern edge of the Huquf, where the bitter water was nastier than any I had ever drunk. We had emptied our water-skins the night before and had some difficulty in finding the well, since our Afar guide was confused by dunes, three or four feet high, which he said had not been there when he passed that way ten years earlier. To me it seemed that these tongues of sand were the only landmarks on the level plain that we had been crossing for the past two days.

At Farai there was a busy crowd of Wahiba, Junuba, and Harasis watering their camels and donkeys, and flocks of sheep and goats. I had an anxious moment when a Wahiba boy recognized bin Kabina's camel as one which had been stolen from him a few months earlier, but bin al Kamam reassured me, explaining that by tribal custom the boy now had no claim to it since bin Kabina had bought it. The lad was, however, anxious to get it back as it was his favourite, and after a little haggling bin Kabina handed it over in part exchange for a far finer animal that he had just been admiring. The boy came back a little later with a young fennec fox, which he had caught that morning, and which he now offered to me as a present. It was an engaging little animal, about nine inches long, almost white, and with very large ears. I did not want to take it, thinking we should have difficulty in feeding it, but al Jabari, one of the two Awamir who was with us, assured me that he could find enough mice and lizards for it to eat. Two days later when we stopped at midday the sack in which we carried it was empty. Al Jabari insisted on riding back as far as our last camping place to look for 'our little companion', and when he came back without it the others were strangely upset. I was surprised, for Bedu are seldom sentimental even about human beings.

The evening that we were at Farai an old man came up to us. He was one of the two delightful old Wahiba who had spent the night with us at Haushi two years before when we had slaughtered the *hazmia*. He invited us to his encampment, but as this was some way up the Wadi Halfain and as we intended to travel down it to the coast, we declined his invitation. He offered to accompany us, but was old and frail, and so we suggested that his cousin Ahmad should come with us instead. Ahmad was the same age as bin al Kamam and rather similar to him in appearance. He had recently been to Riyadh with a large party of Wahiba to sell camels. His party had suffered severely from fever and eleven of them had died on the way home. He told us later that the funeral feasts had lasted for many days and that a very large number of animals had been slaughtered. I liked Ahmad as soon as I saw him. Not only was he welcoming and friendly, as were all the Wahiba we met, but he had great personal charm. My Rashid liked him too, and bin Kabina said, 'Let us try to persuade him to stay with us until we get back to Muwaiqih.'

We watered again at Haij near the southern coast. From there we should have been able to see Masira Island, by which I could have checked my position, but a gale was blowing and the air was thick with flying sand. We had bought a camel and had slaughtered her the previous evening. She had a large, suppurating abscess on one of her feet, but bin al Kamam assured me that this would not affect the rest of the meat. In any case, I was too hungry to be fastidious. We hung the strips of raw meat to dry in some bushes and I watched with increasing irritation how the grains of sand formed an ever-thickening crust over them.

SIXTEEN

The Wahiba Sands

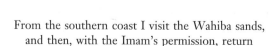

From the southern coast I visit the Wahiba sands,
and then, with the Imam's permission, return
through Oman to Buraimi.

We had crossed southern Arabia from the Persian Gulf to the Indian Ocean, travelling along the edge of the Empty Quarter, but this was the sort of journey to which I was by now well accustomed. From here, however, we had to get back through Oman, a journey which, to be successful, would require diplomacy rather than physical endurance.

I explained to Ahmad that I wished to travel northwards to the Wadi Batha and then to return to Muwaiqih along the foot of the mountains. This route would take me across the Wahiba sands which I was particularly anxious to see, since they were separated from the Sands of the Empty Quarter by more than a hundred and fifty miles of gravel plain. Ahmad said, 'I myself have never been in those sands; I am from the Yahahif and we live on the plains, but I can find a guide from the Al Hiya, the other branch of our tribe. They live in those sands.'

He went on: 'You are free to go wherever you wish in the country of the Wahiba. We are your friends, Umbarak; none of us would try to stop you. But the tribes under the mountains are different; they will certainly make trouble if they find out who you are, just as the Duru did. Anyway, they are all governed by the Imam and they will be afraid to let you pass without his permission.

It's different in the desert; there we could perhaps take you through the land of our enemies, travelling as raiders travel and avoiding the wells. But that is impossible in the mountains; the country is too narrow; we should have to use the paths, and they go through the villages; we could never keep out of sight. I will take you as far as I can, but just you and one of your companions. We will get hold of good camels and keep ahead of the news. As a small party we may avoid attracting attention. We will leave the others in the Wadi Halfain and come back to them as soon as we have been as far as the Wadi Batha. But how you are going to get to Muwaiqih from here I don't know. However, we can discuss that when we return.'

Next day we crossed into the Wadi Andam, which here was only a few miles from the Halfain, and following it northward we arrived two days later at Nafi. The wide valley was well wooded and would have looked like a park had it not been for the drought. Ahmad now found us a man of the Al Hiya, called Sultan, who agreed to guide us across the sands to the Wadi Batha. I decided to take bin Kabina with me. Bin Kamam was anxious to come instead, but I persuaded him to remain in charge of the others, arranging to meet them a little farther to the north in the Wadi Halfain, where the grazing was said to be better.

I hired a fresh camel from Sultan; bin Kabina rode his own, and both Sultan and Ahmad were well mounted. We were riding four of the finest camels in Arabia and if necessary could travel both fast and far. At first we crossed a gravel plain, sprinkled with sand of a reddish tint, and broken up by small limestone tables among which we saw many gazelle, all very wild. Gradually, as we went farther, the sand increased until it entirely overlaid the limestone floor. On the second day we reached the well of Tawi Harian, which was about eighty feet deep. Several Wahiba were there with donkeys, but no camels. We left as soon as we had watered, for we wanted no awkward questions. We were now riding northward along valleys half a mile wide enclosed by dunes of a uniform height of about two hundred feet. A curious feature of these valleys was that they were blocked at intervals of about two miles by gradual rises of hard sand. The sand in the bottoms was rusty red, whereas the dunes on either side were honey-coloured – both colours becoming paler as we travelled farther north. In the evening, having climbed up to camp among the dunes, we looked across waves of sand and small crescent hollows dotted with *abal* bushes.

We had been going for three hours next morning when bin Kabina suddenly exclaimed, 'Who is that?' I glanced back and was relieved to see that it was only a small boy, hurrying along to catch up with us. We waited for him. He was dressed in a white shirt and head-cloth, and wore a dagger; he was little more than four feet high and perhaps eleven years old. After we had formally exchanged the news, he stopped in front of our camels, held out an arm and said, 'You may not go on.' I thought, 'Damn, are we really to be stopped by this child?' The others waited in silence. The boy repeated, 'You may not go on'; and then, pointing to some dunes five or six miles away, added, 'You must come to my tents. I will kill a camel for your lunch. I will give you fat and meat.' We protested, saying that we had far to go before sunset, but the child insisted. Finally, however, he gave way, saying 'It is all wrong but what more can I do?' Then, as we were going on, he asked, 'Have you seen an old grey camel in calf?' Ahmad said 'No.' He thought a moment, and added, 'We passed the tracks of a young camel a little way back, and of three camels before that, none of them in calf.' Sultan asked, 'What are her tracks like?' The boy replied, 'She turns her near fore-foot in a little.' Bin Kabina exclaimed, 'Yes! don't you remember we crossed her tracks beyond that patch of light-coloured sand in the last valley? She had climbed the slope on our right and fed on some *qassis*. It was just before we came to the broken *abal* bush.' The others agreed that these must be the tracks of the boy's camel, and described to him where to find them. The place was about three miles away. Once again I was amazed at their unconscious powers of observation. They had been arguing the rights and wrongs of a recent killing among the Junuba, apparently paying no attention to their surroundings; yet they could now remember every camel-track that we had passed. Sultan said, 'God willing, you will easily find her. The tracks we saw were fresh, made after the sun had risen.' The boy thanked us and turned back down the valley. We watched him as he walked away from us, his clothes very white against the red sand, and Sultan said, 'Ahmad, do you remember old Salih? He died last autumn. That is his son, a good boy.'

Two days later we camped on the top of the dunes, two hundred feet above the Wadi Batha. The valley was about six miles across and was bordered on the far side by a narrow belt of sand. Beyond this were low dark hills, and towering above these the stark range of the Hajar. In spite of the haze I could see the peaks of Jabal Jaalan near the coast at the eastern end of the range. I took bearings with my compass while Sultan pointed out to me the various villages, most of them surrounded by palms, and all easily visible on the yellow plain. I called out to bin Kabina to come and look, adding that I could see some Bedu encampments, but he was busy re-tying the pads on his saddle and called back jokingly, 'What do I want with those Bedu? They did not kill my father.' I joined him where he sat beside the fire, and with his help listed the plants we had seen.

Ahmad and Sultan had brought me across the sands to the Wadi Batha as they had promised. I hoped that now they would not insist on going straight back across the desert to rejoin our companions in the Wadi Halfain, but would first take me westward through the villages that lay among the foothills. When I suggested this to them, Ahmad answered, 'We will show you as much of the country as we can, but from now on no one must discover that you are a Christian.'

In the morning Sultan warned me as we started, 'When we meet Arabs don't say anything.' I asked, 'Who are you going to say I am?' and he answered, 'That will depend on who they are.' Bin Kabina pointed to my watch and said, 'Take that off,' and I dropped it inside my shirt.

As we went up the valley, which is here called the Batha Badiya, Sultan indicated a village half-buried by sand at the foot of a dune, and said, 'In time the sands will swallow this valley. A few years ago that village was inhabited.' We passed several other villages, two or three of which were completely deserted and others partly so. Sultan explained that this was due to the drying-up of the *aflaj*, the underground channels which supplied water to the cultivations. These *aflaj* were probably introduced into Oman from Persia and they are made by sinking shafts every ten yards and joining them up with a tunnel. As they often run for miles, it must need skill to get the level right, working in the dark without instruments. I could see where several of them crossed the plain; the course of each one marked by the mounds of excavated earth.

We were still on foot when we met a party of Arabs, three men and a boy, all armed, leading a string of loaded camels. We stopped and spoke with them. I watched their dark gipsy eyes inspecting us, coming back to me each time, never dwelling on me, but missing nothing. One of them, a middle-aged man with a scar across his cheek, asked Sultan, 'Is he a Baluchi?' 'Yes. He has come from Sur. He buys slaves and is going to Nazwa.' Four pairs of eyes flickered over me again. It was the first of several such encounters, and each time I felt horribly conspicuous, standing there in silence, towering above the others, while they exchanged their news and the long minutes dragged by. Yet even as I waited for my identity to be discovered, I realized that for me the fascination of this journey lay not in seeing the country but in seeing it under these conditions.

Sultan insisted that we should avoid the Harth village which we could see farther up the valley. 'We do not want to meet Salih bin Aisa,' he said. 'He is the Sheikh of the Harth and head of all the Hanawi tribes. He would soon discover who you are, and even if he were friendly the mischief would be done, for news of your presence here would get ahead of us.' To avoid this village he led us round the northern tip of the sands into a maze of bare, broken hills, some of which were of reddish colour, while others were black, slate-blue, or a dirty white. After travelling for two days through these hills we reached the Habus villages in a tributary of the Wadi Andam. We had nearly finished our food, so Sultan and bin Kabina went into Mudhaibi, where there was a market, while Ahmad and I waited for them just outside the village. Several people passed along the track and called out a greeting, but I was thankful that no one came over and spoke to us. If they had done so they might well have remained until the others returned, and would probably have become increasingly inquisitive. Ahmad had told me that a representative of the Imam lived in this village, and I realized that if I roused suspicion here I should be arrested and sent to Nazwa. The others came back an hour later with dates and coffee. They said that there was nothing else to be had in the village, and grumbled that what they had bought had been expensive. We continued down the valley, passing several other villages. Along the edge of the wadi were scattered palm-trees and small gardens irrigated from rivulets bordered with flowering oleanders.

It was a clear day, the first one for weeks, and I could see the ten-thousand-foot summit of Jabal al Akhadar, and seventy miles to the north-west the familiar outline of Jabal Kaur. Around us were many other peaks and mountains. As we rode along I stopped at intervals to sketch their outlines and to take their bearings. Of all these mountains only Jabal al Akhadar was shown on the map.

Sultan told me that from here we must turn southwards to rejoin the rest of my party. Two days later, as we approached a well in the Wadi Andam, my eye was caught by an outstandingly fine camel, fully saddled. At the well a tall man, in a faded brown shirt with an embroidered woollen head-cloth twisted loosely round his head, was talking to two boys and a girl who were watering a flock of goats. I noticed that his dagger was elaborately decorated with silver. Ahmad whispered to me. 'That is Ali bin Said bin Rashid, Sheikh of the Yahahif.' After we had greeted him, he said, 'So you have arrived safely. You are very welcome. Your companions are near my encampment; all of them well and waiting for you. We will go there tomorrow. Tonight we will camp with some Baluchi near here. You must be tired and hungry, for you have travelled far.' Then, turning to Ahmad, he asked, 'Did you have any trouble?' He had steady, thoughtful eyes, a large, slightly crooked nose, deep creases down his cheeks, a straggling beard turning grey, and a closely clipped moustache above rather full lips. It was a good-natured face with no hint of fanaticism, but with unmistakable authority. A Bedu sheikh has no paid retainers on

301

whom he can rely to carry out his orders. He is merely the first among equals in a society where every man is intensely independent and quick to resent any hint of autocracy. His authority depends in consequence on the force of his own personality and on his skill in handling men. His position in the tribe, in fact, resembles that of the chairman of a committee meeting. I had always heard that Ali possessed considerable influence, and looking at him now I could well believe it.

Ahmad fetched Ali's camel, and the five of us rode over to the Baluch encampment near by, where we were to spend the night. It was four o'clock when we got there, but eleven o'clock before we sat down to a large platter heaped with tough meat and dates.

About twenty men and boys collected round our fire. All of them, even the children, wore shirts – for here, unlike Dhaufar, it is not the custom to dress only in a loin-cloth. Ali had told me that these people were in origin Baluchis from Persia, but that they had lived for so long among the Wahiba that now they counted as a section of that tribe. They spoke only Arabic, and I should not have distinguished them from other members of their adopted tribe.

Bin Kabina as usual kept his rifle always ready to his hand. Ali noticed this and said, 'It is all right, boy, you can leave your rifle over there. Thanks to the Imam, God lengthen his life, we have peace here. It is not like the sands where you come from, where there is always raiding and killing.'

We rejoined the others late the next evening near Barida well in the Wadi Halfain, having ridden nearly two hundred and fifty miles since we had parted from them ten days earlier. Ali urged us to go on to his encampment a few miles farther down the wadi, but, instead, we persuaded him to spend the night with us. Bin al Kamam bought a goat; it was long after midnight before we fed. We spent the following day at Ali's tent. This was only about twelve feet long, woven of black goat's-hair and pitched like a wind-break under a small tree. Among these Bedu tribes there is no contrast between rich and poor, since everyone lives in a similar manner, dressing in the same way and eating the same sort of food, and the poorest of them considers himself as good as the richest.

Ali's two wives, with whom, as is the custom here, we had shaken hands on arrival, joined us after we had fed, and sat talking with us while we drank coffee. Before we left the tent they produced a small dish filled with a yellow oil scented with amber and made (I was told) from sesame, saffron, and something called *waris*. We dipped our fingers in it and rubbed it over our faces and beards. I met with this custom only among the Wahiba and the Duru, but bin Kabina told me that he had been anointed with a similar oil before his circumcision.

Ali warned us that the Ghafari tribes to the north had heard of my arrival among the Wahiba and were determined to stop my going through their country. He said, 'Don't think you can slip past them unobserved as you have just done. They will be on the watch for you now. Why don't you travel along the coast to Muscat and then go on through the Batina?' But to do this meant giving up the main object of my journey, which was to explore the interior of Oman. In any case, I was not at all anxious to encounter the Sultan of Muscat. When I had met him in Salala after my first journey through these parts he had been charming. Now after another unauthorized journey I was sure he would be furious. I told Ali that Zayid had given me a letter to Yasir requesting him to help me, and asked him whether he thought Yasir would be able to take me back to Muwaiqih. 'Yes,' he said, 'I suppose Yasir could take you through, but I doubt if he will. He won't wish to offend the Imam.'

There were several Wahiba camped here, some in tents, others in shelters made from tree-trunks and branches. During the next three days we met many more of them watering their stock at the wells which we passed as we rode up the Halfain. The Wahiba seemed to me to be a finer people than the Duru, in the same indefinable way that the Rashid had impressed me as being superior to the Bait Kathir. The Rashid lived harder lives than the Bait Kathir, which perhaps accounted for the difference between them, but the Wahiba and the Duru lived similar lives in the same sort of country. I wondered if the contrast between these two tribes was due to some fundamental difference in origin far back in the past.

I sent Hamaid to Yasir with Zayid's letter when we were near Adam, a small village lying in the gap between Madhamar and Salakh, two mountains which rise abruptly from the gravel plain and run westwards in the shape of a crescent for thirty miles from the Halfain to the Amairi. I had no instruments to calculate their height but guessed that Salakh was three thousand feet and Madhamar fifteen hundred. The limestone of which they are formed had been weathered to leave no prominent features, and no vegetation was apparent on the naked rock. Both of them were dome-shaped, and I thought regretfully that their formation was of the sort which geologists associate with oil. But, even so, I did not anticipate that eight years later an oil company would have established a camp, made an airfield, and be drilling at Fahud not more than forty miles away.

The following day we camped to the north of Madhamar at Tawi Yasir, where we had arranged for Hamaid to meet us. In the evening an elderly villager joined us. He had a disapproving face and an untidy beard, which, according to Ibadhi custom, had never been trimmed. We made coffee for him, and preceded it with a dish of dates. As soon as he had drunk the coffee he prayed interminably and later sat in silence fingering his beard. After dinner bin Tahi tried to enliven the evening by being funny. The result was not happy. Our visitor suddenly got to his feet and declared that bin Tahi was making a mock of him. Shocked, everyone vowed that this was not the case, that he was our guest and that our only wish was to please him. Bin al Kamam tried to mend matters by pretending that bin Tahi had never been right in his head since he had fallen off his camel some years before. The man refused to be pacified, however, and finally made everyone angry by saying, 'This is what happens to Muslims when they travel with an infidel.' Bin Tahi answered immediately, 'I may not be learned in religious matters, but at any rate I don't spend the whole time I am praying scratching my arse.' As the man rode off into the dark, the others said, 'Thank God he is gone.' But I was anxious, and fearful that he would cause us trouble.

Next day we remained where we were, waiting for Hamaid. I

wondered what to do if Yasir refused to help us, and half regretted having sent Hamaid to him, feeling that perhaps had we travelled fast we could have slipped unobserved through the country ahead of us. Now we had hung about here too long, but whatever happened we should be able to get back to the Wahiba.

Bin Kabina was sitting near me mending his shirt. It was worn thin and yesterday it had torn right across the shoulders. I said to him irritably, 'Why don't you wear your new shirt?' He did not answer but went on sewing. I asked him again, and he answered without looking up, 'I have not got another.'

I said, 'I saw the new one with the red stitching in your saddle-bags a few days ago.'

'I gave it away.'

'Who to?'

'Sultan.'

'God, why did you do that when you only have that rag to wear?'

'He asked me for it.'

'Damn the man. I gave him a handsome present. Really, you are a fool.'

'Would you have me refuse when he asked for it?'

'Of course. We could have given him a few more dollars.'

'When I have asked you for money you have refused to give me any.'

This was true. Several times he had borrowed money to give away to people who asked for it; twice recently I had refused to let him have any more, so as to stop this incessant scrounging of money from him which he would later need for himself. I had told him that I would give him his money at Muwaiqih. I would probably need what I had with me before we got there. I said that he could put the blame on me, and tell them that I would not give him the money.

Now I grumbled, 'You will look well if we do meet Yasir, half-naked in that rag.'

He answered angrily, 'Do I have to ask your permission before I can give my own things away?'

Hamaid returned late in the afternoon. Yasir and three other Arabs were with him. Yasir was dressed in a plain white shirt and a large embroidered head-cloth. He wore a dagger and cartridge belt, and carried a .450 Martini. He was a big heavy man, who shuffled as he walked. He had prominent, ill-proportioned features, and a large beard streaked with grey. Hamaid told me later that Yasir had been greatly embarrassed by my arrival, since the Imam, who had heard of my presence in these parts, had given orders that I was to be arrested if I came this way. Yasir had, however, felt obliged to meet me since I had brought a letter from Zayid. He said at once that he could not take me to Muwaiqih without the Imam's permission, but that he would himself go to Nazwa in the morning and see the Imam, and that his son would meanwhile take us to a place in the hills half-way between Nazwa and Izz. I realized that if we went there, and if Yasir then failed to secure me a safe conduct from the Imam, we should be unable to escape. I asked the others what they thought, and bin al Kamam said, 'If you want to get back to Muwaiqih you will have to trust Yasir.' I therefore took Yasir aside and said, 'Zayid, who is my great friend, assured me that only you, the most influential sheikh in these parts, could take me safely through Oman. I have come to you now with Zayid's letter to ask you for your help. I put myself in your hands and am ready to do whatever you suggest.' I then gave him two hundred Maria Theresa dollars, as a present. He answered, 'Go with my son. Tomorrow evening I will meet you, and, God willing, I will have the Imam's permission for your journey.'

We camped next day within ten miles of Nazwa. The town itself was out of sight, hidden behind a rocky ridge, one of many in the broken country that lay between our camp and the foot of the Jabal al Akhadar, or 'The Green Mountain', a name which seemed singularly inappropriate, since its slopes and precipices looked as bare as the hills that surrounded us. The atmosphere was unusually clear and I could see its entire length. For fifty miles it stretched across our front, its face scored by great gorges – streaks of purple on a background of pale yellow and misty blue. The Jabal al Akhadar is a single continuous ridge, and I could not decide which of the bumps and pinnacles that broke its outline was the actual summit. Ten thousand feet high, it forms the highest part of a range which extends unbroken for four hundred miles from the Persian Gulf to the Indian Ocean.

Ahmad named the towns and villages which we could see. Pointing to a town just visible at the foot of the mountain, he said, 'That is Birkat al Mauz – Sulaiman bin Hamyar lives there. He is Sheikh of the Bani Riyam and head of all the Ghafaris. The Jabal al Akhadar belongs to him. They say there is running water all the year round on the mountain, and forests of trees and lots of fruit. It is bitterly cold up there; an Arab from the mountain once told me that in the winter the rain sometimes turns into a soft white powder like salt. No, not hail; we often get hail even down here.' I asked, 'Would Sulaiman allow me to travel on the mountain?' and he answered, 'God knows; he might. They say he is a friend of the Christians who live in Muscat. The Imam, however, would prevent your meeting him. He does not trust Sulaiman.' After a pause, he went on: 'If you could get to Birkat al Mauz without being stopped, I think Sulaiman would take you into the mountain. No one else could take you there.'

Yasir came back at sunset. He had several Arabs with him. He told us that on his way to Nazwa he had met a party of horsemen sent by the Imam to arrest me. He had persuaded them to return to Nazwa, and there, after much angry argument, he had induced the Imam to authorize my journey back to Muwaiqih. The Imam had sent one of his men with Yasir as his representative. I anticipated that this would be some sour-faced fanatic, and was relieved when Yasir introduced me to a friendly old man with an obvious sense of humour. Yasir had also persuaded one of the Duru sheikhs, called Huaishil, to come with us. Huaishil possessed the charm which Yasir so sadly lacked. I knew that accompanied by the Imam's representative, and by *rabias* from Junuba, Duru, and Wahiba, I had no further cause to worry.

I was very busy during the eight days that it took me to reach Muwaiqih. In the desert there had been little to plot except our course, but here there was a great deal of detail to fill in. Except for the outline of Jabal al Akhadar and the position of a few of the larger towns, the existing maps were blank. I was thankful that there was no further need to conceal my identity, and that I could work openly taking bearings and making sketches.

As we were passing under an enormous dome of light-coloured rock which formed a buttress to Jabal Kaur we passed three men on camels. One of them, a small indignant man, smothered under a large white turban, was the redoubtable Riqaishi, Governor of Ibri. At the time I was riding with bin Kabina, bin al Kamam, and the two Awamir some way behind the others. The Riqaishi had just met them. He had immediately warned Yasir that the Christian was in the neighbourhood, and added that he was on his way to Nazwa to inform the Imam. He was horrified when he heard that I was in their company, and left them without further word. The Imam's representative chuckled when later he described the scene to me. Bin al Kamam greeted the Riqaishi as he passed and asked him courteously if there was anything he could do for him. The Riqaishi gave his camel an angry blow and answered, 'You would not have brought the Christian here if you had wished to please me.'

That evening, encamped outside Ibri, we heard that bin Ghabaisha and another Rashid had been there a week earlier. They had visited the Riqaishi, who had publicly insulted bin Ghabaisha, possibly because by now he was a well-known brigand, more probably because he was known to be one of my companions. Furiously angry, bin Ghabaisha got up and left the room. After dark he waylaid the Riqaishi's coffee-maker, a person of importance in an Arab household, threatened to kill him at once if he made a sound and took him outside the town. There he tied the man up and loaded him on a camel. He then roused a cultivator and said to him, 'I am bin Ghabaisha. Tell the Riqaishi in the morning that in return for his insults I have taken his servant, and intend to sell him in the Hasa.'

When I met bin Ghabaisha he told me that the Riqaishi had offered him fifty dollars for the return of his servant. I asked him whether he accepted. 'No. I sent back word that I realized that the man was useless as a coffee-maker. Had he not left me without coffee when I called to pay my respects to the Governor? All the same he would fetch more than that in Saudi Arabia.' Eventually the Riqaishi ransomed his servant for a considerable sum.

From Ibri we rode northward along the foot of the mountains towards Jabal Hafit, passing through the territory of the Bani Kitab and Al bu Shams. Both of these tribes would have stopped me if they could, but now, accompanied as I was by the Imam's representative and *rabias* from the Junuba, Duru, and Wahiba, they were obliged to let me pass. We reached Muwaiqih on 6 April. We had ridden eleven hundred miles since we had left Zayid's fort on 28 January.

SEVENTEEN

The Closing Door

～

Anxious to explore the Jabal al Akhadar I return to
Buraimi the following year, but am turned back
from the Jabal by the Imam of Oman. I leave
Arabia.

I returned from England in November 1949 intending to complete my map of the Duru country, and if possible to visit Jabal
al Akhadar. At Muwaiqih I found bin Kabina, his half-brother
Muhammad bin Kalut, bin Ghabaisha, bin Tahi, and al Jabari of
the Awamir. Bin al Kamam had unfortunately gone back to Dhaufar. The others were ready to go with me, but bin Kabina warned
me that the Duru would prevent my re-entering their territory.
With Zayid's help I sent for Huaishil, the Duru Sheikh who had
been with me the year before. My companions admitted that,
accompanied by him, we were unlikely to have trouble with the
Duru, since he was one of their most influential sheikhs. He arrived
six weeks later, while we were hawking in the Sands to the west of
Muwaiqih, and after much argument he promised to take me
through the Duru country to Birkat al Mauz, where Sulaiman bin
Hamyar lived. Only Sulaiman could take me to the Jabal al Akhadar.

Ten days after we had left Muwaiqih, we had breakfasted and
were saddling our camels when bin Kharas, the same unprepossess-
ing and truculent sheikh who had held me up the year before,
arrived with a large following of Duru, and ordered us to return
at once the way we had come. That night I had been stung by a

scorpion, once in the shoulder as I rolled over in my sleep, and again in the hand as instinctively I reached up. There had been no moon and it had been very dark. I had woken bin Tahi, who was near me, but the old man only muttered, 'I expect it was a mouse,' and went to sleep again. Now, although the pain had stopped, I felt dizzy and rather sick, disinclined to listen patiently to the interminable wrangling of these exasperating Duru. All that day they argued, and the following morning they still refused to let us pass. Huaishil was furious; I have seldom seen a man so angry. Suddenly he shouted, 'By God we are going on, whatever you may say or do, bin Kharas,' and strode off to fetch his camel. Bin Kabina and bin Ghabaisha led me aside, and bin Ghabaisha said, 'Listen to me, Umbarak, Huaishil is mad with anger and will lead you into trouble if you follow him. These cursed Duru mean business and will shoot if we try to go on. You will be the first to die. Why die trying to see their country? What good will that do you? It is not even as if we were raiding. May God destroy these worthless Ghafaris!' So far I had taken little part in the discussion, but now I called Huaishil and suggested that he should go to Ali bin Hilal, the head Sheikh of the Duru, and get his permission for me to travel in their country, the rest of us remaining where we were until he returned. He had already told me that Ali bin Hilal was well disposed towards me. Huaishil and the other Duru eventually agreed to this suggestion, but I heard bin Kharas mutter, 'The Christian is not going through our country even if a hundred Ali bin Hilals give him permission. Who is Ali to give us orders?'

Huaishil rode off, saying he would be back in three days' time, and bin Kharas and his followers left for some encampments near by. In the evening a sheikh of the Afar turned up in our camp, accompanied by a Wahiba and a Harasis. They had heard that we were in trouble with the Duru, and being Hanawis had come to give us their support. They assured us that they would remain with us until Huaishil returned. The weather now turned horribly cold with a tearing gale from the north-east.

Three days later, bin Kharas was back demanding that we should leave, since Huaishil had not returned as he had promised;

we both of us knew quite well that he would not travel in this bitter weather. For the next two days we argued almost incessantly. The Duru did not seem unfriendly. They agreed that I had done them no harm when I had been in their country, but maintained that if they allowed me to travel there at will I should be followed by other Christians in cars, looking for oil and intending to seize their land. The situation was complicated by a tribal feud among the Duru themselves. These particular Duru had been for many years at variance with the Mahamid, the section of the tribe to which the sheikhs belonged. Bin Kharas, although himself of the Mahamid, was bitterly jealous of Ali bin Hilal and Huaishil, and anxious to increase his own authority by lessening theirs.

To divert their attention and to gain a little more time for Huaishil to arrive, I offered a prize of ten Maria Theresa dollars for a camel race. Anxious to win this money and to show off their animals, they agreed to race, after trying unsuccessfully to get me to increase the stakes. A particularly fine camel belonging to bin Kharas won easily. Although the Duru seemed almost cordial after the race, the Afar sheikh advised us to leave, maintaining that they were planning to kill us. They intended, he said, to invite Huaishil's three companions to a discussion, and then to seize and disarm them before attacking us. Like all Duru, they hated the Rashid, and apparently bin Kharas was now saying that it was as meritorious to kill a Christian as to go on pilgrimage to Mecca, and in this case much less trouble.

In the evening bin Kharas came to our camping place and said, 'The Christian must leave tomorrow morning. We are all resolved that he can remain here no longer.' He refused the coffee which we offered him, and left immediately. After he had gone, bin Ghabaisha, who was pouring out coffee for the rest of us, glanced round the hollow in which we were camped and said, 'If we are still here at this time tomorrow we shall be fighting for our lives.' Bin Tahi agreed, and added, 'We must leave; we should not stand a chance, but by God I will come back some time and take that camel off bin Kharas. He is not fit to have one like that.' My companions were certain that the Duru were not bluffing. Even if

I had thought otherwise I was dependent upon them and forced in such a case to follow their advice. So when Muhammad asked, 'What do *you* think, Umbarak?' I said, 'We had better leave in the morning.'

Huaishil rejoined us when we were in the Sands eighty miles to the west. He told us that Ali bin Hilal had agreed to my travelling through their country, and explained that he had waited at Ali's encampment for the wind to drop before coming back to us. I was angry that he had not returned sooner, but said nothing, not wishing to antagonize him. He promised to take us in the morning to the Wadi al Amairi.

The wind had been southerly, but next day it went back to the north-east and blew another gale. Bitterly cold off the frozen uplands of central Asia, it was thick with sand whipped from the dunes around us. We sat throughout the day, without shelter, in a reddish obscurity, half-smothered by the flying grains which, reaching to a height of about eight feet above the ground, rasped our skins, filled our eyes, noses, and ears, and were gritty between our teeth. This continuous discomfort became almost intolerable with the passing hours. Sunset brought relief, for the wind dropped and the stars came out. Next morning I noticed that the dune crests had altered a little, but the general outline of the dunes themselves was unchanged. These sandstorms in southern Arabia must be mild compared with those that occur in the Sahara. One storm in which I had been caught on my way to Tibesti was far worse than any I experienced in the Empty Quarter. But even here these sandstorms sometimes had fatal results; for instance, bin Tahi told me of some Rashid who followed raiders into sands that were unknown to them and died when such a storm wiped out the tracks which they were following.

We travelled back through the Sands and then across gravel plains through country similar to that which I had seen before. In the Wadi al Aswad we met some Duru, one of whom was suffering from fever. I thought it was probably malaria and gave him quinine and aspirin; next day, however, bin Kabina went down with a similar attack. To rest him we remained where we were. In the morning bin Ghabaisha, bin Tahi, and one of Huaishil's Duru were sick. We went on slowly, for our water was getting short, and the evening before we reached the Amairi I myself had a high temperature and a splitting headache, but as our water was finished we could not stop. Next day I was feeling so ill that it was an effort even to keep upright in the saddle, but as I rode along I had constantly to check our course with my compass and note how long we had travelled on each bearing; also I had to write down the names of each water-course that we crossed; otherwise the thread of my traverse would have been irreparably broken. It took us five hours to reach the Amairi. Some Duru fired on us as we approached the well, but Huaishil rode forward and spoke with them. They had been warned by bin Kharas that we might be coming this way and at first they were hostile. However, Huaishil persuaded them to let us pass. I recovered from my fever two days later, but at the time I hardly cared what they said or did, wishing only to be left alone. I think we were suffering from influenza. We heard later that there had been some sort of epidemic in Oman and several deaths. This was the only time I was ill during the years I was in Arabia.

Three days later we were camped in the stony foothills ten miles to the south-west of Izz. Huaishil and al Jabari went off to Sulaiman bin Hamyar at Tanuf to ask if I might visit him. After a further three days they returned to say that Sulaiman had invited me to Birkat al Mauz. On the way back, however, they found that the hue and cry was out, and when they tried to stop in the town of Bahlah for a meal, the inhabitants shut their doors against them. Huaishil had promptly sent a messenger back to Sulaiman asking him to come to our assistance and had then hurried on to warn us. He told us that a pursuit party sent by the Imam was close behind him, and advised us to move across the valley and camp above the village of Mamur where we should be in his own territory. There we were joined by some Junuba, who had been with me the year before, and by some Wahiba who had come to invite me to their country.

Next morning our camel guards reported that a hundred armed

townsmen were collected in a watercourse near by and soon afterwards four of them came to our camp. Their leader, one of the Imam's household slaves, ordered us to leave immediately, saying that the Imam had told them to kill me unless I did so. Huaishil answered that we intended to remain where we were until we heard from Sulaiman. They protested strongly, and a little later were overheard arguing as to which of them should shoot me and claim the reward. We therefore warned them that we would fire at any one who came near us. As I had with me *rabias* from the Duru, Junuba, and Wahiba, I thought it unlikely that they would attack us; but when the situation was getting uncomfortably tense a messenger arrived from Sulaiman bin Hamyar to say that he was on his way. He arrived in the afternoon and camped in Mamur village, a cluster of palm-frond cabins and two or three mud buildings grouped round a small mosque. I met him there, in a courtyard crowded with his own retainers and those of the Imam. A big man, with a sallow complexion and a long black beard, he was dressed in a brown, gold-embroidered cloak of the finest weave, and a spotless white shirt, with an expensive Kashmiri shawl wrapped round his head and sandals on his feet. His dagger was decorated with gold. He impressed me at once as a powerful if not very congenial personality. It was obvious from his bearing and from the behaviour of his retainers that he was not a tribal sheikh ruling by consent, but an autocrat accustomed to obedience. As soon as I had been served with dates and coffee he took me inside the mosque, after stationing a guard at the entrance with orders that no one was to be allowed near. He was obviously angry with the Imam for having prevented me from coming to Birkat al Mauz at his invitation, and by meeting me here he had defied him. I doubted, however, that he would risk a more serious quarrel by taking me to the Jabal al Akhadar. I had always heard that he was without the narrow fanaticism of most Omani townsmen, and that he was interested in and prepared to use the inventions of the West. This lack of orthodoxy and his obvious ambition made him suspect with the Imam.

I soon realized that the Imam had just grounds for his mistrust for after we had talked for a while, sitting close together on a small prayer-rug, he leant closer to me and explained in a whisper that he wished to be recognized by the British Government as the independent ruler of the Jabal al Akhadar, with a status similar to that of the Trucial Sheikhs. I told him that I could not help him in this matter as I was a traveller with no official position, who had come here with no object but to explore the Jabal al Akhadar. He said, 'If you can arrange what I have asked, come back again and I will take you wherever you wish to go.' I suggested that I might have some difficulty in getting away from here, as my camp was surrounded by the Imam's followers, and he said, 'Leave tomorrow and I will stay here for a day and make sure that no one pursues you.'

I was disappointed that I had been turned back when I had so nearly reached the Jabal al Akhadar, for I would have given much to have explored this mountain. I knew, however, that it would be useless to return and try again the following year. Travelling in the desert, we had always been able, when held up, either to profit from the rivalries of the tribesmen, or, if turned back, to reach our destination from another direction. The Rashid who accompanied me were Bedu, at home anywhere in the desert, even in country which was new to them or where the tribes were hostile, but they knew nothing of either the Jabal al Akhadar or of the Arabs who lived there. I had realized even before we had started from Muwaiqih that I could only travel in this mountain with the permission of Sulaiman bin Hamyar. I had reached him, and he had refused me leave to go there.

We arrived back at Muwaiqih ten days later, after travelling by night for the last part of the journey, in order to avoid the Al bu Shams who were on the watch for us. I stayed there for a few days with Zayid before I left for Dibai, taking bin Kabina and bin Ghabaisha with me, for I knew I would not come back and I wanted to have them with me until I left Arabia. On our way to Dibai we stopped for a night in an oil camp that had sprung up near the coast while I had been away in Oman. The 'camp boss' told me that they were nearly ready to drill for oil.

Dibai, where we stayed with Edward Henderson and his assis-

tant, Ronald Codrai, in their house beside the harbour, was happily
still unchanged. At the oil camp bin Kabina and bin Ghabaisha had
not been allowed to share the empty tent which had originally been
allocated to me in the 'European lines', and I had therefore spent
the night with them in the 'native lines'. Henderson and Codrai,
however, were quite willing to treat them as their guests, and gave
us a room together. Henderson asked me what to do about food
and I suggested that he should make no alterations. As we went in
to lunch I said to bin Kabina, 'While I was with you in the desert
I fed and lived as you do; now that you are our guests you must
behave as we do.' They watched carefully to see how we used the
knives and forks and managed with singularly little trouble. They
were far more self-possessed than most Englishmen whom I had
seen feeding with their hands for the first time. Afterwards I said
to them, 'Your hosts wish you to have whatever you want while
you are here. They have asked me to find out whether you prefer
to eat our food or whether you would rather have Arab meals.'
Bin Kabina smiled and answered, 'We shall, it is true, be more
comfortable and able to eat more if we feed as we are accustomed,
but, Umbarak, do not mention this if it would cause embarrassment.
We don't know your customs, and you must help us now as we
helped you in the desert.'

We dined that night with the Sheikh of Dibai on the far side of
the creek. The lad I hired to row us over asked if he should wait
to bring us back and I told him to return at ten o'clock. As we
were coming back to the landing-stage bin Ghabaisha suddenly
said, 'Umbarak, we have done an awful thing,' and when I asked
what was wrong he answered, 'We have forgotten to bring back
any food for our travelling companion.' Puzzled, I asked whom he
meant, and he said, 'The boy who brought us over.' I assured him
that the boy would not expect it, as the customs of the town were
different from the customs of the desert, but bin Ghabaisha shook
his head and said, 'We are Bedu. He was our travelling companion.
Did he not bring us here? and we forgot him. We have fallen short.'
On our first day there bin Kabina accidentally shut himself up

in the sitting-room and was unable to get out until he attracted my
attention by hammering on the wall; but soon both of them were
perfectly at home and were fiddling with the wireless and playing
Henderson's gramophone. Henderson and Codrai were endlessly
good-natured, particularly as in the early morning it amused my
companions, who got up at dawn, to burst into their rooms exhort-
ing them 'Up and pray! Up and pray!' as they beat the beds with
their camel-sticks.

One morning they came back before breakfast from the *suq* in
a state of great excitement. As they buckled on their cartridge-belts
they told me that a kinsman of theirs had been arrested by the
Sheikh of Sharja and that they must go immediately to his assistance. I asked how they proposed to get to Sharja, which was twelve
miles away, and bin Ghabaisha said, 'We will hire a car; give us
some money; you know how much a car will cost.' I suggested that
they should wait and get a lift in a lorry which I knew Henderson
was sending there later in the morning, but they were impatient:
'We cannot wait; we must go now, at once. Tell Henderson to
send the lorry now.' I asked, 'Who is the man? Do I know him?
What is his name?' and bin Kabina said, 'I don't know his name,
but he is a kinsman of ours. Is that not enough?' 'Is he a Rashid?'
I asked. 'No, he is a Sharaifi.' By now I knew enough of tribal
genealogies to realize that this small and obscure tribe was only
very distantly connected with the Rashid, but bin Ghabaisha said,
'What does it matter? He is a kinsman and in trouble; we must go
to his help. Would you have us desert him, Umbarak, when there
is no one else to help him?'

They went off in the lorry and came back in the evening. The
man had been released before they got to Sharja.

Having come to Dibai by car they had no camels to worry
about and were content to remain for a while enjoying this new
experience. It would give them something to talk about when they
got back to the desert. Meanwhile, they found it pleasant to sit
about, fully fed, and with nothing to do but wander into the *suq*
and gossip in the shops. I asked bin Kabina if he would care to live
here permanently, and he said, 'No. This is no life for a man. What

is there to do?' I noticed that when they chatted together in the evenings it was of the desert that they spoke, rather than of the things they had seen during the day.

I have often been asked, 'Why do the Bedu live in the desert where they have to put up with the appalling conditions which you describe? Why don't they leave it and find an easier life elsewhere?' and few people have believed me when I have said, 'They live there from choice.' Yet obviously the great Bedu tribes of Syria could at any time have dispossessed the weaker cultivators along the desert's edge and settled on their land. They continued instead to dwell as nomads in the desert because that was the life they cherished. When I was in Damascus I often visited the Rualla while they were camped in summer on the wells outside the city. They urged me to accompany them on their annual migration, which would start southward for the Najd as soon as grazing had come up after the autumn rains. Only in the desert, they declared, could a man find freedom. It must have been this same craving for freedom which induced tribes that entered Egypt at the time of the Arab conquest to pass on through the Nile valley into the interminable desert beyond, leaving behind them the green fields, the palm groves, the shade and running water, and all the luxury which they found in the towns they had conquered.

Knowing that I should not come back, I advised bin Kabina and bin Ghabaisha to return to their homelands in the south as soon as the weather got cool. Already they had many blood-feuds on their hands, and I feared that they would inevitably be killed if they remained in these parts. The following year I heard that bin Kabina had collected his camels and gone back to Habarut; bin Ghabaisha, however, remained on the Trucial Coast, where his reputation became increasingly notorious. Henderson wrote and told me how he was woken in the early hours to find bin Ghabaisha on his doorstep seeking sanctuary with a badly-wounded man in his arms. They had been raiding camels on the outskirts of the town. Henderson sent the wounded man to hospital in Bahrain, and bin Ghabaisha went there with him. Two years later I saw a report by the Political Resident which stated that the Sheikh of

Sharja had succeeded at last in capturing 'the notorious brigand bin Ghabaisha who had been Thesiger's companion' and that he was determined to make an example of him. I was relieved when I heard soon afterwards that the Sheikh had released him after receiving an ultimatum from the Rashid and Awamir.

One evening the Political Officer who had taken over from Noel Jackson came to dinner. He led me aside and said, 'I am afraid, Thesiger, that I have a rather embarrassing duty to perform. The Sultan of Muscat, His Highness Sayid Saiyid Bin Taimur, has demanded that we should cancel your Muscat visa. I have been instructed to do so by the Political Resident. I am afraid I must therefore have your passport.' I replied, 'All right, I'll get it; but you realize I've never had a Muscat visa.'

Although we joked during dinner about a 'visa for Nazwa,' I realized that it would not be long before visas really were required, even for travel in the Empty Quarter. Even now I was probably barred from going back there. To reach the Sands, I had to start from somewhere on the coast, and I could no longer land in Oman or in Dhaufar; even if I returned to the Trucial Coast my presence would probably be regarded as an embarrassment by the Political Resident. I recalled that the previous year the Aden Government, hearing that I was planning another journey, had sent me a telegram advising me for my own sake not to enter Saudi territory. Although I had no political or economic interest in the country few people accepted the fact that I travelled there for my own pleasure, certainly not the American oil companies nor the Saudi Government. I knew that I had made my last journey in the Empty Quarter and that a phase in my life was ended. Here in the desert I had found all that I asked; I knew that I should never find it again. But it was not only this personal sorrow that distressed me. I realized that the Bedu with whom I had lived and travelled, and in whose company I had found contentment, were doomed. Some people maintain that they will be better off when they have exchanged the hardship and poverty of the desert for the security of a materialistic world. This I do not believe. I shall always remember how often I was humbled by those illiterate herdsmen who possessed, in so much greater measure than I, generosity and courage, endurance, patience, and lighthearted gallantry. Among no other people have I ever felt the same sense of personal inadequacy.

On the last evening, as bin Kabina and bin Ghabaisha were tying up the few things they had bought, Codrai said, looking at the two small bundles, 'It is rather pathetic that this is all they have.' I understood what he meant; I had often felt the same. Yet I knew that for them the danger lay, not in the hardship of their lives, but in the boredom and frustration they would feel when they renounced it. The tragedy was that the choice would not be theirs; economic forces beyond their control would eventually drive them into the towns to hang about street-corners as 'unskilled labour'.

The lorry arrived after breakfast. We embraced for the last time. I said, 'Go in peace,' and they answered together, 'Remain in the safe keeping of God, Umbarak.' Then they scrambled up on to a pile of petrol drums beside a Palestinian refugee in oil-stained dungarees. A few minutes later they were out of sight round a corner. I was glad when Codrai took me to the aerodrome at Sharja. As the plane climbed over the town and swung out above the sea I knew how it felt to go into exile.

Arabic and Botanical Names of Plants
Mentioned in the Book

Abal   Calligonum sp.
Ailqi   Dipterygium glaucum Decne.
Arad   Salsola cyclophylla Bak.
Birkan   Limeum arabicum Friedr. and L. indicum Stocks
Ghaf   Prosopis spicigera L.
Had   Cornulaca monacantha Del.
Harm   Zygophyllum spp.
Harmal   Rhazya stricta Decne.
Ilb   Ziziphus spina-christi (L.) Willd.
Karia   Heliotropium digynum (Forsk.) Aschers ex C. Christens.
Qassis   Cyperus conglomeratus Rottb.
Rahath   Eremobium aegyptiacum (Spreng.) Hochr.
Rimram   Heliotropium Rotschyi (Bunge) Gürke
Sadan   Neurada procumbens L.
Saf   Nannorrhops aribica Burret
Shanan   Seidlitzia rosmarinus (Ehrenb.) Boiss.
Zahra   Tribulus spp.

A List of the Chief Characters
on the Various Journeys

1945–6

The Journey from Salala to Mughshin

Salim Tamtaim
Sultan
Musallim bin Tafl
Mabkhaut

} of the Bait Kathir

The Journey from Salala to the Hadhramaut

Sultan
Musallim bin Tafl

} of the Bait Kathir

Musallim bin al Kamam
Salim bin Kabina

} of the Rashid

1946–7

The First Crossing of the Empty Quarter

Salim Tamtaim
Sultan
Musallim bin Tafi
Mabkhaut
Bin Turkia
Bin Anauf (son of bin Turkia)
Said

} of the Bait Kathir

Salim bin Kabina
Muhammad al Auf
Amair
Mahsin
Salim bin Mautlauq
Bin Shuas

} of the Rashid

The Journey from Salala to Mukalla

Bin Kalut
Musallim bin al Kamam
Muhammad (son of bin Kalut and
   half brother to Salim bin Kabina) ⎫ of the Rashid
Salim bin Kabina
Salim bin Ghabaisha
Salim bin Mautlauq

Mabkhaut
Bin Turkia ⎫ of the Bait Kathir
Bin Anauf

Bin Duailan (nicknamed 'The Cat')   of the Manahil

1947–8

The Second Crossing of the Empty Quarter

Salim bin Kabina
Salim bin Ghabaisha ⎫ of the Rashid
Muhammad
Amair

Salih ⎫ of the Saar
Sadr

1948–9

The Journey to Liwa

Salim bin Kabina
Salim bin Ghabaisha
Musallim bin al Kamam ⎫ of the Rashid
Amair
Bin Tahi

The Journey through Oman

Salim bin Kabina
Musallim bin al Kamam ⎫ of the Rashid
Bin Tahi

Al Jabari
Mahalhal } of the Awamir

Hamaid   of the Mahra
Salim bin Habarut   of the Junuba
Ahmad
Sultan } of the Wahiba

Yasir   of the Junuba
Huaishil   of the Duru

1949–50

The Journey in Oman

Salim bin Kabina
Salim bin Ghabaisha
Muhammad } of the Rashid
Bin Tahi

Al Jabari   of the Awamir
Huaishil   of the Duru

Index

Abal, 111, 118, 151, 218, 219, 298
Abd al Aziz ibn Saud. *See* ibn Saud, King
Abdullah bin Nura. *See* bin Maiqal
Abdullah, one-eyed, of the Rashid: 196; anxiety over raiders, 197
Abha, 62, 235
Abhebad, Lake, 13
Abida, the: 173, 197; raiders from, 207; wounded from, 207; fight with, 269
Abr, al: 202; raids around, 205
Abu Bahr, plain of, 221
Abu Dhabi: 129, 140, 143, 144, 145, 234, 235; weariness on journey to, 251; arrival at, 251; stay in, 252–6; second visit to, 270–2
Abyssinia: Great Rebellion of 1916 in, 4; Haile Selassie's coronation, 5; exploration in, 5ff.; campaign in, during World War II, 22
Abyssinians, ancestors of, 97, 186
Acacia, 74, 167, 180, 263
Ad, lost city of, 226
Adaaimara, the, 10
Adam, 304
Addax, 17
Addis Ababa, xix
Adnan, 159
Adobada, Lake, 13
Aelius Gallus, 30
Afar, the: 163, 311; sick tribesman from, 181; guide from, 292
Aflaj, 300
Africa, central, 96
Ahl al Hadara, the, 33
Ahmad, of the Saar, 194, 197
Ahmad, of the Wahiba, 294–5, 298, 301
Ahsaba, Wadi al, 61
Aidam, Wadi, 247
Ailqi, 218

Ain, al, spring, 67, 172
Ain, al, Wadi: 65, 161, 172, 288; wrongly marked on map, 185
Aiwat al Saar, the, 195
Aiyun, pool of, 69, 176, 178
Ajman, the, 79
Akaki plains, 13
Akhadar, Jabal al: 164, 170, 301, 306; desire to explore, 310; turned back from, 316
Akhwan, the, 228, 238
Al bu Falah, the, 101, 111, 140, 144, 150, 256, 271, 284
Al bu Shams, the, 284, 309, 316
Al bu Said dynasty, 262
Al Hiya, the, 297
Al Kathir, the, 68
Aleppo, 22
Alhambra, 85
Ali, of the Duru, 161–2, 289
Ali, of the Hatim, 206 *passim*
Ali bin Hilal. *See* bin Hilal
Ali bin Said. *See* bin Said
Ali bin Sulaiman. *See* bin Sulaiman
Amar, of the Rashid: 63, 88, 208; quarrel with bin Mautlauq, 99; joins Umbarak at Tamis well, 202; presented with rifle before Western Sands crossing, 213; ruthlessness of, 215; remains at Buraimi, 284
Amairi, al, Wadi, 162, 163, 165, 314
Amarjid, the, 186
Amir, of Salaiyil: 229–30, 234; of the Wadi, 232
Andam, Wadi, 297, 300, 301
Andhur: 167; ruins at, 179
Arab, al Araba: 78; *al Mustaraba*, 78
Arabia: early civilizations in, 29; rainfall on south coast, 32; breaking down of tribal life in, 79–83; wealth from oil, 81

Arabia Felix, 25, 29, 78
Arabic: 33, 37; as great cultural
  language, 84-5
Arabs: system of government among, 32;
  treatment of slaves, 64; dress, 66;
  attitude to camels; 69-71 (*see also*
  Camels); feeding habits, 71-2, 153-4,
  155; generosity to guests, 75, 155;
  burial sites, 75; number of, in Arabia,
  77; racial divisions of, 78; effect of
  desert life on, 82; influence on world
  history, 83-4; and dignity, 156;
  greetings, 89; effect of thirst on, 140;
  attitude to women, 182-3, 260;
  divorce among, 182; attitude to
  bastards, 182; circumcision among,
  65, 91-3, 111, 150; feuds between
  tribes, 94-5; admiration for modern
  architecture, 199; indifference to pain,
  244; as sailors, 266-7. See also Bedu
Arad, 98, 291
Aradh escarpment, the, 210, 222, 226,
  231, 232
Arussi Mountains, 7
Ass, wild, 151, 263
Assaaimara, the, 9
Assal basin, the, 14
Assir, the, 1-2
Assyria, 78
Aswad, al, Wadi, 163, 313
Attila, 84
Auf, Muhammad al, of the Rashid:
  description, 88, 89, 90; and proposed
  crossing of the Empty Quarter, 97,
  101, 103-5; on the Al bu Falah, 111;
  agrees to go on, 119; offered rifles,
  120; leads way across Empty Quarter,
  121ff.; recites from Koran, 124;
  interest in depth of rainfall, 127;
  reconnoitres sand-dunes, 132; as
  guide over sand-dunes, 133-4ff.; on
  thirst, 140; on difficulties of
  concealing Umbarak, 144; and
  journey to Mukalla, 172; and
  preparations against attack, near
  Fughama, 188
Augustus, Emperor, 30
Aussa, 11-12
Awamir, the: 51, 53, 140, 144, 196, 198,
  259; inquisitiveness, 145
Awash, River, 5-6, 7

Baboons, 7, 62
Babylonia, 78
Badayat, 20
Badgers, honey, 250
Baggara, the, 15
Baghila, 265
Bahdu, 10-11
Bahlah, 314
Bahr al Safi, the, 105, 288
Bahrain, journey to, by dhow, 265-7
Bai: 101, 111, 165; distance from
  Mughshin to, 128-9; reunion at, 166
Baish, Wadi, 61
Bait al Sheikh, the, 178
Bait Imani, the, 53, 109, 122
Bait Kathir, the: 32-3, 34, 172; attitude
  to Christians, 36-8; dialect of, 37;
  prayer among, 39-40; as guides on
  Salala-Mughshin journey, 63ff.; as
  animal owners, 74; jealousy of the
  Rashid, 97, 98; and proposed crossing
  of the Empty Quarter, 103; love of
  news, 111; turn back from Empty
  Quarter, 120, 121; refusal to cross,
  166; avarice of, 194
Bait Khawar, the, 173, 184
Bait Musan, the, 63; changing of camels
  with, 103, 107, 109, 114, 128ff.
Bait Qatan, 68
Bait Saad, 68
Bakhit al Dahaimi. See Dahaimi, al
Balagh well, 145, 153, 250
Baluchi, encampment of, 301-2
Bani Ad, the, 226
Bani Hilal, the, 61, 79
Bani Kitab, the, 257, 263, 309
Bani Maradh, the, 223-4
Bani Ramh, sands of, 226
Bani Yas, the: 144, 150, 251, 252-3,
  260, 261; uncouthness and selfishness
  of, 177-8
Barbary sheep. See Sheep
Bardai, 21
Barida well, 302
Barton, Sir Sidney, 5
Batha Bidiya, the, 299
Batha, Wadi, 296; 299
Batin, the, 145
Bedu, the: nature of, 36, 47-8, 50; daily
  life among, 39ff.; attitude to their
  camels, 41-5, 69-70; love of

conversation and news, 47, 72–3, 122, 158, 166; coffee-drinking, 46; smoking, 46; camping habits, 46–8; breadmaking, 47; skill at reading camel tracks, 51–2, 197; generosity of, 50, 57, 65; Southern Bedu contrasted with Northern Bedu, 54; love of poetry, 73; numbers of, in Arabia, 77; moral and physical ascendancy of, 79; tribal society, 80–1; attitude to money, 81, 82, 156; effect of oil discovery on, 82; refusal to eat hare, 99; enjoyment of arguments and disputes, 99, 241; cauterizing as remedy for ailments, 100; *hamrar* rememedy, 100; attitude to food, 101, 165; gregariousness of, 108; vigour of, 112; swearing by, 112; reality of God to, 129; regard for human dignity, 156; ease with which offended, 151; indifference to human life, 181, 216; keen observation of, 222, 298; refusal to express opinion on weather, 235; strong position of outlaws among warring sheikhs, 271; division of spoil after raids, 277; preference for hard nomadic life, 319; their way of life doomed, 320–1

Bent, Theodore and Mabel, 31
Bernard, Capitaine, 14
Bianchi, 8
bin Abdullah al Khalili. *See* Oman, Iman of
bin Aisa, Salih, Sheikh of the Harth, 300
bin al Kamam, Musallim, sheikh of the Rashid: 52–3, 58, 59, 63, 90, 113, 173, 289; and proposed truce with the Dahm, 173–4; asked to join in crossing of Western Sands, 193; unable to join, 196; describes effort to kill Umbarak after Manwakh, 217; mistrust of the Duru, 290
bin Anauf, of the Bait Kathir: 67, 71, 119; reunion with, at Bai, 166; and journey to Mukalla, 172
bin Arbain, Mabkhaut, of the Bait Kathir, 65, 71–2, 110, 119; his family, 74; and Empty Quarter crossing, 101; and journey to Mukalla, 172
bin Daisan, of the bin Maaruf: as *rabia*

for Western Sands crossing, 205–7, 208; on route to the Hassi, 221
bin Duailan, of the Manahil ('The Cat'): 90, 174; description of, 176; personality of, 180; and proposed attack on the Dahm near Fughama, 188–9; attacks on government posts, 193; killed in raid on the Yam, 196; account of his death, 232–3
bin Duailan, Jumaan, brother of 'The Cat': 276; steals camels, 293
bin Ghabaisha, Salim, of the Rashid: description of, 176; as hunter, 176–7, 179, 180, 182, 214, 217, 263; his brother, 180; and preparations for attack near Fughama, 188; asked to join in crossing of Western Sands, 193; unable to join, 196; with father at Mudhail, 198; is flown to Riyan and driven to Saiwun, 199; buys black camel from the bin Maaruf, 204; competence of, 214–15; night in the stocks, 232; finds Dhiby well, 248; accidentally knocked out, 256; collects ten shillings from Sultan of Muscat, 260; steals Riqaishi's servant, 308; remains at Buraimi, 284; agrees to join Jabal al Akhadar exploration, 311; attack of fever, 314; stays with Europeans in Dibai, 317; becomes brigand on the Trucial Coast, 319
bin Hamyar, Sulaiman, sheikh of the Bani Riyam, 307, 310, 315
bin Hanna, Hamad, sheikh of the Rashid: 139, 143–4, 145; as guide to Ibri, 152; returns home, 163
bin Hilal, Ali, sheikh of the Duru, 311, 312
bin Jalawi. *See* ibn Jalawi
bin Kabina, Salim, of the Rashid: 54–9; shoots at raiders, 58; at Shishur, 88, 90, 92, 93; and proposed crossing of the Empty Quarter, 98, 101, 108, 109, 110; agrees to go on, 119; leads way across, 122; gives away his loin-cloth, 124; as cook, 129, 138, 155, 219; fails to buy stores in Liwa, 145–7; and journey to Mukalla, 172; sudden illness, 177; and preparations for attack near Fughama, 188; and parting at Mukalla, 190; invited to

bin Kabina – *cont.*
join Western Sands crossing, 193, 196; collapse of camel after 900-mile ride, 198; welcome from, at Manwakh, 203; buys camel from the bin Maaruf, 204; preparations for the crossing, 211–13; loses two camels to the Abida, 215; put in stocks, 232; accompanies Umbarak to Dam, 232; collects ten shillings from Sultan of Muscat, 260; hunts tahr, 263–4; rejoins Umbarak at Muwaiqih, 270; harrying of Bani Kitab, 270, 273; begs for release of *saiyid*, 271; goes to collect camels at Dhafara, 277; hands over camel, 294; accompanies on journey to the Wadi Batha, 298; gives away new shirt, 305; agrees to join Jabal al Akhadar exploration, 310; attack of fever, 313–14; stays with Europeans in Dibai, 317; returns to Habarut, 319

bin Kalut, sheikh of the Rashid: 168, 173; as guide for Mukalla journey, 172; decision as to Dahm-Rashid truce, 176; on trouble with the Bait Khawar, 183

bin Kharas, Sulaiman, sheikh of the Duru, 290; orders Umbarak out of Duru country, 310–11

bin Maaruf Saar, the, 203, 204; fear of attack by Yam, 202, 203; greeting from, at Manwakh, 203; return of scouts, 205

bin Madhi, Amir of Najram, 235, 269

bin Maiqal (Abdullah bin Nura), of the bin Maaruf Saar, 201–3, 208

bin Maktum of Dibai, the, 101, 140, 271

bin Mautlauq, Salim, of the Rashid: 88, 94; quarrel with Amair, 99; reported death of, in raid, 206–7; wounded, 269

bin Murzuk, of the Abida: 197, 206; pursuit of, 206

bin Nura, Andullah. *See* bin Maiqal

bin Rashid al Kharusi, Salim, former Imam of Oman, 262

bin Said bin Rashid, Ali, sheikh of the Yahahif: 301; his wives, 303

bin Saiyid Muhammad, Ahmad, release of, 271–2

bin Shuas, of the Rashid, 88, 94, 97, 101

bin Sulaiman, Ali, of the Hatim, 201

bin Sultan, Zayid: 255, 257–60, 263, 270; help given to Bird, 261; agrees to help Umbarak to explore Oman, 263; further hospitality from, 276; hawking with, 278–84; helps Umbarak to enter Oman, 285; final stay with, 316

bin Tafl, Mussalim, of the Bait Kathir: 46, 51, 64–5, 67; as hunter, 100, 112, 177; as cook, 101, 110, 126, 129, 146; and cure for constipation, 100; conversation of, 111; and crossing of the Empty Quarter, 111; agrees to go on, 119; jealousy of al Auf, 132; fear of travelling in Duru country, 148–9; blood-feud with Mahras, 172

bin Tahi, of the Rashid: 272; reads the sands, 293; annoys the Ibadhi, 304; attack of fever, 314; agrees to join Jabal al Akhadar exploration, 310

bin Timur, Saiyid Said. *See* Muscat, Sultan of

bin Tanas, sheikh of the Manahil, 188, 189

bin Turkia, Salim of the Bait Kathir: 65, 67, 71–2, 114; and proposed crossing of the Empty Quarter, 101; wishes to go on, 119; reunion with, at Bai, 166; and journey to Mukalla, 172

Bir Halu, 51, 107, 109

Bir Natrum, wells of, 16

Bird, Dick, 258, 261

Birkat al Mauz, 307, 310, 315

Boom, 266

Boscawen, T. M., 193

Buraimi: journey to, 256; control of villages in, 206–1; occupied by Wahabis, 261

Bustard, MacQueen's, hunting of, 279–83

Butterflies, 33, 117

Camels: in the Danakil country, 9, 15; in the Sudan, 16; in Arabia, 41–5; recognition of tracks, 52, 214; food for, 65, 98; milk, 66; attachment to Bedu owners, 70; watering of, 87–8, 113, 116, 145, 208, 211; stampede of, 97; choice of, for crossing Empty Quarter, 101; kicking by, 102; poor condition of, 105, 244; grazing for,

105, 114–17, 248; cast a calf, 114; mating of, 123; milking of, 66, 123, 220; fall, on steep slope, 125; exhaustion of, 136–7, 218, 225; hunger and thirst of, 138; of the Manasir, 152; inability to walk straight, 164; killing of, for food, 165; for drawing well-ropes, 195; litters on, for transport of small children, 203; loading of, 213; patience of, 242; ulcers on, 244; Batina, 256; *Banat Farha*, 256; *Banat al Hamra*, 256; Bedu killed by bull camel, 269; division of, after raid, 277

Caper bushes, 74

Castration, 6, 9, 244

Cat, wild, 151

Cattle. *See* Cows

Cauterizing, to cure ailments, 100

Caves used by Qarra, 33, 67

Cheesman, Colonel R. E., 5, 105, 240

Chercher Mountains, 7

Circumcision. *See* Arabs

Codrai, Ronald, 317

Coffee, as made by the Saar, 195

Cold, in the desert, 124, 131, 135, 202, 216, 311, 313

Coot, 168

Cows, 33, 74

Cox, Sir Percy, 262

Crocodiles, 7–8, 14

Dagger, 67, 94, 175, 253, 315

Dahaimi, Bakhit al, of the Rashid, 94, 155, 157, 163, 255

Dahal well, 187

Dahana sands, 242, 243

Dahm, the: 53, 90, 173–4; raids by, 59, 112, 172, 174–6, 188–9; truce with the Rashid, 173; break truce, 175; fail to overtake and kill Umbarak, 217; one man from, living among the Yam, 235; renewal of truce with Rashid, 269

Dakaka sands, 113, 133, 205

Dam, 230

Damascus, 22

Danakil, the, 6, 7–10, 13, 14

Danakil desert, 6, 7–8

Darbat, pools of, 168

Darfur, 15, 17, 20, 21

Daru plateau, the, 183

Date palms, 98

Dawasir, the: 90, 193, 196; massing to attack the Saar, 205

Dawasir, Wadi: 113, 201, 205, 227, 232; Amir of, 232–3

Desert, Arabian, size of, 24

Dessie, 22

Dew, in the desert, 151

Dhafar, 68

Dhafara, 103–4, 114, 137, 277

Dhala, 30

Dhaufar Mountains: 29, 178; trilithons on, 76; great flood in, 247

Dhiby well: 245; arrival at, 247–8

Dhow: 65, 255, 265; voyage on, 266–8

Dibai, 152, 250, 264, 269, 316–17

Difin, Wadi, 82

Dikil, 14

Dinka, the, 19

Divers, Bani Yas with pearling fleet, 251

Donkeys, 251, 294, 297

Doon crater, 21

Drums, priests': in Abyssinia, 3; in the Tihama, 61, 93

Druze, Jabal al, 22

Dugong, 255

Dupuis, Charles, 15

Duru, the: 101, 256, 258, 261; treachery of, 144; hostility to Christians, 149; enmity with Rashid, 159; hostile meeting with, 161–2; they pursue Umbarak's party in Wadi al Ain, 289–90; desire to keep Umbarak out of their territory, 310–14

Eagles: lawful as food, 151; chasing gazelle, 187; killing fox, 273; attacking peregrines, 283

Eastern Aden Protectorate: journey through, 170ff.; raid from, 174

Egypt: 22, 96; Ancient, 78

Elephants, 19

Eloy, Aucher, 262

Emi Koussi crater, 20

Empty Quarter, the: 24ff., 39, 62ff.; first view of, 69, 95. *See also throughout Chapters 7 and 11*

Execution of a Habad, 113

Exploration, reasons in favour of, 267–8

Fahad, Amir of Laila, 236
Fahud, 304
Falcons: saker, at Laila, 236; the training and using of, 278–84; the catching of, 278–9
Farai, 294
Fasher, 16
Faswat al Ajuz, well of, 274
Fennec. *See* Fox
Fig-trees, 32, 168
FitzGerald, Vesey, 26, 27
Floods, 52, 170, 247
Flycatchers, Paradise, 33
Fox: 127; steals meat, 106; lawful food, 151; killed by eagle, 273; Fennec, 250, 294
Frankincense, 29, 178
Fughama: 188; anticipated attack near, 188

Galifage, 11
Gazelle: 94, 99, 100, 106, 117, 167, 180, 187, 297; becoming rare, 221
Genghis Khan, 84
Ghaf, 98, 106, 160, 263
Ghafari, the: 159, 186, 262, 271, 284, 285; hostility to Umbarak's journey through Oman, 303
Ghaidat, 111, 185, 196
Ghail ba Yamin, 189
Ghanim, 50, 62–3, 106, 141, 152
Gharbaniat sands, 291
Ghazala, a camel, 263, 281
Ghudun, Wadi, 69, 75
Giulietti (Italian explorer), 8
Gloucester, Duke of: mission to Ethiopia, 5
Glubb, Sir John, 95, 112, 158
Goats, 56, 59, 71, 160, 234, 294
Gojam, 22
Granite, 222
Grasshoppers, swarming of, 27
Grazing. *See* Camels
Greece, Ancient: influence of, on Muslim Empire, 84–5
Gumsait Mahra, the, 185
Gypsum: 107, 114; flats, 139

Habab, the, 113
Habarut, 180–2
Habasha, 186

Habashiya, Jabal, 186
Had pastures, 223
Hadara. *See* Ahl al Hadara
Hadhramaut, the: 33, 53, 59, 193; architecture of, 75, 198–9; raids around, 173–4
Hadoram. *See* Ahl al Hadara
Hafit, Jabal, 263, 272, 309
Haig-Thomas, David, 7, 9
Haij, 295
Haile Selassie, Emperor of Abyssinia: coronation of, 4, 186; restoration of, 21
Hajaz Mountains: 1, 61, 226; villages in, 37; travels in, 192
Halfain, Wadi, 193, 299, 303
Hamad bin Hanna. *See* bin Hanna
Hamaid, of the Mahra: 285, 286, 289, 292; arrested at Tawi Yasir, 304–5
Hamasa, 271; sheikh of, 272
Hamdu Uga, 11
Hanawi, the, 159, 163, 262, 271, 311
Hands, cutting off of, 231
Hanu, stream bed of, 226
Harasis, the, 33, 167, 311
Hares: 117, 137; as forbidden food, 99; the catching of, 154, 273; the hunting of, 282
Harm: 118; as camel food, 152, 153
Harmal, 76
Harth, the, 300
Hasa, the, 221
Hassi well: 209–10; arrival at, 225ff.
Haushi, well at, 165, 166
Hautas, 98
Hawking, 278–84
Hazaramaveth, 33
Heat, in the desert, 127, 136, 145
Hebrews, 78
Heliotrope. *See* Rimram
Henderson, Edward, 264, 316
Himyarite civilization: 29–30, 78, 186; languge of, 33
Hiza, sheikh of Abu Dhabi, 252–3, 256, 257
Homosexuality, 113–14
Honeysuckle, 2
Huaishil: sheikh of the Duru, 307; as guide to Birkat al Mauz, 310; anger with Duru, 311; gets support from Ali bin Hilal, 313

Hulaiya, 58
Humum, the: 53, 183, 193–4; trilithons
    in their country, 76
Hun, Wadi, 188
Hunger, in the desert, 131, 146–7
Huquf, the, 294
Hurr, 278
Hussain, Saif al Islam al, Governor of
    the Jauf, 217
Hyenas, 168

Ibadhis, the, 262, 304
Ibex, 71, 176, 180, 187
Ibn Jawali, Governor of the Hassa, 109,
    140, 144
Ibn Saud, Abd al Aziz, King of Saudi
    Arabia: 27, 79, 174; permission to
    Philby to cross Empty Quarter, 109;
    his tax-collectors, 139–40, 144;
    refuses permission to cross Western
    Sands, 192–3; acknowledged as
    overlord by the bin Maaruf Saar, 201;
    post at the Hassi, 210; permission to
    tribes to raid Mishqas, 227; orders
    detention of Umbarak and
    imprisonment of his companions, 228;
    anger at Umbarak's journey to
    Sulaiyil, 236; and the Akhwan, 238;
    control over Murra, 261
Ibri: 149, 260; hostile Duru from, 161;
    diversion to collect stores from,
    162
Ilb, 194
Incense, 96
Ingrams, W. H., 193, 199
Iraq Petroleum Company, 261, 264
Islam, 39–41, 83–5, 238
Izz, 285, 306, 314

Jaalan, Jabal, 299
Jabal. See under individual names of
    mountains
Jabari, al: of the Awamir, 284; and the
    fennec fox, 294; agrees to accompany
    Jabal al Akhadar exploration, 310
Jabrin: 105, 221; Umbarak offers to act
    as guide to, 237–9; journey to, 239ff.
Jackson, Noel, 264
Jaddat al Harasis, the, 118, 167, 193
Jadid, of the Rashid: 143, 145; leaves the
    party, 152

Jarbib, 32, 69
Jasmine, 2, 32
Jasper, 222
Jaub, 245
Jauf, the, 174, 217
Jaul, al, tableland of, 189
Jaulbaut, 265
Jayakar, Dr., 264
Jerboas, 117
Jibuti, 5
Jidda, 26, 61, 174
Jilida plain, the, 214, 222–3
Jira, volcanoes of, 13
Jiza, Wadi, 185, 186; drought in, 90
Jizan, 62
Johnson, E. R., Assistant Political
    Officer in the Hadhramaut, 199
Joktan. See Qahtan
Juasimi pirates, 266
Jumaan bin Duailan. See bin Duailan
Juniper, 1
Junuba, the, 100, 314

Karab, the, 140, 202, 203, 214
Karia, 273
Kashgai, the, 265
Kaur, Jabal, 160, 301, 308
Khaba well, 144–5
Khalid, sheikh of Abu Dhabi, 252–3
Khalili, al. See Oman, Imam of
Kharijites, the, 262
Khartoum, 15, 16
Khaur bin Atarit well, 107, 141
Khaur Sabakha, 140
Khaur Wir, 167
Khautim, 122–3
Kidyut valley, 184
Kismim pass, 68, 176
Kites, 5, 252
Koran, the opening verse, 40
Kudu, 17
Kutum, 16, 20

Lahamma well, 273
Laila: plan to go to, 234; arrival at,
    235–6; given no food in, 237; failure
    to find guide in, 237; as stronghold of
    the Akhwan, 238; supplies from, 240
Lammergeyer, 62
Larks, 117
Lawful food, 150

Lawrence, T. E.: 69, 83; on Bedouins, xxi; *Revolt in the Desert*, 25; *The Seven Pillars of Wisdom*, 112
Lean, O. B., 22
Leopard, 67
Libyan desert, 16, 17
Limestone, 34, 165, 222, 304
Lions, 19
Liwa: 103, 140; as centre for buying food, 144, 145; decision to look for, on way to Abu Dhabi, 249; found, 250; exploration of, 272ff.
Lizards: 117, 167, 219; monitor, 250; lizard skins for carrying butter, 71
Locusts: in the Sudan, 25; in Abyssinia, 25; 'desert locust', 27; Locust Research Centre, 25–8, 169–70, 192
London, Umbarak's homesickness in, 192
Lucerne, 60, 227

Mabkhaut bin Arbain. *See* bin Arbain
Madhamar, Mt., 304
Mahalhal, of the Awamir, 284
Mahra, the: 33, 53, 96, 167, 172, 180, 184, 185, 196, 203, 206; descent from the Habasha, 186; circumcision among, 111–12; assist in attack on Abida, 207
Mahrat, Wadi, 185, 186
Mahsin, of the Rashid: 88–9, 94; accident to, 97ff., 123; recovers, 102; in Salala, 168
Maidob, Jabal, 16
Main, 217
Makhia, the, 202
Mamur, 315
Manahil, the: 53, 59, 90, 140, 172, 173, 203, 204, 205–6; raids on, 59; as sheep owners, 74; fight with the Dahm, 187; attacks on government posts, 193; hatred of the Saar, 197; raid the Yam, 190; raid the Manasir, 276
Manasir, the: 144, 150, 152, 260; encampments of, 153; Liwa encampment of, 250; guide from, for Abu Dhabi, 250
Mankhali, well mounds of, 226
Manwakh well: 195, 203; lovely girl at, 195; well runs dry, 209

Maria Theresa dollars. *See* Riyals
Ma Shadid well, 75
Masila valley, 185, 186
Matrah, battle between Omanis and English, 262
Maxwell, Wedderburn, 19
Meat, division of, by lots, 71–2, 138
Mecca: 84, 96; sanctuary around, 99; face towards, when praying, 40
Michail, Negus, 4
Miles, Colonel, 262, 265
Minaean civilization: 29, 78; langue of, 33
Miram Muhammad, 11
Mishqas, the: 197; attacks by, 233
Modra valley, 21
Monsoon, 32
Moon eclipse of, 139
Moore, Guy, 15
Mosque, 315
Mudhaibi, 300
Mudhail: 178–9; discovery of neolithic axe-head at, 178; old buildings at, 179
Mughair well, 57
Mughshin: 28, 31, 51, 95ff., 143, 193; prolonged drought around, 52; Sultan of Muscat's claim to, 62
Muhammad al Riqaishi. *See* Riqaishi, al
Muhammad bid Abdullah al Khalili. *See* Oman, Imam of
Muhammad, of the Duru: acts as *rabia*, 162; returns home, 163
Muhammad, of the Rashid (son of bin Kalut): 173, 196, 206; offers to join Western Sands crossing, 196; anxiety over raiders, 196; suggests alternative crossing, 206; presented with rifle before crossing, 213; inefficiency of, 215; offers to guide from Subkhat Mutti to Abu Dhabi, 243; agrees to accompany Jabal al Akhadar exploration, 310
Muhammad Yayu, Sultan of Aussa, 11
Mukalla: 53, 119; plan to travel to, 169; arrival at, 189–90; return to, 193
Munzinger, Werner, 8, 14
Muqaibara well, 293–4
Murra, the 109, 140, 193, 228, 229, 239–40, 243
Murri, Ali al, 271, 273

Murzuk, a renegade Saar, 197
Musallim bin al Kamam. *See* bin al
   Kamam
Musallim bin Tafl. *See* bin Tafl
Musandam peninsula, 260
Muscat: 162; as capital of Oman, 262
Muscat, Sultan of (Sayid Saiyid bin
   Taimur), 28, 62, 109, 261, 303,
   320
Muslim Empire, 78, 84–5
Muslim faith. *See* Islam
Mutair, the, 79
Muwaiqih, 257, 261, 263, 270, 277, 284,
   307, 310

Nabi Hud, shrine of, 187
Nafi, 298
Nafud sands, 242
Najd, the, 37, 78, 319
Najran, 174, 192, 196, 201, 204, 230,
   269
Nasrani, al, 228
Naukhada, 265
Nazwa, 163, 300, 306, 307
Nesbitt, L. M., *Desert and Forest,* 8
No, Lake, 19
Nuer, the, 19, 20, 33
Nura, 181, 182

Oil, effects of discovery of, 82–3
Oil used to anoint guests, 303
Oleanders, 301
Olive, wild, 1, 62
Oman: 62, 111; route through, 144;
   interior of, 259, 261–2; bitterness of
   feuds in, 271; Umbarak's
   determination to return to Buraimi
   through, 296
Oman, Imam of (Muhammad bin
   Abdullah al Khalili): 63, 149, 161,
   260–1, 262, 284; authorizes journey
   back to Muwaiqih, 307, 315–16
Omdurman: 15; camel ride from Jamal
   Maidob to, 16
Ophir, 29
Oryx, 16, 17, 167, 217, 218–19; search
   for, 291, 293; missed by Umbarak,
   217; becoming extinct, 221; the
   stalking of, 222; Awadh shoots forty,
   269
Ostriches, 16, 221

Palmetto. *See Saf*
Palms: date, 98, 150, 152, 167, 181, 185,
   198, 227, 242, 250, 252, 257; coconut,
   29
Pelicans, 219
Peregrines. *See* Falcons
Persians, 78
Philby, St. John: 24, 230, 235, 236–9;
   and crossing of the Empty Quarter,
   108–9; work along Yemen border,
   193
Phoenicians, 78
Pinks, 2
Pintails, 168
Pirate Coast, 266
Plant distribution in the Empty Quarter,
   170
Porphyry, 222
Prayer: 39; call to, 40
Primulas, 2

Qahtan (or Joktan), descendant of
   Shem, 33, 78, 159
Qahtan, the, 61
Qaid, 106
Qaimiyat, the, 218
Qamaiqam, a camel, 145, 256
Qariya: well, at, 226; ruins at, 226, 237
Qarra, the: 31, 32–3; customs with
   cows, 33; as cattle owners, 68
Qarra Mountains, 28, 32, 109, 167, 174
Qasaiwara well, 285, 286, 290
Qasm, 271
Qassis, 137, 218, 219, 248, 273, 298
Qatar peninsula, 243
Quff, palm groves at, 198
Qurn Sahma, 293
Qutuf, 250

Rabadh, 153, 154
Rabia, the, part played by, 159, 162,
   163, 173, 185
Rai, of the Afar, 163–4
Raidat al Saar, 194, 203
Rainfall, in the desert, 115–16, 127,
   169, 245–9
Ramadhan, fast of, 130
Ramlat al Ghafa, 11, 114, 132
Rashid, the: 38, 53, 65, 90; prayers
   among, 40, 58; contrasted with the
   Bait Kathir, 53; small numbers of, 54;

Rashid – *cont.*
   signal of peace among, 57; raids on,
   59; raid on Saar, 95; lead across the
   Empty Quarter, 121ff.; enmity with
   Duru, 159–60; as guides to Mukalla,
   169; anger at truce-breaking by the
   Dahm, 175; agree to attack the
   Dahm, 188; discuss truce with the
   Saar, 196; buy camels from the bin
   Maaruf, 204; youthfulness of guides,
   205; two herdsmen killed by the
   Abida, 206; attack on the Abida at
   Thamus, 206; renewal of truce with
   the Dahm, 269
Rashid, son of Sheikh of Dibai, 284
Ras Lul Seged, 3
Ravens: 117, 135; eaten as cure for
   stomach ache, 151; attacked by
   peregrine, 282–3
Rhyolite, 222
Rift Valley, 7
Rim, 116, 218, 219
Rimram, 111, 118
Riqaishi, Muhammad al, 163
Riqaishi, the, Governor of Ibri, 149,
   308
Riqaiya. *See* Walia
Riyadh, 109, 113, 232
Riyals, 67, 147
Romans, the: 77–8; attempt to invade
   Arabia, 30
Roses, wild, 2
Royal Air Force: 28, 34, 35; in the
   desert, 168, 172, 199, 244, 261, 264
Rub al Khali. *See* Empty Quarter
Rualla, the, 54, 319
Rustaq, 262

Saad, Sheikh, tomb of, 178
Saar, the: 53, 95, 97, 173; trilithons in
   their country, 76–7; murder of Saar
   boy, 94; nature of, 194; discuss truce
   with the Rashid, 196; camels bought
   from, 201; encampment near
   Manwakh, 202; credulity of, 203;
   bitterness towards the Rashid, 205
Sabaean civilization: 29, 78, 186;
   language of, 33
Sabkhat Mutti salt-flats: 243, 248; the
   crossing of, 248ff.
Sabyia, 62

Saddle camel, Omani, 43
Sadr, of the Saar, 209–10, 211, 214,
   219, 225–6
Saf, 73, 74
Sahail, killing of, 94
Sahara desert, 20
Sahma sands, 98, 291
Said of the Bait Kathir and evil spirit,
   96; and proposed crossing of Empty
   Quarter, 101, 103; and stomach ache,
   110
Said, of the Rashid (brother of bin
   Kabina), 118, 184, 188
Saif al Islam al Hussain. *See* Hussain
Saints, oaths sworn on tombs of, 99
Saiwun: 193; Sultan's palace at, 198;
   modernization of, 199
Saiyid Said bin Timur. *See* Muscat,
   Sultan of
Saiyids, the: 199, 203, 204; overcharging
   by, 204
Saker. *See* Falcon
Salakh, Mt., 304
Salala: 29, 50, 121, 169; description of,
   29–30; Wali of, 31, 34, 168; stay at,
   170ff.
Salih, of the Saar, 209–10, 211, 214,
   222, 224, 227
Salih bin Aisa. *See* bin Aisa
Salim bin Ghabaisha. *See* bin Ghabaisha
Salim bin Habarut. *See* bin Habarut
Salim bin Kabina. *See* bin Kabina
Salim bin Mautlauq. *See* bin Mautlauq
Salim bin Rashid al Kharusi, former
   Imam of Oman, 262
Salt-bushes. *See* Harm
Salt-flats, 128, 130, 135
Salukis, 273
Sambuk, 265
Sanau well, 57
Sandford, Colonel (later Brigadier)
   D. A., 6
Sands, the. *See* Empty Quarter
Sands: colours of, 115, 125, 128, 136,
   139; 'the singing of', 154; reading
   the, 293
Sands, Western. *See* Empty Quarter
Sandstorms, 313
Sardines, 29, 56, 182; fed to camels, 65
Saud, brother of Salim bin Mautlauq,
   207

Scorpions: 110; Umbarak stung by, 310–11
Scott, Captain Robert Falcon, 267
Second World War, 21–2
Sedge. *See* Qassis
Semitic race, 78
Shaghham well, 206
Shahara, the, 33, 68
Shahin, 278–9
Shanin, 124
Shakhbut, Sheikh of Abu Dhabi, 252–3, 255, 260, 270; authority over tribes, 261
Shammar, the, 54
Sharaifi, the, 318
Sharja: 264, 318; R.A.F. aerodrome at, 265; arrival at, 264
Sharja, sheikh of, 318, 319–20
Sheep: 78, 164, 234, 294; Barbary, 17
Sheppard, C. H. J., British Resident in Mukalla, 189, 193
Shibam, 193, 201; stores bought at, 201
Shield, Qarra, 67
Shihr, 189
Shilluk, the, 19
Shanan, 139
Shisur, 50, 87
Shrines, offerings left at, 195
Sib, Treaty of, 262
Skink, 150
Slaves: 64, 92, 112, 227, 230, 315; price of, 271–2; caravan of, 273
Snakes: 110; Bedu bitten by, 74
Somaliland, French, 14
Somalis, the, 6, 9, 265
Special Air Service Regiment, 22
Spiders, 110
Spirit, evil, possession by. *See* Zar
Springtime, rareness of, in the desert, 247
Staiyun, of the Duru: 162–3; offers to guide Umbarak in Oman, 289, 290–1; returns to encampment, 292
Stick: Qarra throwing-stick, 67; camel-stick, 111
Stocks, Umbarak's companions put in, 230
Sudan, the, 15, 19, 96
Sudan Defence Force, 21
Sudd, 19
Sulaim, of the Mahra, a *Rabia*, 186

Sulaiman bin Hamyar. *See* bin Hamyar
Sulaiman bin Kharas. *See* bin Kharas
Sulaiyil, 196, 208, 227–8
Sultan, of the Al Hiya, 297ff.
Sultan, of the Bait Kathir: 37, 42–3, 46, 64, 66, 67, 114; personality of, 37; points out trilithons, 77; and proposed crossing of the Empty Quarter, 98, 101; on the crossing, 111; refuses to go on, 118–19; brooding, 167
Sumeria, 78
Sword, Qarra, 67
Syria, 22

Tagrud, 280
Tahr, the hunting of, 263–4
Taif, 62, 254
Taj Mahal, 85
Tajura, 14
Tamarinds, 32
Tamarisk, 98, 188
Tamis well, 197
Tamtaim, Salim, of the Bait Kathir: 34, 35, 36, 46, 51, 69, 71; age and vigour of, 34, 64; at prayer, 40; as abritrator, 99; reunion with, at Bai, 166
Tamudic script, 76–7
Tarim, 60, 70, 199
Tawi Harian well, 297
Tawi Yasir, 304
Temperatures: in summer, 75; in the sands, 127
Tents, Arab, 74, 84, 157, 203, 302
Thamud well: 57; fighting at, 206, 207, 269
Thesiger, Wilfred. *See* Umbarak
Thomas, Bertram: 28, 31, 63, 168, 243, 288; *Arabia Felix*, 25, 29; remembered by Bait Kathir, 35, 37–8, 253; on trilithons, 77; on Umm al Samim, 105; and crossing of the Empty Quarter, 108–9
Thunderstorms, 245
Tibbu, the, 20
Tibesti Mountains, 20ff.
Ticks, leathery. *See* Dhafar
Tieroko, Mt., 21
Tihama, the, 61, 92, 231
Timkat, 3
Toadstools, edible, 256

Tracks, recognition of, in desert, 51–2
Trenchard, Marshal of the R.A.F.,
 Viscount, 24
Tribulus. *See* Zahra
Trilithons, 76–7, 178
Trucial Coast, the: 53, 63, 201, 232;
 fighting on, 111; authority on, 261
Trucial Oman Scouts, 261
Truffles, 256
Tubaiq range, 232
Tumuli, 9, 75–6, 178, 242
Turks, 78

Uainat, seized by Italians, 16
Umbarak (the author): 77; extra food
 given to, 138; difficulties of
 concealing, in hostile country, 144,
 149; faces starvation, 146; poses as a
 Syrian, 162, 163; trouble in Bait
 Khawar on way to Mukalla, 184–5;
 unrecognized by Rashid in European
 dress, 190; telegram to Ibn Saud, 229;
 interrogated by Amir of Wadi
 Dawasir, 229; release of, 232; chases
 raiders, 274; finds they are friends,
 275; obstacles to his entering Oman,
 284; in disguise among foothills of
 Oman, 299ff.; attack of fever, 314
Umbrausha, a camel, 41, 42
Umm al Hait, the, 73, 95, 98, 116
Umm at Samim quicksands: 98, 105,
 133, 162, 170, 286ff.; path across, 292
Uruq al Shaiba, the, 103, 105, 131ff.,
 147
Uruq al Zaza sands, 216
Uvarov, Dr., 27, 28, 62, 170

Villiers, Commander Alan, 265
Vines, 2
Von Wrede, Adolph, 288

Wad Medani, 17
Wadi. *See under individual names of
 Wadis*
Wahiba, the: 33, 163, 311, 314; desire
 to cross their country, 292, 297;
funeral feasts of the, 295; contrasted
 with the Duru, 303

Wahabis, 261
Wali of Dhaufar, 29, 30–1, 34, 168
Walia Riqaiya, 194
Ward, Rowland, *Records of Big Game*, 4
Water: the carrying of, 71; scarcity of,
 75, 113–14. *See also* Camels, watering
 of
Water-skins, 71, 201
Watts, A. F., Political Officer in the
 Hadhramaut, 193, 199
Wellsted, J. R., 262
Western Aden Protectorate, 185
Western Sands. *See* Empty Quarter
Widgeon, 168
Wind-turrets, 265
Wingate's Gideon Force, 21
Wolves, 187, 225

Yahahif, the, 296, 301
Yahya, Imam, 217
Yam, the: 90, 192, 193, 214; raided by
 the Manahil, 174, 196; massing to
 attack the Saar, 201; raiding parties
 of, 205; possible danger from, after
 crossing Western Sands, 209, 269;
 meeting with, 227; killer of bin
 Duailan from, 232; attacks on the
 Mishqas, 233–4
Yamin. *See* Ghail ba Tamin
Yarmuk, battle of, 84
Yasir, of the Junuba: 285, 304; asks
 Imam for permission for Umbarak to
 cross Oman, 306–7
Yemen, the: 29, 54, 63, 77–8, 90, 174;
 encouragement of raiders by
 goverment, in 174; Imam of, 269
Yisbub, 167

Zaghawa, 20
Zahra: 111, 115, 118; as camel food,
 126, 131
Zamakh well, 194, 202
Zanzibar, conquest of, by Oman, 262
Zar, 96
Zarzura, 22
Zayid bin Sultan. *See* bin Sultan, Zayid.
Zifr wells, 225
Zuaqti watercourse, 291